AF605861

THE YEAR'S WORK IN THE PUNK BOOKSHELF

OR, LUSTY SCRIPTS

BRIAN JAMES SCHILL

INDIANA UNIVERSITY PRESS

This book is a publication of

INDIANA UNIVERSITY PRESS
Office of Scholarly Publishing
Herman B Wells Library 350
1320 East 10th Street
Bloomington, Indiana 47405 USA

iupress.indiana.edu

The paper used in this publication meets the minimum requirements of the American National Standard for Information Sciences—Permanence of Paper for Printed Library Materials, ANSI Z39.48–1992.

Manufactured in the
United States of America

Library of Congress
Cataloging-in-Publication Data

Names: Schill, Brian James, author.
Title: The year's work in the punk bookshelf, or, lusty scripts / Brian James Schill.
Description: Bloomington : Indiana University Press, [2017] | Series: The year's work: studies in fan culture and cultural theory | Includes bibliographical references and index. | Description based on print version record and CIP data provided by publisher; resource not viewed.
Identifiers: LCCN 2017010177 (print) | LCCN 2017011598 (ebook) | ISBN 9780253029447 (eb) | ISBN 9780253029232 (cloth : alk. paper) | ISBN 9780253029300 (pbk : alk. paper)
Subjects: LCSH: Subculture. | Punk culture. | Punk rock music—Philosophy and aesthetics. | Influence (Literary, artistic, etc.)—History—20th century. | Reading interests—United States. | Reading interests—Great Britain. | Youth—Books and reading.
Classification: LCC HM646 (ebook) | LCC HM646 .S35 2017 (print) | DDC 306/.1—dc23
LC record available at https://lccn.loc.gov/2017010177

1 2 3 4 5 22 21 20 19 18 17

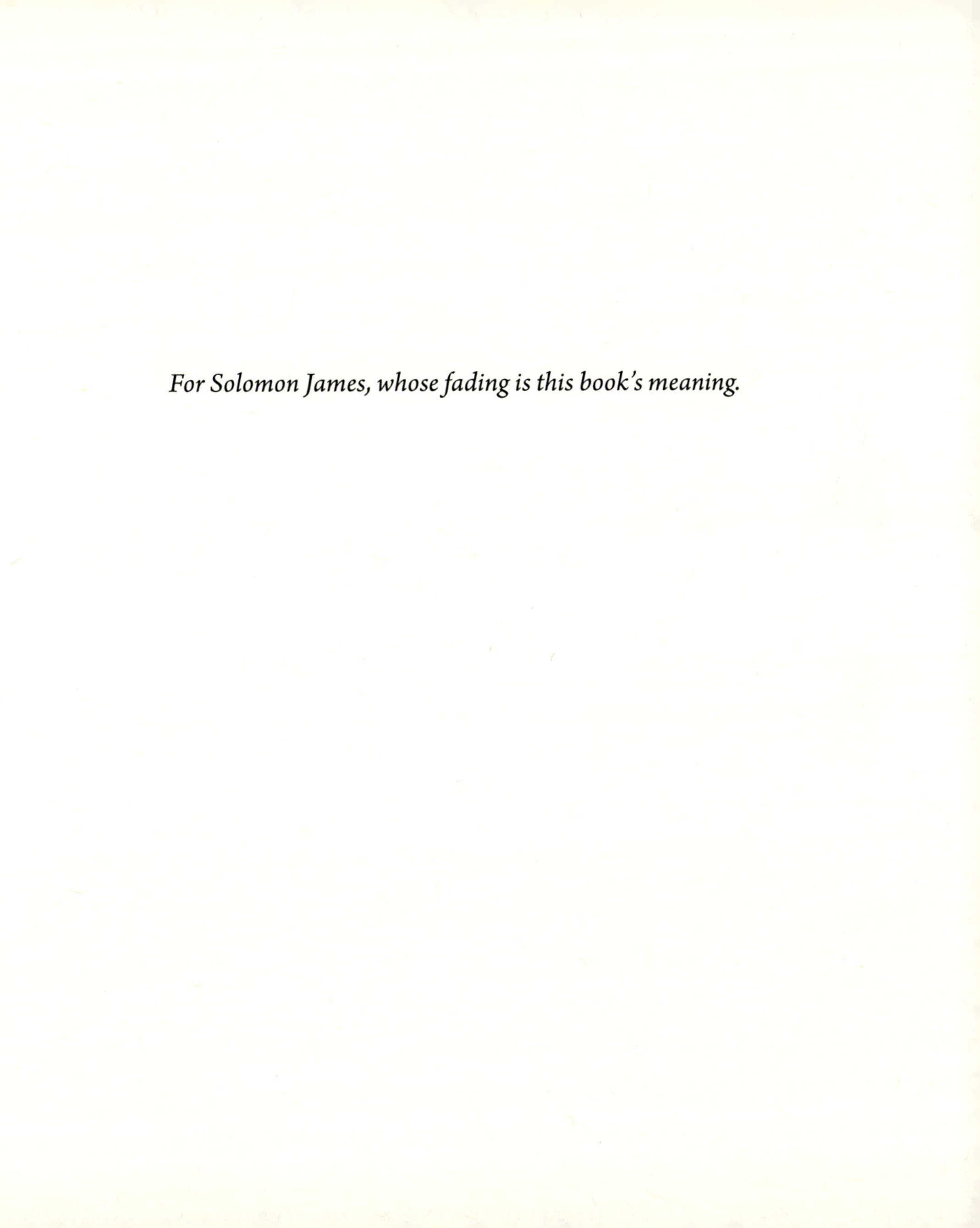

For Solomon James, whose fading is this book's meaning.

CONTENTS

ACKNOWLEDGMENTS

Robin David and her gorgeous children—Elias, Ezra, and Evelina—for their irrational, bottomless love and support, everyone at *Arizona Quarterly,* Mäts Backer, Roberta Bayley, Michael Beard, Erin and Nick Berthelsen, Russell Bestley and Matt Grimes and all at the Punk Scholars Network, Amanda Boyd, Bill Caraher, Sharon Carson, Anne Cecil and everyone at PCA/ACA, Daniel Chang, Melanie Crow, Hugh D'Andrade, Arlene David, Kathleen Dixon, Andrine and David Evers, Janice Frisch, Eric Fundingsland, Chris Gable, Green Gartside, Sean Gohman, Greg Graffin, Julene Griffin, Sam Gruenberg, Richard Hell, Emily Hill, David Hulsey, Mark Joseph, Chris Jury, Lloyd Kaufman and John Brennan at Troma Entertainment, Kaitlyn Kelly, Adam Kemp, Carol A. Kennedy, Diane Kinney, Merie Kirby, Phil Kiszley and everyone at *Punk and Post-Punk,* Adam Kitzes, Jason Lay, Shawn Leake, Joseph Leiss, Steven A. Light, Nancy Lightfoot, Damon Locks, Ian MacKaye, Rhodri Marsden, Nate Marshall, Jim Mochoruk, Dan Mohr, June Panic, Raina Polivka, Sally Pyle, Peter Quinn, Dan Schill, James and Judy Schill, Kathryn and Eric Schommer, Dan Sinker, Lonna Skoog, Jeremy Swisher, Michelle Sybert, Nathan Thompson, Isaac Turner, Rebecca Weaver-Hightower, Jack R. Weinstein, Wendy Wendt, Aaron Wentz, Dana Williams, everyone on the University of North Dakota Senate Scholarly Activities Committee:

Thanks.

THE YEAR'S WORK IN THE PUNK BOOKSHELF

OR, LUSTY SCRIPTS

PROLOGUE

The scene is straight out of an early Sergio Leone film, something probably featuring Clint Eastwood: grunting and poorly dubbed savages enter, with bravado, the main hall of Tromaville High and begin tossing hapless underclassmen aside, threatening to overrun the heretofore well-ordered oasis of Knowledge in a postmodern wasteland of primitivism. "It may just be my woman's intuition, you guys, but somethin's goin' *ahn*. Look around you!" a short-skirted blonde frets, eyeing the brutes early in Lloyd Kaufman's and Michael Herz's campy 1986 film *Class of Nuke 'Em High*, a cross between Mark Lester's exploitation flick *Class of 1984* and Ted Post's revenge western *Hang 'Em High*. Remembering the straight-A student who only a day earlier had without warning retched up a noxious green phlegm before throwing himself out a third-floor classroom window, the Valley Girl is remembering the nuclear power plant upwind from her high school (the recent meltdown of which had been covered up by local officials) and spying suspiciously this ramshackle collection of outlaws known as the Cretins. "Remember those guys?" she asks her clique with a nod. "*They* were the Honor Society. *Now* look at them."

Flaunting wild and variegated Mohicans, tattered tees, scuffed leathers, and a fundamentally oafish demeanor, these brigands, *Class of Nuke 'Em High* suggests, are not just any fugitive mob, but have been converted by radiation into a gang of mindless *punks*. And just what sort

0.1. Spike assesses the literary canon in *Class of Nuke 'Em High* (1986). Used by permission of Troma Entertainment Inc.

of threat do these barbarians pose to the developed world? "I remember in debating class they suddenly stopped debating and they *beat up* Mr. Bluick," the blonde continues in a whisper to her rapt friends as around her grunting confederates stalk her classmates. "Yeah—the change was instant," the girl's letterman boyfriend Warren adds with a start, like a groundskeeper remembering where he mislaid his keys. He had been watching distractedly as one Cretin molested a coed. "I mean, there they are one day a bunch clean-cut preppies, and the next day they're a bunch of violent, perverted cretins."

These punks are, the film contends, the blood pouring from the elevator, the embodied return of the repressed. Embedded within this return is not only an obscene (sexual) violence and general misanthropy, but an aversion to intellectual activity of any sort. Serving as heralds of the purported cultural senescence captured by dozens of handwringing headlines from the previous decade ("Decline in Reading of the Classics Causing Concern about Students' Intellectual Grasp" warned the May 29, 1977, edition of the *New York Times* as punk raged), the Cretins make clear that *reading* in particular is a pungent punk allergen.[1] In a droll tracking shot preceding the film's title sequence, two Cretins are shown seated alongside a series of teen archetypes: bimbos and jocks, nerds and preps. Gonzo, the bone-carrying, nose-ringed creep whose entire face has been tattooed pitch black, chews his mouthpiece and looks around maniacally while using his pen as an awl, engraving his notebook and shredding several sheets of paper in a one sweeping motion. Sitting to Gonzo's left, a skunk-haired punk named Spike steals a textbook from the classmate behind him and tears out pages one after another, examining them briefly through narrowed eyes—his head assuming the angle of an expectant dachshund—before handing the creased papers to his dingy punk muse who completes the crumpling of the book's inscribed knowledge, throwing the pages off-camera with a flick of her studded wrist.

By the time of *Class of Nuke 'Em High*, youth on both sides of the Atlantic engrossed in punk rock were desensitized to this ugly depiction of their cognitive and social faculties, having been told for years by their parent culture that they were useless, dimwitted, *anti*-intellectual even. "He had never seen the inside of a library," Caskie Stinnett smirked self-righteously in the pages of *Atlantic Monthly* as early as August 1977 of a punk rocker whose identity he holds secret, "had never read a book that was not written by Harold Robbins or Jacqueline Susann." Upholding his status as the vainglorious defender of high society earned in the pages of *Travel & Leisure*, the *Saturday Evening Post*, and *Ladies' Home Journal*, Stinnett was lamenting not merely rock music, but the eruption of *punk* rock in England and America. "They wear hand-ripped clothes and plastic garbage bags, mascara, swastikas, chains, dog collars, and they have pierced nostrils through which safety pins are fastened," Stinnett wrote disgustedly, documenting with a shudder how punk songs "are interspersed with torrents of four-letter words, and the groups have such names as The Sex Pistols, The Damned, The Vibrators, and Clash." Seizing on this dread were Kaufman and Herz, who proffered the mutated version of a stereotype that since the late 1970s had portrayed punk as nothing less than the bastion of what to the vanguard seemed an entire generation of destructive, foul-mouthed youth loath to express an intelligent thought or be caught reading a book. Caricaturing Stinnett's horror, Kaufman and Herz proposed that punks, in their vulgar hysteria and philistinism, go so far as to annihilate not only pop culture but *the literary canon*.

Feeding this dread, this misrepresentation, were often punks themselves, many of whom baited such reactions, reveling in the fear they had generated in their elders and recognizing the satire embedded within films like *Nuke 'Em High*. "Instead of studying theory, we're going to get up and go," Teen Idles singer Nathan Strejcek screamed in "Get Up and Go" on the first record produced by Washington, DC's Dischord Records, a label known for its punk ethos. The Teen Idles' record came out the same year that anarcho-punks Crass lampooned in "Where Next Columbus?" not only Freud but Jung, Marx, Sartre, and Einstein and warned listeners not to take theory too seriously. Of course punk was "empty, shallow and trivial," English historian and *novelist* Stewart Home, an early punk proponent, argued in *Cranked Up Really High* fifteen years after Crass and Teen Idles but one year before including one of his short stories in a punk fiction anthology whose title page notes that "Punks Can't Read."[2] Rolling his eyes at several writers for attempting to intellectualize punk and postpunk subculture, Home calls punk rock a calculated doltishness, thinking perhaps of the Sex Pistols' "Pretty Vacant" and the Ramones' ode to idiocy "Pinhead," wherein

Joey Ramone chants "D-U-M-B / Everyone's accusing me!" Even Nirvana's Kurt Cobain got into the act, Home recalled, mugging meatheadedness repeatedly, from admitting "I feel stupid and contagious" on his band's breakthrough record *Nevermind* to moaning "I think I'm dumb" and "I take pride as the king of illiterature" on his band's terminal album *In Utero*. "After all," continues Home, "if punk rockers had preferred 'analysis' to 'rhetoric,' they'd have been attempting to organise a revolution instead of pogoing to three minute pop songs."[3] To claim otherwise, suggests Home with reference to Greil Marcus and Neil Nehring, is to engage in an intellectually dishonest mystification of punk that may be popular among highbrow necrophiles in the academy but misses the point of punk praxis. Or, as John Roderick, singer with Seattle group the Long Winters, put it as late as 2013 in a polemic essay for the *Seattle Weekly*, far from honing its adherents' critical thinking strategies, punk subculture created a caste of kids who merely "internalized [punk's] laundry list of pseudo-values—anti-establishmentarianism, anti-capitalism, libertarianism, anti-intellectualism, and self-abnegation disguised as humility," resulting in an intellectual ghetto where "dumbasses were teaching dumbasses."[4]

The consensus thus seems to be that to be punk means to oppose oneself to literature, erudition, even functional thought. But to conclude as much is a mistake. Home's invective and Stinnett's grousing at the impropriety of his progeny notwithstanding, a parade of song lyrics, interviews, and performances since the 1970s signal instead that "proto-punk," punk, and postpunk culture was and remains interested in not only critical thinking but literature, philosophy, and avant-garde art and theater broadly. Moreover, this attraction to books both contributes to punk aesthetics and politics generally and has held up over time, if not increased, in several punk scenes around the world. In addition to the literary pretentions of American proto-punks Iggy Pop, Lou Reed, Tom

Verlaine, Patti Smith, and Richard Hell, for instance, consider the art schooling of English first-wavers Wire and the Mekons. Likewise, early California hardcore acts Bad Religion and Descendents were dismissed by "Dean" of the rock critics Robert Christgau, who called these groups "thesaurus rock" for their often forced use of polysyllabics—anechoic, enthalpic, irascible, pusillanimous—and their pedantic tone on record and in concert.[5] "When I was in high school I was looking for an origin narrative. I read Darwin's journal of his travels and that was very inspiring to me. I read *Origin of Species* in college and that helped me understand my own origins," explains Bad Religion's Greg Graffin, a graduate of the UCLA doctoral program in evolutionary biology whose father was an English professor and whose band referenced, over the course of several records, Hemingway, Henry Miller, Kerouac, Ludwig Boltzmann, Diogenes Laërtius, Spinoza, Richard Leakey, James Hutton, and other writers and scientists. "Fiction came later," Graffin adds, Salman Rushdie in particular.[6]

Long before the singers of Bad Religion, Descendents, and Offspring earned their doctoral degrees, though, Cleveland punks Pere Ubu named themselves after an Alfred Jarry play and Johnny Rotten noted his affinity for not only Oscar Wilde but Shakespeare—*Richard III* in particular.[7] In his widow's words, Joy Division singer Ian Curtis's reading list included "Dostoyevsky, Nietzsche, Jean Paul Sartre, Herman Hesse and J. G. Ballard."[8] Taking their name from the writings of Italian Marxist Antonio Gramsci, English postpunks Scritti Politti would reference French theory in the songs "Jacques Derrida" and "The Word Girl," calling their publishing imprint "Jouissance, Ltd."—a reference to one of French psychoanalyst Jacques Lacan's more seminal concepts. All of this came before Birthday Party and Bad Seeds front man Nick Cave turned his affection for southern American gothic writing—William Faulkner, Flannery O'Connor—into a handful of grotesque novels, poems, and plays. For his part, Simon Reynolds notes repeatedly in his celebratory *Rip It Up and Start Again* how many punk and postpunk figures were "ravenously well-read" and steeped themselves in the prose of Dostoevsky, Kafka, Joseph Conrad, and Samuel Beckett, among other writers, paving the way for groups like Michigan's Bear vs. Shark, named for the Chris Bachelder novel of the same title.[9] Finally, Sonic Youth's Kim Gordon recalls having taken to "Nietzsche, Sartre, Balzac, Flaubert, Baudelaire, and all the other French thinkers, writers, and poets my high school felt it unnecessary to teach" long before she went on to include the ideas of Philip K. Dick and William Gibson in the music she made with her future- and ex-husband Thurston Moore, who too is a published author.[10]

"My life has been surrounded by books—growing up we were seriously *choked* by books," Minor Threat/Fugazi/Evens singer and Dischord Records cofounder Ian MacKaye, whose grandparents and parents were writers, told me, acknowledging a fondness for the work of Kurt Vonnegut, C. S. Lewis, and James Baldwin. "My grandfather, Milton MacKaye, wrote a series of true crime books in the 1930s and wrote for the *Saturday Evening Post*, and my grandmother Dorothy Cameron Disney wrote mysteries and then later did the 'Can This Marriage Be Saved' column for the *Ladies Home Journal*." According to MacKaye, during his time in Fugazi, a band whose name was taken from Mark Baker's Vietnam War memoir *Nam*, after his grandparents' deaths "[Fugazi would] drive up to my grandparents' house in Connecticut to rehearse and write songs, and their house was full of books. So, playing in the living room we'd do a song and then just look at the wall of books for a working title to use for the song. A lot of those titles we swapped out, but something like 'Lusty Scripps' [the title of Gilson Gardner's biography of newspaper publisher E. W. Scripps] was a song we never finished and so the title stayed."[11]

Long before Fugazi, this choking appetite for books was fundamental to perhaps the most successful punk exponent of the 1970s as well. In 1978 the practice of "gobbing," reciprocated among fans and performers, had reached an apex at punk shows around the globe. It is perhaps inevitable, then, that an easy target like the Clash, who toured incessantly, would catch more than others' mucus. "See, either you're a junkie or you've been licking toilet bowls out or something—or people have been spitting at you hours on end all over the country," Joe Strummer told Howie Klein, then writing for San Francisco punk zine *Search & Destroy*—"the authoritative guide to punk culture"—from London's rank Western Hospital. "You can understand it if you think about it, but it gets a bit boring when you get one down your throat and you have to swallow it coz the next line's coming up. It kind of puts you off a bit." Not one to let a typically curable case of hepatitis keep him from working, Strummer adds that the whole nauseating affair has inspired the poet in him: he is spinning a yarn of his own. "It's called *Saliva Missions*. There's a lot of saliva going around! I'm not saying it's particularly healthy—that's my excuse why I'm here. I'm writing a book 'cause I have nothin' else to do.[12]

Contrary to media headlines of the time, rather, most of this interview's readers knew as they pored over Strummer's words in 1978 that such talk was hardly remarkable for punks; literature was central to *Search & Destroy* editor Vale's documentarian approach to punk music and its exponents. Such a focus felt natural, after all, as Klein notes while methodically listing the texts sprawled throughout Strummer's cramped room: "The Strummer library included: *The Long Goodbye* (Raymond Chandler), *334* (Thomas Disch), *M'Hashish* (Mohammed Mrabet), *The Greatest* (Muhammad Ali), *Black Players—The Secret World of Black Pimps* (Christina Milner), *Mexico City Blues* (Jack Kerouac), *History of the Russian Revolution* by Leon Trotsky, *Crash* by J.G. Ballard, *USA* (Dos Passos), and 3 books by Jean Genet."[13]

Beyond Strummer, punks' broader literary influences often served as the hub around which *Search & Destroy* articles revolved. "What are your favorite books?" "Read any good books lately?" "What's your favorite book?" "What are you reading now?" "Are there any writers you admire?" Each of these questions was asked of several interviewees in the magazine's dozen issues. Answers from performers and groups as varied as Iggy Pop, Blondie, Devo, Screamers, the Damned, the Dickies, and Throbbing Gristle run the gamut: philosophy to science fiction to poetry—Antonin Artaud, Edgar Allan Poe, and the Marquis de Sade to Terry Southern, Germaine Greer, Philip K. Dick, Andre Breton, Vladimir Nabokov, Herman Hesse, and Jean-Paul Sartre. Plus countless Friedrich Nietzsche and William S. Burroughs references, the latter of whom was interviewed for *Search & Destroy* #10.

The focus on books seemed so intense by early punk writers, in fact, that at least one agitated performer grew tired of the question: "Then there are journalists who only want to know all the fuckin' books I've ever read, and all the albums I've listened to, they take inventory!" complains Alejandro Escovedo, guitarist of San Francisco's Nuns, who opened the Sex Pistols' final show at Winterland. "And it's not even which books I've read, but which books I *have*. So I like a lot of fuckin' books and movies, big deal, you know? I don't think anybody really cares. . . . 'Looking at your bookcase,' that's a good title for a song."[14]

Certainly there had been references to poetry, philosophy, and fiction in pop music before punk, whether Dylan singing about Shakespeare, Ezra Pound, and T. S. Eliot or David Bowie (whose affection for literature was well-known) crooning, "Beware the savage jaw of 1984" on his Orwell-themed 1974 record *Diamond Dogs*. And there have been such references since: the Police referencing Nabokov's *Lolita* and Homer's *Odyssey* over the course of several records, headbangers Metallica reimagining Dalton Trumbo's *Johnny Got His Gun* on "One" from their 1988 record . . . *And Justice For All,* American hip-hop artists Mos Def and Talib Kweli rapping on *Moby-Dick* in their *Black Star* album, or the Faulkner-referencing metal band As I Lay Dying. But not before or since punk and postpunk have such citations, such bookishness, constituted the *fabric* of commercial music itself, the core ideological and aesthetic kernel of a pop program.

To Escovedo's chagrin, then, the obsession by scores of punk writers and fans who *still* care about the punk bookshelf did not end with *Search & Destroy*: a quarter century after Nuns, Tim Midgett of Seattle-Chicago postpunk group Silkworm even seemed to channel not only the Talking Heads' Tina Weymouth, who in 1978 beat Sting to the punch by telling *Search & Destroy,* "I love Nabokov," but English postpunks the Fall, which entitled its 1986 album *Bend Sinister* after Nabokov's novel.[15] In a 2002 interview with North Dakota–based punk zine *Agricouture,* Midgett uses a literary question by interviewer Isaac Turner—himself a member of postpunk groups Straphanger, Out, Minutes, and Imipolex G (whose name was a hat tipped in Thomas Pynchon's direction)—as a reason to talk Nabokov. "Have you ever read *Infinite Jest* by David Foster Wallace?" Turner asks, hoping to have a serious conversation with a fellow punk reader about the thousand-page novel. Midgett's excited reply veers off course quickly, linking literary criticism to the motivations behind independent record making:

> [Silkworm guitarist] Andy [Cohen] had "I.J." in his manpurse the other day. I think he was reading it. . . . Historically, my main men are W. S. Burroughs and Nabokov. I love Nabokov. Mainly I just devoured the books, but I also admire his technical brilliance. Formally, he doesn't

> make the ultradramatic leaps that Burroughs does. I mean, he's not particularly subtle, being a virtuoso. But when he does something grand, he usually takes accepted means of communication and transforms them by changing their content. *Pale Fire* is the best example, and it may be my favorite book ever. *Bend Sinister, Despair, Laughter in the Dark*—they're impossible targets if you're trying to write a book, less matchable than most any record I can think of. If I were a novelist, I'd be demoralized by those books, and I've never felt that way as a musician about a record.[16]

Demoralized, says Midgett, by the brilliance of the Russian synesthete's metafictional tale of literary obsession, madness, and friendship, by the technical prowess of Nabokov the stylist. Musing on the different aesthetic and methodological choices that separate novel writing from record production, Midgett is here less an aging punk kid from Montana than an autodidact and incredibly thoughtful critic of one of the most important writers of the twentieth century. Speaking thus, Midgett, one is tempted to propose, becomes not a contemporary Christgau so much as a punk Edmund Wilson, that celebrated American crank and literary critic, turning underground music itself into criticism and becoming a high-volume man of letters in the process.

It is, in fact, Wilson's critique of Nabokov and the pair's subsequent feud following more than two decades of trading genial letters that Silkworm reimagines in "Lily White and Cherry Red," a taut track included on the group's posthumous record *Chokes*! "This record begins where the world began / This weak-cheeked little animal has crawled onto land," sings Cohen over his own distorted guitar in a voice both fey and bitter, comparing Wilson to a skulking lungfish and watching the Nabokov-Wilson alliance implode again from a distance of forty years. Or, if not the writers' relationship, Cohen is speaking of the

Marxism remembered in Wilson's socialist saga *To the Finland Station*. "They tried to attack you but Edmund stepped in," Cohen sings. "Even though we make fun of him, he's a good friend." Not quite a dirge, the brittle, driving track—an exasperated Cohen barely stops to catch his breath between verses in a song without a chorus—is nonetheless elegiac, celebrating first the writers' deep affection for each other before lamenting their friendship's death (and the cultural consequences of the falling-out) for what seems to be *no reason*. For despite relishing paper arguments with his colleague over Dickens and Tolstoy, despite waiting anxiously for the postman to deliver his friend's reply to his defense of Lenin and Trotsky, Wilson skewered unexpectedly, in 1965, Nabokov's translation of Alexander Pushkin's novel-in-verse *Eugene Onegin*—Nabokov's first major work after *Pale Fire*—in the *New York Review of Books*. The review was a glinting blade, Silkworm reminds its audience, a distorted reflection that turned Nabokov himself into the shadow of the waxwing slain and severed a bond that had lasted a quarter century. "Aside from this desire both to suffer and make suffer—so important an element in his fiction—the only characteristic Nabokov trait that one recognizes in this uneven and sometimes banal translation is the addiction to rare and unfamiliar words," wrote Wilson of Nabokov's *Onegin*. "To inflict on the reader such words is not really to translate at all, for it is not to write idiomatic and recognizable English."[17] Calling the review full of "ghastly blunders," Nabokov replied that "Mr. Wilson's didactic purpose is defeated by the presence of such errors (and there are many more to be listed later), as it is also by the strange tone of his article. Its mixture of pompous aplomb and peevish ignorance is certainly not conducive to a sensible discussion of Pushkin's language and mine."[18]

Both aggrieved by and seeing the irony in the exchange are Midgett and Cohen, who, smirking at the absurdity of the assault that made hardly a blip on the American literary scene at the time and remains neglected outside scholarly circles, convert the feud into a devastating portrait of American cultural politics in the 1960s for a twenty-first-century audience. Speaking as American postpunk's elder statesmen forty years later, Silkworm, the long-suffering group who like Wilson never seemed to catch a break, to become *popular,* exhumes the friendship's corpse, offering the last—only—pop word on Wilson's sudden, inexplicable betrayal (and apparently taking his side) with all the disaffected resentment of a comrade left behind:

> You were the King and Queen rolled into one
> But the rabble stoned the temple in a desperate lunge
> Tiny Edmund Wilson drove us to your gate
> But none of us could figure out the source of his *hate*

"Cuz everyone pretty much seemed to love you cherry red / We all see the beauty and we're in your debt," continues Cohen in "Lily White" before seeming to needle his bandmate in doubting Nabokov's skill. "But Edmund is immune—his wisdom gave us a clue / He showed us it was *stupid* to suffer for you."

Whether Cohen is referencing Marx or Nabokov, that such a bit of literary esoterica could become the subject of a (post) punk song in the twenty-first century, one played live or on college radio to both agitated American youth in a Chicago club and Heineken-slurping punk punters lounging in pubs across Western Europe, is as astonishing as it is curious. In making such a statement available for purchase, for broadcasting, Midgett and Cohen were breaking no molds but building on a tradition that has given an entire subculture its motivation, its center, since Lou Reed and John Cale named their avant-garde rock ensemble after Michael Leigh's book-length account of sexual deviance published in 1962 as *The Velvet Underground.* This literary quality, unique in popular culture, confounds the pigeonhole foisted upon the bands and records loosely branded as "punk" almost from the moment Iggy Stooge taunted a Detroit-based group of Hell's Angels in 1974 with a lewd forty-five-minute version of "Louie, Louie" whose revised lyrics once ran, "A fine little girl is waiting for me / But I'm as bent as Dostoevsky."[19] It also serves as a defense against the simultaneous snubbing and exploitation of punk by the culture industry, the effect of which has been the decades-long disarming of a rich *intellectual* movement that only happened to use very loud and abrasive music as its medium of choice for the communication of its well-read and sober critiques of capitalism, organized religion, and the State. So do Silkworm and its cohorts show just how backward Stinnett and even Home are. From Lou Reed and Iggy Pop in the late 1960s to Joy Division to the Charles Bukowski–reading groups Nirvana and Modest Mouse in the 1990s to Silkworm and the Derrida- and Franz Kafka–referencing postpunk group Deathfix in the new century, musicians affiliated with punk represented and continue to represent not the deterioration of intellectualism in popular culture, but the *injection of literary thought into it.*

This clandestine truth was also broached in passing by the screenwriter whose film was the basis for Kaufman's and Herz's parody of wholesome honors students gone bad. "And the amazing thing—I think that Stegman's actually a brilliant kid," music instructor Andrew Norris tells his biology colleague, the cynical Mr. Corrigan, played by Roddy McDowall, in Mark Lester's *Class of 1984,* a sort of punk *Blackboard Jungle.* "So was the Marquis de Sade," replies Corrigan with a sneer of the student who seems to be forsaking gleefully a promising future in Medicine or Law by affiliating not with Students-of-the-Month but burnouts, addicts, and imps. The men are referring here to the charismatic sociopath Peter Stegman, leader of a gang of teen criminals and sexual deviants who had been terrorizing the Lincoln High student body: "We are the future! . . . And Nothing Can stop Us" the caption atop a stylized quartet of punks clothed in threadbare sadomasochistic garb—leathers, chains, spikes—had read in the film's promotional poster.

In calling Stegman brilliant, Norris was remembering the astonishingly beautiful piano composition produced by the punker only moments after he had pounded the keys of the music room upright in a discordant fury early in the film; this kid is clearly more sophisticated than he lets on. Setting the stage for *Nuke 'Em High, Class of 1984* suggested to audiences in 1982 that the punk lieutenants Stegman commands are not only crude and sadistic advocates of aggressive music, but surprisingly well-read. As the punks lounge and survey their underground empire later in the film, one of Stegman's cohorts, the leather-jacketed Fallon, can be seen reading the 1980 edition of *Adventures in Time and Space*—"The Single Best Volume of What Science Fiction Is All About!" according to the book's dust jacket—featuring short stories by Isaac Asimov and Robert Heinlein. Unlike *Nuke 'Em High*'s Spike and Simon Reynolds's postpunks, Fallon does not rip this text apart, but rather regards it intently, looking annoyed when Stegman gives him a depraved task to perform.

Both *Class* films are today cult classics, two in a parade of kitschy B movies from around the world that followed Roger Corman's *Rock and Roll High School* in associating the snide eruption of punk rock with Armageddon—Derek Jarman's *Jubilee,* the *Mad Max* franchise, *Dead-End Drive In, The New Barbarians.* Such films remain current in analyses of punk for the same reason the spaghetti Western still attracts an audience: their reactionary and melodramatic typecasting was so overblown, so far removed from what most "real" punks and postpunks said and did in public or private, that these films did a better job than punks themselves of illustrating the horrors that a shameless postindustrial market economy had unleashed upon communities, whose growing political fragmentation, social isolation, and desertification were evident by the 1970s. In exaggerating punk's style and symbolic power, rather, these films simultaneously neutralize, in what Lacan called the Imaginary order, the reality of punk at the same time as they *make punks' argument for them,* illustrating for the viewer the "no future" punks had been merely yowling on about.

Falling into this trap as well was Lester's overdetermined screenplay, which only broadened the audience for punks' critique of what Walter Benjamin called "the phantasmagoria of capitalist culture"—spectacle, anomie—even as it scapegoated and then murdered those voicing this critique.[20] Having challenged Norris's rule, all of the offending punks in *Class of 1984* are rewarded with a series of brutal deaths worthy of Eastwood's drifter (dismemberment, hanging, immolation) at the hands of the more refined music instructor. So it is that Lester's defense of the cultural, political, and socioeconomic status quo that had created punk in the first place, and his decision not to explore how it is that smart, highly literate kids end up being seen by the community as pollutants in need of eradication, not only signals a failure of imagination on the film's part, but serves as a rather emetic apology for hierarchy and tradition—the Name of the Father—by pitting a *classical music teacher* against a series of rapist "punks" whose afterschool haunts include back alleys and raucous nightclubs.

The question Lester's film was consciously exploring—What is to be done about this scourge of punk-inspired anti-intellectualism and violence plaguing North American public schools?—is not the right one in any case; rock and roll has, long in advance of punk, been considered the harbinger of cultural decline and the citadel of idiocy, youth rebellion, and licentiousness. To highlight punk in this regard in 1979 or 1982 said nothing new. Better questions go in the opposite direction and recognize the intellectual innovation punk represented for popular culture: How is it that punk rock effectively introduced literature and dramaturgy into pop music? How is it that punk created the conditions whereby, as Greil Marcus once put it, "teenagers screamed philosophy; thugs made poetry"?[21] Why are punks attracted to Baudelaire, Dostoevsky, Salinger, Kafka, and Burroughs—to the point of quoting these writers in lyrics and interviews—but not other "canonical" writers and poets, or even the pulpish writers Stinnett cited (although members of X once claimed that their "favorite books" were "*Valley of the Dolls* and *Once is not Enough* by Jackie Susanne" [*sic*]).[22] Finally, why is it that, as several of these films suggest, *reading books* seems to be the actual source of so many kids' devolution into monsters?

Answering these questions—broadening the literary context in which punk music is performed and heard—is this book's aim. By and large, punk and postpunk are and have been from their beginning cerebral, intellectually astute, if confounding, music subcultures made by often smart and well-read people. And it is these musicians' reading that has shaped punk aesthetics and politics in a variety of ways. Or so this book argues, considering how, why, and to what effect young people with ragged clothing and perforated faces have for decades absorbed, debated, and reintroduced into popular culture not only continental philosophy but French poetry, American literature, and avant-garde theater—or gone on to pierce their faces *after* reading such texts. With psychoanalysis and the Marxism of writers like Benjamin as its guides, *Lusty Scripts* documents punk's literary roots, connecting punk not only to Hegel, Nietzsche, and Freud, but Arthur Rimbaud, Henry Miller, Antonin Artaud, Kafka, Burroughs, Genet, Dick, and Gibson. It catalogues and interprets the subculture's bookshelf—what punks read and write—making sense out of the literary history of one of the twentieth century's most maligned and misunderstood cultural movements. In so doing, this book posits a new theory of punk, teasing out Lester Bangs's throwaway line from a 1977 article on the Clash that claims most punk music "merely amounts to saying I suck" in order to argue that punk's intellectual interests and radical politics can ultimately be traced to the *shame*—whether physical, socioeconomic, cultural, or sexual—many of the genre's advocates feel in the face of a shameless market economy and the First World's swelling consumer largesse that generated the punk polemic in the first place.[23]

By articulating this humiliation, also a central concern for most of the writers cited above, from Dostoevsky to Bukowski, each individual punk serves as a symptom indicating the presence of disease in a market culture numb to the disgrace of its historical failure to follow through on its own rhetoric, to generate opportunity, dignity, and an ethic of freedom and self-worth among its tenants. Each of the references that punks and postpunks have made to fiction, poetry, philosophy, and theater is a clue to the etiology of an infection that has been festering for over forty years. This book is an attempt to diagnose what amounts to a rash on the skin of contemporary culture, in other words, and give shape to punk's literary history in so doing.

Such an endeavor is inevitably fraught, of course, for no pop phenomenon has been plagued by as much vociferous debate as to what does or does not constitute the subject in question. "The word 'punk' seemed to sum up the thread that connected everything we liked—drunk, obnoxious, smart but not pretentious, absurd, funny, ironic, and things that appealed to the darker side," says *Punk* magazine founder Legs McNeil. To this Dead Kennedys singer Jello Biafra later replied, speaking of the debate over the definition of punk that emerged among journalists, promoters, and fans of punk and postpunk in the 1980s, "If 'Holiday in Cambodia' were released today, it would be banned from [hardcore magazine] *Maximum Rock n Roll* for not sounding punk."[24] This very debate over what is or is not "punk" demonstrates the value punks place on the precise use of language, of *Logos*, of articulating what it means to associate oneself with an idea both in practice and on paper. Such dispute is embedded deep in the punk bookshelf—as is a desire, moth-eaten and yellowed though it may be, harbored by artists, writers, and radicals the world over to express just how disgraceful and absurd it is to have to live like "dying animals on a doomed planet," as Burroughs once put it, to be forced to explain why they mutilate themselves and wear trash bags and other shabby coverings while ranting on about their alienation and antipathy.[25] You have made of us trash, punks accuse the Name of the Father—capitalism, government, Church, and family—not merely objects (which at least have value) but subordinate *abject* subjects, to quote Judith Butler, disallowed from entertaining an original thought, engaging in meaningful work, or expressing any human emotion.

For the purposes of this book, then, Ellen Willis's description of the Velvet Underground as "rock and roll artists who had no real chance of attracting a mass audience" will serve as a working definition of "punk": music not merely subscribing to a specific volume or speed, but pop music as a self-defeating contradiction, pop culture that intentionally flies in the face of the popular in an array of contexts, usually to its own disadvantage (say, by musing at length on Edmund Wilson and Vladimir Nabokov).[26] Punk and postpunk here are not subcultures associated with any specific style but musical movements whose form and/or content make their likelihood of achieving traditional measures of (commercial) "success" highly unlikely even as they toy with pop formulae. For as novelist and pop critic Chuck Klosterman reminds punks and his typically less-than-punk readers, this contradictory approach to an aesthetic is often taxing on the arbiters of the popular; it is quite irritating for the cultural dominant when a caste of subjects fed up with both pop's inanity and their own miserable condition *speaks* up. "I hate punk rock," begins the cultural critic and erstwhile *New York Times* ethicist, anticipating John Roderick in his 2004 collection of shallow criticism and poor philosophy, *Sex, Drugs, and Cocoa Puffs*:

> Actually that's not true; I kind of like punk rock, sometimes. What I hate are people who *love* punk rock. There has never been a genre of anything that has made more people confused about what art is capable of doing, and they all refuse to shut up about it. A few years ago, one of my favorite humans of all time died of bone cancer. A few hours after the funeral, I found myself in conversation with someone who was as depressed as I was and almost as drunk. But—in order to avoid talking about our friend, probably—we started talking about pop music, and this guy kept saying, "Punk rock saved my life." He said it like four times in ten minutes. "When I was in high school," he insisted, "punk rock saved my life, man." I have heard those exact words said thousands of times by hundreds of people, and none of them are ever joking. They exist in a culture of certainty. They want to believe what they are saying *so much*. They want to believe that this sentiment is literally true. And all I could do while I listened to this dude tell me how punk rock saved his life was think, Wow. Why did my friend waste all that time going to chemotherapy? I guess we should have just played him a bunch of shitty Black Flag records.[27]

His smug and puerile sarcasm notwithstanding, in correctly identifying what has become something of a cliché among many fans of punk and postpunk, Klosterman nevertheless smirks his way past the intellectual, socioeconomic, and ethical context in which much of punk is created and consumed, failing to engage the politics of a music culture that, as the artists and musicians incorporated into this book suggest, has for decades provided embittered abject subjects like Klosterman's colleague with egress and at least the semblance of autonomy in a world that is trying to shame them to death.

"Well, you gotta talk or you'll die," Tilden puts it in Sam Shepard's *Buried Child*, echoing both Scheherazade, whose voice went long into the night, and Freud.[28] Punks and postpunks are alienated and marginalized human beings who have simply, finally, opened their mouths, putting an end to the silencing they felt has been forced upon them by Klosterman and his benefactors and making a necessary enunciation with their guitars, mouths, and pens that, as Klosterman's interlocutor tried to get across, both helps them come to grips with their status as dispossessed abject subjects and sometimes saves their lives: punks need to demonstrate to the executioner—as much as the analyst or themselves—their humiliation and the literature that helps them understand and respond to their abjection, lest they die in silence of shame, if not the axe. So have they turned to literature to help them do so for four decades, pulling verse out of the gutter and attempting to overcome their indignity and anomie by consulting and then rebroadcasting the philosophy, poetry, and prose that shares their apprehension over their dehumanization and demotion—and maybe even silence the master in the process. To these broadcasts Church, State, and political economy should listen, for they are an alarm, anticipating the future in store for even those who like Klosterman hear but do not listen, who make no attempt to understand the punk polemic even as the infection it has symptomatized for decades—disenfranchisement, pauperization, abjectification—becomes pandemic in a world of emerging markets, perpetual war, and disintegrating communities.

Notes

1. Beverly Crandall, "Decline in Reading of the Classics Causing Concern about Students' Intellectual Grasp," *New York Times*, May 29, 1977, A1, A36.

2. Stewart Home, *Cranked Up Really High* (Hove, UK: Codex, 1995), 20. See also Home, "Cheap Night Out," in *Gobbing Pogoing and Gratuitous Bad Language*, ed. Robert Dellar (London: Spare Change, 1996), 76–78.

3. Home, *Cranked Up*, 24.

4. John Roderick, "Punk Rock Is Bullshit," *Seattle Weekly*, March 6, 2013, Sound Publishing, Inc., http://archive.seattleweekly.com/arts/830007-129/punk-rock-music-art-culture-self.

5. See Christgau's review of Bad Religion's *All Ages* and *The Gray Race* ("Spins: Platter Du Jour") in *Spin*, March 1996, 107. Despite his rolled eyes, Christgau nonetheless agrees that Bad Religion's vocabulary signals its "disinclination to condescend."

6. Greg Graffin, personal communication with the author, November 3, 2015.

7. John Lydon, *Rotten: No Irish, No Blacks, No Dogs* (New York: Picador, 1994), 17, 154.

8. Deborah Curtis, *Touching from a Distance* (London: Faber & Faber, 2007), 90.

9. Simon Reynolds, *Rip It Up and Start Again* (New York: Penguin, 2005), 2.

10. Kim Gordon, *Girl in a Band* (New York: Dey/HarperCollins, 2015), 50.

11. Ian MacKaye, personal communication with the author, September 2, 2015. See also Fugazi, "Lusty Scripps," *Instrument*, compact disc, Dischord, DIS120CD, 1999; and Gilson Gardner, *Lusty Scripps: The Life of E. W. Scripps (1854–1926)* (New York: Vanguard, 1932).

12. Howie Klein, "Clash in the Hospital," *Search & Destroy* #6, 1978, in *Search and Destroy 1–6: The Complete Reprint*, by V. Vale (San Francisco: V/Search, 1996), 123. Strummer is here being disingenuous. As Chris Salewicz documents in *Redemption Song*, Strummer likely contracted the disease from shooting heroin with a dirty hypodermic needle.

13. Ibid.

14. Lynn X, "Alejandro Is a Maverick," *Search & Destroy* #6, 1978, in *Search and Destroy 1–6: The Complete Reprint*, by V. Vale (San Francisco: V/Search, 1996), 116.

15. Lynn X, "Talking Heads," *Search & Destroy* #6, 1978, in *Search and Destroy 1–6: The Complete Reprint*, by V. Vale (San Francisco: V/Search, 1996), 133.

16. Isaac Turner, "SKWM," *Agricouture* #2, July 2002, 8–9.

17. Edmund Wilson, "The Strange Case of Pushkin and Nabokov," *New York Review of Books*, July 15, 1965, 3–6.

18. Vladimir Nabokov, "Letters: The Strange Case of Nabokov and Wilson," *New York Review of Books*, August 26, 1965, 25–26.

19. This story is recounted in Lester Bangs, *Psychotic Reactions and Carburetor Dung*, ed. Greil Marcus (New York: Vintage, 1988), 206. See also Iggy Pop, "Louie, Louie," *American Caesar*, compact disc, Virgin, 724383900220, 1993.

20. Walter Benjamin, "Paris, the Capital of the Nineteenth Century," in *The Writer of Modern Life*, ed. Michael W. Jennings (1935; Cambridge, MA: Belknap, 2006), 37.

21. Greil Marcus, *Lipstick Traces: A Secret History of the Twentieth Century* (Cambridge, MA: Harvard University Press, 1989), 6.

22. Black Randy, "Black Randy," *Search & Destroy* #3, 1977, in *Search and Destroy 1–6: The Complete Reprint*, by V. Vale (San Francisco: V/Search, 1996), 39.

23. Bangs, *Psychotic Reactions*, 225.

24. Legs McNeil and Gillian McCain, *Please Kill Me: The Uncensored Oral History of Punk* (New York: Penguin, 1996), 204. See also David Grad, "Jello Biafra," in *We Owe You Nothing*, ed. Dan Sinker (1997; New York: Akashic, 2001), 44.

25. William S. Burroughs, *The Ticket That Exploded* (New York: Grove, 1967), 151.

26. Ellen Willis, "The Velvet Underground," in *Out of the Vinyl Deeps* (1978; Minneapolis: University of Minnesota Press, 2011), 56.

27. Chuck Klosterman, *Sex, Drugs, and Cocoa Puffs* (New York: Scribner, 2003), 173.

28. Sam Shepard, "Buried Child," in *Seven Plays* (Toronto: Bantam, 1986), 78.

1 NIETZSCHE'S LISP

"Why *shouldn't* people be frightened by this music?" The question comes by way of *The Tomorrow Show* host Tom Snyder late on a cold February night in 1981, long after most of Johnny Carson's viewers had drifted off to sleep. It is the latest in what has been a string of patronizing and superficial queries that included "Do you hear your own voice when you're singing back there?" and "If you toned it down a little bit maybe you'd have more fans—do you think about that at all?" He is marking time, Snyder, picking lint from his coat and looking for a way of filling space until the next advertising break. Bored by his own interview with Iggy Pop, and apparently having learned little from his disastrous conversation with John Lydon and Keith Levene of Public Image Ltd six months earlier, the interviewer is trying if not to provoke then at least to amuse the jittery and sometimes jumbled guest opposite him who had only minutes earlier performed "Dog Food" and "T.V. Eye" for an in-studio audience. As his disinterested line of questions suggests, Snyder has come to regard Pop—still bleeding after butting himself in the face with an NBC microphone—as a freak, a numbskull, certainly not someone to be taken seriously or engaged *intellectually*. The interview had been beset by fits and starts to that point, with, as a result, awkward moments that even had Snyder held his interlocutor in more esteem would likely have emerged naturally from the juxtaposition of the well-heeled patriarch of late-late television and the shoot-from-the-hip former Stooge who explained comfortably only seconds before this latest question that his effort to tax his own flesh with broken glass during a 1973 performance was an attempt to express a certain existential principle: "the truth of that moment was that I ought to be cut."

Snyder, frowning now, is nonplussed; he is tired of the guest's incoherence and lack of professionalism. "I was talking to your chick who works for you the other day . . . is this mic working?" Pop had mumbled in between sips of water as a shrill voice in the audience orders Pop, "Take off your clothes!" Trying to rein things in, Snyder presses on, refusing to let his initial question die a natural death: "Just as some people were very terrified of rock and roll when it started, and then they got terrified of the Beatles, there are some people who get scared by any new trend in music—" he continues before being cut off.

"Okay, fair enough," admits Pop finally, ignoring Snyder's suggestion that punk was somehow *new* in 1981. "One terror is that if you played music like the way I do, okay, obviously, already, if I put as much into a song as I possibly can on your show, automatically for five, ten minutes, it is very hard for me to speak articulately or to talk to you—"

"You're pumped up back there," Snyder offers, nodding in feigned understanding.

"You see, because I've quite given myself totally to that," Pop says soberly, gesturing to the stage behind him. Then, grinning like a little boy about to voice a dirty word, Pop returns his gaze to Snyder and after a pause almost whispers, "It's *Dionysiac*."

Snyder's posture, his entire carriage, shifts at the sound. "You know the difference between Dionysiac and Apollonian art?" Pop asks his host quickly, sensing immediately the freeze the question brings into the studio. Snyder's own smile, as if through a certain sublimation, evaporates: this is not Lydon smoking and smirking but nonetheless deferring to Snyder's lead—Snyder has himself become the object of his own program. Snyder is disoriented by Pop's query, his heretofore smug regard for his guest replaced by an expression of confusion. Silence. He sits up a bit straighter, searching for a reply.

The lag lasts only a moment, but in the profound void that follows Pop's question to a respected news reporter and anchorman, who, knowing instantly that he has been duped (again), can only manage a meek, "I'm not too good on that," everyone—interviewer, interviewee, studio audience, television viewer—recognizes instantly the transference that has occurred in the room.

Without hesitating longer, Pop, simultaneously trying to save his host from too much embarrassment and recognizing that he has cleared the ground completely, launches into a discourse on Friedrich Nietzsche's 1872 foray into dramaturgy, *The Birth of Tragedy*. The broken-toothed, scrawny punk, astute enough to know just how narrow is the opening in this window, drives the discourse forward, now lecturing the television man: "Dionysiac art in Greek times was where, like, a bunch of people would get together and they'd erect a paper phallus 50 feet long and carry it around and chant to some god they believed in, right?" Snyder is getting visibly nervous, uncertain of where this is all going. He has no reply save a subtle "mmhmmm." Pop advances with confidence, returning finally to the question that began the interview. "You know . . . the creation of an event—it's eventful art. Apollonian is when you just make a statue and it's there forever and it's set out very clearly. There's a Dionysiac element to my art that does . . . I suppose a lot of people might be frightened to be me. But I'm quite happy to be me."

In a space of ninety seconds, Iggy Pop, the self-debasing, skittish, and bloodied former Stooge—who made a name for himself by crawling about a stage singing, "I Wanna Be Your Dog" and coating himself in peanut butter on stage—has swept away all frivolity, all the trite commercial pandering typical of late-night television and pop schlock that even at the height of early punk dominated the airwaves, and replaced it with dramatic theory, with *philosophy*. On NBC. Perhaps even more stunned than was Bill Grundy when the Sex Pistols unleashed "the filth and the fury" on Thames TV in 1977, Snyder, confounded as to how to continue when his guest failed to act like the crude monkey he was expected to be, has little recourse but to move on quickly, to search for a way of keeping things light—"All right. In the world of music, who are your favorites?"

Although Pop entertains the question, citing Sun Ra, Cab Calloway, and Howlin' Wolf, his answer is irrelevant. The point has been made: to misjudge punk's intellectual ceiling, to dismiss it as mindless violence and atonal noise, is a precarious, and potentially fatal, move. That a conversation on continental philosophy and the phallus as a signifier—on Nietzsche as the basis for an international pop subculture—is so disarming to a member of the elite *and* advanced not by an academic, politician, or establishment critic but a *punk rocker*, is an astounding commentary on the sad state of pop music, broadcast journalism, and American culture broadly in 1981. This Snyder and his advertisers learned the hard way, with cameras rolling.

Perhaps even more remarkable, however, is the fact that Pop, in 1981, was but the latest in a long line of punks to have made direct reference to Nietzsche since the 1970s. "I like philosophers on a literary level rather than—like Nietzsche—he's got flair!" So enthused the Dickies singer Leonard Graves Phillips two years in advance of Pop's interview. "Sure he contradicts himself all the time but . . . I always got the impression that Nietzsche was a real Quasimodo virgin guy—in the daytime he'd, 'Uh, hi, how are you, I-I'm really a ni-nice guy,' but at night he'd go into his room and Wham: THE MASTER RACE! THE SUPER MAN!"[1]

"Western values mean nothing to her," crooned Mark Stewart of the Pop Group through a red kerchief a year after Phillips in "She Is

Beyond Good and Evil," a disjointed single that unfolds like a Nietzschean wet dream and anticipates the group's later single "Where There's a Will There's a Way," in referencing the philosopher's most polemic work. Not to be outdone, Germs singer Darby Crash confessed to having filled countless notebooks with homespun poetry, prose, and philosophy in high school. "I [still] work on some philosophy stuff. Just Scientology and Nietzsche like *Thus Spake Zarathustra* and *The Prince* by Machiavelli."[2]

Or, as Richard Hell had put it to *Punk* magazine's Legs McNeil years before Germs, the Pop Group, or the Dickies had pulled themselves together, "Did you ever read Nietzsche?" McNeil only laughs. "Legs, listen to me, he said that anything that makes you laugh, anything that's funny indicates an emotion that's died. Every time you laugh that's an emotion, a serious emotion, that doesn't exist with you anymore . . . and that—that's why I think you and everything else is so funny." "Yeah, I do too, but *that's* not funny," responds McNeil, stifling a laugh. "That's 'cause you don't have any emotions," Hell shoots back, sending both young men, barely out of their teens, into a fit of hysterical guffawing.[3]

Nietzsche notwithstanding, punks' interest in philosophy, Snyder would have been shocked to learn, runs the gamut from aesthetics to phenomenology to epistemology, as Eugene Hütz implies when he sings in gypsy-punk band Gogol Bordello's drunken "Start Wearing Purple" that "I know it all from Dio-*gee*-neez to the Foucault." Or consider that almost lost in the very fine print that typified *Search & Destroy* is that San Francisco group Screamers directs readers, in a 1978 interview, not only to Susan Sontag and Basil Bernstein but to Foucault's *Madness and Civilization*.[4] Building on Screamers' ostensible poststructuralism, English postpunks Scritti Politti demonstrate their reading of not only Jacques Derrida but French psychoanalyst Jacques Lacan over several singles in songs such as "The Sweetest Girl" and "The Word Girl." Ian

Curtis's widow Deborah likewise documents in her memoir *Touching from a Distance*, the former Joy Division singer obsessed over numerous philosophers, particularly Nietzsche and Sartre.[5]

Further east, Slovenian industrial-postpunk group Laibach lent a blurb to the back of Slavoj Žižek's sophomore English title *For They Know Not What They Do* two years in advance of the philosopher's public defense of the group against charges of fascism. Finally, American postpunk June Panic made an effort to bring each of these disparate threads together in 2003, telling *Punk Planet* magazine, "I'm reading a guy called Žižek. I guess you'd call him a Marxist-Lacanian philosopher. The main guy I constantly go back to is Wittgenstein. I read a lot of Heidegger too—I actually wrote a song for him that will be on my new album. I'm reading some essays by T. S. Eliot, Emerson, a lot of Thoreau and stuff like that."[6]

As such examples suggest, punks and postpunks have, across time and place, taken philosophy quite seriously. Even Stewart Home, the writer and founder of the band White Colours, who rejects the intellectual qualities of punk with venom in *Cranked Up Really High*, concedes that he "spends his time pursuing an interest in Hegelian philosophy" and references by name Marx, Freud, Lacan, Derrida, and Deleuze in his novel *Cunt*.[7] So does it come as no surprise that a handful of writers—academic and not—have explored the question of whether or not there is an identifiable "punk philosophy." In 1999, anarchist imprint AK Press officially published Craig O'Hara's widely circulated pamphlet originally penned in 1992, *The Philosophy of Punk: More Than Noise*. Dealing mostly with the historical context and definition of punk, O'Hara's book, many readers noticed, uses "philosophy" loosely as metonymy for "way of life," failing to make a single reference to political, continental, analytic, or postmodern philosophy and exploring instead punk's connections to anarchism, veganism, and the mass media.[8] The same critique can be made of Lars Kristiansen's *Screaming for Change: Articulating a Unifying Philosophy of Punk Rock*. Despite his assertion that "punk should be understood as a way of seeing the world, as a way of reasoning, or, essentially, as a philosophy on its own terms," Kristiansen brushes aside all questions of ontology, political economy, and ethics to focus primarily on punk *rhetoric*.[9] Finally, in 2014 Situation Press published *The Truth of Revolution, Brother*, an interview collection that brought together many of punk's leading voices to discuss their personal philosophies of Being, aesthetics, and politics. It is ironic, then, that although the book's subtitle is "an exploration of punk philosophy," like its predecessors *Truth* shies away from actually defining or discussing philosophy proper, or any thinkers-writers dead or alive, in any detail. Although the book's editors argue that "punk brought to life some profound philosophical ideas that largely remained parked on the pages of worthy tomes," these ideas and the tomes from which they emerged are almost *nowhere* mentioned in the book.[10]

Although one can imagine, in each of the above titles, bibliographies ripe with texts by Hegel, Arendt, and Foucault, Kropotkin, Sartre, and Heidegger, Chomsky, Kant, and Judith Butler, no such citations emerge in any of them—save a handful of throwaway references to Nietzsche and a vaguely defined "existentialism" in each. This absence accounts for these books' bitter aftertaste for readers expecting punk thoughts on the love of wisdom: in ignoring speculative philosophy of the more customary variety these books ignore the fact that many, many punks are often demonstrably—sycophantically—interested in the thinkers cited above, in philosophy as a tradition.

Arguing that punks' actual reading of philosophy forms the basis for what might be called the "punk philosophy," this chapter posits that one cannot articulate a sensible punk philosophy in the absence of understanding the philosophers punks and postpunks have internalized and espoused, the philosophy that heralds punk music and aesthetics. For in identifying the works of philosophy punks have cited in their lyrics, in interviews, on album covers, and from stage, in cataloguing the variegated philosophies punks tend to exploit (if not endorse) in the practice of their art, a pattern emerges: continental rather than analytical philosophy tends to be valorized; the philosophers most often cited were at one time, and at times still are, those marginalized—if not dismissed outright—within much of academic philosophy; and with Iggy leading the way, punks often craft an aesthetic out of their reading of philosophy, even when the texts in question have little to do with aesthetics. For example, on Scritti Politti's Lacan-referencing "Wood Beez," Green Gartside, playing the role of analyst, transfers Derrida's *différance,* the infinite delay in signification implicit to language, to the pop love song, singing, "I'm a would be / W.O.O.D. / I'm a would be would be / B.E.E.Z.," making of language a plaything and musing on his conjectural proposals for future being, each of which morphs into frustratingly indefinite deferrals of signification, unfulfilled desires that like a swarm of buzzing insects drive the speaker mad. Out of this particular reading, the punk philosophy that comes to be embodied by punks and their descendants is less a nonconformist philosophy of deviance, as Kristiansen puts it, than a celebratory and often self-flagellating valorization of punks' chronic alienation, mortification, and silencing vis-à-vis what Lacan called the institutional Names of the Father—capitalism, Church, family, government, ideology—they reject who are the collective source of punks' humiliating marginalization. Beginning with Hegel and ending with punks' reading of psychoanalysis and poststructuralism, this chapter posits that the punk and post-punk philosophy, prefigured not only by Hegel, Marx, and Nietzsche, but also by Freud, Lacan, Derrida, and Foucault, is one that articulates punks' ongoing attempt to stage, make sense of, and ultimately escape the abject selves created by a series of what Lacan called "master signifiers" that punks come to oppose as a matter of course for the shame they beget in the punk subject.

Tarrying with the Negative

Nietzsche's attraction for punks is therefore obvious: he is one of their own. Renouncing his Prussian citizenship in 1869, Nietzsche wormed his way into the academy in Switzerland—at age twenty-four—despite lacking both a terminal degree and a teaching credential. Cultivating a reputation as a rabble-rousing nonconformist and "nihilist" (though he would also warn of nihilism's harms) he produced increasingly bold tracts attacking the establishment wherever he encountered it, the Church, high culture, and his intellectual predecessors. "Like Luther, like Liebniz, Kant was one more clog for German honesty," Nietzsche wrote sardonically in his most antagonistically entitled work *The Antichrist*—which perhaps caught Johnny Rotten's eye somewhere along the way—before concluding that as a result of his scrupulousness, "Kant became an idiot." The philosopher infamous for drawing attention to the death of God would go on in the same essay to call Hegel's notion of "pure spirit" a "pure lie" and argue that the unfolding of consciousness from his *The Phenomenology of Spirit* is so much time wasted: "The development of consciousness, the 'spirit,' is for us nothing less than the symptom of a relative imperfection of the organism; it means trying, groping, blundering—an exertion which uses up an unnecessary amount of nervous energy."[11] Nietzsche's aphoristic and narrative style, moreover, today remains remarkably readable compared to the turgid cryptographs of Kant, Hegel, Schopenhauer, and other thinkers Nietzsche attacked in print. "I think of Nietzsche as the first great punk philosopher. I see him there in the pantheon with a safety pin stuck through his nose and two fingers thrust up in the general direction of the philosophic pantheon," English novelist Will Self once put it. "And that is a *positive* aspect of him, as it were, paradoxically. In his most apparent nihilism he seems to me also to be the most apparently positive of thinkers because he's enjoining people to do it themselves, in that way. His philosophy is not a guide that you should think like him; it's a guide that you should think for yourself."[12]

The irony of punks' ingestion and citation of Nietzsche—accomplished as they simultaneously model his ethic—is that in associating with one of Hegel's less diplomatic critics punks on both sides of the Atlantic nonetheless engage Hegel directly as well. A full generation before Nietzsche attacked and dismissed the cultural, political, and moral intelligentsia, Hegel launched an entire philosophical method wherein the subject is consumed with "putting itself to the test at every point of its existence," a system based on the subject's relentless negation of its own assumptions, conclusions, perceptions, and subjectivity. Hegel encouraged the externalizing and interrogating of the contradictions embedded within both what he called the world-historical Spirit at each stage of its development and the abstraction of the individual consciousness, which too was expected, with each step, to critique its own inconsistencies in thought and action. The life of Spirit "is not the life that shrinks from death and keeps itself untouched by devastation, but rather the life that endures [devastation] and maintains itself in it. It wins its truth only when, in utter dismemberment, it finds itself," Hegel prophesied in the famous preface to *Phenomenology* as he laid out his case for a militant ontological *negativity* couched primarily in the self-alienation typical of punk and summarized by punks from Iggy and Hell to John Lydon, Ian Curtis, and Kurt Cobain.[13]

Consider, in a specific example—if not Washington, DC, postpunkers the Dismemberment Plan, Penny Rimbaud's suggestion that with

Crass "everything had to basically contradict itself, be self-devouring," or the Pixies' "Where Is My Mind?"—Akron's earliest and best group Devo.[14] "Take a step outside yourself—then you turn around," Mark Mothersbaugh advises on "Turnaround," the B-side of his band's "Whip It" single and perhaps the most concise translation of Hegel's *Phenomenology* in history. "Take a look at who you are. It's pretty scary." Advocating not merely self-alienation, but the subject's estrangement from her city, country, and planet, Mothersbaugh blazes through a description of Spirit's unfolding in time wherein Spirit is repeatedly *revolted* upon seeing itself from the other side: "You're so silly," Mothersbaugh laughs at both himself and History in a tune that sounds like it was lifted from some crude gaming console. "You're not much / If you're anything." Sloughing off Bob Dylan and D. A. Pennebaker, the chroniclers of the postmodern epoch's devolution (which in 1990 would release an album entitled *Post Post-Modern Man*) then ask, "Who said don't look back? Don't believe them," promoting instead a perpetual shedding of one's skin and a habitual moving away from the wastefulness and foolishness of a given historical moment.

For Hegel, such a revolting progression toward Truth, toward (self-) knowledge, is unspeakably traumatic. "Thus consciousness suffers violence at its own hands," he writes. "When consciousness feels this violence, its anxiety may well make it retreat from the truth, and strive to hold on to what it is in danger of losing. But it can find no peace."[15] Nor can Devo, who explained to one interviewer, "that's why we chose DE-EVOLUTION—taking apart all the assumptions of the past decade and synthesizing them, mutating them, putting them back together with a new attitude."[16] It is this very taking apart, this "tarrying with the negative" as Hegel put it in advance of Devo, that converts Spirit and Consciousness, including that of the individual, from mere abstraction into Being itself. And as Nirvana's "Negative Creep,"

Einstürzende Neubauten's "Negativ Nein," Bad Religion's "The Positive Aspect of Negative Thinking," and the groups Negative Trend, Negative Approach, Negativland, Against Me!, Subhumans, and the Negatives confirm, punk as a cultural project can be understood as emerging directly out of this specific tarrying with the negative as much as Nietzsche's general DIY pessimism. If Hegel sought the unveiling of the contradictions endemic to any idea, subject, system, or epoch, punk was and remains the externalization and embodiment of the inconsistencies contained within not only the pop regime but capitalism, the Church, the family, ideology, and the punk subject herself, Devo and its cohorts demonstrate. Punk is, as such, the self-alienating apparition haunting each of these "masters" whose rabid negativity in the service of Reason is characterized by a terrific violence directed both externally and internally. And although their advocates may not have read *Phenomenology* or *Logic* cover to cover, Home notwithstanding, punk and postpunk in many ways seem to be attempting to "act out" Hegel's chronicle on stage and record, whether they are expressing an almost pathological bent toward violence and self-alienation, spewing often "incoherent" and cryptic discourse in an attack on the extant manifestations of world-historical Spirit, or valorizing the negative as an ontological category in itself.

Moreover, in the violence of this absolute negativity performed in the face of and in response to a condescending cultural and political status quo, in this movement of the subject from consciousness to self-consciousness to bondsman to unhappy consciousness (and even to the impotent "beautiful soul" Hegel describes as a purely negative being "devoid of Spirit"), the significance of punks' physical incorporation of the trappings of bondage, violence, and disinheritance is illuminated. From Richard Hell's "Please Kill Me" and the Sex Pistols' "Pretty Vacant," to the stifling stylings of Malcolm McLaren and Vivienne Westwood to X-Ray Spex's "Oh Bondage, Up Yours" and Cobain's "I Hate Myself and Want to Die," punks' bondage fetish, their self-injury and negative agency, are not merely markers of some petty, fatuous sadomasochism or reactionary and juvenile cry for attention, but punks' rather cheeky incorporation of the bondsman from Hegel's master-slave dialectic. In the aesthetics of groups like Suicide, in Pop's desire to be cut (or as Lester Bangs put it, Pop's performance of his own "'idiocy,' torment, and, most of all bondage"), and in the Bromley Contingent's tattered and trussed style, the analyst can see the punk self-consciousness showing itself and the master signifier that it is willing to stake its life not only in an effort to earn its freedom, but to show the Father the paralyzing and humiliating subject position into which it has been placed by him.[17]

Combining an emphasis on bondage with at times an irrationally aggressive demeanor and anti-aesthetic, punks assume Hegel's claim that through its self-conscious negation the subject "procures for its own self the certainty of its freedom, generates the experience of that freedom, and thereby raises it to truth."[18] The truth of this freedom is nothing but pure negativity, Hegel concludes in advance of hardcore group F-Minus's smoldering forty-five-second "Party's Over," a dentist's drill of a song whose lyrics include "[I] Don't believe in anarchy / Don't believe in democracy / Don't believe in communist / Don't believe in fascist / I walk the dark path." It is such negativity and the refusal of categorization and ideology that creates the conditions for punk *work* and punk's material gesture toward the universal by publicizing itself, on stage and record, as the filthy underside of capitalism, patriarchy, and political and religious orthodoxy. In serving as a cracked mirror, reflecting the ugliness of power back upon itself as a distorted version of itself, punk demonstrates its capacity for Reason and reveals the corruption and unreason of the master's discourse at the same time as punk moves itself, and the parent culture, toward Truth.

In so doing, punk realizes the self-flagellating Spirit that Hegel notes is the very wound and weapon that *heals* the subject through its alienation and thus "leave[s] no scars behind."[19] That is to say, like an insect undergoing metamorphosis or the spear in Wagner's *Parsifal* that both caused and cures the cut that has afflicted the king for years, punk is simultaneously the wound and the salve, having since the 1960s tormented the (pop) cultural dominant, bled it, but representing and catalyzing also its renewal. With apologies to avant-garde prog-punk group Sleepytime Gorilla Museum, who included the *Phenomenology*-referencing "Sleepytime (Spirit Is a Bone)" on their debut record—"Spirit is a bone / Bone is a tree / Tree is alive / Inside of me" Nyls Frykdahl chants, remembering Hegel's comments on phrenology—this concomitant hurting-healing is the "Positive Aspect of Negative Thinking" that Bad Religion's Greg Graffin had in mind when he encouraged his audience to "gather 'round the carcass of the old deflated beast," speaking of not only History but punk. In Bad Religion's rambling, syntactically challenged effort to understand its own slave morality in fifty-seven seconds (!) the listener begins to understand what Hegel means when he repeats throughout *Phenomenology* that such absolute negativity is, in essence, *positive*—it is productive for the subject. On the one hand, as the ineffectual lament of a beautiful soul, "Positive Aspect" merely identifies the sources of its desolation before quitting the game too soon, thus investing in these master signifiers a specific authority and enduring power over the punk subject. As Hegel explains the situation, the beautiful soul, "being conscious of this contradiction in its unreconciled immediacy, is disordered to the point of madness, wastes itself in yearning and pines away in [self-] consumption."[20] This is especially true of hardcore: not only Graffin's but much of hardcore punk's social critique from without is as wasteful as it is angry (and too often fascist) so far as the institutions on trial remain in power long after the punk has exhausted her rage. On the other hand, because the punk's desire is not necessarily the direct dissolution of such adversaries anyway, but one's own self-negation in the service of Truth, the suicidal act, the anti-pop pop song, is a demonstration of the bondsman's freedom, her shaking off the fears and anxieties of bondage and assuming agency and moving History forward.

"Positive Aspect" is in this way representative of punk's typically Left Hegelianism in that it refuses to believe that History and Freedom reached a developmental end in either 1805 or 1977, in either the Prussian state or Western capitalist democracy: the consensus by so many punk first-wavers themselves that "punk is dead" signals punk's willingness to pierce themselves further (believing after all in the maxim "No Future [in punk]") and in so doing to advance world Spirit in the form of postpunk as a continuing attack on the status quo, which punk was becoming. "It's dead. It's a disease. It's a plague. It's been going on for too long. It's *history*. It's vile. It's not achieving anything. It's just digression," Lydon described not only rock and roll but *punk* to Snyder during his own visit to *The Tomorrow Show* six months before Iggy made his appearance, almost embarrassed at having been associated with the Sex Pistols. "The Sex Pistols was going to be the absolute end of rock and roll." But when it was not the end, the band blew itself up, Lydon moaning his way through a cover of Iggy's "No Fun" and eventually asking his audience at San Francisco's Winterland Ballroom, "Ever get the feeling you've been cheated?" The question was not merely rhetorical but existential and ideological—historical even: Does the audience understand punk is the cut it is trying to cure, and that punk, which was a failure in Lydon's eyes, too must be abandoned?

So did Rotten make the necessarily dialectical move to alienate himself from not only himself but his art, to throw it all away and establish not a new band, he tells to Snyder, but a limited liability corporation.

1.1. Public Image Ltd confounds Tom Snyder on *The Tomorrow Show* in 1980.

"We ain't no band. We're a company. Simple. Nothing to do with rock and roll. Doo daa," Lydon, straight-faced, says of Public Image Ltd, a group so far removed from the Sex Pistols, from early punk, that it all but guaranteed Lydon the self-alienation Spirit demanded in the subject's becoming. "The cassette played *pop*tones / I can't forget the impression you made / You left a hole in the back of my head," Lydon would sneer on his new band's second album mere months before he told Snyder, "History does not matter." He is at the very enunciation of these words healing the very wound he symbolizes, alienating himself from himself in a record whose guitars have been subverted and whose formerly externally directed rage has turned inward. Lydon in this moment is refusing the inevitability of History, announcing that "hindsight does me no good." As he put it with finality to Snyder, "We've tried very hard to break down those barriers [erected by the master], but it's not working. So we have to think again. So in the meantime we'll put our attention somewhere else."

A Bone to Pick with Capitalism

In so arguing, Lydon was far ahead of the curve even among his colleagues: in elevating mere complaints but stopping there too soon, in doubling down on punk, the abject subject reinforces the masters in question and remains if not "dead," whether physically, politically, or ideologically, then at the untenable and useless level of beautiful soul. Recognizing and seeking escape from this contradiction, many groups and scenes within punk and postpunk have sought a less deterministic response to such immediate social crises, finding "somewhere else" not only in Nietzsche and Hegel but in the ideas of the philosopher who hoped to use Hegel's bones to craft not a scaffold but a pickaxe, reading the dialectic described in *Phenomenology* not as a method of approaching Spirit but as a way of understanding the subject's own material conditions and agency *on the ground*. Even underground. Out of this critique of Hegel coalesced two camps that have been of particular importance to punk subculture: Marxism and anarchism. But where the "anarchism" of punk has been mostly feigned and melodramatic—not only Lydon's taunting and disingenuous "Iiiee yam an anarch*ist*!" and the Exploited's gauche "I Believe in Anarchy," but the nominal anarcho-punk ethos of groups such as Chumbawamba and Crass (whose Penny Rimbaud once admitted, "I'm not actually interested in what Bakunin or Proudhon said")—punk's Marxism has been more resolute.[21]

Bracketing punks' reading of Marx for a moment, the long and detailed history of academic writing connecting punk to Marx should be recalled. Before punk was declared dead by its own advocates, Dick Hebdige and David Laing, among others, penned readings of punk heavily influenced by Marxist theory. Greil Marcus, who leans on Theodor Adorno and Herbert Marcuse, and Neil Nehring too rely on Marx throughout *Lipstick Traces* and *Flowers in the Dustbin*, respectively, if not for method, then for atmosphere—as one of many specters haunting punk and postpunk praxis. In the twenty-first century Stacy Thompson expanded on these analyses by offering an explicit economic analysis of punk labor couched in Marx's algorithms from *Capital*, arguing that the "noncommercial" activity of punk record labels reverses industrial capitalism's M-C-M' sequence, making money the vitiated middle term in the punk version of exchange: C-M-C'.[22] Such scholarship tells readers more about the state of the academy and criticism in the West since the late 1970s and 1980s than it does about punk, however. Valuable as these analyses by various partisans of the Birmingham or Frankfurt Schools may be, none of them tell readers much about whether or not punks actually *read* Marx or his acolytes.

For read Marx they have—much more than they have read the gatekeepers of anarchist thought. At times dismissive of the contemporary theorizing noted above, scores of self-identified punks nonetheless promote a matter-of-fact familiarity with Marx's oeuvre and indicate Marx as the inspiration behind their band names, lyrics, and, as Thompson suggests, "punk" production processes. Whereas groups like the Proletariat, Killdozer, Randy, and Das Kapital engage in explicitly "Marxist" discourse—singing songs like "Religion Is the Opium of the Masses," "Das Kapital," and "Karl Marx and History"—other punks eschew overt references to Marx but make the critique of capitalism their object, as in the Dils' "Class War"; Gang of Four's appropriation of Mao; Modest Mouse's broad despair at the desertification of nature and human relationships wrought by consumer capitalism across several records (particularly *The Lonesome Crowded West*); Kathleen Hanna's "Riot Grrl Manifesto," the thirteenth entry of which calls for "Revolution Girl Style Now" "Because we hate capitalism in all its forms"; or Big Black and Shellac founder Steve Albini's admission that "I spend most of my time either playing cards or trying to end capitalism now."[23] Some groups treat Marx ironically or with a certain levity, as in the (International) Noise Conspiracy's "Capitalism Stole My Virginity" or NOFX's "The Marxist Brothers." Others take both Marx and themselves too seriously, including future Noise Conspirators Refused, who argue inelegantly in the liner notes of *The Shape of Punk To Come,* "The theory that Marx recognized from Feuerbach, and now we, the people, need to see the spectacle that binds us to our 'destiny.' Alienation is not commodity, figures, statistics or make believe but very much a real tool of oppression and seclusion." Finally, some punks simply repeat the mistakes of the most cynical vulgar Marxists of the nineteenth century, as with Delaware hardcore band BoySetsFire, which tries to convince its supporters in a tract entitled "American Civics 101," included in a reissue of the group's maudlin 1996 album *This Crying, This Screaming, My Voice Is Being Born,* that "the American populace is taught to be passive. They learn at an early age that obedience and submission will lead to a reward, often unattainable and almost always to their own detriment. Marx discussed this idea in *Das Capital* [*sic*] when he refers to religion as being the opiate of the people." Mistaking *Capital* for Marx's *Contribution to a Critique of Hegel's Philosophy of Right,* the band, which cares little for the two texts' specifics, alludes casually to *The Communist Manifesto* as well, later scribbling clumsily, "Citizens must learn that the truth will not be spoon-fed to them. All must learn the beauty of doubt, for what can be lost but their chains."

BoySetsFire's almost nonsensical conflation of a series of Marxian chestnuts notwithstanding, the referencing of these three seminal documents is instructive so far as it encapsulates well the Marx punks have read and signals the ease with which punks tend to assume Marxian ideas and discourse. While most punks' interest in Marx hinges on the framework he offers for a critique of capitalism broadly, punks see in Marx's *Contribution* a seat for their rejection of religion expressed not only in Lou Reed or the Ramones miming Marx's repudiation of his familial Judaism but in Patti Smith's "Jesus died for somebody's sins, but not mine," the Sex Pistols' "Iiiee yam an anti*christ*," Dead Kennedys' *In God We Trust, Inc.*, Crass's *Christ—The Album*, the Vaselines' "Jesus Wants Me for a Sunbeam," and Bad Religion's entire discography.[24] As the Proletariat's full-throated appropriation of *Contribution* suggests, punk and postpunk too tend to regard religion as a distorting liniment that estranges subjects from themselves and reinforces a "false consciousness" best jettisoned. Or, as Green Day later suggested, the punk subject should consider putting a bullet in a Bible. Following Marx's own intellectual development, punks make the criticism of religion the foundation of their criticism of political economy, which emerged concomitant with postpunk and hardcore, whose advocates found themselves not only quoting the *Manifesto* but echoing many of *Capital*'s more familiar critiques of estranged labor and alienation (see the several punk songs referencing "alienation" by Citizen Fish, Youth Brigade, Green Day, Viet Cong, and others), the fetishization of commodities, the mystical way capitalism melts all that is solid into air, and the commodification of both desire and the human subject, the latter two notions of which are best exemplified in tracks such as the Slits'

"Spend Spend Spend" and multiple tracks by the Clash, the Raincoats, Gang of Four, Fugazi, and Refused, whose Dennis Lyxzén, recognizing that "Human life is not [a] commodity," decides he has "a bone to pick with capitalism / And a few to break." As with many of their antecedents, particularly the mechanical and "industrial" sounds of groups like Cabaret Voltaire, Throbbing Gristle, Devo, and Big Black, these songs make explicit their attempt to turn the tables on capitalism by alienating the consumer from her own objectified desire, alienating pop culture from itself, making of pop music not an aphrodisiac but an acid bath.

In framing their art as such, punks often lift openly from *Capital*, wherein Marx uses several ghoulish metaphors—vampire, werewolf, monster—to describe if not the capitalist, then capitalism as a system. Above and beyond Rancid's "The Wolf" and . . . *And Out Come the Wolves*, TV On The Radio's "Wolf Like Me," or Black Eyes' "Pack of Wolves," note Rudimentary Peni's "Vampire State Building" and Bad Brains' "Fearless Vampire Killers," a sixty-second stake to the heart of capitalism from 1982 that warns:

> The bourgeoisie better watch out for me
> All throughout this so-called nation
> We don't want your filthy money
> We don't need your innocent bloodshed
> We just want to end your world
> Well, my mind's made up
> Yes, it's time for you to pay
> Better watch out for me
> I'm a member of the F.V.K.

Taking its name from the 1967 Roman Polanski film of the same name starring Sharon Tate, "Fearless Vampire Killers" combines Marx's eschatological hope for a revolutionary dictatorship of the proletariat with

Haile Selassie's Gnosticism, the result of which is a menacing rebuke of capitalism, later coded by the band as Babylon, whose pitch is all the more poignant in that it comes from not disenfranchised middle-class white kids but a quartet of militant black youth who were banned from most clubs in their hometown Washington, DC, and England both for the ferocity of their concerts and fans and for telling the ruling class, without irony, that they intend to *end your world*.[25]

With such a reading of political economy leaking into their aesthetics, lyrics, and lives, many punk bands began—often simultaneous to their incorporation—taking the production process into their own hands as well, circumventing the record industry's commodification of music in an effort to put into practice Marx's final thesis on Feuerbach: "The philosophers have only interpreted the world in various ways; the point is to change it." Snubbing overtures from established record companies, booking agencies, and managers, bands following punk's first wave (Smith, the Sex Pistols, the Clash, the Ramones, and Iggy, who all relied on multinationals for the production of their records) founded their own imprints—Rough Trade, SST, Touch & Go, Factory, Fast Product, Subpop, Kill Rock Stars—for the express purpose of retaining control over their aesthetics, politics, product distribution, and, as Public Image Ltd might put it, "communications," hoping to revolutionize the record industry in the process.

"I'm actually fairly good at delegating work. That's not a problem for me. But overall, there's still much work that I do. I still do things like take out the trash. I still rake the leaves," Ian MacKaye explained of his administration of Dischord Records, a punk label he cofounded in 1980 dedicated to documenting the Washington, DC, hardcore scene, particularly his early bands Teen Idles and Minor Threat.[26]

Although MacKaye does not sleep with a copy of *Capital* under his pillow, he concedes to having been influenced by the writing of

American Marxists Abbie Hoffman, Jerry Rubin, and the Diggers: "Emmett Grogan's [*Ringolevio*] is a great fucking book," MacKaye told me of the autobiography of the leader of the San Francisco anarcho-socialist theater troupe.[27] Such reading paved the way for MacKaye's post-hardcore group Fugazi, which earned notoriety in the 1990s for managing to tour extensively for Dischord despite insisting that concertgoers for most shows pay a meager five-dollar admission price, even those occurring in large halls. Speaking of Fugazi, MacKaye adds, "One aspect of Do It Yourself is that you really have to do it yourself. It's work! We manage ourselves, we book ourselves, we do our own equipment upkeep, we do our own recording, we do our own taxes. We don't have other people do that stuff. This is what we do and it takes time. You can't tour every day of the year because someone has to come home and book [shows] sooner or later. I think there's a lot of infrastructure work that we do that people are unaware of."[28] By cultivating such an ethic, MacKaye and his colleagues—such as the editors at hardcore punk zine *Maximumrocknroll*, who maintain the open access *Book Your Own Fucking Life* tour registry—push back against the commodification, fetishization, and alienation Marx describes, undermining the very premises of capital by, for example, refusing to ask bands whose records are released by Dischord to sign contracts. (Such bands include Nation of Ulysses and the Make-Up, whose draftsman Ian Svenonius has read Marx and made a point of throwing references to Marx into not only his lyrics and interviews but several books, *The Psychic Soviet* being only the most obvious.) Transferring the retention of the means of production to their bands' politics and aesthetics, MacKaye and his mates make explicit their collective effort to elide the division of labor typical of capitalism by refusing even to identify the roles—guitars, drums, lyrics—of respective contributors to any given album, noting, in simple alphabetical order on the sleeves of each of the band's records, "Fugazi is Brendan Canty, Joe Lally, Ian MacKaye, and Guy Picciotto." So is MacKaye, for instance, as vital to Dischord as a phone-answering packer of seven-inch records as he is as a tour manager or performer with his several bands on the label. But he is nowhere identified as filling any *specific* role within either the organization or the bands he helped establish. Like De Tocqueville musing that Americans, despite their having no interest in actually reading Descartes, are better at putting him into practice than are the French, Fugazi—in no way as "Marxist" as, say, the Proletariat or the Dils—does a better job of articulating really existing Marxism than the more explicit punk readers of Marx cited above, some of whom would go on to take up residence within the gilded corridors of the very culture industry that Adorno long ago argued "debased" human beings by converting them into objects as exchangeable as any commodity.

Bringing such politics home, punks the world over have also founded a variety of communal "punk houses" dedicated to group living; sharing of resources such as food, books, tools, and even personal care items; and use of such space tactically as a locus for coordinating persons and events dedicated to redistributive politics: Food Not Bombs, benefit concerts in support of free clinics, and "die-ins" or other events expressing solidarity with groups Marx would have labeled the *lumpenproletariat*. Articulating the complex nature of such an arrangement is Elliot Rosenberg, narrator of Abram Himelstein's and Jamie Schweser's riff on the Washington, DC, punk scene *Tales of a Punk Rock Nothing*, who lives with a half-dozen other squatters, artists, activists, runaways, and queer youth in a punk house in DC. Speaking of the community, which shares not only living space but work tasks from housekeeping to record stuffing to political organizing, Elliot tells his diary: "Came home, kids were all in the kitchen and living room Food

Not Bombing. Talked to [my brother] Colin on the phone. Hard to explain to someone at college what's going on here. Zines, music, politics, three local labels, everyone is up to something. Even the show tonight is raising money for a rape crisis center, not to mention it's all-ages. Feels like Haight-Ashbury in the 60's, except no one's doing drugs or talking about sex (or doing it as far as I can tell) Plus people don't have lice."[29]

Encapsulated in this short scene is the core of what Marx's materialism offers punk in response to the master that Hegel does not: in retaining agency and control of the products of their labor, in critiquing religion, public education, and capitalism through their rhetoric *and* praxis, in trying to implement a sustainable and active "communist" alternative within the confines of a market economy, punks draw attention to the horrors of capitalism—its manufacture of poverty, its dehumanization of the subject, its commodification of life itself—at the same time as they make a serious attempt at building an alternative and participatory economic system around reimagined (noncoercive) human relationships. Thinking perhaps of Marx, who in his 1844 manuscripts calls sex work "only a *specific* expression of the *general* prostitution of the *laborer*," punks in Elliot's house (who may or may not have heard the Pop Group's "We Are All Prostitutes") see themselves as Subhumans, as the Exploited subject to a "phallogocentric" economy and global elite that propositions, consumes, and discards—fucks—them daily.[30] So do they incorporate into their bodies the signifiers of such treatment at the hands of various pimps whose behavior they are unable to influence: not only Iggy smearing himself with peanut butter in 1970 but punks' buckles, belts, chains, and dog collars, tattered trousers, trash-bag blouses, and self-deprecating pseudonyms that signify the subject's degradation, commodification, and disposability—Rat Scabies, Beki Bondage, Poly Styrene, Alice Bag, John Doe, and Dee Generate. Such aliases get at the generalized shame that capitalism breeds so far as it implicates all subjects in the commodification of life, of desire itself, making of everyone always-already either a prostitute or a john.

But even in their responding to the status quo with Marxian alternatives, a contradiction emerges for punk. As *Tales of a Punk Rock Nothing* suggests—describing a Puritan punk house wherein no one consumes drugs, engages in sex acts, or even talks meaningfully about the profound interpersonal problems of desire exacerbated by political economy—punk Marxism speaks to the desire produced and commodified by capitalism not by circumventing or dissipating it, but by *repressing* it. Seeing only embarrassment in desire writ large, in capital's injunction to enjoy, punk Marxism posits a conundrum: the infinite suspension of the desire sold by a capitalist milieu that encourages the subject to "seize the day" or "just do it" paired with the creation of a novel desire—that a better world is possible—that punk either has no interest in fulfilling or immediately recognizes as impossible. Although most punk and postpunk have moved beyond the "No Future" rhetoric typical of punk's first wave, this paralysis, *Tales* demonstrates, is the inevitable consequence of BoySetsFire's haphazard vivisection of Marx's *Contribution, Manifesto,* and *Capital*: not revolution of an oppressed class, not a dictatorship of the proletariat, but a vulgar Marxism that often struggles to go beyond the subjugation of desire and the glossing of its own middle-class revolutionary fantasy. So it is that in seeking an escape from the repression and alienation he feels more keenly as a punk than when he lived with his parents, Elliot abandons the "straightedge" punk house that had become as controlling as the Church or State punk was supposedly resisting, noting on the day of his departure, "Had the urge to smoke a cig, eat a burger, shoot some smack, read some porn. But the fact that I could do any of this stuff and not get yelled at by my housemates suddenly made it seem unappealing again. Ahhh, freedom."[31]

Jouissance Music

This layered paradox—not only that refusing capitalism requires punk's recapitulation to what Nietzsche called Hegel's slave morality, but that abandoning Marx and accepting capitalism's invitations to pleasure and self-satisfaction ironically kill desire itself—helps elucidate why later punks (including those in former Eastern Bloc nations unable to commiserate with Western punks' critique of capitalism) have made an effort to demonstrate their allegiance not to Marx but to Freud and his interpreters, particularly French poststructuralist thinkers who also speak to the desire produced concomitantly by an increasingly regimented, isolating, and bureaucratic "society of control" as Gilles Deleuze once put it. Direct references to Freud or Freudian concepts by Iggy, Crass, the Cramps, Offspring, and Deathfix notwithstanding, English postpunkers Scritti Politti included a torn bit of French psychoanalyst Jacques Lacan's anthology Écrits on the cover of their "The Word Girl" single, calling also their ASCAP imprint "Jouissance Music," a reference to Lacan's term for a transgressive, surplus enjoyment that the subject experiences as discomfort. Having read their Lacan back in the early 1980s, Scritti Politti had in fact set the stage for postpunks' interest in the critics of psychoanalysis whose thinking has come to be known as poststructuralism (Foucault, Derrida, and Deleuze in particular) by including the song "Jacques Derrida" on their début album *Songs to Remember.* "Thank you for the flowers and the book by Derrida," quipped Canadian postpunks Weakerthans in "Our Retired Explorer (Dines with Michel Foucault in Paris, 1961)" two decades after Scritti Politti on their sardonically entitled nod to Derrida *Reconstruction Site,* "but I must be getting back to dear Antarctica." Later, Australian "screamo" band Ohana, reminding its listeners of Foucault's notion from 1963 that the physician's speaking gaze objectifies his patients, yelped, "What goes in my mouth comes out yours! / Birth of the clinic!" just as Geoff Rickly of post-hardcore group United Nations boasted, "When I was a boy they called me kid Lacan." Finally, as Amherst, Massachusetts, band Orchid sizes up the situation in "Tigers" from their break-up record *Gatefold*, which also includes the dialectically infused tracks "Let's Commodify Sexuality" and "Discourse in Desire":

> I kiss the girls that speak Marcuse
> I kiss the boys that speak Foucault
> I love the kids that know Adorno
> And snub their nose at kids who don't

Warbling through this most lucid of several unintelligible songs, with only guitars behind him, Orchid's Jayson Green, one of the architects of screamo, is less endorsing such reading than patronizing punks especially who seem to have lost themselves in critical theory, bourgeois exhibitionists who like so many milk teeth—white and shallow—cite Marcuse and Foucault in passing but express little interest in taking their comments on dialectics and power, Hegel and Freud, seriously.

As Orchid's who's-who of critical theory demonstrates, however, punks since the 1980s tend to associate several of the aforementioned twentieth-century writers, carelessly at times, often conflating and misusing theory in what appears an attempt to strike an erudite pose. This critique notwithstanding, (post)punks are right to associate and internalize these writers so far as they each speak to the common denominator—madness—that links Nietzsche (who did go mad), Lacan, Foucault, Deleuze, and Derrida to Freud. More specifically, the ways in which the depression, anomie, hysteria, and schizophrenia explored habitually in punk connect to language, power, and the Superego have become a virtual obsession among postpunks. Punk songs notwithstanding—Black Flag's *Nervous Breakdown* EP and "Depression,"

Descendents' and Sonic Youth's versions of "Schizophrenia," Bad Religion's "Sanity," Green Day's "Basket Case," and both Joy Division's and Preoccupations' (formerly Viet Cong) entire discographies—consider not only the groups Madness or Suicidal Tendencies but the several punk institutionalizations on record (Lou Reed, Iggy, Joey Ramone, Television guitarist Richard Lloyd, and Slint drummer Britt Walford to name a few); Nick Blinko's punk novel *The Primal Screamer,* conceived as the dictation of a psychoanalyst engaged with a morbid punk subject; and Nick Cave's analysis-oriented film *20,000 Days on Earth.* Grasping almost instinctually Freud's *Civilization and Its Discontents,* which had argued in 1930 that the repression of desire that civilization requires produces the neuroses for which punk is but a symptom, punks the world over began seeking, as early as the 1970s, psychosocial and socioeconomic rather than medical answers to the reasons why, as Hell told *Punk,* "I always feel uncomfortable and I just want to . . . walk out of the room."[32] So has an increasingly "schizophrenic" punk subculture—dividing into dozens of variants—turned to everything from Lacan to Foucault's *Madness and Civilization* to Deleuze's and Guattari's two-volume *Capitalism and Schizophrenia,* reading widely and patiently, dropping French names into interviews and turning poststructuralist and psychoanalytic notions into songs in an effort to make sense of their anxiety and discomfiture.

This "splitting" of the subject explored by punk has long been part of psychoanalytic discourse, from Freud's earliest work to the contemporary critics of Freud and Lacan, such as Deleuze, Butler, Alain Badiou, and Žižek. Particularly important to the notion of a split in the ego in the context of punk is Lacan's "The Signification of the Phallus," which volunteers that if the unconscious is structured like a language, it is through the speaking subject that both the signifier, as an Other, and desire come into being. The "privileged signifier" that connects the Logos to desire is the phallus, which is not a physical object but a "signifier that is destined to designate meaning effects as a whole," and can be possessed or lacked by both biologically male and female subjects, the former "having" the phallus and latter typically "being" the phallus. In the case of the parent-child relationship, for example, the child's demand for love from the parent exceeds her need, generating a gap between demand and need that can be understood as desire—the signification of which is the phallus the child ostensibly lacks, leading to "her" libidinal investment in the parent and thus her *aphanisis* or "fading" in the face of her emerging "meaning" as a signifier alienated from herself in an objectified form. Such signification and splintering repeats itself in the dialectic of myriad social relations, including those involving the institutions of State, Church, economy, and education. The subject's subordination to the signifier and subsequent evaporation is prompted first and foremost, if indeed the signifier is phallic in origin, by the symbolic paternal, the Name of the Father, who in speaking first and inscribing Logos/Law silences the child, threatening her with punishment (castration) for violating his Law.

In Butler's reading, such emasculation creates an entire class of "abject subjects," whose Being consists entirely of an objectified marginalization. Punks, for obvious reasons, can be included in the castrated grouping of individuals "who are not yet 'subjects,' but form the constitutive outside to the domain of the subject. The abject designates here precisely those 'unlivable' and 'uninhabitable' zones of social life which are nevertheless densely populated by those who do not enjoy the status of the subject, but whose living under the sign of the 'unlivable' is required to circumscribe the domain of the subject." In this way, punk and postpunk are quite literally not only the spear that both hurts and heals or the repressed returned, but the physical incorporation of psychoanalysis so far as the subculture's self-applied title signifies its self-conscious subordination to and silencing/castration by the master signifier, its identification as an abject subject who has been "punked" and who has turned to the violence of language, of noise, in response.[33]

It is here, then, at the intersection of Hegel and Marx, Lacan and poststructuralism, that punks' interest in psychoanalysis especially is clarified. Lacanian psychoanalysis—which reads Hegel *through* Freud by emphasizing that Freud's discovery was to see *Phenomenology* as Hegel's attempt to articulate human consciousness through the signifier in a way Freud's patients were encouraged to do—is particularly useful for punk in that it allows the composers of the songs above (including not only the queercore community generally but transgender performers such as Jayne County or Laura Jane Grace from Against Me!) to understand their relation to power as that of the debilitated and "hysteric" slave under the thumb of the master signifier whose Law conditions their very being, as Lacan put it early in his seminar *The Other Side of Psychoanalysis*. So it is that the hysteric (whose origins Freud explored as early as 1893) is best, perhaps obviously, framed as feminine: "Let's give him the gender under which this subject is most often embodied," says Lacan, who would go on to call woman a "symptom" of man so far as the feminine subject position reveals the repressed truth of the dominant discourse. "She doesn't give up her knowledge. She unmasks, however, the master's function . . . which she evades in her capacity as object of his desire."[34] Like punks' identification as Hegelian bondsmen, then, Lacanian psychoanalysis not only allows punk to understand itself productively as the "castrated" hysteric, evident in MacKaye's "I don't fuck" from *Out of Step*, Cobain's visions of "a man lying in a gynecological chair with legs up in sturrops," and its necessary and significant progression to Riot Grrrl and queercore, but helps punk see, subsequently, itself as the location of cultural knowledge generally, as the seat of Truth whose work unmasks the shameless and exploitive phallogocentrism implicit to rock and roll.[35] Although this latter notion carries with it the air of a very old con—the master telling the slave how noble her labor is as he exploits her—it creates the justification for punks' efforts to move past the emasculated objectivity they suffer under capitalism, Church, government, and nuclear family by "becoming" themselves through several satisfying transgressions designed to assume the phallus for herself: protesting the master's discourse; subverting his modes of production and distribution; "hystericizing" rather than repressing their anger, despair, and anomie; and committing ritual violence, often against the subject herself.

Each of these ejaculatory acts of jouissance by the punk subject functions as a direct transgression symptomatic of her loss of knowledge, power, and subjectivity, all stolen from her by the master. "For psychoanalysis, the symptom is not a 'disorder,' it is a silenced truth that needs to be heard," writes Agnès Aflalo in the wake of punk in a book that calls psychoanalysis a public good whose survival despite myriad attacks speaks to its strength and continuing methodological value. "The symptom includes the paradoxical satisfaction that leads to suffering ('jouissance'). Treatment is a dialectical procedure, which brings to the surface the weight of jouissance that words carry. Words encircle the truth without the subject being aware of it. Grasping the two faces of the symptom—language and jouissance—allows the subject to read his story and make it his again."[36]

Or hers. Such an argument Foucault had infused into his *History of Madness*, which if it shows punks anything it is that the legacy of their hystericization, their "madness," has been *silence*, and it is here the punk subject specifically directs her efforts. That is to say, from the seventeenth through nineteenth centuries, leaders in the religious, political, and economic worlds went to great lengths to incarcerate and muzzle not only the mad in what Foucault calls "The Great Confinement," but anyone demonstrating "unreason" in the Age of Enlightenment: sex workers, the poor, blasphemers, criminals, political radicals, or other agents connected to those marginalized groups with whom punks early and late tend to associate and from which punk often recruits. "A whole region became isolated, grouping together the practices and decisions through which madness was denounced and offered for exclusion," writes Foucault, describing the ostracizing of any person or idea deemed by power to be undesirable. "All elements in it that were uncomfortably close to reason, and which threatened reason by a derisive similarity, were violently separated and rigorously reduced to silence."[37]

Building too on Freud's project, which Foucault hailed as the breakthrough that finally allowed madness and unreason to speak, is punk. Feeling that little has changed since the seventeenth century, punk, reading Freud and Hegel through Lacan, comes to believe Lacan's suggestion that it is only through language that the subject comes into Being.[38] In so doing the punk hysteric or abject subject obliterates the repressive limits put on her jouissance-knowledge and attempts to reclaim her subjectivity through not merely speech but a shrill and abusive *singing*, an ejaculatory screaming at unprecedented volumes, as if punks are making up for three centuries of shushing, speaking on behalf of the millions of radicals and runaways, misanthropes and madmen, branded for centuries as irrational—abnormal—for daring to challenge the established order. San Francisco's Screamers, Washington, DC's Scream, Seattle's Screaming Trees, and screamo punk notwithstanding, this is the environment wherein Henry Rollins entitled the first record by his post–Black Flag band *The End of Silence*; it is why BoySetsFire was right to draw attention to *This Crying, This Screaming, My Voice Is Being Born*. Or, in perhaps the most memorable reversal of the Great Confinement, Blinko's *The Primal Screamer*, after describing its punk subject Nat Snoxell's "scream therapy," silences the paternal psychoanalyst; at novel's end Nat's therapist abandons his profession and becomes a monk, ultimately taking a vow of silence himself: the master made mute by the slave's speech.

"I feel like I'm disappearing / Getting smaller every day" Kim Gordon put it in "Tunic (For Karen)" early in Sonic Youth's arc, ostensibly speaking for Karen Carpenter. "But when I open my mouth to sing / I'm bigger in every way." For this reason, Gordon implies, the critique of punk by vexed oldsters the world over that "you can't even understand the words" misses the point of a punk speech-act couched in Hegel, Freud, and French philosophy: the unintelligibility of the words and music are an angry and often overflowing response to the punitive and silencing institutions punks have finally worked up the courage and energy to shout down. "This violent liberation of speech is possible and can be pursued only in the extent to which it keeps itself resolutely and consciously at the greatest possible proximity to the abuse that is the usage of speech," Derrida adds in his review of Foucault's *History* (but remembering Freud and Lacan), "just close enough to say violence, to dialogue with itself as irreducible violence, and just far enough to live and live as speech."[39] So it is in punk, where the violence of speech erupts not merely in the form of a liberated unconscious delivering unrestrained speech at an unreasonable volume—Rotten's "Fuck this and fuck that fuck it all and fuck her fucking brat"—but as a repressed returned whose user assaults the very language she is finally allowed to employ. With all apologies to Nirvana, whose fragmented "Endless, Nameless" and "Tourette's" both exemplify such speech, the eponymous debut album from Washington, DC, punks Black Eyes experiments repeatedly with the syntax and semantics of pop, offering a parade of brutal sounds supporting often nonsense phrases that achieve the violence Derrida describes at the same time as they put into practice both *Of Grammatology* and Lacan in constructing a series of self-conscious pop aporiae.

Caricaturing the glossolalia typical of evangelical Christianity, Daniel McCormick and Hugh McElroy shout two verses worth of incoherent, highly stylized exclamations and accusations over each other in "Speaking in Tongues" before McCormick drops out—symbolically silencing himself—and McElroy pronounces finally not only that "Some words, if you use them enough, lose all meaning," but the reverse:

> If you
> Use them
> Lose their
> Too much
> Meaning enough
> Enough.

Too much meaning, says McElroy in an echo of Derrida, who had told an audience at Johns Hopkins University in 1966 that "there is too much, more than one can say" of signification. Literally—for the frothing hysteric subject unused to speaking. "One cannot determine the center and exhaust totalization [in interpretation or critique of the text] because the sign which replaces the center, which supplements it . . . occurs as a surplus, as a *supplement*."[40] Accepting such logic, that there is nothing *outside* the text, McElroy is not, in this song, speaking of his own verse, but of language as a medium, and worrying that after so long a silence he has more to say than can even be said to an audience supposedly interested in his string of signifiers.

In this "fucking with language," as Kathleen Hanna put it apropos her post–Bikini Kill record *Julie Ruin*, which includes the track "On Language," punk confirms its interest in both Lacan's signifying chain and the decentering of signification that marked Derrida's thought, making punk a sort of "deconstructionist" movement too bent on decentering the pop subject (whether the "rock star" or the audience) and ultimately displacing the centrality of enjoyment and desire in rock music by being *un*musical, hyper-rhythmic, and often phonologically muddled.[41] In other words, Derrida's *différance* becomes, in punk, not merely "fuck all" or "DIY," but the explicit attempt to defamiliarize the language of pop from within it.

"A word for you to use / A girl without a cause," Gartside croons in what may be Scritti's best attempt at such a defamiliarization, "The Word Girl," seeming to speak directly of the castrated punk hysteric bent on dismantling her master's tongue. "A name for what you lose / When it was never yours." The hysteric subject of this tune has outgrown her own name, Gartside argues of punk in front of a reggae beat, a name that was never authentic in the first place, following Derrida, but a surplus signifier that "stands for your abuse." So it is that "in a world of broken rules"—linguistic, social, ethical—the punky word girl "found a place for you along her [signifying] chain of fools."

In drawing attention to the abuses of the master signifier and refusing him, punk reclaims—or at least attempts to find—its own voice, its subjectivity, and demonstrates why the hysteric's discourse is, as Lacan puts it, the sister of Truth—the feminine sibling linked by blood to the ineffable Absolute.[42] Taking back her voice from the master and exploiting his language (taking possession of and inverting the master's phallogocentric discourse), the hysteric reifies not only her freedom but Spirit and History in a way that not even Marx was able to accomplish in his historical materialism. Giving form to language, Truth, and jouissance, the hysteric sweeps aside the silence and shamefaced refusal of the castrated body that has been the hysteric's legacy for most of recorded history. In so doing she authenticates her allegiance not only to Nietzsche, but to the Marquis de Sade, whose *Philosophy in the Boudoir* had advised the young hysteric, "tied down too long by the absurd and dangerous bonds of an imaginary virtue and a disgusting religion," to

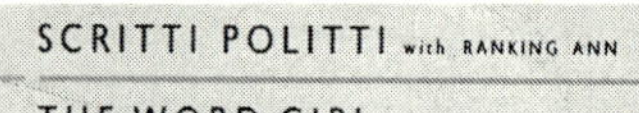

1.2. Scritti Politti's "The Word Girl" single (1985) with reference to Jacques Lacan's notion of the signifying chain. Used by permission.

imitate the work's heroine Eugénie: "Destroy, trample, as quickly as she, all the ridiculous precepts inculcated by moronic parents."[43] Accepting such advice is the punk who too has attached herself to Sade, publicizing her degradation and founding bands such as Marquis de Sade, whose "Back to Cruelty" warns of increasingly sadistic behavior of the "fat men cut off from real life," and Justin(e), whose tune "Médisance après" (After slander) reminds the listener that where patricide is concerned, "Le pistol est superbe, Deleuze génial." Or, as Nico Ordway put it admiringly in *Search & Destroy*, in a brief article entitled simply "De Sade," "In a world grotesquely oppressed by religion, feudal stratification, and privileged uselessness, Sade shouted at the top of his lungs the orgasmic cry of freedom."[44]

Finally, if linguistics—the signifier—is the recurring punk predilection, we should not be surprised to see on the punk bookshelf a handful of texts by linguist and political philosopher Noam Chomsky, whose name and words pop up in records by not only Screeching Weasel, BoySetsFire, and NOFX, but the (International) Noise Conspiracy, and Subb, whose campaign against silence "A Little More of Chomsky (A Little Less of You and Me)" preaches "Think for yourself! / And raise your voice / And change the things they've done." All pedantic false modesty aside, Winnipeg punks Propagandhi gave Chomsky his own spoken-word track on their compilation record *Where Quantity is Job #1*, while *Maximumrocknroll* produced a split Bad Religion/Noam Chomsky vinyl record in response to the impending Persian Gulf War. "Back in 1990, I got a letter from a punk rock group called Bad Religion," recalled the linguist behind the theory of generative grammar.

> I liked the name. So, they asked me to talk for eight minutes about the invasion of Iraq. At that time, you couldn't say a word about it, literally it was banned—like North Korea. So I thought, okay. They sent me a tape and somebody had a tape recorder, so I took the tape and I talked for eight minutes and mailed it back to them. And in a little while they sent me a [seven] inch record with my eight minutes on one side and what they called an anti-war song on the other. I couldn't make head or tail out of the anti-war song, so I sent it to a friend who had a fourteen year old daughter, and she sent me back a lengthy disquisition on the

> meaning of the song and where it fit in popular culture and so on. But I later discovered—when I give talks people wanted books signed, for years, the main thing that people wanted signed, all over the world, was that record.[45]

"Chomsky and I have a lot of ideas in common and I wasn't even aware of him for many years until about the time of the Gulf War," Bad Religion's Graffin quipped in 1996, recalling the split single. "I've read five of his books in the last year. Hey kids, get smart and read Chomsky."[46]

Although Graffin has maintained a sporadic correspondence with Chomsky, and earned a doctorate in evolutionary biology from UCLA in the years following the release of the record, his interest in Chomsky, like that of Propagandhi, NOFX, and the scads of punkers directing their friends to the dissident's books in the 1990s, is usually less linguistic than political. That is to say, despite their interest in language, punks are not reading Chomsky to better understand his minimalist program so much as to get an alternative take on American foreign policy and to learn more about Chomsky's "anarcho-syndicalism." Sympathizing with the articulate and tireless critic of the American political economy, media system, and military-industrial complex, punks more interested in politics than the philosopher's comments on Descartes, Wilhelm von Humboldt, or Foucault too find in Chomsky the intellectual base for much of their less-than-academic and at times rambling critique of authority. Punks see in Chomsky a public figure who understands both the pressure to adjust sobering analyses of power, which do not fit the governing narratives, to a commercial media system, and the marginalization that results for those who refuse to do so.

All of this is why not only elites but the bourgeois class *should* be frightened by punk and postpunk. This taking seriously of philosophy and psychoanalysis, of the violence of speech and a critique of the cultural dominant, is what Iggy was unable to articulate to a dismissive Snyder with concision. Punk rock, that shrewd, loud, and abusive—intellectually, politically, linguistically—subculture has for a generation not merely documented "the decline of Western Civilization," as Penelope Spheeris put it, but has actively sought its reconfiguration, basing such a program on its reading of a collection of both radical and canonical philosophical texts, many of which have little to do with anarchism proper, but nevertheless make the unblinking contestation of the status quo their purpose. Punk and postpunk have done so under the auspices of not only Nietzsche but Sade, Hegel, Marx, Freud, Adorno, Foucault, Lacan, Derrida, Chomsky, and Deleuze, bringing these philosophers' often disquieting ideas into a pop regime that cannot help but see such disruptions as dangerous to its bottom line, to its own ontology, which typically profits by marginalizing dissent and critical thought, profits by keeping the phallogocentric star system in place and the subject distracted from class consciousness and the isolating and castrating effects of power. Seeing alienation as the bridge connecting their interest in Hegel to their appropriation of Marx, and madness and the refusal of silence as a path from Nietzsche to the twentieth century—and French theory in particular—punk fashions for itself a way out of a relationship with the Name of the Father, with power, that is always-already imbalanced, exploitive, and antiquated. This is the "punk philosophy" embedded in punks' lyrics, aesthetics, interview quips, and style. And as the remainder of this book will document, these texts populate only the top spot on a punk bookshelf filled with volumes that punks see as sympathizing with the shame they feel in having been tossed aside by the dominant discourse that subordinates the hysteric (abject) subject without even trying. Particularly important in this last, in punks' aestheticizing of shame, has been a writer whose work has been charged with pounding in the footings of what would come to be known as existentialism: Fyodor Dostoevsky. Taking especial interest in *Notes from Underground,* whose grotesque characterizations of humankind and questioning of the moral, political, and aesthetic status quo also help them frame their own emphasis on existence as opposed to essence, punks turn to Dostoevsky's fiction on an astoundingly regular basis, and it is to Dostoevsky that this study turns.

Notes

1. V. Vale, "Dickies: LA Band Leaps to Punk Preeminence," *Search & Destroy* #5, 1978, in *Search and Destroy 1–6: The Complete Reprint,* by V. Vale (San Francisco: V/Search, 1996), 108.

2. Brendan Mullen, Don Bolles, and Adam Parfrey, *Lexicon Devil: The Fast Times and Short Life of Darby Crash and the Germs* (Los Angeles: Feral House, 2002), 26.

3. John Holmstrom, "Richard Hell," in *Punk: The Best of Punk Magazine,* by John Holmstrom and Bridget Hurd (New York: HarperCollins, 2012), 63. Hell's notion is either a reference to Nietzsche's *Human All Too Human* maxim #202, which states, "Wit is the epitaph of an emotion," or the philosopher's *Mixed Opinions and Maxims,* also maxim #202—"A joke is the epigram on the death of a feeling."

4. V. Vale, "Screamers from LA: A Better World Begins with You," *Search & Destroy* #5, 1978, in *Search and Destroy 1–6: The Complete Reprint,* by V. Vale (San Francisco: V/Search, 1996), 90.

5. Deborah Curtis, *Touching from a Distance* (London: Faber & Faber, 2007), 90.

6. Brian James Schill, "June Panic," *Punk Planet* #57, September–October 2003, 64. The Heidegger song Panic refers to is his "On H's 'They,'" from the album *I Hope You Fail Better.* Furthermore, Panic's record *Horror Vacui* mimics Kant's *Critique of Pure Reason,* unfolding as a series of pro and contra arguments for the existence of God.

7. Stewart Home, *Cranked Up Really High* (Hove, UK: Codex, 1995), n.p. See also Home, *Cunt* (London: Do-Not Press, 1999), 25, 36, 79.

8. Craig O'Hara, *The Philosophy of Punk: More Than Noise!* (1999; Oakland, CA: AK Press, 2001).

9. Lars J. Kristiansen, et al., *Screaming for Change: Articulating a Unifying Philosophy of Punk Rock* (Lanham, MD: Lexington, 2010), 2, 145.

10. Lisa Sofianos, Robin Ryde, and Charlie Waterhouse, *The Truth of Revolution, Brother* (London: Situation Press, 2014), 21.

11. Friedrich Nietzsche, "The Antichrist," in *The Portable Nietzsche*, ed. Walter Kaufmann (1888; New York: Penguin, 1976), 575, 577–78, 581.

12. "Beyond Good and Evil," *Human, All Too Human*, directed by Simon Chu, et al. BBC Television. EuroArts, 1999.

13. G. W. F. Hegel, *Phenomenology of Spirit*, trans. A. V. Miller. (1807; Oxford: Oxford University Press, 1977), 19.

14. Sofianos, *The Truth of Revolution*, 58.

15. Hegel, *Phenomenology*, 51.

16. "Devo's De-Evolution Decade," *Search & Destroy* #2, 1977, in *Search and Destroy 1–6: The Complete Reprint*, by V. Vale (San Francisco: V/Search, 1996), 30–31.

17. Lester Bangs, "Iggy Pop: Blowtorch in Bondage," in *Psychotic Reactions and Carburetor Dung*, ed. Greil Marcus (New York: Vintage, 1988), 205.

18. Hegel, *Phenomenology*, 124.

19. Ibid., 407.

20. Ibid.

21. George Berger, *The Story of Crass* (Oakland: PM Press, 2009), 170. See also Sofianos's *Truth*, wherein Crass's Steve Ignorant confesses that "I've read two pages of [Errico] Malatesta and I've had to put it down because it was so boring" (51).

22. Stacy Thompson, *Punk Productions* (Albany: SUNY Press, 2004), 121–22, 151.

23. Kathleen Hanna, "Riot Grrrl Manifesto," *Bikini Kill* #2, n.p, n.d. (ca. 1991). Albini quoted in Robert Rodi and Dennis Polkow, "Music 45: Who Keeps Chicago in Tune 2015," *Newcity* 30, no. 1330 (July 16–23, 2015): 9.

24. For comments on the Ramones' or Reed's Judaism see Steven Lee Beeber, *The Heebie-Jeebies at CBGB's* (Chicago: Chicago Review Press, 2006).

25. This song would generate the English punk band Fearless Vampire Killers.

26. Dan Sinker, "Ian MacKaye," in *We Owe You Nothing*, ed. Dan Sinker (1999; New York: Akashic, 2001), 21.

27. Ian MacKaye, personal communication with the author, September 2, 2015.

28. Sinker, "Ian MacKaye," *We Owe You Nothing*, 19.

29. Abram Himelstein and Jamie Schweser, *Tales of a Punk Rock Nothing* (New Orleans: New Mouth from the Dirty South, 1998), 26.

30. Karl Marx, "Private Property and Communism," in *The Economic and Philosophic Manuscripts of 1844*, ed. Dirk J. Struik (New York: International Publishers, 1964), 133.

31. Himelstein and Schweser, *Tales of a Punk Rock Nothing*, 57.

32. Holmstrom, "Richard Hell," *Punk*, 62.

33. Judith Butler, *Bodies That Matter* (New York: Routledge, 1993), 3.

34. Jacques Lacan, *The Other Side of Psychoanalysis*, trans. Russell Grigg (1970; New York: Norton: 2007), 94.

35. See Kurt Cobain, *Journals* (New York: Penguin/Riverhead, 2002), 265.

36. Agnès Aflalo, *The Failed Assassination of Psychoanalysis: The Rise and Fall of Cognitivism*, trans. A. R. Price (2009; London: Karnac, 2015), 137.

37. Michel Foucault, *History of Madness*, trans. Jonathan Murphy and Jean Khalfa (1961; London: Routledge, 2006), 170.

38. See Jacques Lacan, "Discourse To Catholics," in *The Triumph of Religion*, trans. Bruce Fink. (1960; Cambridge: Polity, 2013).

39. Jacques Derrida, "Cogito and the History of Madness," in *Writing and Difference*, trans. Alan Bass (1967; Chicago: University of Chicago, 1978), 61.

40. Derrida, *Writing and Difference*, 289.

41. Sinker, "Kathleen Hanna," in *We Owe You Nothing*, 64.

42. Lacan, *Other Side of Psychoanalysis*, 61–68.

43. Marquis de Sade, *Philosophy in the Boudoir*, trans. Joachim Neugroschel (1795; New York: Penguin, 2006), 13.

44. Nico Ordway, "De Sade," *Search & Destroy #4*, 1977, in *Search and Destroy 1–6: The Complete Reprint*, by V. Vale (San Francisco: V/Search, 1996), 68.

45. Jeff Jetton, "The Secret of Noam: A Chomsky Interview," *Brightest Young Things*, BYT Media, Inc., March 9, 2011, see Chomsky.Info, Anthony Arnove Admin., http://chomsky.info/20110309-2/.

46. Orange County Keith, "Good Times with Bad Religion," *The Orange County Keith Netzine*, The Bad Religion Page, January 1, 1996. http://www.thebrpage.net/media/item.asp?itemID=558.

"I COULD'VE BEEN RASKOLNIKOV" 2

Punk Reads Dostoevsky

> The entire goal here on earth toward which mankind is striving consists of nothing more than . . . two times two makes four, that is, a formula, and after all, two times two makes four is already not life, gentlemen, but the beginning of death.
>
> Dostoevsky, *Notes from Underground*

> Punks constitute a form of passive resistance to a slick social order . . . in an era when there are plenty of voices who would tell you that all human behavior can be reduced to a formula.
>
> Lester Bangs, "The Clash," *New Musical Express*

On a gray January day in 2012, eight young women, donning only nylon tights and skirts and concealing their faces with crudely fashioned pastel balaclavas, startled anyone stubborn enough to be waltzing about Moscow's Red Square in the freezing temperatures by climbing atop the Lobnoye Mesto platform—the traditional site of the tsar's proclamations—and unfurled the purple flag of anarcha-feminism. Distressed at the increasingly likely reelection of Vladimir Putin, the tiny band of artists-radicals had chosen, quite logically, to take command of the master's phallic lectern by claiming the entire square as their own by decree. "A rebellious column moves toward the Kremlin!" the octet screamed, carrying no weapons save their own sharp voices, two trebly electric guitars plugged into tiny hip-mounted speakers, and a lavender smoke bomb. "Bitches piss behind the red walls." So went the opening lines to Pussy Riot's "Putin Pissed Himself," a song inspired by the pan-commonwealth protests in December 2011 opposing the fraught second coming of the man American president George W. Bush had christened Ostrich Legs. Performing a choreographed mini-ballet on the massive stone stage and banging away on cheap instruments, the women directed their pithy complaint directly at the administrators who, were they to step to their office windows, might witness the performance only meters away. "Revolt in Russia—the charisma of protest!" the women screeched as tourists abandoned Red Square in haste. "Revolt in Russia: we exist!"[1]

The event was like a dream, a moment precious for its fleeting and fragmented nature and symptomatic, as André Breton put it in *Nadja*, "of the repercussion such recollections, provided one surrenders to them with a certain violence, may have on the course of one's thought."[2] For the scant witnesses, some remembering perhaps the Ukrainian national who had told London's *Daily Telegraph* less than a decade before, as Kiev became ground zero of what was later called the Orange Revolution, that "we should have got rid of the bandits that run this country in 1991, but we were fooled. Now we have had enough," Breton's sentiment seemed inspiringly on point.[3] The performance, observers would remember, was as unforgettable as the revolutionary moment it referenced, despite the fact that it lasted but ninety seconds before the women, unmasked, were forcibly removed by Moscow police.

Although the happening catalyzed no broader revolt in Moscow at the time, to the chagrin of the Russian oligarchs, many of whom were the same former KGB agents and Putin lackeys who would later send

Russian soldiers into Crimea (and perhaps even meddle in the 2016 American presidential election), Pussy Riot's antics in Red Square were not the last such protest. In February, five of the eight members of the ensemble entered Moscow's Cathedral of Christ the Saviour and, sporting again their balaclavas, lined up along the gilded priests-only altar before chanting what they later characterized as a "punk prayer," dancing and punching the air as icons of Russian Orthodox saints watched on in horror. Crossing themselves melodramatically and, on their knees now, asking the Virgin Mary to save the country from a second Putin presidency—"Virgin Mary, Mother of God, put Putin away!"—the women railed against the Church's tacit support for the Russian president as guards rushed the altar and cathedral officials accosted, in vain, anyone who had taken to recording the performance. "The Church's praise of rotten dictators," the women shouted in unison as they were escorted outside. "The cross-bearer procession of black limousines!"[4]

Charged with "hooliganism" for the cathedral performance, motivated supposedly by their hatred of religion, three of the five women—Nadezhda Tolokonnikova, Maria Alyokhina, and Yekaterina Samutsevich—were arrested days later only to be held in a Russian jail for months awaiting a formal hearing. At a July trial, as they gave their closing statements from inside the glass box that served as the prisoners' holding cell, the trio signaled its musical bias less by virtue of its radical politics or variegated couture than its literary acumen. Railing against the Russian Church, the State educational system, and the Russian news media, each of the women cited, in self-defense, several Russian philosophers, Montaigne's *Essays*, Kafka, large swaths of the Christian Bible, Plato, and Solzhenitsyn. And as Tolokonnikova asked her judge and anyone watching the proceedings, "Do you remember why young Dostoevsky was sentenced to death? His entire guilt lay in the fact that he was fascinated by socialist theories, and during meetings of freethinkers and friends—who met on Fridays in the apartment of Petrashevsky—he discussed the writings of Fourier and George Sand. On one of the last Fridays, he read Belinsky's letter to Gogol aloud, a letter that was filled, according to the court that tried Dostoevsky—*listen*!—'with impudent statements against the Orthodox Church and the State government.'" Demanding not merely to be heard but to be *listened to*, Tolokonnikova with a smirk called to mind the great Russian novelist, appreciating finally the conditions that contributed to his grotesque narratives and imagining his own shame and fear at the state-sanctioned dehumanization and mock execution he suffered at the hands of an earlier tsar.[5]

In making such references—and claiming common cause with Dostoevsky in particular—the members of Pussy Riot were engaging in a practice common to punk and postpunk advocates at least since Iggy Pop had entitled his debut solo album *The Idiot* in 1977. A year following Pop's record, Lester Bangs asked a maudlin Richard Hell bluntly, "Did Dostoyevsky sit around mewling about I, I, I?"[6] The next decade Magazine singer Howard Devoto cited *Crime and Punishment* anti-hero Raskolnikov in "Philadelphia" from his second band's third record *The Correct Use of Soap* ("I could've been Raskolnikov / But Mother Nature ripped me off") and the Karamazov-referencing instrumental punkers Stinking Lizaveta—who are from Philadelphia—debuted. And in his terse autobiography *Rotten*, John Lydon's ruminations teeter on plagiarism of Dostoevsky's underground man, who introduces himself with a sneer: "I am a sick man. . . . I am a spiteful man. A truly unattractive man."[7] Inspired, perhaps, Lydon replies in a staccato delivery that mimes the underground man's, "I'm a spiteful bastard. I always have been. If I can make trouble, then that's perfect for me. My school reports show this thoroughly. Negative Attitude. Well, of course."[8] Finally, in her memoir Deborah Curtis includes Dostoevsky on a list of her late husband's literary influences, as Henry Rollins elsewhere responded to

Search & Destroy editor Vale, "I love the Russians; I love Dostoyevsky, but after ten pages I'm winded, because it's so heavy and I need a break."[9]

If humankind truly is rebellious by nature, as his Grand Inquisitor declares, perhaps no novelist's body of literature is more appropriate to read in the context of punk and postpunk than Fyodor Dostoevsky. By itself *Notes from Underground,* a proto-existentialist work that bewitched Nietzsche, who called the novella "really a piece of music . . . a stroke of genius,"[10] has been appropriated repeatedly by those who consider themselves members of these particular music subcultures, as this sampling suggests: Stephen Duncombe's analysis of the punk/zine subculture *Notes from Underground: Zines and the Politics of Alternative Culture;* Steven Taylor's punk ethnography *False Prophet: Field Notes from the Punk Underground;* Magazine's "A Song from Under the Floorboards"; the New York–based Notes from Underground punk group and their disbanded Canadian analogue *the* Notes from Underground; the 2002 Underground Operations Records compilation album *Notes from Underground;* punk-industrial band Pigface's 1994 record *Notes from Thee Underground;* and the (defunct) American magazine *Punk Planet,* whose editor Daniel Sinker made "notes from underground" his magazine's subtitle in 2002. "We thought the literary reference was important," Sinker told me not long before his operation folded, feeling the phrase would add intellectual weight to the project. "We liked the double meaning the phrase held—written notes or musical notes. It's not a direct endorsement of the book, but certainly some of its themes—alienation, the underground—are applicable to punk culture."[11]

Recognizing the cheapness of such talk, punks have for years couched allusions to Dostoevsky in what might be considered the musical interpretation of the novels from which they arise. A Sex Pistols song, or perhaps an entire hardcore record, sounds like Dostoevsky's shortest novel, with its badgering, rapid-fire misanthropy and screeching rant at the vanguard, whereas Public Image Ltd's postpunk touchstone *Metal Box* or Hüsker Dü's "punk opera" *Zen Arcade* unfold much like Dostoevsky's ungainly and under read volumes *Demons* and *Raw Youth*: too long, disjointed, cumbersome, but subversive nonetheless and weighed down by a glut of political, aesthetic, and ethical insights. These interpretations too carry over into both punk philosophy and punk style: while not necessarily endorsing Raskolnikov's theory on the moral right of "exceptional" individuals to transgress the master's Law with impunity, punks share much with Raskolnikov's shabby couture, ideological predilections about seeking always to say something new, and, in so doing, their demanding, as he puts it, the "destruction of the present reality in the name of one that is better."[12] Or, describing Stavrogin, Dostoevsky's narrator in *Demons* (alternately *The Devils* or *Possessed*) seems to anticipate punk in noting how at one time the womanizing radical who too sought the subversion of his bourgeois heritage "was living in strange company, associating with the dregs of the Petersburg population, with some down-at-heel Civil Servants, retired army officers who had to beg for a living, and drunkards, that he visited their families, spending days and nights in slums and goodness only knows what other disreputable places, that he had sunk very low, walked about in rags, and that apparently this life was to his taste." While Stavrogin would ultimately come up for air after sinking so deep, his youthful indiscretions, which heralded the Sex Pistols, were legend in the provincial Russian town of his birth: leading an elderly aristocrat about by the nose, kissing married women on the lips in public, biting a governor's ear, and generally repudiating the middle class that had groomed him.[13]

Stavrogin's defense? "I really was—indisposed . . . do you really think that I'm capable of attacking people while in the full possession of my senses?" he asks a colleague even as the narrator would go on to end his novel by noting that "the verdict of our doctors after the post-mortem was that [Stavrogin's behavior] was most definitely not a case of insanity."[14] Indeed, as the reader had sensed long before the novel's end, there is more to Stavrogin's mania than mental illness; he is in many ways, like so many punks in his wake, the demonic swine driven out of the self-flagellating hermit in Mark's Gospel, implies Dostoevsky, one of an entire generation of youth rejecting their own middle-class values and out to undermine the philosophical, economic, and theological mooring of Russian society, whose inconsistencies and brutality had triggered its youths' "devilish" demeanor. So it is that the motley adoption of Dostoevsky's characters and style, politics, and "philosophy," is neither coincidence nor caprice, but part of a well-conceived punk construction-of-self that was established early in punk history and serves as one of the foundational literary threads that have linked several otherwise disparate punk scenes both aesthetically and ideologically. Or so this chapter shall argue—with help from psychoanalysis and Russian writer M. M. Bakhtin, who long ago identified the "carnivalesque" quality of Dostoevsky's fiction that punk adopted. Taking punks at their word, this chapter explores a trio of scenarios, which emerge sequentially, to show how and to what effect Dostoevsky has repeatedly emerged in punk and postpunk as they challenge not merely musical or cultural but political orthodoxy in all its forms: first, as an attempt to identify and grapple with punks' self-hating obsession with disgrace and depravity; then, as a touchstone for the often paralyzing "intensified consciousness" that follows punks' disgrace, modeled after the underground man, and perhaps Raskolnikov and Stavrogin; and, finally, as a way of approaching the killing of all manner of symbolic fathers who *generate*, even in their absence, punks' depravity, shame, (self-) consciousness, and paralysis.

Grotesque Realism

In his magisterial work of literary criticism *Problems of Dostoevsky's Poetics,* Bakhtin describes the "carnivalesque" as a complex and symbolic literary form that takes its cues from not only Greco-Roman festivals of antiquity but Medieval events such as *Mardi Gras*. Such festivals were notable for their obscenity, ritual spectacle, dreamlike suspension of the Law, and inversion of religious and social hierarchy generally. In Bakhtin's summary, carnival is a "pageant without footlights" that turns spectators into performers, a "counter-hegemonic event" wherein everyone is a participant and in which a grotesque realism is less performed than reified. Language misuse is particularly important to the carnivalesque, which elevates abusive language, blasphemy, and the "language of the market" to an art form while denigrating high diction. In this way, writes Bakhtin, carnivalization of the Logos "facilitated the destruction of epic and tragic distance and the transfer of all represented material to a zone of familiar contact," which "exercised a powerful transforming influence on the very verbal style of literature." In art and literature specifically, carnivalization served as a subversive negation of the master signifier whose effects went beyond the temporary festival space, an annual attempt to take Hegelian dialectics seriously and carry what the philosopher called the "dismemberment" of consciousness past the holiday.[15]

Although sixteenth-century French writer François Rabelais's epic *Gargantua and Pantagruel* was, for Bakhtin, the epitome of carnival, the preponderance of Dostoevsky's fiction too contains the characteristic accessories of the literary carnival. Divided between a mocking, irreverent monologue and a disgraceful, self-loathing tragicomedy, *Notes from Underground* is only the most obvious example. As his fame grew and his style evolved, however, Dostoevsky's stories almost seemed to become increasingly carnivalesque; *The Idiot, Raw Youth, The Dream of a Ridiculous Man,* and *The Brothers Karamazov,* all of which rely on several voices and styles throughout their often satirical and shape-shifting narratives, too display not merely overstated, grotesque characters and scandalous (even seditious) literary and political transpositions, but signal the author's—and thus reader's—inherent "multiplicity." Consider one exemplary scene from *Demons*: having arranged a literary fete and ball to raise funds for poor governesses, local governor's wife Julia von Lembke is horrified when a drunken General Lebyadkin appears and recites aloud an obscene poem. The matinée devolves from there as elderly novelist Karamazinov replaces the drunkard on stage to read a masturbatory account of his own legacy as a man of letters that ends in his exchanging insults with the audience, and a "professor" from St. Petersburg pipes up, attacking the Russian political and religious establishment. So does the event descend into a riot as the mortified governess wilts with dread.[16]

To wit, several scholars have explored already the degree to which punk resembles such a scene, a connection that seems to have reached its apex not merely in the Sex Pistols' familiar antics but in bands such as Gogol Bordello or the entire "circus punk" subgenre. According to Peter Jones, punk is infused with a carnival spirit so far as it is "fluid, heterogenous, and transient, marked by irreverence, dissent, and symbolic resistance through music, dress, and behavior." Particularly important in connecting carnival to punk is its "everyman" quality in which anyone can participate, needing no special training or belief system to contribute to the subculture whose participants "live in it," as Bakhtin put it.[17] Pointing to punk's dismantling of social hierarchy, vulgar speech, and demotion of high art, Jones notes too the intentional elision of sexual categorization in much of punk and postpunk subculture, which has drawn attention to its own gender-bending, cross-dressing, homosexuality, and symbolic castration for years, if inconsistently.

As Jones's focus on English punk suggests, most important to punk's version of carnival is the subculture's ongoing "multi-voiced dialogism," in Bakhtin's phthisic phrasing, which creates a forum for the voices of those the parent culture has either left behind or silenced: the disaffected, dispossessed, abject, and alienated. Punks have for decades (in)articulated this estrangement—here the underclass, there women or various minority groups such as the Muslim punk subcult known as "Taqwacore"—not simply through abusive language and profane behavior on stage or vinyl, but through a robust network of cut-up and intentionally unedited fanzines, pseudonyms, and neologisms that not only invert and distort pop and political discourse, but amplify the multifarious voices of the subculture's shrieking advocates. Even punk fiction has adopted this deconstruction of language, cultivating what Deleuze and Guattari called a minor literature. "And likewise we did a sharpened bamboo pongee stick palisade with rat poison on the tips nine steps times two above the ninth-floor landing in honor of the English band 999," Thorn Hillsbery's narrator Rockets Redglare puts it in *What We Do Is Secret,* at the same time as English punk poet and novelist Billy Childish constructs a dialogue with himself, not unlike the underground man, calling his grotesque *Notebooks of a Naked Youth,* "Words piled on top of words, yet others shout at me to take notice of them, and together they jostle over the page, ill-formed, illogical and mis-spelled. A great vomit of half-formed consciousness."[18]

Only two examples in a growing list of increasingly satisfying punk novelists, Hillsbery and Childish epitomize their genre's carnivalesque resolve to twist and invert its mother tongue, to deconstruct the Father's phallogocentrism. Through a flexible, creative use of diction, such enunciation itself destabilizes the literary status quo, the master's Logos that creates punks as abject subjects, inverting the hierarchy of thought and forcing the vanguard to at least engage with its externalities, its festering symptoms, if not grudgingly acknowledge their cause.

The Idiot

So it is that the emergence of "punk fiction" as its own mutinous genre—which will receive a full treatment in chapter 7—signals an important component of punk carnivalization that earlier analyses ignore: the subculture's appropriation and distortion not only of literature generally but of Dostoevsky's characters and style in particular. As a glimpse into the world of punk fiction shows, punks' interest in Dostoevsky extends beyond mere name-dropping. Many punk and postpunk musicians, writers, and fans have internalized a shelf's worth of Dostoevsky explicitly, self-styling as "underground" men and women or presenting themselves as contemporary "idiots," Stavrogins, or Raskolnikovs, harboring "almost physical disgust for everyone he met and everything around him. . . . If anyone had addressed him, he would have been quite capable of simply spitting on him."[19] Aesthetically, too, we see in punk fashion not merely an embodiment of the underground man's anxious "existentialism" and apparel—which he admits appears "old, threadbare, soiled" with "a huge yellow spot on my trousers"—but Stavrogin, as we have seen, and Raskolnikov, whose shabby clothing is described at one point as increasing the likelihood that its wearer "might have been mistaken for a professional beggar."[20]

Paving the way for later punks' appropriation was none other than Iggy Pop, whose seminal grotesquerie onstage was once characterized by Bangs as "repeatedly [twisting] his face and body up into masks and gestures symbolic of 'idiocy,' torment, and, most of all bondage."[21] By all extant accounts, James Osterberg's interest in literature as a youth was genuine. Noted for carrying around Gibbon's *Decline and Fall of the Roman Empire,* Iggy had not only talked Nietzsche with Tom Snyder on television but confessed to *Search & Destroy* his interest in Burroughs in 1977, calling *Naked Lunch* and *Junky* "great books."[22] And if one takes seriously Iggy's claim that "I'm as bent as Dostoevsky," the brooding Russian novelist too topped Iggy's reading list.[23] Or as Angela Bowie once quipped, "I suppose Lou [Reed] was a little more sophisticated than Iggy, but whereas Lou didn't do the reading, Iggy . . . actually read, you know, Dostoevsky and all that kinda crap."[24]

So it is that the melodramatic and obscene histrionics of Dostoevsky's characters became part of Osterberg's persona, embedded in Iggy's crass lyrics and vulgar public behavior, to the degree that Iggy literally became something of a Myshkinesque chump: sensitive and intelligent, yet exceedingly fatuous—an idiot savant playing the Princely role of escaped mental patient whose brilliance and self-confidence were matched only by his naive, and often depraved, ridiculousness. In Bangs's telling, during one Stooges show near the end of the group's career, Iggy responded to the Hell's Angels in the audience who wanted to hear his infamous "Louie, Louie" by singing a forty-five-minute version of the song, the revised lyrics of which included "You can suck my ass you biker faggot sissies."[25] The bikers would eventually put Iggy, who had gone into the crowd to confront the gang, in the hospital. Like Myshkin, then, Iggy, whose twitching onstage mimicked the Prince's (or Smerdyakov's or Dostoevsky's) epileptic fits, was well-read and perceptive, ahead of his peers intellectually and aesthetically, but also given to an almost puerile thoughtlessness. Or, as Paul Trynka asks less rhetorically than disconcertedly in his Osterberg biography, at one point noting specifically Iggy's interest in Dostoevsky's *Idiot,* "how could one

2.1. Iggy reads. Photo by Mäts Backer, 1977.

man be so clever, and so stupid?" Trynka is here remembering the parade of embarrassments that Iggy seemed to collect like totems: performing in a dog collar on his knees, rolling in broken glass, coating himself with peanut butter, stumbling about the stage like a child who had just revolved around a baseball bat with his head on the heel, squirming about lasciviously with his pants nearly on the floor, routinely goading abuse by concertgoers, and his eventual institutionalization in Los Angeles. "The slow, painful, heroic death of the Stooges started with humiliation and ended in a hail of bottles," Trynka summarizes of Iggy's early career. Of the two assaults, "The humiliation hurt more."[26]

When combined, Iggy's bestial music, literary pretentions, and degrading antics onstage and off mark the beginning of a broad punk predilection with disrepute and disgust that finds its literary analogue in Dostoevsky. As Deborah Martinsen explains in *Surprised by Shame*, from his earliest work to *Karamazov* Dostoevsky "provides countless case studies of shame—shame turned inward, as in the case of the underground man, or shame directed outward."[27] The Underground Man's countless humiliations notwithstanding, *Demons* is again a poignant case: Lebyadkin's incorrigible drunkenness, Julia von Lembke's failed gala and plummeting social standing, Stavrogin's secret marriage to a simpleton he despises and his prurient pedophilia, Lisa's unmarried pregnancy, Mrs. Stavrogin's shame in her far-from-the-tree son, Shatov's abandonment by his wife, and so on, all describe not only these characters' shame but the readers'—the *Russians'*—collective dishonor. Or, as the *Demons* narrator recalls the conversation of several interlocutors—"I wonder the Lembkes are not ashamed to look on!" "Why should they be ashamed? You are not." "Yes, I am ashamed, and he is the governor." "And you are a pig"—following Julia von Lembke's humbling fete, "I don't remember all the absurd tricks they played, however; it was all in the same style, so that I felt at last painfully ashamed. And this same expression, as it were, of shame was reflected in the whole public, even on the most sullen figures that had come out of the refreshment-room. For some time all were silent and gazed with angry perplexity. When a man is ashamed he generally begins to get angry and is disposed to be cynical."[28]

The humiliation so many of Dostoevsky's characters experience—and especially the audacity they often display in the face of such disgrace—has three effects on the novels' readers, says Martinsen: disruption, disorientation, and an increased self-consciousness. Each of these effects can be observed in punk's paterfamilias Iggy, whose public persona accomplished for a twentieth-century American and European audience what Dostoevsky's fiction did for a nineteenth-century Russian one.

Leaping over his most obviously self-loathing Stooges songs such as "I Wanna Be Your Dog" and "Dirt" (which seems to have internalized Stavrogin's mother's claim to her son that "Your idea of heaven is disorder. Your idea of enjoyment is dirt"), Iggy's painfully awkward debut solo record, *The Idiot,* serves as a perfect punk example of such disruption, disorientation, and self-consciousness. Written and recorded in France and Germany with David Bowie (who too was astoundingly well-read), the record documents the experiences of some hideous and brooding Myshkin-Stavrogin hybrid both tired of and disgusted by his degradation, but also unwilling to change and even celebrating his corruption as he lurks about some twentieth-century European city flooded by postwar capital, cheap sex, and amphetamines. "Calling Sister Midnight / I'm an idiot for you," the record's speaker begins with a self-loathing belch in "Sister Midnight," drawing out his early-morning syllables, "I'm breakage inside." His bloodshot eyes narrowed to slits, the singer drawls on a telephone to his estranged sibling, who picks up but is scarcely listening. "Can you hear me at all?" The song is a drunk-dial, an incestuous cry for help to The Night, whose wicked charms have turned the singer into a slobbering fool and forced him to confess with chagrin that:

> I had a dream last night
> Mother was in my bed
> And I made love to her
> Father he gunned for me
> Hunted me with his six-gun

Acknowledging the Oedipal origins of both his sleaze and his desire for abuse, Iggy's crooner admits too his dislocation, his desperation under the Father's Law and attempted assumption of the Father's position as keeper of the phallus. "What can I do about my dreams?" Pop pleads to the oracle, blaming her for selling him out on the Father's behalf and his conversion into one of Dostoevsky's shiftless anti-heroes: "You've got me walking in rags . . . you put a beggar in my heart."

The speaker's dignity only dissolves from there. "Nightclubbing," "Funtime," and "China Girl" detail his craving for what he knows is a decadent late-1970s nightlife while deeper in the album the lounge act–inspired "Tiny Girls" offers listeners the story of a red-faced pederast who like Stavrogin "don't want to live," but continues to do so simply to spite himself, pursuing not mature companions but the tiny girls "Who have got no tricks, who have got no past." In the end, "Though I try to die," moans the baritone-voiced, arthritic old man of the record's closer "Mass Production," he keeps finding himself physically alive but essentially dehumanized—"back on the [production] line / Again and again," unable (or unwilling) to reclaim agency in his life, to genuinely and consistently assume the Name of the Father and make of himself Lacan's privileged signifier, realizing like the man in Kafka's "Before the Law" that such an assumption was always-already impossible.

It leaves you feeling dirty, *The Idiot,* both depraved and depressed, as if you have just witnessed a snuff film whose subject's eyes reflect not horror but resignation and ambivalence. Extending the listener's discomfort, "Mass Production," at nearly nine minutes, pushes the repeated synthetic buzz the song starts with all the way though to a Nashville fade whose end cannot seem to come, like the end of *Demons* or *Raw Youth,* soon enough. This is, of course, the album's goal. In articulating a failed attempt to occupy the place of the master signifier, to become one who "has" rather than "is" a phallus, Iggy demonstrates his own shame in the face of the shameless Father. In so doing Iggy resurrects Dostoevsky's characters' embarrassing exhibitionism, self-loathing, sharing of their depravity with the community, and at times the *jouissance* they experience from their transgressive shame, all of which serve to engage readers and make them complicit in the book's bent-headed narrative. Like his characters, for example *Raw Youth*'s teenage protag Arkady, who is brought to a certain epiphany as a result of the disgusting incontinence *and* Catholicism of his biological father Versilov, Dostoevsky's readers too "experience the disruption of shame—the effect of surprise. Like them we experience the disorientation of shame . . . we find ourselves in a state of *aporia,* a liminal state in which we are particularly open to shame's third effect: self-consciousness."[29] Martinsen is at this writing of these words remembering the "confession" Stavrogin offers a priest in a chapter originally censored from *Demons.* "Every extraordinarily disgraceful, infinitely humiliating, vile, and, above all, ridiculous situation in which I happened to find myself in life, invariably aroused in me not only intense anger, but also a feeling of intense pleasure," the Russian proto-punk admits to a monk in the apocryphal chapter: "It was the same in moments when I was committing a crime and in moments when my life was in danger. If I were to steal something, I should at the time of committing the theft have felt like dancing with pleasure at the thought of the depth of my villainy. It was not the villainy that I loved (here my mind was absolutely clear). What I liked was the feeling of rapture caused by the agonizing consciousness of my baseness."[30]

As Bangs documented decades ago and Iggy's *The Idiot* suggests, Pop for most of his career operated on such a level, even admitting to mimicking Stavrogin in corrupting—repeatedly—a thirteen-year-old girl.[31] "What we need are *more* rock 'stars' willing to make fools of themselves, absolutely jump off the deep end and make the *audience embarrassed* for them if necessary," Bangs wrote of Iggy in 1970, "so long as they have not one shred of dignity [remaining]."[32] Much in how Myshkin's, Stravrogin's, or the underground man's appropriation of the Father's phallogocentric exhibitionism allows the reader to engage with the narrative in a more palpable, horrified, and perhaps titillating way, Pop's self-abuse and humiliating, sordid performance allows Iggy's audience, Bangs, and even Bangs's readers a greater consciousness of not only themselves but their own degradation so far as they remain (abject) subjects under the master's thumb in the twentieth and twenty-first centuries. And once such humiliations in the face of the symbolic paternal's repression have been experienced communally, abject beings—that is to say, each of us subject to the Law—emerge more conscious of their status as lesser-than and the marginalizing environs through which they stumble. As Iggy and Bangs demonstrate, then, punk's chronic return to Dostoevsky functions as both an ideological and a performative strategy that not only expresses and reenacts the speaker's disruptive and disorienting—humiliating—self-consciousness, but serves as an attempt at taking the symbolic paternal space, "not to assume it," says Judith Butler, "but to show that it is *occupiable,* to raise the question of the cost and movement of that assumption."[33]

Or if Iggy fails to convince, take Peter Laughner. The creative force behind Cleveland's Rocket from the Tombs, Laughner took his cues from Iggy in helping design American punk's debauched literary aesthetic in the middle 1970s with songs such as "Ain't It Fun" ("somebody came to me and they spit right in my face / But I didn't even feel it—it was such a disgrace") and "Life Stinks."

A notoriously quick-witted and tactless essayist, Laughner often went out of his way to publicly document his own writer-cum-boor methodology and baseness. As Laughner confessed in a mawkish and hilarious review of Lou Reed's *Coney Island Baby*:

> [After hearing the record] I didn't go to work. I had a horrible physical fight with my wife over a stupid bottle of 10 mg Valiums. . . . I called up the editor of this magazine . . . and did virtually nothing but cough up phlegm in an alcoholic stupor for three hours. . . . I came on to my sister-in-law: "C'mon over and give me head while I'm passed out." I cadged drinks off anyone who would come near me or let me into their apartments. I ended up the whole debacle passing out stone cold after puking and pissing myself at a band rehearsal, had to be kicked awake by my lead singer.[34]

This rehearsal notwithstanding, Laughner was a manic, intense presence on stage, echoing both Iggy Pop's self-deprecating performance art and Lou Reed's songwriting acumen. He was also an immoderate drug user and music fanatic whose poor judgment and wantonness, documented by Lester Bangs in a 1977 *New York Rocker* obituary, led to his premature and depraved death.

The shameless exhibitionism typical of Laughner and Iggy "aggressively transgresses and collapses the intersubjective boundaries" that separate readers from characters and texts, Martinsen contends, suggesting too that the shameless attempt to assume the Name of the Father demonstrated by subjects like the speaker of Iggy's *The Idiot* "is an aggressive defense against shame or the anticipation of shame."[35]

Likewise, much as how Dostoevsky's characters' ignobility allow the reader to engage with the narrative in a more palpable, reflective way—to see the Father's shamelessness trickling down his leg—Laughner's self-abuse and callow demise allow Bangs and his readers a greater consciousness of not only themselves but their own degradation in a patronizing world so malign that its wanderers require sedatives simply to function, as Marx long ago mused. Or, as the Ex-Workers' Collective and punk proponents CrimethInc. puts it in their twenty-first-century field manual, essentially summarizing *Notes from Underground*, "I would like to tell the story of the most antisocial, indefensible man, to give voice to his untold treasures and torments, to expose his wretched humanity in so compelling a portrait that you would be made to see the absoluteness of his needs as you see the absoluteness of your own. Then all his unforgivable sins would be on your conscience, and you'd have to find a way to wash the world of shame once and for all or else perish with the untouchables you're so proud to outrank."[36]

Confessing that being around Laughner made him feel "embarrassed," Bangs writes that he too feels "a certain complicity" for Laughner's death.[37] For Bangs, rather, Laughner's ruin generated in his colleagues and fans an instructive aporia, as Martinsen puts it, a serious consideration of not only one's own doubts, fears, and failures, but those of the penetrating lawgiver who has put the subordinated subject in her miserable position, intentionally or not. Once such humiliations, such debasing thoughts and actions, have been expressed publicly and collectively, the subjects of such depravity—and their witnesses—emerge more conscious of themselves and the institutions and systems by which they are beset, including history and political economy. "They're just shy people," Iggy told *Rolling Stone* of his early audience, recounting their beaten and battered psychology and his "list of thirty-two important transgressions—my stations of the cross" as a Stooge, sympathizing with his fellow hysterics and idiots. "And there are people who hate what they are, who want to get rid of that part of themselves, to scrape it away. They look to me, especially twenty years ago, as someone who did that."[38]

All of this is to say that punk depravity functions as a political and performative (attempted) occupation of the Name of the Father that not only expresses the speaker's disorienting and humiliated self-consciousness as a subject subordinated to the Law, but challenges the hearer to recognize her own subordination and self-hate, to make her complicit in the thoughts and words of the moaning singer and thus a participant in the often unsettling punk performance or artifact. And to act up in response. Furthermore, such an orientation serves as a defense against the anticipated (or deeply felt) shame in Being itself, which is a direct result of the master signifier's rule. And writhing at the center of it all, for dozens of punks, is Dostoevsky, who in at least one spiteful instance noted the subsequently *paralyzing* consequences of such self-consciousness.

Going Underground

Useful as her analysis is, Martinsen fails to explore in great detail the underside of the self-consciousness that depravity and shame produce in the subordinated or abject subject-reader, the audience. After all, if the history of punk (and the suicides of several of those punk agents mentioned above) is any indication, this underside includes not only the depression, madness, and substance abuse that killed or nearly killed Iggy, Laughner, Sid Vicious, Darby Crash, Bangs, Kurt Cobain, and scores of punk enthusiasts, but a paralyzing inability to function among the living *when* living. Taking their cue from Iggy—whose "1969" and "I'm Bored" drew attention to boredom as a facet of abject being early in its history—punk has for decades filled its records and concerts with songs that explore the inactivity that results from the pensive self-consciousness that its predilection with disgrace generates. Take, as early examples, the Buzzcocks's "Boredom," the Clash's "I'm So Bored with the U.S.A.," the Adverts's "Bored Teenagers," the Ramones's "Now I Wanna Sniff Some Glue," and GG Allin's "Bored to Death." Later examples include Green Day's "Longview," whose speaker is "so damn bored I'm going blind," Cobain's "Teenage angst has paid off well / Now I'm bored and old" from *In Utero,* and Mr. T Experience's "Boredom Zone." Their content notwithstanding, even the very delivery of such songs, both the music and lyrics, is often casual or slurred, as in Hell's "New Pleasure" or the many songs by Jonathan Richman and the Modern Lovers. Such torpor is the result, punks seem to proffer in these songs, of their very consciousness of their own depravity and the marginalizing, dehumanizing, castrating nature of a postindustrial and bureaucratic society—and their resigned inability to extirpate themselves from or overcome their disenfranchisement and shame.

In articulating such boredom, hysteric punks from Rotten to Crash, Laughner to Curtis, and Rollins to Cobain deliberately cultivate in themselves what Dostoevsky's underground man calls an "intensified consciousness": a being deeply cognizant of both one's own deformities and "your own degradation." Early in his monologue, in fact, the underground man calls consciousness a sickness and explains how rather than finding himself uplifted and enlightened by a greater self-consciousness that education and experience provided, the narrator acted increasingly erratic and base, explaining, "The more conscious I was . . . the deeper I sank into my morass and the more apt I was to be completely bogged down in it." The cause of his baseness, says the writer, is the self-doubt and inaction that result from his surplus of consciousness and contemplation of his "abjectivity." As opposed to the reactionary bull—the stupid "normal man"—the thoughtful and sensitive "mouse" paralyzes itself through indecision, its "stinking muck" of doubt, shame, and endurance of "the spittle showered upon it by the matter-of-fact men." Consciousness of both one's self and one's abject status *causes* the mouse's habitual inaction and, ultimately, its marginalization and chronic (self-) degradation, the underground man insists through sharpened teeth.[39]

Following Iggy's own base antics, several punk figures have explored the subculture's paralyzed embodiment of this state of being on paper, developing their own "notes from underground" that both echo and update the underground man's blood spitting and anxious refusal of the status quo. Richard Hell is but one obvious example. Although Hell claims no special attraction to Dostoevsky, he agrees it is "doubtless" Dostoevsky influenced his own writing and philosophy. "I tried to read NOTES FROM UNDERGR . . . [*sic*] when I was a kid," Hell wrote in 2007, verifying Bangs's rebuke above and adding that he later slogged through *The Idiot,* "because [Robert] Bresson made movies from Dostoevsky and I love Bresson (he said the idea of *Au hasard Balthazar* came from the scene where the protagonist of *The Idiot* is moved by the sound of a donkey's braying)."[40] So it is that Dostoevsky played at least a supporting role in what would become Hell's hyperconscious version of punk, explored in both his touchstone record *Blank Generation* and his 1973 novella *The Voidoid,* which alternates between often incoherent musings on shame, love, and self-hate and the awkward tale of a skeleton and vampire named Skull and Lips, respectively. At one point, in fact, *Voidoid* reiterates the underground man by noting that "laziness" is the natural consequence of a life of thought: "Consciousness intensifies life. Self-consciousness more so; but activity declines. Therefore, inactivity is a sign of life."[41]

But Hell's example is far from exceptional. While Hell was futzing about pretending to be a vampire in New York, Billy Childish was slogging around Chatham reading Dostoevsky and gathering material for what would become a series of intensely self-aware novels, including the "creative confession" *My Fault* and *Notebooks of a Naked Youth*, a "fantastic biography" that reads like a postpunk *Notes from Underground*. Given its grotesque characters, hallucinatory scenes of degradation, and disjointed and contradictory discourse, *Notebooks* especially evokes much of Dostoevsky's work, documenting the almost chronic humiliations aspiring writer and punker William Loveday suffers at the hands of a carnivalesque collection of English brutes and phantoms: trembling and croaking grandparents, the yeasty tease Kursty, a skeletal hag pushing a gimpy shopping trolley, the half-giant Blue and his absurd hat, the oblivious café ghoul who refuses to challenge William's impossible yarn about the Medway Bog Man, and the grunting punk ogre with a tattooed face. "I still thieve and I still lie, and I admire myself and admonish myself pitilessly," William admits early in his notebook, sounding not unlike Dostoevsky's narrator in describing also his tattered garments, unsightly acne, and chronic headache—and ultimately rejecting his own craft: "The disgusting thing about writing, in my opinion, is that it's aggressive and unnecessary and proves nothing but the conceit of the person who writes," admits the writer and musician not long after arguing too that "poets and musicians, as is well-known, are a bunch of vile, gaudy show-offs!"[42]

More than a fantastic autobiographer, though, Childish—who compares himself to Raskolnikov in his poem "I Am the Strange Hero of Hunger" and admitted to *Search & Destroy*'s Vale that each of Dostoevsky's major works can be found on his bookshelf—seems to have borrowed much material from the Russian writer.[43] In the same way that Dostoevsky's *Notes* is a parody of Nikolai Chernyshevsky's leftist novel *What Is to Be Done*?, so is Childish's *Notebooks* a punk update of Dostoevsky's novella. Structurally and thematically, *Notebooks* follows

Notes in offering the intimate and desperate journal of a raving urchin marginalized by power and reactionary in his self-hate. Both document their poverty and impishness in the face of not only their so-called "superiors" but their intellectual *inferiors*, their disgust with the status quo and their birthright, and their almost spastic ejaculations in the face of the deep shame thrust upon them by political economy. "I realize that, yet again, it has happened to me, that I must after all carry an invisible sign round my neck welcoming all the disadvantaged, the shambling and the lost, to come barding in and harass me with their impudent and pointless questions," William laments at one point, just as the spoken curse of a passing mutt forces the youth's right arm involuntarily up—where it stays, locked in position, for days, drawing to him all manner of sniggers and heckles.[44]

Stumbling about some coastal English municipality, searching for love and recognition in a world wholly disinterested in anything he has to say, William nonetheless soldiers on in his determination to write "the story of a man who is a man, but then again is not a man. A man ostracized by his own people for daring to show them the blackness of their souls. . . . A zombie man." Losing his manuscript, William confesses to his notebook his growing paralysis in the face of such humiliations: "From this day on I will quit trying to prove my intelligence and self-worth, and will instead only endeavour to show the depths of my idiocy." In so doing he joins his rock band on the continent—following a harrowing sea voyage—and performs a series of underwhelming gigs in sloshing pubs and bottomless burlesque houses, all bursting at the seams with pimps and whores, drunkards and madmen.

Wandering about Hamburg's Reeperbahn after midnight—following his band's complimentary admission to the sex show elsewhere within the club where his band had played—William concludes his notebook, again, not unlike Dostoevsky, by employing a prostitute. As with the underground man or Iggy, he is trying to escape his boredom and "uncastrate" himself, William, to assume the Name of the Father whose licentiousness and mastery over the abject, "feminized" world had just been performed for him at the Star Club: "He really lies there like some disgusting hairy old bear sprawled out on a bed of stinking goose feathers," William had remarked of the Zeus figure who had just had his way with a young femme. "And even though I pretend to examine myself and understand what it is that I find so repulsive in this heathen man, really I am just excited by his maleness and am dreaming of the day that it will be me who stands naked upon that stage with the maidens of the world gathered to my loins, suckling my great God-like phallus, whilst I spray my seed into their open mouths and gratefully upturned faces." Even as he entertains such flights of fantasy, William knows they will remain the impossible product of his imagination. Nonetheless, it is this performance William recalls as he propositions a streetwalker in Hamburg's red-light district, ashamed at his desire to want to be as grotesque as Zeus and belittled even by the disinterested sex worker who just wants the task over and done, wants to be paid. "And I look down, shamed by my maleness, by my filthy desires, by my lies and lack of humanity," William admits as the notebook reaches its final page and its author rebukes himself for only wanting to take on a prostitute in order to dominate her. Failing in even this, in reproducing the Father, William turns his attack inward, writing that "I rip into myself with a vengeance and call myself a whore-lover and a dog-fucker with a limp dick! I torture myself mercilessly, until I'm sure that I'm squirming with utter contempt and hating myself with total abandon, with absolute assuredness." And so does the red-faced Englishman, exceedingly self-conscious of his own "shameful and crude" character, see in the same Zeus who keeps this "truly great young writer" in chains, an impenetrable—and even unassumable—signifier, who can never really be displaced but only imitated unconvincingly and with shame, leaving the abject hysteric subordinated and even more humiliated than he had been before attempting to assume the master's role.[45]

"What if I commit suicide?" William asks himself throughout his notebook, thinking such thoughts again as the notebook runs out of pages and realizing that if activity is fruitless, one might as well try paralysis, if not death. "If I want to, I tell myself, I can hang myself."[46] Such, after all, seems to be the only reasonable response to one's failure, one's ineffectual, if noble, desire to make the carnival's inversion of order a permanent installation. Dostoevsky regularly suggested as much, leading several characters to such ends: Kirilov, Stavrogin, Smerdyakov.

But William does not kill himself, finding himself instead paralyzed by the experience. So, beyond suicide, with which not only Dostoevsky but the punkers cited above dabble, how can disgrace and the subsequent immobilizing self-consciousness that punk underscores be overcome? Iggy, Laughner, Hell, and Childish, like the underground man, all sought to nullify their emasculation by owning it, trying to become shameless "commanding" masters by anticipating, facing, and moving through the baseness and intense self-consciousness that they feebly assumed as that of the Father. We can read the Sex Pistols as having made a similar move in conning several major record labels into subsidizing their aggressive critique of the record industry itself, and the spectacle of rock and roll "stardom" in particular, amassing tens of thousands of pounds by upping the ante on public degeneracy and the culture industry's standard operating procedure, cashing in on acerbic and offensive songs like "Belsen Was a Gas" and Iggy's "No Fun" along the way.

As we have seen, though, such an act cannot help but end in failure if, as Butler thinks, both suicide and the less extreme displacement of the master signifier "culminates paradoxically in a weakening of the very constituency it is meant to unite." The irony of the abject subject's attempt to become the keeper of Logos, says Butler, is that occupying such positions "is not a matter of ascending to preexisting structural locales within a contemporary symbolic order; on the contrary, certain 'occupations' constitute fundamental ways of rearticulating . . . possibilities of enunciation." Such action on punks' behalf, in other words, automatically changes what and who the master is and the site and scope of his decrees, not the hysteric's station.[47] Dissatisfied both with failing to occupy the master's position and with paralysis and suicide, many hyperconscious punks have taken a different tack: not to try to assume the phallus and its shamelessness or pull the trigger on the self but to eliminate in full the source of humiliation, the master signifier that calls the abject subject into being only to marginalize her. Recognizing the Father as the source of shame, many punks have sought to bury him outright in the hole whence he emerged. And it is in the spirit of patricide that many punks have appropriated, in one form or another, Dostoevsky's capstone.

Smerdyakov, with a Guitar

Dostoevsky's crowning achievement, the multivoiced, grotesque *Brothers Karamazov,* is never transparent on the identity of Fyodor Karamazov's murderer—or the story's narrator; each of the Karamazov brothers, never mind others in the community, had reason to hate the old man. Although Dmitri, the eldest Karamazov brother, who had expressed hatred of his lying, lustful, and shameless father more explicitly than his brothers, is ultimately convicted of the crime, it is the servant Smerdyakov, the illegitimate, epileptic son of Fyodor and the homeless "Stinking Lizaveta," who confesses to middle brother Ivan to killing the patriarch. Following his passionate confession to Ivan, Smerdyakov, who claims to have simulated an epileptic fit to distract Fyodor's servants and gain access to the Father's room, hangs himself. But Smerdyakov's confession is problematic from the start; flippant and self-aggrandizing, the embarrassing "son of the stinking one" may be a bastard and servant, but a murderer that does not make him. This, though, is what makes him one of the novel's most compelling and complex characters, particularly for patricidal punks and postpunks who cannot help but recognize that the novel ends on the suggestion that the self-hating Smerdyakov did the deed only to end up a corpse himself.

Without question, *Karamazov* is not the first time Dostoevsky had framed a novel around cunning, grotesque, and manic characters most readers would hold at arm's length. The reason Dostoevsky fixates on characters who display "boundless egoism and a strong destructive urge," Freud posits in "Dostoevsky and Parricide," is because Dostoevsky himself retained similar tendencies and transfers onto his characters his own neuroses, be they obsessional, hysterical, or melancholic. Like these characters, Dostoevsky's destructive urge was less external than internal, "directed mainly against his own person" and thus "found expression as masochism and a sense of guilt," argues Freud. It is with *Karamazov* most clearly that Dostoevsky not only expresses his guilt and shame over the latent joy he felt his whole life over the death of his own strict father, for which Dostoevsky feels responsible, Freud observes, but documents the hold his superego held over him unto death.[48]

While Freud's reading of Dostoevsky never caught on among psychoanalysts or literary critics, his essay is in line with his earlier and more influential theory in *The Ego and the Id* that absent a disciplinary Father the subject internalizes the lawgiving master signifier in the form of the superego, multiplying its severity in so doing. In other words, by internalizing the founding link in its signifying chain, which has "obtained a hold upon consciousness" especially following the external

Father's disappearance, the subject becomes hypercritical of itself as its superego "rages against the ego with merciless violence, as if it had taken possession of the whole of sadism," says Freud in anticipation of William Loveday, leading the subject toward "destructive intentions."[49] For Dostoevsky too, the disappearance of the Father did not lessen his power over the future writer, but only emboldened the "father's deputy," the consequences of which are documented in not only Dostoevsky's fiction, but his own epilepsy and neuroses—his paralyzing guilt, compulsive gambling, and affinity for criminals and derelicts. All of this, writes Freud, is tied to Dostoevsky's missing father and chaperones Dostoevsky's masochism and unconscious desire for castration as an adult. As such, Dostoevsky, like punk and postpunk in his wake, is also "innately bisexual," often adopting the feminine (hysteric) role in relation to the powerful, controlling superego.[50]

The significance of Freud's theory to punks, particularly Dostoevsky's characterization of Smerdyakov, cannot be overstated. His alleged patricide notwithstanding, Smerdyakov is frequently described as exceedingly "punk." When we first meet the blasphemous, self-hating misanthrope, he is called by the narrator a "terribly unsocial and taciturn" young man who "seemed to despise everyone": "You are not a human being, you were begotten of bathhouse slime," his guardian once noted. A stubborn critic of institutions who "hates[s] all of Russia," the bastard is also a gender-bending masochist and anti-nationalist who is called a foreigner in his own land. Most significantly, Smerdyakov is characterized as a singer-songwriter who revels in his own lack of talent and carnivalesque dismissal of formal training. He is, unabashedly, a flunky belching out little more than "a lackey tenor, with a lackey trill."[51] The resemblance many punks—and their songs—have to this characterization is remarkable, and the connection Ian Curtis alone has to Smerdyakov signals how pointed this discovery may be: both are brooding, "patricidal" (Ian had an uneasy relationship with his policeman father) epileptics who hang themselves following a conniption—one of them doing so in the shadow of Dostoevsky's *The Idiot,* the other while listening to Iggy's *The Idiot* on vinyl.

Suicide notwithstanding, what makes the Smerdyakov allusion most appropriate for punks generally is their broadly vicious response to the master signifier. As we have already seen, the parent-child relationship itself proves fertile ground for the cultivation of an unbearable tension and shame that are, Lacan posits after reading Hegel and Freud, indefatigable so long as both master and castrated hysteric-child exist as opposed signifiers. Hoping to terminate this dialectic, punks accomplish their murder in several ways. Some punks seek to neutralize the Father by displacing him—by internalizing him and exaggerating his humiliating severity against the ego, as in the case of Iggy, Sid Vicious, Laughner, or William Loveday. Some of these same punks also undermine the master by falling on their swords if not literally then metaphorically as in the case of Lydon and Suicide. Still others take an alternative approach to patricide: attempting to kill the Name of the Father himself—capitalism in the case of Refused, corrupt government in the case of Fugazi or Propagandhi, or religion as with Bad Religion or Crass—through an array of aggressive strategies.

Such symbolic paternals notwithstanding, consider first that punks' biological (or step-) parents, and fathers in particular, serve as the categorical subject of reproach in many punk songs. "The first song I wrote with the band was . . . about a girl called Mandy who wanted to kill her parents," Lydon continues in his autobiography. "It went something like, 'There's blood on the carpet, blood on the stairs, And dear old Mandy's got blood in her hair.'"[52] Or consider if not the Raymond Pettibon–crafted cover of Sonic Youth's *Goo,* the caption of which reads "I stole my sister's boyfriend. It was all whirlwind heat, and flash. Within a week we killed my parents and hit the road," then the spoken-word introduction to Black Flag's *Family Man* wherein Rollins seethes in his coarse baritone, "Family man, I want to crucify you to your front door . . . Saint Dad / Father on fire / I've come to incinerate you." Building on such sentiments, several of the novels filling the aforementioned punk fiction genre hinge on their subject's antagonistic relationship with their deadbeat, abusive, or overly permissive parents, including a handful of (dead) fathers whose absence or belligerence, as in Frank Portman's *King Dork* or Nick Cave's *The Death of Bunny Munro,* respectively, generates a hysteric (often shameless) subject who grapples with an overbearing, neurosis-inducing superego. Finally, many punks go so far as to make even more explicit Oedipal moves in their lyrics and performances, as in Iggy's "Sister Midnight" or GG Allin's "Kill Thy Father, Rape Thy Mother."

Although differing in both scope and purpose from Dostoevsky, punk parricide in the twentieth and twenty-first centuries mirrors Dostoevsky's life and fiction in several ways. To Freud's analysis of Dostoevsky's bittersweet relationship with his father one should add that although he ended his life a Christian, like many punks Dostoevsky dithered between faith and doubt, offering scathing appraisals of both Roman Catholicism and Judaism in both his novels and nonfiction. He was likewise critical of the Russian status quo, including its government, finding himself mock-executed, as Pussy Riot reminds us, during an internment in Siberia for associating with a collection of socialist intellectuals opposed to the autocratic administration of Tsar Nicholas I. And while he was not an anti-capitalist by any means, his work is a damning testament to the destructive power of capitalism as a system. As Bakhtin put it, Dostoevsky's multivoiced, grotesque novels "could indeed have been realized only in the capitalist era." Specifically, "The most favourable soil" for the narratives Dostoevsky developed was

Russia, where capitalism emerged quite suddenly—"catastrophically" says Bakhtin—compared to its more gradual advance in the West.[53] So it is with punk: in a liberalizing market economy whose subjects find themselves alienated from themselves and each other, punk becomes an especially necessary critique, as the emergence of a heretofore negligible punk underground in much of the "developing" world suggests.

Ever Get the Feeling You've Been Cheated?

All of this is to say that Dostoevsky for decades has proven exceptionally expedient for punks and their fans. First, punks' appropriation allows them an understanding of the parallels between Dostoevsky's Russia and contemporary Western society, specifically what the respective speakers see as the decline of each at the moment of their (polyphonic) enunciation. His proto-existentialism notwithstanding, which too has set the stage for punks' aforementioned interest in Nietzsche and Sartre, Dostoevsky's characters and grotesque style herald and legitimize punks' social criticism and exploration of alternatives to the (middle-class) status quo, allowing them to spotlight the failures of capitalism, government, religion, and the nuclear family. Related to this critique, Dostoevsky gives punk a more "practical," readable intellectual foothold than does Hegel, Marx, Foucault, or Chomsky so far as Dostoevsky's narrative obsession with shame in a turbulent social environment undergoing both intellectual and economic upheaval serves as the legend on a map that allows punks to interpret more effectively the repressive and marginalizing shamelessness of their own symbolic paternal in a variety of contexts.

These benefits notwithstanding, punk's Dostoevskianism presents the subculture with a series of ironic challenges. Most significantly, if psychoanalysis is the method in question, even Freud admits early in his work that the patricide detailed above is hardly a solution, given that the Father's absence only increases his overbearing demeanor in the form of the internalized superego's despotism. Especially in death, the Father humiliates the child as patricide becomes the source of a heightened guilt and shame in the increasingly hysteric subject, as Smerdyakov demonstrates. And if such shame and exaggerated shamelessness (brought about by Freud's "brutal" superego) does not kill the hysteric, as it killed Vicious, Curtis, Crash, and Cobain, "then you're left with a life of shame by the bucketful, by virtue of the fact that [the master signifier] is not worth dying for," Lacan would later argue.[54] The Father is not worth dying for or killing for so far as his murder would be, in the end, not even a meaningful event, as patricide only confirms the impossibility of the hysteric's Lacanian Real: because punk requires the master's discourse to help it shape its own identity and speech, the independence and escape the hysteric sought in patricide are ineffable, even nonexistent, and had always been so. More than this, in Lacan's reading of Freud's *Moses and Monotheism*, such a murder "is the fertile moment of the debt by which the subject binds himself for life to the Law, the symbolic father, insofar as he signifies this Law." That is to say, patricide itself is the source of the inscription of Logos, or the symbolic Law upon which civilization is built and which punk still refuses but to which it remains subordinate.[55]

Furthermore, when punks cite Dostoevsky in concert or on record or characterize themselves as blasphemous underground men, rabid Raskolnikovs, or raw youth, they are building their personae and cultural capital around a writer who despite his critique of religion was ultimately a Christian thinker. For example, in spite of the fact that Dostoevsky was initially an admirer of Belinsky, having read his "Correspondance with Gogol" (which attacks the Russian Orthodox Church) to the Petrashevsky group in 1847, Konstantin Mochulsky reminds us that Dostoevsky broke with Belinsky thereafter. In Dostoevsky's words, "I read [the essay] at Petrashevsky's because I had given my word and at that point was unable to retract it. I read it . . . as a literary monument, neither more nor less."[56] Ignoring such nuanced affiliations, punks like Pussy Riot, Childish, and Iggy only seem to see in Dostoevsky a sympathy for rebels, outcasts, derelicts, and nonbelievers—and the notion that, as Alexander Gibson puts it, "There are few documents in literature which look less Christian than *Notes from Underground*."[57] But it is the underground man's very despair, self-hate, and egocentrism, Gibson continues, that Dostoevsky wished to argue (in a chapter of the novella censored by Russian officials) can be overcome only through a belief in the Christian messiah. This too is the point of *Crime and Punishment,* the conclusion of which describes Raskolnikov's "rehabilitation" by the reformed prostitute Sonya, who had earlier gifted a cross to the disgraced murderer. Lastly, it goes without saying that despite its theological equivocations *Karamazov* ultimately outlines Dostoevsky's faith and intellectual conservatism, all of which paved the way for not only fascist punk but "Christian punk" and Johnny Ramone's *endorsement* of George W. Bush early in the new century.

Thus does punk's well-documented and very broad and critical response to not only religion but Christianity especially stand shakily beside its devotion to a writer whose defense of the Christian ideal is well known. This fact is particularly true if one explores further Dostoevsky's ultimate rejection of the Gnosticism that emerged in opposition to the Roman Church very early in Christian history and that Greil Marcus used to frame his punk analysis. Despite developing characters who entertain "Gnostic" convictions—believing the fallen material world is at its core a bleak, evil place whose only escape is through esoteric knowledge—Dostoevsky time and again ends his stories with the destruction of such characters. In Gibson's reading, not only does

Dostoevsky "dissipate" the dualist philosophy in *Notes from Underground*, but in "The Dream of a Ridiculous Man" Dostoevsky takes a firm stand against the "Manichees and other dualists."[58] Building on Gibson is Malcolm Jones, who feels that appearances notwithstanding, an honest reading of Dostoevsky will "dispose of the idea that [his stories are] essentially gnostic in orientation."[59]

Despite their affinity for Dostoevsky, then, punks appear to have missed this critique by at least implicitly endorsing Gnosticism in a variety of ways at the same time as they endorse Gnosticism's most prolific critic. Even if Marcus's compelling narrative strays too far from the second-century definition of Gnosticism proper, he was right to see in punk a certain Gnostic bias—evident also in the punk bookshelf if punks' interest in Dostoevsky, Henry Miller, Burroughs, and Philip K. Dick is any indication. From the first Clash record to Bad Brains to the 1990s "ska-punk" revival, many punks have for decades done little to confound Marcus's argument, continuing to challenge orthodoxy and materialism, appropriating the Rastafari faith's reggae rhythms and critique of Babylon, and bemoaning the atomization of community and self that follows capitalism wherever it stomps. The difficulty of punk's persistent Gnosticism and its attraction to Dostoevsky's most "Gnostic" figures is that it stands in stark contrast to Dostoevsky's rejection of these characters' Manichaeism in favor of a more orthodox theology, giving only ammunition to the scores of critics who have dismissed punk for its *conservatism*.

What this final irony signals is that punks seem to have misread much of the satire and grotesquerie of Dostoevsky's pointedly parodic novels. As Bakhtin makes clear, Dostoevsky's highly carnivalesque fiction is pregnant with parody, especially the novels cited here. Much as *Raw Youth* should be read as parody, *Notes* too goes beyond a mere rebuke of the Russian "nihilism" of the 1840s or Chernyshevsky's *What*

Is to Be Done? Several Dostoevsky scholars, Joseph Frank among them, have noted the degree to which Dostoevsky is duplicating, for example, Chernyshevsky's prose and narrative structure, as both the underground man's monologue and entire scenes from the novella's second half resemble portions of *What Is to Be Done*? Such is also the case for *Humiliated and Insulted* and portions of Dostoevsky's epics. Iggy, Devoto, Hell, Rotten, Childish, and many other punks seem to have forgotten, despite their affinity for parody and carnivale, that Dostoevsky was not advocating the underground man's lifestyle, attitude, or philosophy—nor Raskolnikov's, Stavrogin's, or Ivan Karamazov's. In fact he was satirizing in order to repudiate many of those very characteristics punks have assumed unironically: intentional irrationality, boredom, heresy, a smug and juvenile "nastiness," and the refusal of love.[60]

Perhaps this critique misses the point, however, for if Pussy Riot is any indication punk and postpunk have been and on occasion remain a threat to the master signifier and his phallogocentric economy at specific historical moments and in particular places. Whether Dostoevsky would go on to denounce Belinsky and claim a more orthodox theology is irrelevant to a trio of incarcerated anarcha-feminists and the tens of thousands of people, particularly women, they have inspired to challenge patriarchy today. The fact that Dostoevsky's writings give voice to those organizing against autocracy, challenging religious fundamentalism, or attacking capitalism now is what matters to these and scores of other punk partisans around the globe. In the end, punk and postpunk continue to affect their culture as much as their advocates are motivated by the worst excesses of the dominant culture—and the disgust and disgrace it triggers—to act. And Dostoevsky has played a considerable role in catalyzing this action. In any case, perhaps appropriating, inverting, and parodying the literary canon is exactly what punk and postpunk always intended to do and, like Rabelais and Dostoevsky, have been doing self-consciously for decades. Punks, one could argue, are obviously reveling in Dostoevsky's satire and parody and broadening their scope—converting pop into a carnivalesque riff on itself akin to "Weird Al" Yankovic, who we must remember was called by Cobain "America's modern pop-rock genious [*sic*]" for his biting attack on pop culture and the status quo in songs like "Happy Birthday."[61] For if in claiming to belong to the "blank generation" or praying mockingly that "God save the Queen" and "Saint Maria, Virgin, become a feminist," Hell, Lydon, and Pussy Riot, respectively, opened up "temporary autonomous zones," as Gnostic eccentric Hakim Bey once put it, and reclaimed agency on their own terms by refusing the conditions of a postindustrial consumer culture that creates such shame and resistance, punk was and remains significant and transformative to its participants and the broken world they inhabit.[62]

Notes

1. Amy Scholder, ed., *Pussy Riot: A Punk Prayer for Freedom* (New York: Feminist Press/CUNY, 2013), 36–37.

2. André Breton, *Nadja*, trans. Richard Howard (1928; New York: Grove, 1960), 50.

3. Julius Strauss, "We Will Face the Tanks If We Have to," *London Daily Telegraph*, November 24, 2004, 14.

4. Scholder, *Pussy Riot*, 14.

5. Ibid., 100.

6. Lester Bangs, "Richard Hell: Death Means Never Having to Say You're Incomplete," in *Psychotic Reactions and Carburetor Dung*, ed. Greil Marcus (New York: Vintage, 1988), 268.

7. Fyodor Dostoevsky, *Notes from Underground*, trans. Serge Shishkoff (1864; New York: Thomas Crowell, 1969), 3.

8. John Lydon, *Rotten: No Irish, No Blacks, No Dogs* (New York: Picador, 1994), 3.

9. Deborah Curtis, *Touching from a Distance* (London: Faber & Faber, 2007), 90. See too V. Vale, "Henry Rollins," in *Real Conversations No. 1: Henry Rollins, Jello Biafra, Lawrence Ferlinghetti, Billy Childish* (San Francisco: RE/Search, 2011), 68.

10. Friedrich Nietzsche, "Letter to Overbeck," in *The Portable Nietzsche*, ed. Walter Kaufmann (1887; New York: Penguin, 1976), 455.

11. Dan Sinker, personal communication with the author, November 2004.

12. Fyodor Dostoevsky, *Crime and Punishment*, trans. David McNuff (1866; London: Penguin, 2003), 310.

13. Fyodor Dostoevsky, *Demons*, trans. David Magarshack (1870; London: Penguin, 1971), 56.

14. Ibid., 66, 669.

15. M. M. Bakhtin, *Problems of Dostoevsky's Poetics*, trans. Caryl Emerson (1963; Minneapolis: University of Minnesota Press, 1984), 122–24.

16. Dostoevsky, *Demons*, Book 3, chapter 1.

17. Bakhtin, *Problems*, 122.

18. Thorn Hillsbery, *What We Do Is Secret* (New York: Villard, 2005), 8. See also Billy Childish, *Notebooks of a Naked Youth* (Northville, MI: Sun Dog, 1998), 79.

19. Dostoevsky, *Crime*, 115.

20. Dostoevsky, *Notes from Underground*, 66, and *Crime*, 118.

21. Lester Bangs, "Iggy Pop: Blowtorch in Bondage," in *Psychotic Reactions*, 205.

22. Lynn X, "Iggy Pop," *Search & Destroy* #4, 1977, in *Search and Destroy 1–6: The Complete Reprint*, by V. Vale (San Francisco: V/Search, 1996), 64.

23. Iggy Pop, "Louie, Louie," *American Caesar*, compact disc, Virgin, 724383900220, 1993.

24. Legs McNeil and Gillian McCain, *Please Kill Me: The Uncensored Oral History of Punk* (New York: Penguin, 1996), 125.

25. Bangs, "Iggy Pop," 206.

26. Paul Trynka, *Iggy: Open Up and Bleed* (New York: Broadway Books, 2007), 9, 151, 211.

27. Deborah Martinsen, *Surprised by Shame* (Columbus: Ohio State University Press, 2003), xv.

28. Dostoevsky, *Demons*, book 3, chapter 2.

29. Martinsen, *Surprised by Shame*, 217.

30. Dostoevsky, *Demons*, 684.

31. McNeil and McCain, *Please Kill Me*, 54.

32. Lester Bangs, "Of Pop Pies and Fun," in *Psychotic Reactions*, 34 (emphasis added).

33. Judith Butler, *Bodies That Matter* (New York: Routledge, 1993), 36.

34. Peter Laughner quoted in Bangs, "Peter Laughner," in *Psychotic Reactions*, 218–19.

35. Martinsen, *Surprised by Shame*, 10, 218.

36. CrimethInc., *Expect Resistance* (Salem, OR: CrimethInc. Workers' Collective, 2008), 247–48.

37. Bangs, "Peter Laughner," 222.

38. David Fricke, "Iggy Pop," *Rolling Stone*, April 19, 2007, 54–59.

39. Dostoevsky, *Notes from Underground*, 7, 8, 11.

40. Richard Hell, personal communication with the author, November 14, 2007.

41. Richard Hell, *The Voidoid* (1973; Hove, UK: Codex, 1996), 28.

42. Childish, *Notebooks*, 13, 35–36, 146.

43. Wild Billy Childish and the Chatham Singers, "I Am the Strange Hero of Hunger," *Heavens Journey*, compact disc, Damaged Goods, DAMGOOD255CD, 2005. See also, Vale, *Real Conversation No. 1*, 126.

44. Childish, *Notebooks*, 107.

45. Ibid., 45, 80, 145, 199, 225, 238, 241.

46. Ibid., 209.

47. Butler, *Bodies*, 113–14.

48. Sigmund Freud, "Dostoevsky and Parricide," in *The Standard Edition of the Complete Psychological Works of Sigmund Freud*, vol. 21, ed. James Strachey (1927; London: Hoggarth Press, 1961), 178.

49. Sigmund Freud, "The Ego and the Id," in *The Standard Edition of the Complete Psychological Works of Sigmund Freud*, vol. 19, ed. James Strachey (1923; London: Hoggarth Press, 1961), 53.

50. Freud, "Dostoevsky and Parricide," 185–86.

51. Fyodor Dostoevsky, *The Brothers Karamazov*, trans. Richard Pevear and Larissa Volokhonsky (1880; New York: Vintage, 1991), 124, 223, 225.

52. Lydon, *Rotten*, 78.

53. Bakhtin, *Problems*, 19–20.

54. Jacques Lacan, *The Other Side of Psychoanalysis*, trans. Russell Grigg (1970; New York: Norton: 2007), 181.

55. Jacques Lacan, "On a Question Prior to any Possible Treatment of Psychosis," in *Écrits: A Selection*, trans. Bruce Fink (1956; New York: Norton, 2002), 189.

56. Konstantin Mochulsky, *Dostoevsky: His Life and Work*, trans. Michael A. Minihan (1947; Princeton, NJ: Princeton University Press, 1967), 123.

57. Alexander Gibson, *The Religion of Dostoevsky* (Philadelphia: Westminster Press, 1973), 78.

58. Ibid., 86, 166.

59. Malcolm Jones, *Dostoevsky and the Dynamics of Religious Experience* (London: Anthem Press, 2005), 50.

60. See Joseph Frank, *Dostoevsky: The Stir of Liberation 1860–1865* (Princeton, NJ: Princeton University Press, 1986).

61. Kurt Cobain, *Journals* (New York: Penguin/Riverhead, 2002), 252.

62. Hakim Bey, *T.A.Z. The Temporary Autonomous Zone, Ontological Anarchy, Poetic Terrorism* (Brooklyn: Autonomedia, 1991), 95.

3 DEPARTURE IN NEW NOISE

Punk Poetry

There were only a few of them
In all the earth
Each one thought he was alone
They sang, they were right
To sing
But they sang the way you sack a city
The way you kill yourself.

Paul Éluard, *Les Yeux fertiles*

Back, evil-doer with your hair awry.

Comte de Lautréamont, *Maldoror*

Long before lamenting how "it's too late to fall in love with Sharon Tate" on his band's début record *Catholic Boy* and recounting the dozen-plus friends he had lost before age thirty in "People Who Died," before adding his voice to songs by Lou Reed and Los Angeles punk band Rancid (who reference him in their 1995 album . . . *And Out Come the Wolves*), before even giving director Scott Kalvert permission to use his "basketball diaries" as the basis for a film starring a very young Leonardo DiCaprio, Jim Carroll was a poet. An astonishingly good poet. Having published his first chapbook in high school and seen his writing accepted by the *Paris Review* and *Poetry* magazine by age twenty, Carroll, born and raised in New York's Lower East Side, began attracting comparisons to Allen Ginsberg, Frank O'Hara, and, given his youth, Arthur Rimbaud. "For years the idea of Rimbaud was more important to me than the work," Carroll noted in 1981. "Baudelaire had wisdom with intelligence, and Rimbaud had the intelligence without the wisdom. He just wanted to crash through."[1] Then, as now, the Rimbaud reference feels particularly apt for a poet also committed to crashing through. Recording in detail the violence, deceit, schizophrenia, and depraved corruption at the heart of the American metropolis in the late twentieth century, Carroll's *Living at the Movies,* published when Carroll was twenty-five, reads like Rimbaud in remembering the boredom of adolescence, the sterile, demonic faces of his Catholic school lecturers, the disorienting horrors of capitalism, the muddle of sex, and what Brooklyn postpunks TV On The Radio would later call the "desperate youth, blood-thirsty babes" borne of a market economy. "You want to whisper, mainly of fear, / 'Who are they?'" Carroll explains in "Withdrawal Letter," his own version of Rimbaud's "Departure,"

> and 'They,' well, they surround you in N.Y.C.
> on subways and park entrances near the plaza
> but can you turn your head to the fountain?
> I sit with my long hair breathing spray
> And can I bear all those other scenes
> So many other words might shoot up?
> I want my hands and neck to be free and clear
> No crucifixes and no rings.

It can break a young spirit so easily, the City, suggests Carroll with simmering contempt, remembering not only the icebox that is Manhattan in the spring, but Rimbaud's attitude toward beautification. Still a *kid*, the poem's speaker already feels fragmented and penitent—he is looking for clemency after "treating someone I love badly."[2]

Taking the comparisons perhaps too seriously—or maybe trying to trivialize them—the lithe and leather-jacketed Carroll, his pale cheeks sunken after shooting up more than words, imagines a series of scenes from Rimbaud's short life in his *Movies* follow-up *The Book of Nods*, not published until after Carroll had both dabbled in and then abandoned punk rock. The scenes are hilarious, envisioning the poet's visit to a nineteenth-century clinic ("There is a tiny German whose clothing is in flames running in circles along the back of my jaw," Rimbaud tells his dentist of the pain in his mouth), his provocative swallowing (and passing) of a totem belonging to Paul Verlaine that the elder poet believes to be a fragment of Jesus of Nazareth's crucifixion cross, and Rimbaud's dealings with the Abyssinian ambassador whose liege desires "many bullets . . . whatever amount our bearers might safely transport; 16 Russian mortar launchers . . . or, as I suspect you prefer, a like number of American bazookas; and, finally, yet in the sacred eyes of our great Chieftain, most important of all these things, a Gatling gun." Consider it done, the wordsmith from Charleville, no longer young, replies with confidence as his knee swells, admiring how the almost beatific lyrical labels for such weapons mask the violence of their purpose: "Gatling gun, dear Sire Ambassador . . . it is not unlike 'Gathering grain' . . . no?"[3]

This forsaking of poetry for pop music, for *punk rock*, even if for only a moment, struck more than a few observers in the literary world as crass and ill-advised. "Mr. Carroll now chants his poetry over a loud rock backdrop," *New York Times* critic John Rockwell groaned in 1980. "On Thursday, most of the words were indecipherable, and the rock itself was decidedly perfunctory."[4] What Rockwell and other such critics missed, though, was that *Catholic Boy*—the "last great punk album" according to William Grimes—not only anticipated Chatham-born punk-poet Billy Childish, who would go on to argue that "people don't need poetry," but was a duplication of the very action Rimbaud had taken a century earlier.[5] For Rimbaud too had abandoned his own youthful denunciations of form and decorum in the service of art to become, of all things, a lord of war in Ethiopia. "What can I lose, when all I have is my own self," Rimbaud wrote his mother of his new profession from Yemen in 1882, en route to the Horn of Africa. "I'm a capitalist with nothing to fear from his own speculations, nor from other peoples.'"[6]

Boasting in advance of the cancerous tumor in his right leg that resulted in the limb's amputation a decade later, Rimbaud recognized as he wrote home that in such activity—in warmongering—he was quite intentionally dropping bombs upon the literary trail he had blazed. For Carroll the same held true; his transition to punk was as unexpected (at least to the literati) as it was self-lacerating. But such was the self-consciously dialectical point in each case: as both young men knew, the crushing adolescent art they had produced did little but earn them praise; it did not change the conditions both described. So did Rimbaud and Carroll opt not to inscribe but to demonstrate, to become, the horror they had recorded in verse, not selling out so much as buying in and consciously making themselves into the commodities Rimbaud described in "Clearance Sale" from his *Illuminations*: "Clearance sale of diamonds without control! For sale anarchy for the masses; irrepressible satisfaction for superior amateurs; excruciating death for the faithful and the lovers! For sale settlements and migrations, sports, fairylands and perfect comforts, and the noise, the movement and the future they create!"[7] Weapons and splendors, bodies and voices, even the future will be for sale in the coming liquidation, Rimbaud prophesies with glee a century in advance of Carroll. In so saying he anticipated not only his own cynical profiteering, but punk itself ("Yes—I'd be a gun-runner,"

Joe Strummer told one interviewer of a profession he might consider pursuing. "Organize the sale of guns."[8]) and the explosion in human trafficking, mass culture, state and nonstate terrorism, and debt that capitalism would usher into to the twentieth and especially twenty-first centuries: "The vendors have not reached the end of their clearance sale! The travelers will not have to render their commission for some time to come!"[9] And so it goes.

It was this recognition of the insidiousness of capital, identified by Rimbaud the *voyant* in 1874 and picked up by Carroll a century later, that a collection of European punks repeated also with reference to Rimbaud as the twentieth century stumbled to a close. "And how can we expect anyone to listen if we are using the same old voice? We need new *NOISE*," cried Dennis Lyxzén of Refused in "New Noise" from their break-up record *The Shape of Punk To Come*, resurrecting the poet who, when only a boy, had already seen enough. "Masterly music disappoints our desire," Rimbaud had written in *Illuminations*, speaking directly, Refused felt, to the Scandinavian radicals from the grave of his disenchantment with Romanticism and the aesthetics of masters so-called by age nineteen. For this reason he too pleads for something new, advocating a "departure into new affection and *new noise*."[10] This desire for the new Rimbaud had been stoking for years. "Let us ask the *poet* for *something new*—ideas and forms," he had proposed to Paul Demeny in 1871, asking of poetry nothing less than a revolutionary pivot in process and consciousness: a full derangement of self. "A poet makes himself a visionary through a long, boundless, and systematized *disorganization* of *all the senses*."[11] Twelve decades later, it is not the dope-sick Carroll but the fanatically clean-living Lyxzén and crew who in the record that also contains the track "Worms of the Senses / Faculties of the Skull" play the seer in making of punk a deranged mélange of poetry, Marxism, heavy metal, electronica, anarchism, jazz, folk, and found sounds (spoken in multiple languages) that would have confounded even Rimbaud's senses. His nod to Rimbaud notwithstanding, Lyxzén is in this track actually talking back to Carroll's most celebrated fan, Allen Ginsberg, who had insisted to Carl Solomon in 1956 that "I'm with you in Rockland / where the faculties of the skull no longer admit / the worms of the senses."[12] That Lyxzén and Ginsberg, both of whom rely on obscenity and the refusal of the cultural and political status quo as methods, would find common ground comes as no surprise. "I like the Nuns. They're like Kabuki Theatre," the poet, whose poem "Bop Lyrics" was later appropriated by Washington, DC, punkers Smart Went Crazy, told *Search & Destroy* excitedly in 1977, seeing in punk an activist Luddism. "I've been to CBGB's 15 or 20 times. . . . The new wave music is protest music, but its chief concern seems to be the Mockery of television, machinery, and decadence."[13]

In name-dropping Rimbaud, in quoting Ginsberg, both Carroll and Lyxzén were, decades removed, following the lead of not only Richard Hell and Patti Smith—who in her poetry volume *Auguries of Innocence* calls Rimbaud "the rats' poet laureate"—but English anarcho-punks Crass, whose Jeremy Ratter took the surname Penny Rimbaud, and Seattle punk poet Cynthia Genser of the group Chinas Comidas, who told an interviewer in 1978 that she was influenced by the "Symbolists mostly . . . Mallarmé, Nerval, Baudelaire, Rimbaud, Gerard Manley Hopkins, Shakespeare."[14] As Genser indicates with her list, almost pretentious in its length, poetry too has held a special place in the punk arsenal almost since the word "punk" was first applied to the clamor generated by disillusioned and angry youth in Europe and the Anglophone world in the 1970s. Smith, Hell, and punk ranter John Cooper Clarke—who had performed with the Sex Pistols, Joy Division, the Buzzcocks, and Elvis Costello—have identified Arthur Rimbaud, Paul Verlaine, Dylan Thomas, Ted Berrigan, and Charles Baudelaire as particularly influential to their own thought and writing. Other punk and postpunk groups, for example the Ex, Madison-cum-Brooklyn postpunkers Rainer Maria, and Black Eyes, have pointed to Lucille Clifton, Bertolt Brecht, Edna St. Vincent Millay, Rainer Maria Rilke, Lucebert, and a throng of other poets in their lyrics and album art, if not published books of poetry themselves, as has Sonic Youth's Thurston Moore, ex-con and CrimethInc. affiliate Raegan Butcher, and Lungfish's Daniel Higgs. And as Daniel McCormick of Black Eyes told *Punk Planet* magazine in 2003, explaining why his band included so many poetic references in its eponymous record, "I think a number of my favorite bands—the two that come to mind are the Ex and Raincoats—reference poets in their songs, and it seemed fairly natural for us to do so as well."[15] So does McCormick insert here Langston Hughes, there Yusef Komunyakaa, into a record whose own lyrics bleed out of their speakers' mouths a shockingly taut glossolalia—"and I can feel no black and white, no 1 2 3 no humor me," McCormick squeals cyclically in "King's Dominion," referencing also James Baldwin: "I'd like to fire you from my life / Like a cannonball out of me / I'd like to fire you from my life / So light the fire next time"—equal parts nonsense and mystagogical maxim, the stuff of cosseted sophists and feckless opium eaters alike.

Taking early American punk as its point of entry, this chapter resurrects Walter Benjamin, whose musings on Baudelaire, Rimbaud, and André Breton give shape to punks' continuing interest in these specific writers, to discuss "punk poetry" more generally in the twentieth and twenty-first centuries. As Benjamin helps the analyst appreciate, punk's poetic influences—typically the French Symbolists and European and American modernists—are of a particular ideological and *moral* type best summarized by Breton in his first manifesto as writers demonstrating "psychic automatism in its pure state, by which one proposes to express—verbally, by means of the written word, or in any other manner—the actual functioning of thought." Punk poetry is an attempt at a linguistics "dictated by thought, in the absence of any control exercised by reason, exempt from any aesthetic or moral concern."[16] This "immoral" and often irrational affront to semantics and syntax, like the words of those poets who inspired it, do to pop music what not only Baudelaire and Rimbaud but Breton and his collaborators did to bourgeois art culture in the nineteenth and twentieth centuries: not merely blow it up as did Dada, but move it forward by integrating into their anti-art both the stuff of culture—Freud's dream analyses, bourgeois fashion, literary criticism, science, and a radical take on love—and an often irreparable abuse of self and the class from which punk typically emerges.

Time of the Assassins

As their repeated references to Rimbaud suggest, then, there is much in the French poet's style, philosophy, and experience with which punks and postpunks identify. Rimbaud is in many ways punk's intellectual godfather and elemental versifier. Punks see in the writer who had renounced his own calling and once claimed, "Morality is the weakness of the brain," a template for their own rejection of authority and history, their violent *détournement* of art and pop in the service of prophecy, sneering through performances with a vulgar, self-consciously naive pessimism and contentious repudiation of self, family, God, and country typified by punk missiles from "God Save the Queen" to "Smells Like Teen Spirit" to Green Day's "Good Riddance (Time of Your Life)," the last of which remains an absolute (Hegelian) denunciation of the band's own audience and history. In such songs, punks, many of whom continue to have nothing to lose, too play the assassins Rimbaud references in "Morning of Drunkenness," conspiring through narrow eyes and on behalf of an invisible crowd to scrawl, "We have faith in the poison. We know how to give up our entire life day after day."[17] Targeting progenitors of all types and abilities and injecting into pop a bitter venom that would reveal the emperor's nakedness through a certain electrolysis—coarse hair dropping off in clumps—punks worldwide, Carroll, Clarke, Childish, Exene Cervenka, Lydia Lunch, and Lyxzén demonstrate and continue to see theirs as the time of the assassins, a time whose idols and architects deserve to be not only exposed but *put down.*[18]

In basements and slums, crumbling clubs and abandoned warehouses, punks began plotting such acts of less physical than intellectual violence against pop; they have not ceased scheming. And for these plotters Rimbaud has always been near—if not literally, slavering dog-eared in the torn pocket of some tarnished trousers, then in memory, a gritty smog floating in the air swirling about dirty urban children and aesthetes of all stripes. Of this there is no better example than Patti Smith. Behind the creation of the poems set to music that serve as two of American punk's most important documents—Patti Smith Group's *Horses* and *Radio Ethiopia*—is Rimbaud. "I had found solace in Arthur Rimbaud," Smith explains early in her memoir *Just Kids,* noting she discovered the poet at age twenty-one when she *stole* a copy of *Illuminations* from a Philadelphia street vendor, struck by the "haughty gaze" of the author on the book's cover: "Rimbaud held the keys to a mystical language that I devoured even as I could not fully decipher it. My unrequited love for him was as real to me as anything I had experienced. . . . It was for him that I wrote and dreamed."[19]

Smith literally fell in love with Rimbaud, she insists, fixating on his photograph and imagining herself heiress to the poor-born French Catholic, writing squalid and quarrelsome words opposing not only the cultural status quo but herself. Out of this impossible love emerged

Smith's desire to be worthy of her fantasy lover, leading her into an extraordinary ocean of words that includes the surreal "Dream of Rimbaud," wherein Smith imagines herself making love to "the One," and her frantic rejection of manual labor, "Piss Factory." The other subjects of Smith's early poems run the gamut: the waking sex fantasy, Harry Houdini, pagan myth, Joan of Arc, exploitation. In each, Rimbaud's sour scent lingers. "Everything is shit. the word art must be redefined. this is the age where everyone creates," Smith later scribbles in "Neo Boy" in advance of Patti Smith Group's *Horses*, imitating Rimbaud in calling for the demise of the old regime and ascendance of a new species of stylist: "milky spirals boring in a clearing and ooze a message significant only to happy boys celebrating twin births. the frolic w/buck in miles of icing. pausing to let arrows fly from their birthday bows. a million darts pierce the ice forest evaporating crystal deer leap like melting eye of butter. Neo boy just nods and laughs then slides deep in his machine messing with the multi-colored controls and merging with blue fish space." Nothing less than the derangement of the cultural landscape can be accepted, Smith contends in 1975, whose One has by now shifted from Rimbaud to another young and aggressive rabble-rouser: the punk rocker. Having performed in front of musicians for years, Smith increasingly came to see rock—particularly the nascent new wave—as the "neo boy" capable of inaugurating a sweeping terraform program to revitalize a dying planet: "arise in/health new niggers and celebrate the birth of the one," continues Smith associating punks with other marginalized, abject subjects; "this is your calling and this is your psalm. rise up niggers and reign w/your instruments of fortune."[20]

From page to stage, Smith brought both Rimbaud's rhythm and tone into her own verse, making Rimbaud a founding partner in what would become punk's contentious aesthetic project. Accordingly, the debt punk owes Rimbaud is perhaps most evident in Patti Smith

Group's second record, *Radio Ethiopia,* whose surreal ten-minute title track imagines Rimbaud's last days, before merging into a track called "Abyssinia," Ethiopia's historical name. "I'll send you a telegram. I have some information for *you,*" Smith, speaking as Rimbaud, cautions in advance of Lenny Kaye's guitar and Jay Dee Daugherty's drums, which alternate—as does contemporary Abyssinia—between order and chaos, love and violence. "There will be no famine in my existence—I merge with the people of the hills, O people of Ethiopia." Dismissed by many critics, the record is a compelling, if not an easy, listen: overwrought, under-rehearsed, and contradictory all at once. As such, *Radio Ethiopia* offers no traditional singles, despite its several well-conceived and passionate tracks. But in trying to be both radical and commercial, catchy and unlistenable simultaneously—see "Ain't It Strange" where the singer degenerates into a snarling badger—Smith and her conspirators sought the derangement of the senses encouraged by Rimbaud, creating a modern pop version of the sort of thing Rimbaud sought to do with poetry. It is *Illuminations* on vinyl. "One of our goals is to do a *single* that *everyone* in the world gets off on regardless of what they're into. It translates immediately. Short circuits all their logic banks and goes right to the heart of them," Kaye told Legs McNeil in 1976 as the band was writing and recording *Radio Ethiopia,* tapping into Smith's obsession with the poet whom she was, as the recording sessions went on, again dreaming about: "[Last night] I dreamt I was at a concert," Smith interjects, building on Kaye's vision a decade after she stole her imaginary lover's chapbook. "I dreamt there was all these beautiful Rimbaud-like boys at this concert and I went in the bathroom and looked in the mirror—there were like twenty mirrors and in every one these Rimbaud-like boys—god it was great."[21]

In humoring such fictions, feeding an obsession that would generate such dreams, Smith followed Rimbaud's lead in deranging her own senses and turned rock music into a disorienting assault on its own audience, a negation best exemplified if not by Iggy's or Suicide's self- and crowd-abuse then by Smith's twirling offstage and falling some fifteen feet down into an orchestra pit during a hot 1977 performance in Tampa; she awoke with a shattered spine.

Sidelined by the manic stage persona she attributed to her reading of *Illuminations*, which nearly killed her, Smith found herself both thrilled and frustrated to see her fellow punk poet Richard Hell take his simultaneous reading of Rimbaud and other French poets in a more abrasive and dark direction that same year. A former member of the group Television—which included his childhood friend Tom Miller, who took the handle "Verlaine"—Hell had, like Smith, come to New York with aspirations of being a poet. After a few years of meager success as a publisher and writing poems under the alias Theresa Stern—Hell's and Verlaine's composite persona who in 1976 told *Punk* magazine that she was inspired by André Breton and encouraged *Punk* readers to "cultivate [their] most 'shameful' traits"—Hell released perhaps the most important American punk record, *Blank Generation*, in September 1977 with his group the Voidoids.[22]

Where Smith, on *Radio Ethiopia*, puts *Illuminations* to music, channeling Rimbaud's lyrical style and emotional timbre, Hell reinterprets, on the bitter and unhinged *Blank Generation*, the poet's *A Season in Hell*. Finding inspiration in Rimbaud's "Foolish Virgin," whose young male speaker feels that "love needs reinventing," Hell begins *Blank Generation* with the double entendre "Love Comes in Spurts," describing how at age fourteen Hell had experienced all the shame and torment of Rimbaud's "Les Desérts de l'Amour," the author of which "fled from every moral law."[23] So does Hell, in his dissonant and ironic take on the classic pop love song, abandon love as a concept and posit that "love comes in spurts / in dangerous flirts / and it murders your heart / they didn't tell

3.1 Arthur Rimbaud with chopped hair, age seventeen. Photo by Étienne Carjat, ca. 1871.

you that part," setting the stage for Agnieszka Holland's overwrought dramatization of the Rimbaud-Verlaine affair *Total Eclipse*, whose rakish Rimbaud—again, Leonardo DiCaprio—tells David Thewlis's Verlaine, to Patti Smith's chagrin, "Whatever it is that binds families and married couples together, that's not love. That's stupidity or selfishness or fear. Love doesn't exist."

Whether or not such words were ever uttered by Rimbaud—and Hell would, many years later, update the Frenchmen's affair in his novel *Godlike*, casting Rimbaud and Verlaine, respectively, as a street-smart New York poet and washed-up academic who fall in and out of love in the 1970s—the bulk of *A Season in Hell* boils with similar sentiments. "I can laugh at the old false loves," Rimbaud puts it in the book's final entry, "Farewell," "and smite with shame those deceitful couples."[24] Reading such lines a century after their composition is Hell, who, joining Carroll and Smith in aping Rimbaud, challenges the morality of his progenitors in "New Pleasure" and "Who Says?" ("Who says it's good to be alive? / Same ones who keep it a perpetual jive") and updates *Season*'s "Bad Blood" ("Life is the farce all have to perform") by penning one of punk's most poignant and concise policy platforms ever put on record.[25] As Hell begins in the title track from *Blank Generation*,

> I was saying let me out of here before I was
> even born—it's such a gamble when you get a face
> It's fascinating to observe what the mirror does
> but when I dine it's for the wall that I set a place

"I belong to the *blank* generation and / I can take it or leave it each time," the singer concludes in the song's chorus, satirizing both the Who's "My Generation" and Bob McFadden's 1959 novelty tune "Beat Generation." "I belong to the __________ generation / But I can take it or leave it each time." The song, a rejection of bourgeois life and determinism, is a pop parody—and almost a parody of a parody; as such is has a condensed shelf life, making sense only to those hearing it at a particular moment in time. It does not, as did France's July Revolutionaries of 1830, stop the passage of time with a musket. But it is just vague and catchy enough, just esoteric enough in its novelty and reliance on Rimbaud and Ginsberg, to retain a certain currency. Keeping the song relevant today, then, is not its anxiety, its wailing refusal of Being, but that excruciating silence—that space in the refrain that, like moving at the speed of flight, at least *slows* time at the very moment that it solidifies the openness, the radical space, punk created for itself sui generis.

It is this mute openness that Hell has tried repeatedly to induce on paper as well, both before and after *Blank Generation*. Theresa Stern and *Godlike* notwithstanding, Hell's 1973 novella *The Voidoid* set the stage for much of Hell's later poetry and prose, offering a dialogue between a skeleton and a vampire who trade thoughts on masturbation, love, and self-hate before one of them finds himself convulsing on a New York City street muttering on about his love for his apartment wall and telling passersby "please kill me."[26] By his own admission, Hell's novella is an attempt to merge the styles of Rimbaud's contemporaries Joris-Karl Huysmans and Comte de Lautréamont (Isidore Ducasse). Having once called Huysmans's *Against Nature* his "favorite book," Hell admits in the afterword to *The Voidoid* that at the time of the book's writing he was likewise obsessed with Lautréamont, the French poet who had warned his readers at the outset of *Les Chants de Maldoror* that "it would not be good for everyone to read the pages which follow; only the few may relish this bitter fruit without danger."[27] Thus unfolds the hallucinatory and grotesque succession of scenes detailing the lives and passions of gravediggers, pedophiles, freaks, and amputees that influenced both Hell and Tom Verlaine, who for his part told *Search & Destroy*, "I read *Maldoror* when I was 21; thought it was the best book I'd ever read."[28]

As the designation *Chants* reveals, the entire piece is conceived as an assemblage of vicious and offensive *songs* whose intentional discord the ostensibly evil author claims to have cultivated in an attack on bourgeois values. "One should let one's fingernails grow for a fortnight," Maldoror, who had read his Marquis de Sade, later notes in the first of his six cantos. "Oh! How sweet to snatch brutally from his bed a boy who has yet nothing upon his upper lip, and . . . all of a sudden, just when he least expects it, to sink your long nails into his tender breast, but not so that he dies, for if he died you would miss the sight of his subsequent sufferings."[29] As Hell put it in the afterword to the 1996 reprint of *The Voidoid*, "I still like this book a lot. It's balled up with *Maldoror*, but I relished that and flaunted it because Lautréamont was my brother."[30]

His fraternity with Lautréamont notwithstanding, it was Rimbaud who provided Hell, and scores of early punks, with not only a method but an entire satchel full of pince-nez useful in seeing the world anew, of understanding the perspective of the Other, of deranging the self: "It's like Ralph Ellison's book *Invisible Man*—punks are niggers," Hell told Lester Bangs matter-of-factly in 1978, repeating Smith's casual use of the problematic word and seemingly ignorant of the knotty equivocation both punks were making in their attempt at solidarity. "The treatment that you would classify as being prejudicial to minority races is precisely the same accorded to people who go around dressed like me."[31] Hell is here not merely referencing but remembering again *Season*'s "Bad Blood," wherein the Frenchman laments his own invisibility: "In the morning my eyes were so vacant and my face so dead that the people I met *may not even have seen me*," Rimbaud insists. "I am an animal, a nigger."[32] Cultivating that dead-faced look—that blankness—as part of a larger attempt to see and be seen anew, Hell began demanding that the crowds of New York *see* him as they did not see Ellison, a demand that, as Hell rightly suggests, brought with it a parade of degradations and dangers.

3.2. Richard Hell writes in 1977. Photo by Roberta Bayley.

This demand included primarily a quite visible, violent style that likewise looked to Rimbaud, who was punk's covert clothier, for inspiration. As Rimbaud had prophesied in a sequence of lines from "Pageant" that perhaps stuck in Hell's reminiscence years after he first encountered them:

> There are some young ones . . . possessed of frightful voices and some dangerous expedients. . . . In costumes improvised with nightmarish taste they enact mournful ballads, tragedies of brigands and of demigods spiritual as history or religions have never been . . . they mix popular, maternal tricks with bestial poses and caresses. They would interpret new plays and 'sentimental' songs. Master jugglers, they transform the place and the characters and employ hypnotic theater. Eyes ablaze, blood sings, bones broaden, tears and red rivulets stream down. Their raillery or their terror lasts a minute, or entire months.[33]

The words arrest the reader still, less for their novelty or ferocity than for their foresight, for anticipating Iggy Pop, the Sex Pistols, Black Flag, and both X and the Ex. They likely arrested Hell too, whose performance aesthetic, clothing, and haircut came to resemble the "nightmarish taste" of the brigand Rimbaud describes: "And yeah, what I was talking about was the haircut," Hell told an audience at New York's Fashion Institute of Technology in 1988, gesturing to a journal in his hand. "I don't know whether you can see this, but this is the last issue of the magazine that I was publishing at the time. It came out in 1971. You see it has Rimbaud and Artaud on the cover. Does that haircut look familiar?"[34]

Baudelaire Splits His Trousers

All of this is mere prelude, though, for if Rimbaud is the punk's poet laureate, if Lautréamont influenced half of Television, it is Charles

Baudelaire who is punk's true patron saint. Despite their denunciations of self and reader, their often puerile and immoral nastiness, neither Rimbaud nor Lautréamont can match Baudelaire's vindictive disregard for his audience and craft, his violence and expression of boredom in Being. "Baudelaire was my hero," John Cooper Clarke once put it plainly to the *London Independent,* thinking perhaps of Baudelaire's setting the stage for punks' reflections on boredom and violence via *Les Fleurs Du Mal.* "Baudelaire was the baddest motherfucker on the block."[35] Decades after Clarke first opened for dozens of English punks, Hell referenced Baudelaire in his novel *Go Now,* while American group AFI set Baudelaire's "De Profundis Clamavi" to music in their fin de siècle record *Black Sails in the Sunset* and Texas postpunks . . . And You Will Know Us by the Trail of Dead included the bludgeoning "Baudelaire" on their third album, *Source Tags & Codes.*

Laying the foundation for punk's combative relation with its own clientele, the poem that prefaces Baudelaire's book-length meditation on evil, boredom, and modernity is really a deft attack on the reader—not a warning akin to Lautréamont, but a *taunt* to continue reading despite the insults Baudelaire spits at those holding his book (which is simultaneously an attack on himself, his class, and poetry as an art form): "Reader, you know this squeamish monster well, /—hypocrite reader, my alias, my twin!"[36] Conflating himself grudgingly with his yawning, disingenuous patron, Baudelaire signals both his solidarity with the working-class pedestrians not reading his poems whose agency has been obliterated by the swarming crowd of the modern city and his defense of the listlessness of the *flâneur*—the bored loafer—generated by such an environment, which was primarily that of early punks on both sides of the Atlantic who in song after song railed against urban blight and tenement housing while simultaneously emphasizing their own city-born lethargy and anomie. In so doing, punks from Rotten and Rollins to Cervenka and Cobain recreate the wayward speaker of Baudelaire's "Even She Who Was Called Beatrice by Many Who Knew Not Wherefore" who wanders about in an industrial wasteland of threadbare imps and wild-haired madmen, howling out a Jeremiad to no particular listener, lamenting his "modern" condition:

> Take a good look at this caricature
> of Hamlet or—with his dishevelled hair,
> his indecisive gaze—of Hamlet's ghost!
> Who could keep from laughing at the sight—
> this shabby aesthete, this artistic sham,
> this ham, this clamorous comedian
> who knowing his abracadabra inside out
> attempts to interest eagles (crickets too),
> even flowers and fountains in his ranted woes,
> reciting his routine at the top of his lungs
> to us as well, who hatched the whole damned thing![37]

More than even Rimbaud's description of the nineteenth-century youth, "possessed of frightful voices and some dangerous expedients," Baudelaire is not only identifying but simultaneously celebrating and judging the lunatic youth later generations of critics and cranks would call "punks" for their misdirected complaints, their lack of ambition, their ridiculous hair. For this Jeremiah is the writer himself, the anti-bourgeois bourgeois intellectual, the master signifier, who "hatched the whole damned thing" and in so doing generated punks' disgust and shame. And it is in such a frame of mind that Baudelaire too anticipates punk style. "I am adept at making do with two shirts layered under torn trousers and a jacket which lets in the wind, and I am so experienced at using straw or even paper to plug up the holes in my shoes that moral suffering is almost the only kind I perceive as suffering," Baudelaire had written his mother. "Yet I must admit that I have reached the point where I don't make any sudden movements or walk a lot, because I fear that I might tear my clothes even more."[38]

In Walter Benjamin's reading, Baudelaire's disheveled flâneur "is someone abandoned in the crowd. He is thus in the same situation as the commodity. He is unaware of this special situation, but this does not diminish its effect on him; it permeates him blissfully, like a narcotic that can compensate him for many humiliations." Baudelaire is, for Benjamin, the *flâneur principale,* the premier lethargic urbanite-object who both identified with the proletarian but also refused to become her in labor, who resisted capital *and* the masses by demanding a leisurely elbow room and performing, if anything, intellectual rather than physical work: "His verse supported the oppressed, though it espoused not only their cause but their illusions as well. It had an ear for the songs of the revolution and also for the 'higher voice' which spoke from the drumroll of the executions." So it is with punk, whose verse and volume, whose talking back to a dehumanizing political economy and demand to be *heard* and *seen* in a city of millions are likewise revolutionary and illusory, as prone to making radical denunciations of the State—as in the Clash, Dead Kennedys, Refused, Crass, Fugazi, or Propagandhi—as reveling in boredom and the activity such conditions beget: delinquency, apathy, and the deliberate abuse of controlled substances.[39]

In context, then, Baudelaire, who wrote *Les Fleurs du Mal* in the immediate wake of *The Communist Manifesto,* can be read as doing with poetry (and bourgeois morality) what Marx and his comrades were attempting to do to philosophy, economics, and history: turn it on its head. Both are an attempt to theorize the emergence of the prole from the point of view of the bourgeoisie. So do Baudelaire and his nineteenth-century analogues Mallarmé, Lautréamont, and Rimbaud serve as a sort of bridge connecting the political philosophies of Marx and

Bakunin to the artifacts that emerge from punk praxis in the next century. Baudelaire and Rimbaud, in other words, more even than Marx, Hegel, Nietzsche, and Dostoevsky, established what would become not the ideological or ontological base of punk rock, but the aesthetic, moral, and linguistic core of a largely middle-class movement at war with itself.

It is for this very reason that attacks on punk that stop at the charge that punk is ultimately a bourgeois project akin to Modernism, while accurate, miss the point. Even if Jello Biafra is correct to argue that around the world punk is ignored by the people living in the slums—"It didn't speak to them, they thought of it as a bourgeois art form they didn't want to have anything to do with," Biafra told *Punk Planet* magazine in 2000[40]—it is important to remember that like Baudelaire's writing, punk was and remains a bourgeois artist's attack on both herself (Alan Suicide or Iggy cutting themselves with glass, Cobain's head thrusting into an amplifier) and her audience (Sid Vicious or Trail of Dead beating their audience with their guitars, Devo repeating the "Jocko Homo" intro ad nauseam until its crowd is frothing, GG Allin). "The only sin in this world corrupt / Where passions erupt / And end abrupt / Is a crime / With no great gesture's cry / Its eyes, with no great evils shine," announces Trail of Dead bassist Neil Busch throatily in "Baudelaire," his mates banging away behind him. Busch is here taking a stand against a conservative and morally tepid middle class, using Baudelaire as his bellwether and arguing that the only true evil is to refuse to commit to an ideological, aesthetic, even theological program—to be unexceptionally middling. "You'll never see the light / In the darkest night / Never see the light / When the boredom comes / If *you're* one of the boring ones." To whom is Busch speaking here if not his own relatively privileged, bourgeois, and predominantly white audience, those really existing flâneurs of the postmodern scene? Channeling Baudelaire's

Sadean "Heauton Timoroumenos," Busch's tortuous punk poem, performed by a group notorious for their self-injurious gigs, is a squealing and unsettling combination of Baudelaire's "Spleen" series and his provocative "A Martyr" ("a headless corpse emits a stream of blood / the sopping pillows shed / onto thirsty sheets which drink it up / as greedily as sand") that reimagines Baudelaire's self-hating elitism on the club stage for a twenty-first-century middle-class punk audience.[41] That such a band seeks the annihilation of their own class, of themselves as an art collective, is punctuated by their end-of-show destruction of the overpriced tools that make their art, their very critique of capital and industry, possible each night. Such is the action of a group that has faith, as Rimbaud put it, in the poison; that knows how to give up their entire lives day after day. In updating Iggy's, Hell's, Suicide's, or the Sex Pistols' onstage violence, rather, Trail of Dead conjures, with palpable antagonism, the aggression, blasphemy, and boredom identified by Baudelaire as the natural products of the modern world's "proletarianization" of the city through the entirety of *Source Tags & Codes*. Punk, Busch suggests in his sickly delivery, internalizes and reminds its listeners of the notion attributed by Benjamin to Constantin Guys that "anyone who is capable of being bored in a crowd is a blockhead. I repeat: a blockhead, and a contemptible one." So do punks respond to the boredom of modernization and sprawl, advertising and alienation with not just a version of Baudelaire's violence and obscenity, but his "urban allegorical" style, that which is a product of the city, the proletarian mass, but is simultaneously Gnostic in tone and scope and as such remains isolated from the working class whose interests and concerns it addresses.[42] Punk is, as Pere Ubu put it, "Elitism for the People."

Writing what might easily be a description of the music and verse of Carroll, Hell, Clarke, Smith, Childish, Thurston Moore, Lunch, or Cervenka, Benjamin notes how "[the work of both Mallarmé and

Baudelaire] shows that the poet no longer supports any of the causes pursued by the class to which he belongs. To found a production process on such a basic renunciation of all the manifest experiences of this class engenders specific and considerable difficulties—difficulties that make this poetry highly esoteric."[43] So it is with punk, whose essential renunciation of self, class, music education, and modern production processes in the creation of a minimalist (anti-) art too mirrors Baudelaire's form and content. Like Baudelaire's verse, punk content comes to resemble a cup of tea steeped too long, a body supersaturated with the bitterest of humors: *spleen*. "I'm like the king of a rainy country, rich / but helpless, decrepit though still a young man / who scorns his fawning tutors, wastes his time / on dogs and other animals, and has no fun," wrote Baudelaire in his third of four "Spleen" poems, anticipating not only Iggy Pop's "No Fun"—the last song the Sex Pistols would perform—but Dwarves' "Oozle," Sum 41's "Billy Spleen," and Gits guitarist Andy Kessler's adoption of the handle Joe Spleen.[44] Or as Cervenka put it in X's "The World's a Mess, It's in My Kiss," one example of several songs' worth of bitter and melancholic poems that lay waste to even Shakespeare's "testy" and "waspish" Cassius, "No one is united / All things are untied / Perhaps we're boiling over inside." In this way Benjamin's reading of Baudelaire helps the analyst see exactly how it is that if, as Henry Miller put it in *Tropic of Cancer*, "Ideas are related to living: liver ideas, kidney ideas," punk is a spleen idea: ill-humored, peevish, acerbic.[45] Punk spleen—evident in punk lyrics, interviews, handbills, couture, and instrumentation—is an erudite defense against its own intractable pessimism and acrid temperament, its violent rejection of middle-class systems and institutions, and its skeptical attitude toward the future that anticipates Rick Moranis's Dark Helmet, who in Mel Brooks's masterpiece *Spaceballs* complains, "Fuck. Even in the future nothing works."

"To interrupt the course of the world—that was Baudelaire's deepest intention. The intention of Joshua," explains Benjamin finally, associating Baudelaire with the Hebrew soldier-seer. "Not so much a prophetic [intention], for he gave no thought to any sort of reform. From this intention sprang his violence, his impatience, and his anger; from it, too, sprang the ever-renewed attempts to stab the world in the heart or sing it to sleep."[46] Because punk, itself prophetic, too holds no illusions about its own efficacy—"I haven't got any illusions about anything," Joe Strummer told Caroline Coon in a 1977 *Melody Maker* interview, "You can show someone what you've done, but you can't show them how to do it"—in few cases does punk seek any sort of serious activist purpose to its violence and blasphemy.[47] As we have seen, the opposite attitude in fact is often the source of punk's contorted mewling: a continual, anti-moralist, "apolitical" articulation of the meaninglessness of not only "art" and agency but its own words, of all signifiers. This, then, is the fuller meaning behind both Clarke's punk poetry—"the fucking beer is fucking flat / the fucking flats have fucking rats / the fucking clocks are fucking wrong / the fucking days are fucking long"—and Johnny Rotten's "No Future": less a pessimism in one's future prospects than an absolute disengagement with prospecting itself, which is an especially bourgeois endeavor.[48]

Bringing this all together is not only Childish, that dyslexic "Remodernist" and punk painter whose untrained and misspelled verse harbors zero faith in either art or the human race—"n she gets up / walks to the bushes / and spits it out / me stood there / wiping myself," Childish writes of the prostitute he had sacked in a park as his girlfriend lolled in some battered flat drinking codeine, "—I haven't washed / for 2 weeks / she says / I hear the venom in / her voise /—good / I say / —good"—but also Exene Cervenka, a middle-class ex-Catholic, like Baudelaire and Rimbaud, who as both a member of X and a writer seems bent on undermining the white-middle-class privilege that is her birthright at the same time as she reifies the latent violence of powerlessness itself in verse.[49] Harnessing the insurgent libidinal energy of deprivation and pouring it into her lyrics and performances, Cervenka, who would coauthor a book of poems with Lydia Lunch, founded X with John Doe in 1977. "Our whole fucking life is a *wreck*," Cervenka shouts of the pair in front of her sprinting musicians on the B-side of her band's first single, "Adult Books / We're Desperate" in 1978, anticipating Childish's "i am a despret man." "John wrote that song," Cervenka admitted to Penelope Spheeris in *The Decline of Western Civilization*, seeing nonetheless the anxiety and violence in the actions and eyes of her fans, most of whom had too repudiated the bourgeois economy. "And it's really weird because at one point I started thinking, there's going to come a point where we keep performing the song and [people will say] '*Suuure*, they're desperate—I just paid six dollars to see this band and *they're* not desperate.'"

"But you don't have money right now," Spheeris responds, gropingly reassuring Cervenka of her song's authenticity and almost seeming to take joy in reminding the singer of her band's insolvency.

"Well, we're not rich—we have enough money to pay our rent," Cervenka clarifies defensively as behind her Doe and their bandmates howl at the suggestion that they are anywhere near financial independence. "[But] there's worse ways of being *desperate* than being *poor*."

They're laughing behind her, Cervenka's band, finding a dark humor in Spheeris's superficial line of inquiry, her confusion at a group of kids choosing hardship over relative comfort. Had the filmmaker not read her Breton, who had explained decades ago that, "Through Surrealism [the artist] will take despair unawares in its poverty"?[50] Feeling incapable of explaining herself to a reporter, Cervenka disengages from the interview, leaving unsaid, even as Spheeris needles her with questions, that "We're Desperate" was but a prelude to X's forthcoming album *Los Angeles,* whose songs top its predecessor in punishing the listener by describing one depraved, violent, and desperate scene after another: the male rape fantasy, the trembling junkie with "poverty and spit" on his lips, the masochist gold digger, the broken woman longing to escape the crumbling landscape that had turned her into a bitter racist ("She started to hate every nigger and Jew" sings Cervenka on "Los Angeles"). The record's final statement to its namesake, "The World's a Mess, It's in My Kiss," gives up all hope in solutions to such insults, instead reveling joyously in a thinly veiled despondence. That is to say, Cervenka's anguished moaning—"down we go, cradle and all"—is made to sound irrational by her musicians' jaunty performance, which is punctuated by former Doors keyboardist Ray Manzarek's carnivalesque organ grinding.

But the contempt Cervenka describes is the only rational response to what, in the book of poems she penned with Lunch, she calls her "perpetual state of disrepair . . . dissolving into despair" that comes from living in the City of Angels.[51] "In the years of the handmade cardboard sign, off-ramp people, & under the freeway families, we will work for the hole in the doughnut. There are thousands of men on the corner. They will work for you in your yard like the old colored jockey holding a lantern," Cervenka writes in her chapbook *Virtual Unreality* of the grift that continues to grow the gap between classes. "The new tuberculosis epidemic in the old, overcrowded prisons, the death penalty. We will be so much safer at night if a few murderers are killed by the state while hundreds are paroled at random. Daggers for eyes, roaming the Reagan sidewalks, in the crumbling, congested, coughing cities, 'neath the junk skylines in the decade of, in the era of, in the good old days of, have we been reduced enough; molecularized; is it still the atomic age? Aren't they done taking us apart yet?"[52]

In articulating this combination of harassment, fatigue, destitution, atomization, corruption, and hatred for one's own caste that in the hands of not the chronic homeless but often bookish middle-class kids generated some of the most visceral and unsettling American pop records ever produced, Cervenka and crew resuscitate Breton's lieutenant Louis Aragon, who had menacingly told an audience of bourgeois students and intellectuals in Madrid in 1925, "We shall waken everywhere the seeds of confusion and discomfort. We are the mind's agitators. All barricades are valid, all shackles to your happiness be damned. Jews, leave your ghettos! Starve the people, so that they will at last know the taste of the bread of wrath!"[53]

"It's a joke you know. When I get out of this plane and get into the real world then it's back to the same shit of not having enough money to make ends meet. We'll be poor and tense until the next tour starts and then we'll get to live again. That is, we get to play and eat again."[54] So stated Black Flag's fast-talking singer and Cervenka's publisher Henry Rollins matter-of-factly in a 1984 echo of Benjamin, who as early as 1929 recognized of surrealism that "no one before these visionaries and augurs perceived how destitution—not only social but architectonic, the poverty of interiors, enslaved and enslaving objects—can be suddenly transformed into revolutionary nihilism."[55] For Rollins, Cervenka, and many of the bands populating the early Los Angeles scene, the chronic poverty and indignity of contemporary architecture, the suffocating and alienating conformity of the suburbs, the desperation Cervenka embodies, all fertilize the seeds of pessimism that soon bloom into a full refusal of bourgeois doctrine. For what have deregulation and the "topless, shapeless, nameless, shameless" neoliberal economy given the majority of Americans except "buckets of blood & buckets of blood & buckets of blood," Cervenka asks finally.[56] One can almost hear, in the silence that follows such reflections, Aragon's rictus creaking with delight as he hears in Cervenka's words his own automatic poem "Red Front," which had advocated in advance of X and Black Flag that his comrades "Kill the cops" and celebrated how "I am here at the elimination of a useless world / Here with intoxication at the destruction of the bourgeois / Has there ever been a finer hunt than the pursuit / of this vermin huddling in every corner of the cities."[57]

"And that response became automatic"

In so writing, performing, and being, Cervenka and X, Clarke, Lunch, and even Henry Rollins, helped create the soundtrack for much of the surrealist poetry and prose that preceded punk and gave flesh to Breton's skeletal suggestion—repeated with satisfaction by Benjamin—that texts like *Nadja* were "a banging door."[58] Punk records and performances too resemble the banging door of surrealism—neither well-wrought nor salable, banging and flapping interminably—and pointing the hearer toward an "irrational," scatological, and often reactionary exit. More than this, the verse of punk poets like Cervenka, Childish, and Butcher—"i hear / i am an easy guy / to get along with / at least / that's what they told / me in prison / which confused me / because I am / always a half-step / from suicide / or murder"[59]—approaches the profane illumination that Benjamin praises surrealism for seeking and reproducing. So it is that in articulating their disinterest in capitalism and reform and advocating a certain anarchy of speech, punk and postpunk soon moved beyond Baudelaire, Lautréamont, and Rimbaud and toward the twentieth-century writers who both were inspired by and sought to overcome not only these particular poets but Swiss linguist Ferdinand de Saussure, whose *Course in General Linguistics* had formalized the very semiotics the advocates of Modernism were working so hard to dismantle following the Great War. Departing from the nineteenth century, the punk and postpunk elide the "or" in Benjamin's "stab the world in the heart or sing it to sleep." Music *is* a knife, punks emerging after those cited above came to believe, taking their cues from futurism, Dada, and surrealism and asserting that there is no difference between stabbing and singing. "I heard of Lautréamont through André Breton's *Manifestoes of Surrealism,*" Nuns' singer Alejandro Escovedo told an interviewer in 1977, connecting literary dots (even as he undermined his musical ancestors) before referring to some of Breton's dreamlike poetry directly and admiring the surrealism of contemporary punk performers of all types: "I saw Chris Burden's show at U. C. Irvine, in which he laid down on a floor surrounded by buckets of water with live electrical wires ominously posed—any spectator could've killed him."[60]

Only months after publishing this conversation, the same magazine that interviewed Escovedo published an article that explored directly the connection between punk and the surrealist verse of Breton (to whom Richard Hell bears a striking resemblance): "For new wave musicians and their audience, the attraction of surrealism is proof not only of the permanent relevance of genuine revolt, but also of the high calibre of surrealist achievements," wrote Nico Ordway in 1978, seeing punk and surrealism corresponding in their attack on "meaning," rejection of logic, cult of adolescence, love of (black) humor, unvarnished style, and intellectual violence. "What brings together surrealism and new wave is the principle of violent non-conformity, of a protest transcending political issues and experiences, a dissent extending from the feet to the hair of daily life."[61] Ordway's punk-as-surrealism thesis was but the beginning of a string of punk arguments in favor of surrealism to come. In 1979 the Raincoats' eponymous debut album included the track "No Looking," an adaptation of Jacques Prévert's "Déjeuner du matin"; that same year, CBGB veterans the Talking Heads included "I

Zimbra"—a song consisting of nonsense words based on German surrealist Hugo Ball's 1928 poem "Gadji beri bimba"—on their third record, *Fear of Music*. Subsequent years saw the arrival of self-described "social surrealist" Attila the Stockbroker (John Baine), who debuted as a solo performer in the tradition of Clarke until his founding of the punk band Barnstormer in the 1990s, and Baltimore-based art collective Candy Machine's conversion of Franco-German poet Jean (Hans) Arp's "The Seat of Air" into the dissonant "Andersons Lookout"—"the air sparks fly by air wheels!"—for the group's Swiftian sophomore album, *"A Modest Proposal."*

Sidestepping for the moment the theatrics of the likes of Burden, which will be explored more fully in the following chapter, the above examples demonstrate the degree to which the literature of surrealism (and its poets in particular) has been read by scores of punks since at least the middle 1970s. Consider postpunk flag-wavers Mission of Burma. "People did not like that man Max Ernst / He was so irrational Max Ernst," Roger Miller reports with a certain contempt for Ernst's critics in the jerky "Max Ernst" from the Boston band's debut record, *Signals, Calls, and Marches,* bringing if not surrealist (and Dadaist) method then at least reference to several surrealist artists into punk as Miller's bandmate Clint Conley rattles off mechanically the titles of Ernst paintings in the background (e.g., "Garden airplane trap!"). An angular, scarcely danceable piece of "artcore," the song, which paves the way for the gaunt, Magritte-referencing "This Is Not A Photograph" and (much later) "Max Ernst's Dream," is representative of the bulk of the group's songs in that it offers the listener no musical or lyrical rationality, no refrain, and comes to an end only after Miller and Conley exhaust their voices in the pagan chant "dada-dada-dada," which both outlasts the guitars' chaotic and squelched dissolution and anticipates the record's lyric sheet: *most*—not all—of the words spoken throughout the album's songs arranged in semi-alphabetical order.

An early version of the postpunk that would come to be categorized as "post-rock" for its jarring rhythms and prickly melodies, Mission of Burma had, before waxing disjointedly on Dadaism, recalled one of Breton's more infamous claims from his *Second Manifesto*—"The simplest surrealist act consists of dashing down into the street, pistol in hand, and firing blindly, as fast as you can pull the trigger, into the crowd"—earlier on the record in "That's When I Reach for My Revolver."[62] Often misattributed to Luftwaffe commandant Hermann Göring, the line is a paraphrased from Hanns Johst's Nazi apology *Schlageter,* wherein Friedrich Thiemann sputters to Albert Leo Schlageter, "When I hear the word culture . . . I release the safety on my Browning!"[63] But unlike Johst's play, Burma's song is no celebration of Nazism; it is, rather, anti-fascist, which is to say surrealist, in its imagery. Lyrically, the verses resemble vaguely the writing method advocated by Breton and Robert Desnos and float uneasily beneath the music, communicating no identifiable message and retaining little internal logic, totalitarian or otherwise, whereas the album's chorus—"That's when I reach for my revolver / That's when it all gets blown away"—fails to make any connection to the verses. It's a nonsequitur, this song, "unconscious" in its signification and suggesting both a flagrant disregard for bourgeois morality—is Miller advocating suicide? murder? the demolition of art?—and the musicians' refusal to become a slave to any single style or master.[64]

Where Burma is more explicitly referential in their aesthetic, Candy Machine simply is surrealism reified. Looking also to the *First Manifesto of Surrealism* for advice, Candy Machine singer Peter Quinn adopts the association-based method of developing verse that resembles what Breton calls "spoken thought": "a monologue spoken as rapidly as possible without any intervention on the part of the critical faculties."[65] As Quinn puts it in "the over under rule in progress," speaking quickly and monotonously, as if in a trance, on the subject of automatic writing itself:

> Then Argo returned to zero and that
> response became automatic, he liked the weather
> pulling words out like a rabbit in language
> with his eye with his water tanks and talking
> pictures, in the air making figure eights
> with his forefinger with his eye he held a
> constant boxing match with his subconscious
> making figure eights and that response became automatic.[66]

Behind Quinn, who is reimagining less busted frigates or Greek mythology than the idiolect of the unconscious, his band's lumbering rhythm section, suspicious guitar, and whispered refrains contribute to the song's automatic quality, as if it was both conceived and birthed in one take. Establishing its members' close reading of Arp, Ball, and Desnos, *"A Modest Proposal,"* which also references *Les Fleurs du Mal,* remains one of the most implicitly surrealist records—lyrically, musically, ideologically—produced by advocates of punk and postpunk music.

"We approached it like Dadaists," says Quinn of his band's methodology and claims that "we saw ourselves as artists crashing into the world of indie rock. In some ways, we didn't belong, but also didn't want to." Acknowledging also the influence of not only F. T. Marinetti and Arp but Galway Kinnell and Robert Bly, Quinn explains how the punk scene in and around Baltimore and Washington, DC, in the early 1990s was a customarily poetic affair. "In fact, I'm just reminded of the time when I met Daniel [Higgs] from Lungfish. We were in the tavern by the art school and got talking at the bar and he gave me one of his poetry zines. That seemed pretty normal at the time. People doing and producing their stuff. It was both punk and high art at the same time."[67] One of those publications might very well have been an early version of Higgs's chapbook of prose poems *The Book of Antennae,* which seems to combine Baudelaire with surrealism in its attempt to "cheat the readership" and "destroy the word cult" by declaring war on meaning in the form of nearly sixty aphorisms of psychic autonomy. As Higgs puts it in his "book of confusion," "The supernatural is the ghetto of uncategorized and absolute natures that proliferate in an independent system of rebellion—History and tradition are merciful to widespread perversion, the ultimate armor being atmosphere—Say nothing, say everything, say what you must—One who hopes, fears—Please understand, I speak without formal authority, but I beg the reader to comprehend the function of these words so that they may hatch in the reader's own determination as to their function." The function of his words, Higgs admits here, is not to clarify but to obscure reality, to derange it in an effort to put into effect surrealism at the same time as it accepts Rimbaud and the psychoanalytic injunction to give the unconscious a certain structure, one unique to each listener, through language.[68]

In lugging surrealism, inelegantly, into the late twentieth century—and, if Deathfix's "Dalí's House" and Quinn's later group Lo Moda are any indication, well into the twenty-first—punk again signaled its silent approval of Benjamin, who in a 1929 essay celebrated surrealism as a "profane illumination" that "push[ed] the 'poetic life' to the utmost limits of possibility."[69] As Mission of Burma, Candy Machine, and a host of bands still demonstrate, punk itself serves as a post-surrealist version of the not hallowed but profane illumination Benjamin had in mind when, thinking of Breton's *Nadja,* he endorsed the surrealists as the only postwar poets to have truly understood—and attempted to address with any urgency—the economic, psychic, ethical, and ideological corollaries of a highly capitalized and hyper-rational modern technocratic state. That is to say, punk (or, to parrot Mission of Burma, *the Obliterati*) builds on surrealism's platform by making a convulsive beauty out of profane words, music, and performance.[70] In valorizing image, reflex, and sound over fixed structure and meaning, in other words, punk poetry signals the latent revolutionary energy embedded within the artifacts of violence and despair that generated both surrealism and punk: terrorism and simulation, crumbling structures and (noise) pollution, decadence and statelessness.

Is this not the point of Baudelaire's own "Albatross," whose limping and droll subject is the poet himself: "How weak and awkward, even comical / this traveler"?[71] Witnessing the radical changes taking place in both industrial and artistic production and consumption in the middle of the nineteenth century, Baudelaire responded to what he saw as the decline in the public's appreciation of lyric poetry in the vein of Samuel Taylor Coleridge's "Rime of the Ancient Mariner"—of his own obsolescence—by composing a book of vicious and bleak poems aimed at the "hypocrite readers" of his day. The modern poet too is this lifeless bird, Baudelaire argues as Romanticism was shriveling up, a scribe burdened with articulating all that she sees in verse, with squawking out of turn, but flightless on the steamer *Modernity*, which increasingly has little use for poetry of any style or subject. Fuming at his redundancy—or as the Jam put it in "The Modern World," "All my life has been the same / I've learned to live by hate and pain / It's my inspiration drive"—Baudelaire delights in being that fowl corpse, in reminding the men and women of his day of the poet's careless murder by hanging about modernity's neck, dripping blood.

Punk too is such a carcass, hanging about the neck of contemporary pop, making of pop culture a joke that laughs in the face of its own audience—attacks them intellectually and physically. In so doing, punk's best poets force their listeners to update Ball's sentiment that "Every word that is spoken and sung [in the Cabaret Voltaire] says . . . that this humiliating age has not succeeded in winning our respect."[72] They also gesture toward Antonin Artaud, who once spoke to "the epileptoid trepidation of the Word which, no matter what the meaning, does not want to be used *without trembling*." Included in Artaud's list of poets whose verse heralds punk in bringing to life the "abyss of the unredeemably filthy and established bestiality" of Being are not only Lautréamont, to whom Artaud dedicates an essay, but Baudelaire, Rimbaud, Breton, and an American popular too with punks: Edgar Allan Poe. These writers' seemingly irrational attack on themselves, on their birthright, was too much for the keepers of high culture to bear, says Artaud; so did priests and policemen, politicians and parents stop the mouths of such soothsayers, "Because people were afraid that their poetry would escape from their books and overthrow reality." This is also why the culture industry, a century after Poe, Baudelaire, Lautréamont, and Rimbaud, moved with a medic's haste to stop the bleeding wrought by punk and make of it "New Wave" almost immediately. The bourgeoisie had learned its lesson after the eruption of Dada and surrealism; were it not to be either recuperated or quashed, such a hysteric social movement threatened to overthrow reality and put an end to political economy as the world then knew it. So it is that with Artaud in mind this narrative turns to histrionics proper and punk's preferred playwrights, particularly Jarry, Brecht, Artaud, and Genet, whose works all took if not the verse then the viciousness of Baudelaire, Rimbaud, Aragon, and Ball and put them on stage to be reenacted in real time night after night for not a single bourgeois reader to consume in the privacy of her or his flat, but an entire hall full of philistines to experience collectively and with tremendous horror.[73]

Notes

1. Carole Corbeil, "Angelic Yearnings from Poet, Rocker," *Globe and Mail,* December 29, 1981, A15.

2. Jim Carroll, "Withdrawal Letter," *Living at the Movies* (New York: Penguin, 1973), 72.

3. Jim Carroll, "Rimbaud Scenes," *The Book of Nods* (New York: Viking, 1986), 33, 35.

4. John Rockwell, "Rock Poet: Jim Carroll," *New York Times,* December 31, 1980, A36.

5. Billy Childish, "People Don't Need Poetry," *Poems of Laughter and Violence*, vinyl LP, Hangman, HANG-16UP, 1988. See also William Grimes, "Jim Carroll, 60, Poet and Punk Rocker Who Wrote 'The Basketball Diaries,'" *New York Times,* September 14, 2009. A19.

6. Arthur Rimbaud letter to his mother dated April 15, 1882, in *Complete Works,* trans. Paul Schmidt (New York: Harper & Row, 1976), 256.

7. Arthur Rimbaud, "Clearance Sale," *A Season in Hell / The Illuminations,* trans. Enid Rhodes Peschel (Oxford: Oxford University Press, 1973), 179.

8. Vermilion Sands and Annette Weatherman, "Clash Landing," *Search & Destroy* #2, 1977, in *Search and Destroy 1–6: The Complete Reprint,* by V. Vale (San Francisco: V/Search, 1996), 28.

9. Rimbaud, *A Season in Hell / The Illuminations,* 179.

10. Ibid., 119, 125.

11. Rimbaud, *Complete Works,* 102–3.

12. Allen Ginsberg, "Howl," in *Howl and Other Poems* (San Francisco: City Lights Books, 1996), 24.

13. No author, "Ginsberg SEZ," *Search & Destroy* #1, 1977, in *Search and Destroy 1–6: The Complete Reprint,* by V. Vale (San Francisco: V/Search, 1996), 13. And as Chris Salewicz notes repeatedly in *Redemption Song* (New York: Faber & Faber, 2006), Joe Strummer was also a Ginsberg fan.

14. Patti Smith, "Mummer Love," *Auguries of Innocence* (New York: HarperCollins, 2005), 57. See also: Annex, "Chinas Comidas," *Search & Destroy* #8, 1978, in *Search and Destroy 1–6: The Complete Reprint,* by V. Vale (San Francisco: V/Search, 1996), 39.

15. Julianne Shepherd, "Black Eyes," *Punk Planet* #57, September–October 2003, 44. See, for example, the Ex record *Dizzy Spells,* which makes music of poems by Lucebert, Heinz Hermann Polzer (Drs. P), and Eduardo Galeano.

16. André Breton, *Manifestoes of Surrealism* (1924; Ann Arbor: University of Michigan Press, 1969), 26.

17. Rimbaud, *A Season in Hell / The Illuminations*, 87, 129.

18. Most obvious in this regard was the Seattle group Popstar Assassins.

19. Patti Smith, *Just Kids* (New York: HarperCollins, 2010), 23.

20. Patti Smith, *Early Work: 1970–1979* (New York: Norton, 1994), 38–43, 73, 77.

21. Legs McNeil, "Patti Smith," *Punk #2*, in *Punk: The Best of Punk Magazine*, ed. John Holmstrom (New York: HarperCollins, 2012), 35–36.

22. Mary Harron, "Theresa Stern," *Punk #4*, in *Punk: The Best of Punk Magazine*, ed. John Holmstrom (New York: HarperCollins, 2012), 90.

23. Rimbaud, *Complete Works*, 133.

24. Rimbaud, *A Season in Hell / The Illuminations*, 105.

25. Ibid., 45.

26. Richard Hell, *The Voidoid* (1973; Hove, UK: Codex, 1996), 38.

27. Lester Bangs, "Richard Hell: Death Means Never Having to Say You're Incomplete," in *Psychotic Reactions and Carburetor Dung*, ed. Greil Marcus (New York: Vintage, 1988), 263. See also Comte de Lautréamont, *Maldoror*, trans. Alexis Lykiard (Cambridge, MA: Exact Change, 1994), 27.

28. LynnX, "Tom Verlaine/Eno," *Search & Destroy # 3*, 1977, in *Search and Destroy 1–6: The Complete Reprint*, by V. Vale (San Francisco: V/Search, 1996), 43.

29. Lautréamont, *Maldoror*, 31.

30. Hell, *Voidoid*, 78.

31. Bangs, *Psychotic Reactions*, 266.

32. Rimbaud, *Complete Works*, 196.

33. Rimbaud, *A Season in Hell / The Illuminations*, 119.

34. "There are some misconceptions about the origins of the hairstyle and torn clothes that have gotten a lot of play in punk journalism. It's often said that I based my haircut on Rimbaud," Hell writes in his autobiography *I Dreamed I Was a Very Clean Tramp*, attempting to walk back this association. "Probably that comes from an interview I did once in which I mentioned that a year or two after I started the hairstyle I noticed that the cover of the final issue of my literary magazine (1971) features pictures of two guys with similar hair: Rimbaud and Artaud. . . . But noticing those was after the fact, though who knows whether there might have been some influence." See "Punk and History," *Discourses: Conversations in Postmodern Art and Culture*, ed. Russell Ferguson et al. (Cambridge, MA: MIT Press, 1990), 235.

35. Robert Chalmers, "No Holds Bard," *Independent on Sunday*, November 8, 2009, 14.

36. Charles Baudelaire, "To the Reader," *Les Fleurs Du* Mal, trans. Richard Howard (1857; Boston: David R. Godine, 1982), 6. "To the Reader" notwithstanding, Baudelaire makes repeated reference to boredom throughout *Les Fleurs Du Mal*. See

also "Consecration," "Destruction," "A Martyr," and "The Wicked Maker of Window Glass."

37. Ibid., 133.

38. Walter Benjamin, "The Paris of the Second Empire in Baudelaire," in *The Writer of Modern Life*, ed, Michael W. Jennings (1938; Cambridge: Belknap Press, 2006), 101.

39. Ibid., 59, 85.

40. See David Grad's interview with Jello Biafra, "Jello Biafra," in *We Owe You Nothing*, ed. Dan Sinker (1997; New York: Akashic, 2001), 43.

41. Baudelaire, *Les Fleurs Du Mal*, 121.

42. Benjamin, *Writer of Modern Life*, 68.

43. Ibid., 133.

44. Baudelaire, *Les Fleurs Du Mal*, 76.

45. Henry Miller, *Tropic of Cancer* (1934; New York: Grove, 1961), 242.

46. Benjamin, *Writer of Modern Life*, 145.

47. Strummer quoted in Salewicz, *Redemption Song*, 185.

48. John Cooper Clarke, "Evidently Chickentown," *Snap, Crackle & Bop*, vinyl LP, Epic, ELPS4071, 1980.

49. Billy Childish, "banging the clay from my knees," "*i'd rather you lied*" (1992; Hove, UK: Codex, 1999), 132.

50. Breton, *Manifestoes of Surrealism*, 31.

51. Exene Cervenka and Lydia Lunch, *Adulterers Anonymous* (San Francisco: Last Gasp, 1996), 22.

52. Exene Cervenka, "Consumption," in *Virtual Unreality* (Los Angeles: 2.13.61, 1996), n.p.

53. Aragon quoted in Maurice Nadeau, *The History of Surrealism*, trans. Richard Howard (New York: Collier, 1965), 111.

54. Henry Rollins, *Get in the Van* (Los Angeles: 2.13.61, 1994), 133.

55. Walter Benjamin, "Surrealism," in *Selected Writings*, vol. 2, trans. Rodney Livingstone; ed. Michael W. Jennings (1929; Cambridge, MA: Belknap Press, 1999), 210.

56. Cervenka, "They Do Everything for Us," in *Virtual Unreality*, n.p.

57. Nadeau, *The History of Surrealism*, 290.

58. Benjamin, "Surrealism," 209.

59. Raegan Butcher, "A Half-Step," in *Rusty String Quartet* (Olympia: CrimethInc. Ex-Workers' Collective, 2005), 158.

60. Vale, "Nuns' Switchblade," *Search & Destroy* #1, 1977, in *Search and Destroy 1–6: The Complete Reprint*, by V. Vale (San Francisco: V/Search, 1996), 10.

61. Nico Ordway, "Anarchy, Surrealism & New Wave," *Search & Destroy* #5, 1978, in *Search and Destroy 1–6: The Complete Reprint*, by V. Vale (San Francisco: V/Search, 1996), 111.

62. Breton, *Manifestoes of Surrealism*, 125.

63. Hanns Johst, *Schlageter* (1933), trans. Ford B. Parkes-Perret (Stuttgart: Akademischer Verlag Hans-Dieter Heinz, 1984), 89.

64. Mission of Burma, "That's When I Reach for My Revolver," *Signals, Calls, and Marches*. Vinyl LP. Ace of Hearts, 1981.

65. Breton, *Manifestoes of Surrealism*, 23.

66. Candy Machine, "The Over Under Rule in Progress," *"A Modest Proposal,"* compact disc, Eastwest/Skene, 1994.

67. Peter Quinn, personal communication with the author, December 8, 2015.

68. Daniel Higgs, *The Book of Antennae* (2000; Chicago: Now Testament, 2015), 1, 17, 23, 28.

69. Benjamin, "Surrealism," 208–9.

70. As André Breton put it at the very end of *Nadja*, "Beauty will be *convulsive*, or will not be at all." Trans. Richard Howard (1928; New York: Grove, 1960), 160.

71. Baudelaire, *Les Fleurs Du Mal*, 14.

72. Hugo Ball, *Flight Out of Time: A Dada Diary*, trans. Ann Raimes (1927; New York: Viking, 1974), 61.

73. Antonin Artaud, "Letter about Lautréamont," in *Antonin Artaud: Selected Works*, ed. Susan Sontag (1946; Berkeley: University of California Press, 1988), 469, 471.

4 "ON PLAY PATTERNS"

Punk's Theater of Cruelty and Alienation Effect

No one in Europe knows how to scream anymore.

Antonin Artaud, *The Theatre and Its Double*

There is a scene late in Bertolt Brecht's *The Threepenny Opera* that a viewer could be forgiven for believing Malcolm McLaren appropriated. In the piece of epic theater, "King of the Beggars" Jeremiah Peachum, who makes a living teaching London's poor how to be more professional in their soliciting and furnishing them with tattered costumes, assembles his retinue in an effort to stage a flash mob at the queen's coronation. He is doing so to protest Police Chief Brown's refusal to arrest Brown's old army pal Mackie Messer, London's most wanted criminal, who had seduced and married Peachum's daughter against Peachum's wishes. "An army of filthy beggars will march up to greet the Queen . . . it won't be a festive sight," Peachum threatens Brown in G. W. Pabst's 1931 film version of the play. "They're not an attractive crowd. How will it look at the coronation if 2,000 cripples are beaten to the ground? A revolting sight." Later learning not only that had "Mack the Knife" Messer been arrested by Brown's men, but that his daughter had used Messer's influence and stolen wealth to acquire a bank to try to bring his enterprise above table—"One can rob a bank. Or one can rob *with* a bank," the young woman reminds Messer's gang in his absence—Peachum tries desperately to call off the mob, whose shuffling and bent deportment anticipated if not Iggy Pop and Johnny Rotten, then Lester Bangs, who had written in 1979 that "so many of the people around the CBGB's and Max's scene have always seemed emotionally if not outright physically crippled—you see speech impediments, hunchbacks, limps, but most of all an overwhelming spiritual flatness."[1]

But Peachum's efforts are in vain. As the queen's caravan makes its way through the narrow London streets, it is forced to stop as the crowd swells and Brown's inept cavalry looks about in confusion. Taking advantage of the disarray, hundreds of dirty and despondent men and women in shabby cloaks, rumpled hats, and torn trousers sidle up to the queen's open carriage. Holding placards inscribed with phrases like "*dem Elend*" ("The Wretched"), the mass of wide-eyed, oily-faced men and women, their chests heaving and faces smudged with grime, stops just short of the carriage and glares at the sovereign. Confounded and alarmed, the queen stares back at the mob for a moment, her bloodless lips sealed tight, before raising a grand bouquet of flowers to her face to shield her eyes from the sight of the mewling mass and mask what must have been the crowd's unwashed aroma of filth and fury. The carriage races away at a clip, the crowd in hot pursuit, as general chaos ensues.

It is hardly an overstatement to suggest that this scene provides a template for virtually everything the Sex Pistols would go on to do half a century later. With McLaren arrogating Peachum's assembly of London's destitute and desperate, the Sex Pistols made every effort to draw such a puckered expression from their queen, going so far as to purse her lips for her with a safety pin and stage a mob of costumed urchins hurling insults at Her Majesty from a riverboat during her Silver Jubilee Celebration. In restaging *The Threepenny Opera* from a barge McLaren too sought to draw attention to the shameless decadence of a monarchy that was celebrating while unemployment in England had

4.1 and 4.2. The queen is confronted by her abject subjects in G. W. Pabst's film version of Brecht's *The Threepenny Opera* (1931).

more than doubled between 1973 and 1977 (and would reach 14 percent by the early 1980s). Following Brecht's lead, McLaren and his early collaborators cultivated a pop aesthetic that situated true power with not royals, aristocrats, or the bourgeoisie, but the underclass: sex workers, beggars, petty criminals, and the dispossessed. In so doing, McLaren also reactivated Brecht's theory of alienation effect, a technique that seeks to defamiliarize a subject, estranging performer from spectator emotionally, but linking them politically in so doing: it was certainly not easy to like Rotten and crew, to invest sympathy in a pop star who yammered on about having "No Feelings" (even as he expressed what

a lot of Brits were feeling at the time). Such a method, wrote Walter Benjamin, is ultimately egalitarian, akin to filling in the orchestra pit, bridging the "abyss which separates the players from the audience as it does the dead from the living."[2] The technique also, says Brecht, necessarily results in a theater of amateurs who are most effective when, like punk, they are "as bad as possible."[3]

Seeing in Brecht's epic theater and alienation effect a way out of the boredom and corruption that characterized both pop and politics in the 1970s—"As for the products of our own time, it held that their lack of any worthwhile content was a sign of decadence," Brecht put it in

1948, accusing Europe's "entertainment emporiums of having degenerated into branches of the bourgeois narcotics business"—McLaren too ornamented an army of runaways, burnouts, scamps, proles, and prostitutes and put them on stage, showing capitalism its own effects.[4] Emboldened by Brecht, by his attack on Aristotle's valorization of theater-as-catharsis, was McLaren, who had learned much about performance and spectacle from having flirted with situationism as well and felt that "frustration is one of the great things in art; satisfaction is nothing."[5]

But McLaren was far from alone among punks in taking his cues from the stage. Punk and postpunk for decades have drawn broadly on theater in crafting their unique response to the Name of the Father. In her memoir, Patti Smith, that book thief who was at one time quite attached to American playwright Sam Shepard and starred in his play *Cowboy Mouth*, references another thief, Jean Genet, repeatedly and remembers of her musical debut, "The reading was scheduled for February 10, 1971 . . . I researched for any auspicious signs connected to the date: Full moon. Bertolt Brecht's birthday. Both favorable. With a nod to Brecht I decided to open the reading singing 'Mack the Knife.' Lenny [Kaye] played along."[6] In framing her own style as an homage to Brecht, to alienation and Genet's criminality-as-art, Smith was paving the way for Cleveland punks Pere Ubu, whose spastic, fleshy frontman David Thomas was so enamored with Alfred Jarry's *Ubu Roi* that he became the absurd liege on stage, eventually adapting the play for his own production *Bring Me the Head of Ubu Roi*. In his own autobiography, John Lydon notes his affinity for both Oscar Wilde and Shakespeare, the latter's *Richard III* in particular—an affinity exploited by Julien Temple in his Pistols documentary *The Filth and the Fury*.[7] And at the same time that England's the Flying Lizards included a cover of the Brecht/Kurt Weill song *"Der Song von Mandelay"* on their eponymous album, San Francisco postpunk group Factrix (familiar with the work of the Snake

Theater in the City by the Bay) were getting way into Antonin Artaud: "We were trying to bring the Theatre of Cruelty to the rock stage," Factrix's Bond Bergland told Simon Reynolds. "It was really about confrontation."[8] Finally, around the time Ian MacKaye was getting his Wilson Players high school theater group banned from public buildings for staging Israel Horovitz's *Indian Wants to Bronx*, Genesis P-Orridge reformed the COUM Transmissions art collective into the sample-based performance art group Throbbing Gristle, who took Artaud to heart in trying to create a musical event that replicates the audience's experience of terror and humiliation, that affects it body as much as its mind. "We're trying to create a sound that is equivalent to the experience," said P-Orridge in 1978. "At the end of one hour of listening to us you feel like you've been through a condensed version of it . . . people do actually come up to us and say they feel physically affected. Not sick—they just feel they've been through something special and strange that they don't understand."[9]

Taken as a compendium, these references by scores of punks to these specific playwrights suggest not only a fondness for the avant-garde—for a theater that challenged the status quo with bravado and violence—but a predilection for the absurdity and depravity of the human condition that each of these playwrights in their own ways dote upon. More than this, and thinking again of Judith Butler, the punk *act* serves as a disquieting resignification of the heterosexist rock scene, which undermines pop by making stooges of what are supposed to be the symbolic paternal's deputies: the larger-than-life objects (both male and female) of an especially phallogocentric desire who speak from on high to the fawning abject subjects below.

Taking the aforementioned writers in their turn, then, this chapter lays out two ideas simultaneously: first, that central to McLaren's construction of the Sex Pistols-as-epic-theater, to Smith's attraction to Genet, to *Ubu Roi* qua punk, is punk's internalization of the wincing shame embedded in these writers' productions and their attempt to "make something out of what is made of [them]" by the symbolic paternal, as Sartre once put it.[10] Seeing in Jarry and Artaud the justification for attacking one's own self and audience, punks have regularly looked also to Brecht and Genet as models for helping them face—and ultimately escape—the horrifying and humiliating subjectivity that has been forced upon them by cultural dominant. Second, the punk performance troubles not so much gender in itself but the cultural dominant, undermining the phallogocentrism typical of rock through what Butler calls "subversive bodily acts." In this way a typically male punk subculture challenges the masculinity of rock not by becoming androgynous like Little Richard or Bowie or dressing in drag like the New York Dolls, but by exaggerating for an audience the master signifier's masculinity, the result of which is the "performance" of his corruption, embarrassment, and disgrace through the hyperbolic and derisive repetition of the discourse of rock.

Merdre, Merdre

Malcolm McLaren as a reader of Brecht: while the documentary evidence for such an association is thin, there is a clear pattern to McLaren's orchestration of the Sex Pistols and a general atmosphere around his band's mythology that make Brecht a likely referent. Consider not only *The Threepenny Opera* but *Baal* in its entirety. From the drama's opening scene wherein the titular poet, surrounded by a gaggle of moneyed publishers, almost literally expects the Sex Pistols' drunken exhibition at A&M Records, to his obscene and shirtless performance later in the play that sends both club owner and audience into frothing fits of rage and gob, the lead in Brecht's first play paves the way for punk performance and the punk response to power in a host of ways. And when one considers the similarities linking Baal and Sid Vicious, the notion becomes almost uncanny: awash in narcotics and increasingly volatile, Baal eventually stabs his best friend with a knife in a fit of passion—this after smashing up a club with his guitar—before going on to drink himself to death. "Who is he anyway?" asks a lolling policeman watching the fallen star from the shadows as Baal stumbles along an alleyway. "In the first place: a murderer. Started out as a cabaret performer and poet," replies his partner. "After the murder, they caught him, but he has the strength of an elephant. It was on account of a waitress, a registered whore." Hesitating, the first cop answers, "A man like that has no soul. He's a wild beast," to which the second officer agrees, proffering, "And yet he's like a child."[11]

The sympathetic description—the pop star as a circus freak and performance artist turned criminal, as a soulless man-child and would-be master out of his league and infatuated with a professional tart—stayed with McLaren, who set out to scandalize London in like manner, particularly after Glen Matlock was forced from the Pistols and Vicious brought on board. But while one can see both Brecht and situationism in McLaren's provocations, in Sid and Nancy, most of what constituted early punk was more akin to theater of the absurd—the dramaturgic response to an existence that appears to have little order or purpose. Before moving into the twentieth century and unpacking the "punk" character of Artaud and Genet, this chapter begins its exploration of punks' interest in theater at Ground Zero of what would evolve into not only theater of the absurd but Artaud's Theatre of Cruelty and Brecht's alienation: Alfred Jarry.

Writer, pataphysician, and "pistol-packing midget bicyclist," as Drew Silver put it, Jarry is known principally for *Ubu Roi,* a parodic conflation of several of Shakespeare's plays wherein the corpulent Pere

Ubu, gluttonous in each of his habits, kills the king of Poland and scores of nobles, accountants, and magistrates with a "debraining machine" in a reign of terror that ends only when Ubu and his wife retreat to France after the deposed king's son drives the pair out of Poland—"that is to say, nowhere," as Jarry sniffs in the prologue to his play's inaugural performance. Irrational, violent, childishly scatological, and contemptuous of history and propriety, Jarry put Freud's Id on stage and reveled in its splattering of "merdre" across Paris—"I'm filling my pants with courage," Ubu admits at one point in a play that begins with the repetition of a variation on the French "shit"—by actors who are not puppets but "pretending to be puppets."

Ubu is, the story goes, a sardonic version of one of Jarry's schoolmasters. But he is also the master signifier more broadly, swollen with sleaze and rotting from the inside-out as La Belle Époque, so-called, came to a festering close at the end of the nineteenth century. Recognizing instantly the insult directed at it, the play's well-heeled first audience—seeing the performance on December 10, 1896—rose up in disgust en masse, some spectators walking out, others pointing and shouting at the actors before threatening the playwright with physical harm.[12] "It is not surprising that the public should have been aghast at the site of its ignoble other-self, which it had never before been shown completely. This other self," Jarry later commented with reference to Catulle Mendès, is composed of "eternal human imbecility, eternal lust, eternal gluttony, the vileness of instinct magnified into tyranny."[13]

In calling such behavior endemic to existence, in attacking his own (bourgeois) audience, Jarry not only declared life a corrupt farce that begins in error and ends often in sudden and humiliating death, but provided the world with what might be considered its first onstage punk speech-act. Having grown up in not New York or London but Cleveland, writer and MC5 fan David Thomas believed as much, seeing in

Ubu Roi a template for responding to the absurdity and decay that characterized his own époque *laide*, which even for those not consumed by paranoia must have felt like the End Times. An early member of Peter Laughner's terrifically important proto-punk group Rocket from the Tombs, Thomas, who at one time called himself Crocus Behemoth and had planned on becoming a literature professor, went on to form Pere Ubu in 1975. Cleveland had inured Thomas to the modern world's—the Father's—preposterousness, allowing him to witness up close the nonsense, violence, and corruption of ostensibly munificent interest groups and institutions—politicians, banks, police, teamsters—that were crooked more often than not. Its "dub housing," crumbling economy, and "acres of flame coming out of the ground" serving as background, Cleveland had been turned into a killing field in the middle 1970s due to a pitched turf war among the city's predominantly Irish mobsters. Cuyahoga County saw thirty-seven bombings in 1976, twenty-one of which were located in Cleveland proper. It had become a running gag, Cleveland, an absurd parody of governance, development, industry, "culture," and even organized crime (the Italian Mafia smirking at its mealy Irish counterpart) whose very name—including its professional athletic clubs—was its own joke.[14]

In this environment Thomas and crew cultivated what must have felt to them a necessarily glib and obsessive attitude toward not only American society but life in general. "I wondered at what point a civilization hits its peak and then begins to decline. All those deserted cities, the jungle overgrows them: at what point does the city die?" Thomas asked Jon Savage rhetorically, thinking perhaps of Oswald Spengler and Freud. "At what point do the people who live there no longer understand the vision of the builders? We felt that we owned Cleveland at that point because nobody else wanted it."[15] Not even the Irish, one is tempted to add. Flippant and disillusioned, Thomas especially took to absurdist literature and vaguely Gnostic works of art that expressed the notion that life is something of a put-on—a ruse wherein what the mind perceived as a free and open space was but a galactic dungeon designed to incarcerate one's soul—and converted it into some of the most original and self-deprecating pop music of any era.

This preoccupation with the absurdity of living amid a decaying civilization is embedded deep in Pere Ubu's *Modern Dance*. Building on the success of their ode to materialism "Final Solution," wherein Thomas groaned, "Seems I'm a victim of natural selection" as his neighborhood depreciated, Pere Ubu released their first long-player in 1978—the year the City of Cleveland defaulted on over $15 million in debt. Singing in a voice borrowed from some fattened farm animal writhing on the chopping block, Thomas, in the record's hissing title song, rolls his eyes at an anonymous sucker who, despite the evidence, foolishly continues to believe he is in control of his own destiny in an environment that not only anticipates but requires decay and poverty in order to function. "Down at the buh-*huh*-husss. Into the town," bleats Thomas, his voice warbling deliberately in simulated nervous laughter. "Our poor boy can't get around." He is, this poor boy who "believes in chance," blind to the fact that despite his positivism he remains subject to magisterial—seemingly supernatural—forces more powerful than he, forces which in myriad ways shape his experience. He has no idea that in a decomposing urban environment he is always-already boxed in by capital, argues Thomas, as behind him his mates interrupt their own spry music with repeated shouts of "Merdre, Merdre." His agency, like life, is shit: a cock-up. It is little more than the trash putrefying in the alleys that city sanitation staffers had refused to collect off and on for years. Closing his eyes to the fact that his Being has been proscribed by political economy, the naive kid continues to act as if his choices are his own as around him the arbiters of the modern dance, the same well-mannered elites who accosted Jarry, now just ignore both the kid and the performance he came downtown to hear, engaging instead in vapid discourse as they applaud listlessly, clinking cocktail glasses and chuckling mechanically at the insulting act that in Jarry's Paris would have started a riot.

This binding, civilization's production of grand-but-impotent structures and its appropriation of the avant-garde, is at the heart of what in "Final Solution," a riff on Eddie Cochran's "Summertime Blues" that Pere Ubu at one point refused to play live due to the phrase's association with Nazism, Thomas calls "sonic reduction." First exploring the idea in the Rocket from the Tombs song "Sonic Reducer," Thomas explains that while ambiguous, the notion of sonic reduction "had something to do with a synthesis of much sound into a moment of clarity."[16] And crucial to using noise as the catalyst spurring the spectator toward a certain lucidity of thought is the image. "We understood the relation of sound to vision," Thomas clarifies of his band, which was explicit in generating often disjointed and unsettling soundtracks (replete with shushing steam pipes, blaring clarinets, and squealing feedback) in an effort to enlarge Thomas's histrionics. "The original idea [of Pere Ubu] was to make sound stimulate the imagination: we always saw what we did in very visual terms."[17]

Out of this notion that sound evokes a certain imagery and (self-) consciousness comes Thomas's explosive, physical emphasis on performing without reserve Cleveland's shame. Footage from early Ubu performances shows a young, corpulent Thomas, whose size and animation call to mind the very puppets Jarry sought to enlarge on stage, *subverting* the rock icon that by 1975 audiences had grown accustomed to salivating over. In rapid succession—often within a single song—Thomas stalks about stage stiffly like a man on stilts as he offers his hand palm-up to his musicians with a scrunched face, mimics a bird attempting its first flight, throws his arms up in confusion and disgust at some invisible antagonist, and seems to be trying to capture and interrogate the very noise his band is creating. He is responding to an absurd existence—to the cult of personality that ignores its embarrassing reality—with absurdity, pulling out his own frazzled hair and grinning at nothing in particular, as in the song "Laughing" from *Modern Dance*, wherein Thomas seeks "the empty spaces of this life" at the same time as he challenges emptiness itself—the devil—to a duel and giggles at the ridiculousness of the very notion of Lucifer as a being.

Like Ubu, like a child, Thomas is an anti-star, less interested than perhaps any rocker before or since in moving units for investors, cultivating sex appeal (which even Iggy and Patti, Strummer and Vicious, were proficient at), or building a following for himself. This spectacle—the performance, the city, and the sounds that generate each—seems designed to add nothing to culture, but only subtract, in other words. This subtraction, then, when wedded to a disruptive musical regime, is the ultimate meaning of Thomas's sonic reduction, of the soundscape that animates and replicates the modern dance that in any other club or hall would be orchestrated by the functionaries of capital and power. The specific combination of Ubu's music with Thomas's dramatization of failure, with Cleveland whining in the background, results in an anti-pop that functions not as gain (financial, sexual, social) for its purveyors and advocates, but as perpetual loss. "We are the longest-lasting, most disastrous commercial outfit to ever appear in rock 'n' roll. No one can come close to matching our loss-to-longevity ratio," Thomas once boasted, reframing his definition of reduction.[18] Or, as Ihab Hassan put it in a commentary on Jarry, in a line that seemed to fit 1970s Cleveland with exactitude, "Reduction leads finally to waste; this is the essential joke of life."[19] And if all the shit and corruption around him is "just a joke, *mon*," as Thomas puts it in the final track on *Modern Dance*, the observer can be excused for laughing in life's face. Or at one's own audience.

Rather, speaking as the shameless, phallic master signifier, Thomas's response becomes a snide and ironic injunction: "Well then humor me," orders Thomas of his own fans, reminding them that they're the ones who have been played. Thomas is here speaking as *and* talking back to the economic and political structures that have turned life into a prank: "For that's the way of the West," he utters finally. Especially the United States—in its mania for markets and freedom, God and guns—has become Ubu Roi and made a joke of life, turning its citizens into coprophagous insects-objects through its immoderate, chronic violence and shameless gluttony, which Thomas, the incarnation of Pere Ubu, stages for those same insects. In showing his audience both the Father and itself, Thomas, like Jarry, finds himself not growing with each performance but shrinking, reducing his size and scope in the faint and ultimately optimistic hope that eventually civilization will right itself and Pere Ubu need not exist at all, at which time Thomas will have simply reduced himself to nothing and disappeared.

Little Anthony

In restaging *Ubu Roi* for a twentieth-century American crowd, Thomas inspired countless imitators. But Thomas and Jarry never attacked their audiences physically. Such would be the task of a collection of Ubu contemporaries under the influence of not Jarry but Antonin Artaud. Writing in the 1930s, alongside Benjamin and Brecht, Artaud seemed to be anticipating punk when he declared that "written poetry is worth reading once, and then should be destroyed." Coming exactly halfway through what until that point had been a rather conventional piece of dramaturgy, *The Theatre and Its Double,* Artaud's line is as invigorating as it is eviscerating even a century later. Like an air-horn, the words startle the reader for their unexpectedness, the volume of their violence. From this moment on, Artaud's earlier etiquette evaporates, his polite critiques of Balinese and Oriental theater forgotten in an instant, lost not in what would later be diagnosed as their author's schizophrenia so much as in his grinding disgust with what he saw as the decline in Western art—theater in particular. Seeing in contemporary drama an overreliance on the text, on written language, Artaud would spend the remainder of *Double* seeking the annihilation of the whole of European theater, developing further what he called the Theatre of Cruelty by challenging the advocates of stage to rediscover everything that made the Greek tragedies and Shakespeare great: spectacle, myth, trance, psychology, spontaneity, and disorder. By "cruelty," explains Artaud, he means not literally sadism or bloodshed, but "dissonance, dispersion of timbres, and the dialectic discontinuity of expression," a theater not pretending at but attaining reality by virtue of its commitment to, "pure and detached feeling, a veritable movement of the mind based on the gestures of life itself."[20]

Such a theater engages the spectator, makes her complicit in the re-creation of violence, melancholy, and debauchery. Or, as Artaud had put it in an early version of his manifesto, "On the Alfred Jarry Theatre," the spectator must be part of the action and learn to "go to the theatre the way he goes to the surgeon or the dentist. In the same state of mind—knowing of course that he will not die, but that it is a serious thing, and that he will not come out of it unscathed." Under the heading "Musical Instruments" in a passage in "The Theatre of Cruelty" that must have made Lou Reed smile as he entered the studio to record *Metal Machine Music,* Artaud demands that the artist seek out "absolutely new sounds, qualities which present-day musical instruments do not possess and which require the revival of ancient and forgotten instruments or the invention of new ones. Research is also required, apart from music, into instruments and appliances which, based upon special combinations or new alloys of metal, can attain a new range and compass, producing sounds or noises that are unbearably piercing." Following his own technique to its logical conclusion, Artaud echoes Benjamin in calling for the abolition of not only the orchestra pit but the stage and auditorium, anticipating punk's confrontational approach to audience interaction and transforming virtually any available space into a concert venue. "A direct communication will be re-established between the spectator and the spectacle, between the actor and the spectator, from the fact that the spectator, placed in the middle of the action, is engulfed and physically affected by it," says Artaud, who wants the action to take place *around* the audience. "Thus abandoning the architecture of present-day theatres, we shall take some hangar or barn." Or, the punk might add, some warehouse, church, or suburban basement. As for sets: "There will not be any set."[21]

Seeing in Artaud's vision a prescription for agitating an audience, for affecting its body and mind in real time, punk went to work four decades later crafting songs and a performance aesthetic that put into practice Artaud's recommendation that theater exploit both physical space and sound to disrupt the pop formula. Burden's influence has been noted already, as has Throbbing Gristle's, Iggy's, and Sid's. And although spoken word artist and punker GG Allin, who did eat his own shit on stage—in addition to parading around naked, sodomizing himself with a banana, and threatening to commit suicide in the presence of his audience—was renowned for attacking his paying customers, he was, in the end, derivative. Long before the leader of the Murder Junkies spewed onto the scene, a host of punks had taken the step of physically engaging their own audience on a Spartan stage. Of this there is no better example than New York's industrial-synth pioneers Suicide.

Rehearsing together since 1971, the New York artist Alan Vega and free-jazz enthusiast Martin Rev settled on the concept of a confrontational ensemble whose minimalism—Vega moaning surreal and disjointed lines over Rev's scuzzy keyboard riffs—formed the core of what amounted to both a physical and psychological attack on its audience. "It was actually like an environmental piece, the music was creating a sound environment, and then with that sound environment—which was driving people nuts—I'd be going out and jumping around," says Vega, who was renowned for skulking about stage like a shaved ape, beating his face with the microphone as he extemporized reverberated lyrics, and taunting his audience. "We were too punk even for the punk crowd. They hated us. I taunted them with, 'You fuckers have to live through us to get to the main band.' That's when the axe came towards my head [in Glasgow, Scotland], missing me by a whisker," Vega told the *Guardian* in 2008. "That became the norm. I started carrying a bicycle chain on stage, figuring, if you can't beat 'em, join 'em. If the violence got really bad, what I'd do was smash a bottle and start cutting my face up. . . . Another ploy I had was to lock the exit doors so nobody could escape. That was the ultimate 'fuck you,' as far as I was concerned."[22] Often terrifying onlookers, and accosting them, Suicide achieved Artaud's vision of recreating reality on stage, reminding the punk participant that, as Artaud put it, to engage this music is to acknowledge "that he is about to undergo a real operation in which not only his mind but his senses and his flesh are at stake."[23] That is to say, Vega and Rev, as their band's name implies, were literally putting their skin on the line for the sake of art every night—as was their audience.

Suicide was a version of what Artaud called the "higher determinism, to which the executioner-tormentor himself is subjected" and from which the audience could not escape, even as it drove them mad. Taking seriously each of Artaud's criteria for resurrecting a dead theater—no sets, piercing instrumentation, visceral danger to both spectator and actor, surrounding the audience, and being willing to perform anywhere under any conditions—Vega and Rev gestured toward the "submission to necessity" that Artaud insisted was essential to generating a novel theater that penetrated its participants' consciousness: "There is no cruelty without consciousness and without the application of consciousness. It is consciousness that gives to the exercise of every act of life its blood-red color, its cruel nuance, since it is understood that life is always someone's death."[24]

The band applies such consciousness in terrific fashion in its signature track "Frankie Teardrop," the hub around which the band's eponymous album *Suicide* revolves and perhaps the most terrifying pop song ever recorded. Telling the story of a destitute husband-father who works ten-hour days in a factory, Vega whispers atop Rev's rapid beat and dark two-note melody, disturbed by what he is about to say. "Frankie can't make it cuz things are just too hard," Vega almost whimpers. "Frankie can't make enough money. Frankie can't buy enough food. Frankie's getting evicted. Let's hear it for Frankie." Increasingly desperate, Frankie takes a revolver and ultimately kills his wife and infant, Vega symbolizing the murders with a succession of unsettling shrieks that fade into Rev's layered drone, the music itself absorbing the violence Vega performs before penetrating listeners' senses. When included in a live set, the genuinely terrifying song, all ten minutes of it, gives Vega's chain-wielding persona the narrative his violence lacks otherwise. To be precise, more than any other Suicide song, "Frankie Teardrop" provides Vega the anarchic license to behave as he does on stage, to become Frankie (who symbolized the failures of capitalism and civilization) and to attack his own cohorts in an America—which like Cleveland was "killing its youth" to quote the group's "Ghost Rider"—that by the 1970s seemed to be crumbling in the wake of Vietnam, record urban violence, and an economic recession that left 10 percent of Americans without work.

"Frankie Teardrop" is the nightmare on a dreamy document that replicates the urban American *un*consciousness broadly. Whether the track in question is the lascivious "Cheree" or "Rocket USA," which reads as a punk version of Flannery O'Connor's "A Good Man Is Hard to Find," the consistently hypnotic *Suicide* is full of wet dreams and night terrors, mutated and often blurred scenes of sex, violence, and collapse. So does the record operate on a subconscious level exclusively, communicating a patchy and inarticulate collection of phallogocentric fantasies that are as impossible as they are disturbing and damaging. It is the soundtrack to Martin Scorsese's *Taxi Driver.* For this reason, the critique that the band's music did not translate well to tape misses the point: *Suicide* is less a pop artifact than a contribution to the fossil record—the Father's chronic shame especially—on magnetic tape. And the political, social, and moral implications of such a document remain unclear, and perhaps untouchable, decades later.

In attacking its own audience, in dedicating nearly an entire side of a debut LP to domestic violence, the dissolution of community, and madness, Suicide too shadows Artaud's valorization of Heliogabalus, that historic "insurgent of genius" whose insurrection, asserts Artaud, "is systematic and shrewd and he directs it first of all against himself. When Heliogabalus dresses as a prostitute and sells himself for forty cents at the doors of Christian churches or the temples of Roman gods, he is not simply pursuing the satisfaction of a vice, he is humiliating the Roman monarch." So it was with Suicide, which seems to have internalized Benjamin's maxim that there is no document of civilization that is not simultaneously a document of human barbarism. Having learned much from Iggy Pop, Suicide is an attempt better than even the Sex Pistols' to degrade and derail pop music's phallogocentrism, assuming

Artaud's belief that, as Susan Sontag puts it, "an image is true insofar as it is violent." This is why Suicide gigs and records are not merely social or political but *moral* in orientation: violence and direct confrontation with the audience are put to use as techniques designed to staunch, in Sontag's words, "the corruption of art, the banalization of suffering."[25] This idea quickly developed cache within the punk community, Suicide notwithstanding. "I have a book to recommend to you: *Antonin Artaud Selected Writings,* edited by Susan Sontag," Screamer Tommy Gear would tell *Search & Destroy*'s Vale in 1978. "There's a pretty long chapter on Heliogabalus—you should read it and keep in mind the concept of anarchy, because that's what it's all about. And Artaud was talking about anarchy and Heliogabalus was the all-time epitome of what anarchy should be about."[26] *This* was what Johnny Rotten meant when he called himself an anarchist in 1976. Or as Henry Rollins scrawled with venom from his suburban "shed" a decade later:

> We will never know the feeling of napalm and that makes me sad. I am losing my human values. The can that holds my humanity has been shot full of holes. Two years ago I was different. Every waking moment is such a dehumanizing experience. I will not struggle to keep it. I choose not to resist the draining and in this draining a new animal will be born. Rational thought is just so ridiculous to me now. I hear them talk and I cannot understand. I used to feel bad that I did not fit in because I thought it was a failing on my part. Now I understand the no one is wrong, including me. Drinking beer and sticking a screwdriver in someone's head are the same thing. One is no worse than the other.

For a middle-class subject whose job it was to perform, endure, and often respond to civilization's barbarism and humiliation, to put a certain anarchism of self into practice while modeling shamelessness for an often depraved audience, Rollins here articulates the shift in morality that

4.3 and 4.4. Antonin Artaud comes to show Renée Falconetti the meaning of cruelty in Dreyer's *The Passion of Joan of Arc* (1928).

Artaud argued is both the necessary and the welcome result of "cruel" theater, particularly for a subject hoping to restage and then undermine the very signifier that he is tasked with representing.[27]

Bringing this all together over thirty years later were Joan of Arc. In 2011, the Chicago postpunkers commemorated the eighty-fifth anniversary of the filming of Carl Theodor Dreyer's *The Passion of Joan of Arc* by giving the film an instrumental soundtrack. Recorded in one take before a live audience during a screening of the film at the Chicago International Movies and Music Festival, the eighty-minute album too looks to Artaud, on screen now, for direction. With droning guitars,

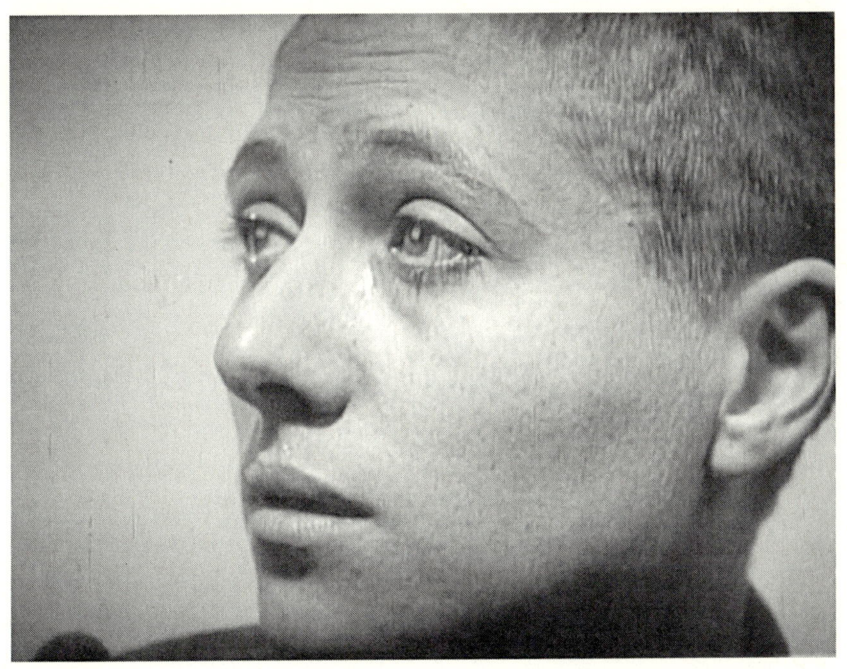

buzzing synthesizers, and ambient electronic beats, Joan of Arc gives an already chilling silent film a painfully unsettling score—subsequently released as an album—designed to give the audience an almost literal feel for the torture to which Jeanne d'Arc was subject by the French Catholic Church and to which Dreyer subjected his lead Renée Falconetti. Even without accompaniment the film is hard to watch, less for its punitive close-ups—which force the viewer to see truly, without the security of distance, Falconetti's anguish and her tormentors' grotesque and hard-boiled malice—than for Falconetti's sweat, tears, and blood that at one point spurts from Jeanne's arm as her warders gouge her with a knife. "Falconetti's blood was actually drawn, her famous hair actually cut," writes James Schamus with shock and awe, "her real tears photographed. One wonders what would have happened had Dreyer actually filmed the torture scene he originally wrote in the screenplay."[28] Joan of Arc's throbbing soundtrack to such images is at times too much, pulling even more anguish and nausea from the audience than the film already tends to evoke on its own.

In providing an equally unsettling "pop" score to Dreyer's already brutal film, Joan of Arc recreates Vega's "sound environment" that with astonishing verisimilitude mirrors the spiritual anarchy and moral disorder that Suicide, with Artaud looking over its shoulder, produced night after night, live and on tape. Consoling Falconetti throughout filming, then, is none other than Artaud himself, whose Jean Massieu, the dean of Rouen, is Jeanne's only genuine sympathizer and who might as well be speaking to the audience when he tells Joan, "*Nous sommes venus pour te preparer à la mort*" (We have come to prepare you for death). The casting was not lost on Joan of Arc, the band, who had perhaps seen Artaud's interview in Sontag's anthology, where Artaud admits to an interviewer the truth, moral or otherwise, that cinema is capable of capturing: "I have unforgettable memories of my work with Dreyer. This time I was working with a man who was able to make me believe in the rightness, the beauty, and the human interest of his conception," Artaud told *Cinémonde* in 1929. "And whatever ideas I may have had about the cinema, about poetry, about life, for once I realized that I was no longer dealing with an aesthetic, a bias, but with a work of art, with a man determined to elucidate one of the most agonizing problems that exists."[29] That problem is, for Artaud, the distortion of the sacred by profane and myopic men. Which is to say, following Jarry, the trivialization and profanation of not only art but life by all of humankind, yes, but the symbolic paternal in particular. Dreyer's punishing and violent attempt to stage this problem, coupled with Joan of Arc's unnerving accompaniment, is only one reason the film pushes viewers to the point of wanting to leave the theater. So it is with Burden, Suicide, Iggy, Throbbing Gristle, and Allin—with punk—whose performances were always less pop or art than a tortuous assault not simply on their own audiences' minds but on their bodies that underscored the simultaneity of truth and violence, the ineluctable horror of Being.

Saint Genet

But if, in punk or theater, the exit doors have been locked, what other options has an audience trying to make sense of its own suffering, of the horror of Being? For Jean Genet, the answer is simple: none. "To escape from horror," Genet put it after Artaud, "bury yourself in it."[30] Overflowing with obscenity, with awfulness, the book whence this line comes, *Our Lady of the Flowers*, was written by the playwright and poet in prison on the coarse paper he was given by his warders to fashion sacks for marketgoers. Twice. The narrator is, at the moment of this enunciation in the semi-autobiographical tale of a drag queen's exploits in the Paris underworld, attempting to rationalize and re-create in memory the actions that had put him in a cage: not only murdering an unsuspecting old man in his own flat, but ejaculating into the dead man's mouth. Such abusive and depraved scenes, above and beyond Sade, mark this "epic of masturbation," according to Sartre, as a work of utter negativity that is at the same time an act "of the rashest optimism" given its author's almost irrational persistence. It is also the purest fantasy, a reverie wherein Genet makes of himself a sand castle dissolving on a beach in the south of France, Sartre theorizes in *Saint Genet*, an eroding and grainy chronicle of obscenity "in constant danger of breaking up or diverging under the pressure of [the author's and readers'] emotional needs."[31] Restarting the narrative after the first draft was set aflame by a turnkey, Genet laughs last, dedicating the published version to his executed fellow convict Maurice Pilorge, a murderer who thumbed his nose at the executioner in an act that "keeps plaguing my life."[32] It is Genet's first and best book, and it is punk through and through.

Such an artist, as Patti Smith understood a decade before she assembled her group, was the epitome of what "punk"—in several senses of the term—had the potential to be. Describing his colleagues' shabby and threadbare style, their refusal of capitalism, and his predilection for the indignity the Name of the Father pushes on its objects, the foundling, criminal, street urchin, and homosexual valorizes in book after book betrayal, theft, treason, and obscenity in opposing the bourgeois, straight culture, repeatedly directing his words at a "you" whose world he rejects, which had in any case already rejected him. "The lice were only a sign of our prosperity, of the very underside of prosperity," Genet later explained in what amounts to a punk manifesto, *The Thief's Journal*. "Using only the pride imposed by poverty, we aroused pity by cultivating the most repulsive wounds. We became a reproach to *your* happiness."[33]

This tattered, almost scattershot, attack on middle-class values is why Dick Hebdige made Genet his principal reference in his early semiotic reading of punk *Subculture*. What punk did, said Hebdige in 1979, already framing punk as an historical episode, is bring Genet's understanding of the seditious potential of style itself into postwar mainstream society, signaling to not only the mass media but parents, priests, police, and professors the world over punks' "unmitigated exile, voluntarily assumed." "Trapped in the paradox of 'divine' subordination like Saint Genet who 'chooses' the Fate which has been bestowed upon him, the punks dissembled," writes Hebdige, "dying to recreate themselves in caricature, to 'dress up' their Destiny in its true colours, to substitute the diet for hunger, to slide the ragamuffin look ('unkempt' but meticulously couture) between poverty and elegance."[34] Like Genet, like Claire and Solange from Genet's *The Maids*, punks saw in the broken glass they used to cut themselves distorted reflections of who and what they were, specifically, *what had been made of them* by the symbolic paternal's bourgeois discourse in which punks were trapped against their will.

So is it no surprise that a version of Genet's line about embracing the shame and horror of one's twisted Being should reemerge on the crumbling walls of Scottish expatriate Brendan Mullen's punk club in late-1970s Hollywood. "The best thing ever written on the wall of the Masque?" asked Mullen rhetorically years after his temporary autonomous zone had evaporated into memory. "'To escape hell you must bury yourself in it.' Taken from Genet. The descent below was well on its way."[35] If Mullen is right in characterizing the goings-on within his basement venue that served as the catalyst for the Los Angeles punk scene as the "revaluation of all values" Nietzsche promotes at the end of *The Antichrist*, Genet is without doubt a natural, even obvious, referent for punks schooled in both Nietzsche and Artaud. Also no surprise, then, is it that as opposed to the American punk scenes in New York and Cleveland, both of which were instinctually artier, *older*, the L.A. scene that reproduced *Our Lady of the Flowers*, that seemed to be trying to act out *The Thief's Journal*, was not only more "English" in its orientation, that is to say younger and poorer, but predominantly comprised of the character types Genet obsesses over: thieves and thugs, drug dealers and addicts, masochists and homosexuals, and street kids abandoned or abused by their parents.

Black Flag, X, and San Francisco group Crime notwithstanding, such a squalid physiognomy was best epitomized in the Los Angeles group Germs and their early associates. Born, like Genet, fatherless, gay, and poor, Jan Paul Beahm was the youngest and likely cleverest of Faith Baker's several children. Seeking escape from the trauma of adolescence and his overbearing giantess of a mother through music, the well-read fan of Nietzsche, Spengler, Rimbaud, Aldous Huxley, and J. G. Ballard found a sidekick and foil in Georg Ruthenberg, a film mogul's son whom Beahm met at the Werner Erhard–influenced University High School in West Los Angeles. Bonding over a mutual interest in David Bowie and acid, the pair was inspired immediately by English punk in the middle 1970s and thus founded Sophistifuck and the Revlon Spam Queens with Teresa "Lorna Doom" Ryan playing bass and a squeaky pre-Go Gos Belinda Carlisle on drums. The name proved too cumbersome—too long to silkscreen on a T-shirt—however. Rechristening themselves Darby Crash (after toying with the alias Bobby Pyn) and Pat Smear, respectively, Beahm and Ruthenberg renamed the group, took on a new drummer who named himself after a journalist murdered in Arizona, and quickly came to epitomize the criminality, loose sexuality, youth, depravity, and calculated and self-injurious incompetence that typified the early L.A. punk scene.

"The punks that came into Licorice Pizza were a combination of idealistic kids who were totally into the scene, and then there were these kids who would create a ruckus in order to distract us so they could shoplift," Matt Groening recalls of his pre-*Simpsons* days, back when he was still formulating his Los Angeles-inspired comic strip *Life in Hell*. "Most of the latter category were associated with the Germs." "None of the Germs could play their instruments whatsoever," added a *Raw Power* review of the band's debut in May 1977, ignoring the problem of the instruments' pilfered status. "They took an hour to get set up and then played for two minutes. The lead singer smeared peanut butter all over his face and . . . they all were spitting on each other until they were kicked off."[36] As Crash even admitted on "Forming," the rudimentary first single by a band that many observers had already come to regard as a joke, "whoever'd buy this shit" is "a fucking jerk." Embedded within such work products, though, was the intellectual, cultural, and familial landscape that generated such "shit" and was too within Genet's purview: not merely Rollins's loss of human values or what Exene Cervenka once called the "poverty and spit" of Los Angeles in the 1970s, but Desoxyn and heroin, the materialism of a hustler culture where kids who had been kicked out by their parents—or had escaped group homes—sold their bodies to survive, police-on-punk violence, and rampant theft.

Such at least is the picture of the L.A. punk underground painted by Thorn Kief Hillsbery in his novel *What We Do Is Secret*. "Before we were punks we were SoCal droogs!" one punker puts it from stage late in Hillsbery's novel, with a reference to Anthony Burgess. "I've got auto theft on my record, burglary, robbery, I'm a goon! I'm a fuckhole!" Or, as the novel's gay, homeless thirteen-year-old narrator Rockets Redglare confesses at one point, after having explained to the reader the dissolute state of his adolescence since fleeing his foster home, "And I don't know much about my parents except both of them were junkies, before and after I was born, they like to rewind-repeat shit like that in group homes so you don't start convincing yourself there's been some terrible mistake, you're the soon-to-be acknowledged love child of Schwarzenegger and Cher. I don't even know if they're still alive. My parents, I mean."[37] Seeing in Los Angeles less razzle-dazzle than desperation and corruption, smelling each night the steaming vats of flavored gelatin cooking high above the hovel he calls home, Rockets finds in Darby Crash and Germs, in the Masque and Cervenka's *Los Angeles*, not merely comfort in Genet's hard underside of prosperity, but a way of converting the horror of poverty, of abandonment to the gutter, into a virtue. "I have thus been that little wretch who knew only hunger, physical humiliation, poverty, fear and degradation," writes Genet, speaking on behalf of

Rockets, Darby Crash, Alice Bag, Exene Cervenka, and Henry Rollins, "but at least I'm aware of it, and such awareness destroys shame and affords me a feeling that few know: pride [and] the knowledge of a force that enables you to stand up to misery—not your own misery, but that of which mankind is composed."[38]

Armed with a sharp tongue, closeted queerness, and an increasing affiliation with wayward boys like Rockets who lie, cheat, and steal their way up and down the Hollywood and Santa Monica Boulevards, Crash followed Genet in making theft, treason, and homosexuality—"the three virtues, which I set up as theological," says Genet—into works of religious art.[39] Of this there is no better example than Germs' second single. The jerky A-side to *Lexicon Devil* is a less-than-subtle call to arms wherein Crash—who only months before his suicide would return from London touting a record whose cover art was simply a dissolve of Antonin Artaud, arms crossed and eyes closed in an apparent death pose—seems to key in on the violence-as-art, martyr-obsessed messianism implicit to his band, to punk as a response to Los Angeles's gilded hedonism broadly, growling,

> I'll get silver guns to drip old blood
> Let's give this established joke a shove
> We're gonna wreak havoc on the rancid mill
> I'm searching for something even if I'm killed

While insurrection was not new to punk in 1978, the ferocity and fluency of Crash's words—those of a steel-toed agitator with murder in his mouth—was.[40] As offended as the English old guard may have been at the Sex Pistols, even it knew that the band was a put-on at some level. But no one could be sure if the same was true of Germs, whose vocabulary and vehemence betrayed its meathead act. "I'm a lexicon devil with a battered brain," insists Crash, the stunning line fighting to escape his equally battered mouth by way of chipped tooth in time as Smear and Doom bang away behind him on stolen instruments. "Searching for a *few-churr*; the world's mah aim."

One can almost hear hardcore punk being invented on this short record, which rather than giving up on the future, as did the Sex Pistols, instead threatens its overthrow. More than this, in *Lexicon Devil* Crash inverts the Gospel of John's valorizing of the master signifier—"In the beginning was the Word, and the Word was with God, and the Word was God"—positing instead the type of discourse the redactors of the Qur'an and Salman Rushdie both called Satanic Verses. Bristling at the doctrine of the word made flesh, Darby Crash suggests in response, after reading up on Scientology's engrams and auditing, that if the symbolic law, if phallogocentrism, comes from God, he will become instead a word devil. In his threat to dismantle both pop and the Logos and take aim at the entire Western world, Crash in this single posits a subtle theology of punk, rearticulating less L. Ron Hubbard—Crash's reading of whom observers like Spitz and Mullen have made much hay over—than *The Thief's Journal*, wherein Genet expressed, quite lucidly and without irony, his desire to be regarded as a saint as a direct result of his "transgression," to be "guided by a will to saintliness until I am so luminous that people will say, 'He is a saint.'"[41] In other words, with the song's chorus—the "Gimme gimme your hands, Gimme gimme your minds, Gimme gimme this, Gimme gimme *thaaaaaaat*," which seemed to become his maxim—Crash ups the ante on Saint Genet's consecration of betrayal and theft, not merely stealing from others as do his associates, but demanding that others relinquish both their possessions and their critical faculties not just to him but to *each other*. "Darby used to make people do things, like he'd make one girl take off a bracelet and give it to another girl, just because he could," Germs manager Nicole Panter once put it, "or he'd say, 'Gimme that button,' 'Gimme that shirt' or 'Gimme a beer,' and five little girls from Beverly Hills would run and get it."[42]

Too often read as a symptom of Crash's obsession with control, of his adolescent fascism, this undermining of the phallogocentric economy that vests power and prestige in those who own and create signals Crash's theological revaluation of Ronald Reagan's American Jesus, of the cult of consumption in the heart of the culture industry whose pearly Logos had been raised high above the Hollywood hills and glared night and day down at the city. As Crash had already implied in "Forming," anyone who would purchase not only a dreadful punk record but anything produced by his shallow city and thus reinforce a corrupt, bourgeois economy, who would render unto Caesar, was to be regarded with extreme contempt. "In the starving sense you worship / the nations of debris," Crash sang of his home in "Land of Treason," "You wear a coat of sewage / that you've never even *seen*." In so singing, Crash, despite his insistence in "No God" from *Lexicon Devil*'s B-side that "there's no god to watch over me," ironically resurrects the Gospel figure who had thumbed his nose at the Roman-occupied first-century Palestinian state and asked followers to abandon all their possessions and riches, telling his own fraught audience, "Empty out your *pah-kets*; you don't need their change / I'm giving you the power to rearrange." So does Crash reconfigure Genet's theft-as-art by imagining the deconstruction of the Word made flesh as anti-capitalism and the renunciation of one's citizenship, acting the messiah figure he was accused of being, turning the desire generated and ideology reinforced by his hometown upside down, and instructing his followers to convert their desire to possess—to "consume" or "marry and reproduce" as Roddy Piper's Nada sees in the Los Angeles billboards in John Carpenter's cinema gem *They Live*—into the desire to reallocate and transgress simultaneously.

Crash set about rearranging staid economic—and thus sociopolitical and interpersonal—relations in Hollywood, in other words, finding, like Genet, Cervenka, and Rollins, revolution not in power or fame but in destitution and poverty. "He found the irreducible nugget of rhetoric for himself right in that word 'gimme,'" Will Amato remembers. "There was a plaintive quality to it that was so kind of Paul Beahm to me."[43] And if Sartre is right in positing that the Genet of *Our Lady of the Flowers* objectifies himself in some sort of politically motivated self-degradation, it is in the *Journal* that Genet, out of prison now, recuperates his agency, becoming again a subject and anticipating L.A. punk in arguing that "the most sordid signs [of destitution] became for me signs of grandeur." From such signs, from poverty and betrayal and theft, Genet sees a method for transcending the dehumanizing structures of bourgeois culture, describing his work—both his betrayal-theft and his art—as an attempt "to rehabilitate persons, objects and feelings reputedly vile."[44]

So it is with Germs and their Masque confederates, who seemed to bury themselves in depravity and objectification, to aggrandize their ignominy, not unlike Dostoevsky or Iggy, in order to transcend it, to move beyond that most profane of cities, Hollywood, and gesture toward something sacred by diving headfirst into the irreverence generated by the city itself to show the city its products. This is the reason for Crash's interest in Scientology, his canonization almost immediately after his death. Or, as Screamer Paul Roessler put it about Crash in the wake of his heroin overdose, remembering Genet, "If I was going to pick one martyred fucking saint artist that I know, he'd be the one!"[45] Saint Darby: the godless patron saint of redistributive destitution, treason, and disgrace, the atheist Heliogabalus who nonetheless seemed to take seriously the Christian Bible's Acts of the Apostles, which stresses that "all the believers agreed to hold everything in common." The notion is as compelling today as it would have been offensive to Crash in

1980, and it has shaped most posthumous accounts of Germs and Darby Crash since his fulfillment of what he called a "five year plan" to state his piece and then exit this world.[46]

The problem with hagiography, though, is that as a genre it's always-already contaminated, too far from dialectical thinking to get at much truth. The same can be said of the many (oral) histories of punk that stop at sainthood and sociology. For as even Genet admitted with a sigh long before Germs began infecting greater Los Angeles, "Never did my broken-down shoes or dirty socks have the dignity that lifts the sandals of the Carmelites and bears them through the dust, never did my dirty jacket accord my movements the slightest nobility."[47] Such an admission flies in the face of not only Sartre's plodding exegesis of Genet, but Roessler's eulogy, which was but one of many Jan Paul Beahm received following his suicide the day before Mark David Chapman murdered John Lennon in December 1980—and overshadowed Crash's own death in so doing. This failure to go beyond a martyr's canonization—which is phallogocentrism at its best—by most documentarians of punk distorts both the etiology and the true theological significance of punk in Southern California, falling into the trap Hebdige laid for himself in his otherwise sterling enquiry: despite his atheism and refusal of God, Crash anticipated Slavoj Žižek's notion that "only an atheist can believe" by being, in practice, the most genuinely "Christian" agent punk has ever seen.

After all, punk, in every scene one could examine, has always been about much more than semiotics, sociology, or style. Left out of Hebdige and most Germs commentary, rather, is the feeling Genet lingers over on page after page: the deeply personal sense of shame he felt in the face of bourgeois culture. "Fatigue, shame and poverty forced me to have recourse only to a world where every incident had a meaning which I cannot define but which is not the one it suggests to you," Genet argues halfway through his *Journal*, articulating, in a book literally awash in its author's humiliation, how his *desire for shame* was borne of the symbolic paternal that both had rejected him and goes about its business of marginalizing dissent and concentrating wealth without embarrassment.[48] Like Jesus of Nazareth turning tables at the Temple or hanging naked on the cross, such shame in the service of desire and a rebellious violence is at the heart of Germs, Darby Crash, and much of the collective Heliogabalus that is Los Angeles punk as well: shame in one's sexual orientation or licentiousness, one's (absent, abusive) parents and parent culture, in capitalism and one's reduction by the State—as Crash snarled in "Manimal," "Sex Boy," and "Richie Dagger's Crime"—into an abject subject. And it is their plunging into the horror of such circumstances on stage (accomplished under the watchful "H" in the Hollywood hills where Welsh-born actor Millicent Lilian Entwistle too plunged to her death in late 1932: "I am afraid, I am a coward. I am sorry for everything. If I had done this a long time ago, it would have saved a lot of pain," Entwistle wrote in a red-faced suicide scrip) that makes Germs and their conspirators, in context, most astonishing and revolutionary as artists.[49]

"Standing in line we're aberrations / Defects in a defect's mirror," Crash belts out in the forty-two-second "What We Do Is Secret," a bleeding tourniquet of a song from the band's only LP. "And we've been here all the time, real fixations / Hidden deep in the furor." The song—chaotic and haphazard, fighting to hold itself together for *that* long—points a crooked finger at the source of Crash's disgrace, that which has made of him a defect, at the same time that it provides a salve to those likewise suffering from the "dementia of a higher order" brought on by Saint Genet's "you." So do Crash and his Circle One crew operate in secret, under the radar, long into the night, cataloguing a community's secret shames—fallen stars, hustlers, junkies, queers, homeless veterans, runaways, and those otherwise sequestered from the shameless master in the land of Reagan—and functioning as the return of what the city had tried so hard to repress, all the while healing the sick and helping the blind see.

The Shame Kid

Theorizing gender and sexual identity as inevitably "performances" established by and within a specific semiotic system, Butler calls not only gender but sex a signifying practice that relies on the repetition of coded rituals and behaviors in a social setting to constitute the gendered subject, which is, ultimately, an *effect* of discourse. "In a sense, all signification takes place within the orbit of the compulsion to repeat," writes Butler in the wake of both Crash and Genet and anticipating Thomas Gabel/Laura Grace of Against Me! As Butler continues, "'agency' then is to be located within the possibility of a variation on that repetition. If the rules governing signification not only restrict, but enable the assertion of alternative domains of cultural intelligibility . . . then it is only *within* the practices of repetitive signifying that a subversion of identity becomes possible."

As we have seen, punk is such a subversion. The predominantly male punk performance confronts the heteronorm—the Name of the Father—not only through androgyny (which rock has been doing for half a century) or drag, but *excessive* and even *feigned* repetition of masculinity. As Iggy, Laughner, Thomas, Vega, and Crash demonstrate, punk ritualizes and enlarges the phallogocentrism embedded within rock and roll as a practice to the point of disgrace, showing the master signifier an exaggerated version of itself on stage in an effort to dramatize the Father's absolutely shameless agency. Taking the phallogocentric discourse of the Church, capitalism, the nuclear family, or the Law—the bourgeoisie—to its logical conclusion, punk, much like Jarry,

Genet, Artaud, or Shepard, repeats and enlarges the abusive violence, horror, and shame of the Father each night for its audience. Such an act confronts directly the discourse that marginalizes women and minorities, that dehumanizes even straight, white subjects to the point of their engaging in what Butler calls the "politics of despair," and inverts it.[50]

This inversion, in the end, is the significance of Alan Suicide's "Frankie Teardrop" and Dave Thomas's Ubu Roi. It is the core of Darby Crash's or Iggy's or GG Allin's repetition of disgusting and debauched acts on stage, not to mention Alice Bag's Castration Squad and Tessa Pollitt's pre-Slits group the Castrators. It is also what Patti Smith's beau Sam Shepard too staged in 1974, essentially heralding punk in the process. Exploring the abject subject's humiliation in *Curse of the Starving Class* and *Buried Child,* both produced at the height of punk, Shepard had already mused on pop's shamelessness in *The Tooth of Crime,* which beat Smith's *Horses* to the punch by a single year. In the piece of musical theater, Hoss, a bloated rock star and alpha male who drives a Maserati and dominates rock music, is confronted by the unconventional Crow, a much younger, tight-jeaned rebel-rocker who arrives on Hoss's scene looking not unlike Iggy, Sid, or Darby, wearing a silver swastika around his neck, an eye patch, steel-toe boots, and sneering lips. Crow has challenged his predecessor, who despite the confidence with which he responds to his contender, intuits that his time has come. "Look at me now. Impotent. Can't strike a kill unless the charts are right. Stuck in my image. Stuck in a mansion. Waiting," the aging star laments, phallus in hand, as Crow makes his way to Hoss's hideout in his black Chevy Impala. "Waiting for a kid who's probably just like me. Just like I was then. A young blood."[51]

Framing pop music as organized crime, as "having degenerated into branches of the bourgeois narcotics business" to quote Brecht, Shepard imagines a showdown between the graybeard and the arriviste, who is characterized as maintaining a more fluid sexuality than his opponent. So do the two subjects put Butler into practice, performing gender by engaging in a verbal battle, hurling insults and accusations across the stage as a variety of (rhetorical) weapons wait on the floor between them. But no sooner than the contest begins does it become clear that the old man is overmatched, that he has no defense against the charge of being the driver of a maudlin pop culture, of "Beatin' meat to the face in the mirror" and profiting on the shame he cultivates in his own clientele. As Hoss retreats, the androgynous "punk" advances, landing a knockout blow when he charges Hoss with humiliating both his audience and himself—imagine if not Elvis Presley in Las Vegas, then his *Having Fun with Elvis On Stage* album—and demanding that he feel the indignity he has been flouting. "Pants down. The moon show. Ass out the window," laughs Crow, accusing Hoss of selling out, of allowing himself to having enjoyed fucking his own audience for so much coin—and creating a culture that encourages emasculated abject subjects to humiliate themselves in myriad ways. "Side slash to the kid with a lisp. The dumb kid. The loser. The runt. The mutt. *The shame kid*. Kid on his belly."

"Never got caught!" Hoss protests to Crow's accusation that he slithered into fame by being a bottom-feeder, by generating in his subjects a disciplinary embarrassment in themselves and propping up an exploitive market economy that does the same. "Never did happen!" But of course it did. And both musicians know that Hoss has become, without embarrassment, corrupt in middle age, swelling in comfortable style and watching with perverse pleasure the emaciating humiliation of the public he birthed through what Butler went on to call the performance of his masculinity made possible by the culture industry's phallogocentric discourse. Sick of being ashamed and marginalized by this particular dick, Crow stays on the offensive, his tone turning violent, assuming and then inverting Hoss's language in order to undermine it:

"Catch ya' with yer pants down. Whip ya' with a belt. Whup ya' up one side and down the other. Whup ya' all night long. Whup ya' to the train time. Leave ya' bleedin' and cryin'. Leave ya' cryin' for Ma. All through the night. All though the night long. Shame on the kid. . . . Scuffle mark. Belt mark. Tune to the rumble. The first to run. The shame kid. The first on his heel. Shame on the shame kid."

"Yeah. You win all right," Hoss admits finally, with a shrug, simply giving up in what appears a sort of broken, resigned epiphany. "All this collection of torture. It's all yours." And picking up a gun from the floor, Hoss—relieved at having an excuse not to accept responsibility of having stylized the enlargement of heterosexual desire, of growing the phallus and abusing his subjects—places the gun to his lips before Crow can do the deed for him.[52] Not so much beaten by the young punk as refusing to reap what he had sown, Hoss demonstrates the end in store for Crow if the youngster cannot find a way to dissipate the shame of not only his discourse but the Name of the Father. In so doing, Hoss gives body to Wallace Stevens's prescient poem "Extracts from Addresses to the Academy of Fine Ideas," which long in advance of Shepard's play concluded that:

> In the end, these philosophic assassins pull
> Revolvers and shoot each other. One remains
> The mass of meaning becomes composed again.
> He that remains plays on an instrument.
> . . . .
> It is the music of the mass of meaning.[53]

Punk as the music of the mass of meaning, as the philosophic assassin Rimbaud celebrated with a juvenile guile before setting his own writing aflame: applying such a reading to a suicidal subculture whose performance of masculinity is always-already subversive cannot be bumped aside as easily as the underground man by the symbolic paternal in the wake of punks' literary predilections. One is tempted here, then, to praise Stevens, Shepard, and Suicide for their clairvoyance, for equating shamelessness and (self-) murder with rock music and capitalism and prophesying the death of the King of Rock and Roll, who would, five years after *The Tooth of Crime* premiered, end his life through what amounts to a rather shameful death—intentional or not—the year punk emerged to point out the king's (and queen's) nakedness.

Perhaps. An equally fitting reading would be to see Shepard's forecasting with his play the death of Danny Rapp. After his time as lead singer of Danny & the Juniors, whose "At the Hop" reached the top of the American pop charts in 1958, Rapp's career had sputtered since the 1960s. Touring the aging rock circuit like Hoss—playing casinos, county fairs, and retirement communities in the American Southwest—Rapp checked in to the Yacht Club Motel in Quartzsite, Arizona, on April 2, 1983. When Rapp failed to show for a performance that day in Phoenix, and after an altercation offstage with a female backing singer for a band that had long since ceased to be relevant, authorities descended on the motel on April 5 and found Rapp dead, like Hoss, having put a gun barrel to his temple before pulling the trigger. "Another motel voice, Arizona 1983," Bryan Webb of Canadian postpunks Constantines sings in "Arizona" twenty years later, not so much eulogizing Rapp as trying to understand what it is about "this sound," this fleeting and intangible music—(punk) rock—that makes it "a terminal condition." "In my hands: a hymn of dispossession," groans Webb in a voice equal parts Bruce Springsteen and Ian MacKaye. "In my head I'm hearing *love* songs." This too Shepard anticipates.

"America is killing its youth," Martin Rev and Alan Vega—as Suicide—had argued in response to Shepard during punk's infancy and Simon Stephens would go on to stage in his play *Punk Rock,* whose young lead unloads a revolver into several of his classmates as the Stooges, Big Black, Cows, and Sonic Youth songs bridge the gaps between scenes. Punk, that terminal condition and rashest of rock subcultures that remains a typically young man's movement, has helped reify Vega's mumbled line: not only Sid Vicious, Crash, Cobain, and Curtis (imploding on the eve of his band's first American tour), but so many abject subjects who have succumbed to the master signifier's politics of despair, to the shamelessness of a phallogocentrism most obvious in the United States of America. All bodies scattered about a terrifically violent and humiliating Western culture which grew cold and stiff after performing for their audience the shame of the Father even as they undermine him in staging his ugliness. America especially, if Henry Miller is right to call the United States a "black curse upon the world" filled with "swiftly decaying people, almost a third of them pauperized, the more intelligent and affluent ones practicing race suicide," seems designed to eat its children.[54] American suicide, Miller suggests well in advance of Elvis, Darby Crash, Rapp, Vicious, Curtis, or Cobain, is not so much tragedy or cliché as *rational*, predictable even if Genet and Brecht are right to equate disgrace with bourgeois consumer culture, if Jarry and Artaud, Samuel Beckett and Samuel Shepard, are justified in gesturing toward the absolute wretchedness and absurdity of humankind, particularly under capitalism.

In facing head-on the same problems as did each of these playwrights, punk made of itself a histrionic, in all senses of the term, movement whose performativity not so much undermines the libidinal investment of desire in the male rock star as it simply makes the typically masculine subject an *undesirable* (humiliated, unattractive, oafish, gauche) subject. In so doing, punk subverts the master signifier himself, at times to the point of abusing the symbolic paternal as the audience either watches in disgust and horror or joins in the action itself.

"The task is not whether to repeat, but how to repeat or, indeed, to repeat and, through a radical proliferation of gender, *to displace* the very gender norms that enable the repetition itself," Butler adds finally.[55] This is exactly what much of punk does. So it is that punk's parodic and performative self-castration and repetition of the Father's shameless violence and libido—his swelling masculinity—ultimately reduce his size and scope, displacing his symbolic law through the appropriation of his own discourse. Punks' performance of masculinity converts, rather, the phallic figure in whom so much libidinal energy has been invested into a shameful subject, undermining the culture industry's selling of both authority and desire to a mass of subordinated subjects. No surprise is it, then, that many punks would go on to fall for a writer who accomplished as much on paper as punks did on stage. Embarrassingly masculine, hyperbolically phallogocentric, and often violently obscene, Henry Miller's prose scandalized the literary world with its brazen shamelessness by taking the discourse of the phallus to its logical and often ridiculous conclusion. And punks ate it up. His fiction notwithstanding, as the loves and deaths of Sid and Nancy, Ian and Deborah Curtis, and Kurt Cobain and Courtney Love demonstrate, the critic can see in punks' infatuation with the Brooklyn-born crank not only an ideological model but a conjugal counselor whose debilitating and brutal marriage to June Miller too shaped what would come to be known as "punk love." Put into practice by scores of punk pairs who had read Miller in the wake of Artaud, Brecht, and Genet, punk love submitted to the love affair Artaud's "necessity of violence," Genet's horror in Being. As such, it is to punks' resurrection of Henry and June that this book now turns.

Notes

1. Lester Bangs, "The White Noise Supremacists," in *Psychotic Reactions and Carburetor Dung*, ed. Greil Marcus (New York: Vintage, 1988), 273.

2. Walter Benjamin, "What Is Epic Theatre?," in *Illuminations*, ed. Hannah Arendt; trans. Harry Zohn (1939; New York: Schocken, 1976), 154.

3. Bertolt Brecht, "A Short Organum for the Theatre," in *Brecht on Theatre* (New York: Hill & Wang, 1964), 187.

4. Ibid., 179.

5. McLaren quoted in Jon Savage, *England's Dreaming* (1991; New York: St. Martin's Griffin, 2001), 9, 30–31.

6. Patti Smith, *Just Kids* (New York: HarperCollins, 2010), 181.

7. John Lydon, *Rotten: No Irish, No Blacks, No Dogs* (New York: Picador, 1994), 17.

8. Simon Reynolds, *Rip It Up and Start Again* (New York: Penguin, 2005), 199.

9. Jon Savage, "Industrial Music for Industrial People," *Search & Destroy #6*, 1978, in *Search and Destroy 1–6: The Complete Reprint*, by V. Vale (San Francisco: V/Search, 1996), 122.

10. Jean-Paul Sartre, "An Interview with Sartre," *New York Review of Books*, March 26, 1970, 22.

11. Bertolt Brecht, "Baal," in *Collected Plays*, vol. 1 (1922; New York: Pantheon, 1970), 26–28, 52–55.

12. Alfred Jarry, *Ubu Roi*, ed. Drew Silver (1896; Mineola, NY: Dover, 2003), vi, 3, 70, 2.

13. Alfred Jarry, "Theatre Questions," in *Selected Works of Alfred Jarry*, ed. Roger Shattuck and Simon W. Taylor (London: Jonathan Cape, 1965), 83.

14. Savage, *England's Dreaming*, 441.

15. Ibid., 137.

16. Jon Allan, "The Rocket from the Tombs Story (1973–1975)," *Late Night Magazine*, Ubu Projex, 2001, http://www.ubuprojex.com/rftt/rfttstory.html.

17. Savage, *England's Dreaming*, 441.

18. Tom Moon, *1,000 Recordings to Hear before You Die: A Listener's Life List* (New York: Workman, 2008), 592.

19. Ihab Hassan, *The Dismemberment of Orpheus* (New York: Oxford University Press, 1971), 52.

20. Antonin Artaud, *The Theatre and Its Double* (New York: Grove, 1958), 78, 113–14.

21. Ibid., 95–97, 157.

22. Jon Wilde, "Every Night I Thought I'd Be Killed," *Guardian*, August 1, 2008, 5.

23. Artaud, *The Theatre and Its Double*, 158.

24. Ibid., 102.

25. Antonin Artaud's "From Heliogablus, or The Anarchist Crowned," in *Antonin Artaud: Selected Works*, ed. Susan Sontag (Berkeley: University of California Press, 1976), 323–24, xxxv, xxii.

26. Vale, "Screamers from LA: A Better World Begins with You," *Search & Destroy* #5, 1978, in *Search and Destroy 1–6: The Complete Reprint*, by V. Vale (San Francisco: V/Search, 1996), 90.

27. Henry Rollins, *Get in the Van* (Los Angeles: 2.13.61, 1994), 202–3.

28. James Schamus, "Dreyer's Textual Realism," in *Rites of Realism: Essays on Corporeal Cinema*, ed. Ivone Margulies (Durham, NC: Duke University Press, 2002), 322.

29. Susan Sontag, ed., *Antonin Artaud: Selected Works* (Berkeley: University of California Press, 1976), 183.

30. Jean Genet, *Our Lady of the Flowers*, trans. Bernard Frechtman (1943; New York: Grove, 1963), 129.

31. Jean-Paul Sartre, *Saint Genet*, trans. Bernard Frechtman (1952; New York: Pantheon, 1963), 447–48, 462.

32. Genet, *Our Lady of the Flowers*, n.p.

33. Jean Genet, *The Thief's Journal*, trans. Bernard Frechtman (1949; New York: Grove, 1964), 26, 55.

34. Hebdige, *Subculture: The Meaning of Style* (1979; London: Routledge, 1999), 66.

35. Marc Spitz and Brendan Mullen, *We Got the Neutron Bomb* (New York: Three Rivers, 2001), 130.

36. Brendan Mullen, Don Bolles, and Adam Parfrey, *Lexicon Devil: The Fast Times and Short Life of Darby Crash and the Germs* (Los Angeles: Feral House, 2002), 55–56.

37. Thorn Kief Hillsbery, *What We Do Is Secret* (New York: Villard, 2005), 31–32, 205.

38. Genet, *Thief's Journal*, 111.

39. Ibid., 149.

40. The album Crash returned from England with was Doll by Doll's *Remember* from 1979. See also Hillsbery, *What We Do*, 213.

41. Genet, *Thief's Journal*, 209.

42. Mullen, *Lexicon Devil*, 115.

43. Ibid., 116.

44. Genet, *Thief's Journal*, 19, 109.

45. Mullen, *Lexicon Devil*, 265.

46. See, for example, Spitz and Mullen, *We Got*; Mullen, *Lexicon Devil*; or Steven Blush, *American Hardcore* (Port Townsend, WA: Feral House, 2010).

47. Genet, *Thief's Journal*, 74.

48. Ibid., 172.

49. No author, "Young Actress Ends Life In Hollywood," *Lewiston Daily Sun*, September 20, 1932, 11.

50. Judith Butler, *Gender Trouble: Feminism and the Subversion of Identity* (1990; New York: Routledge, 1999), 185–86.

51. Sam Shepard, "The Tooth of Crime," in *Seven Plays* (1974; Toronto: Bantam, 1986), 224.

52. Ibid., 235, 249.

53. Wallace Stevens, "Extracts from Addresses to the Academy of Fine Ideas," in *The Collected Poems* (1942; New York: Vintage, 1990), 256.

54. Henry Miller, *Black Spring* (1936; New York: Grove 1963), 24; and *The Air-Conditioned Nightmare* (New York: New Directions, 1945), 228.

55. Butler, *Gender Trouble*, 187.

5 LOVE WILL TEAR US APART,

OR, HENRY AND JUNE MEET SID AND NANCY

"I saw the sleeves for *Slip It In* and *Family Man*," beamed Henry Rollins to his tour journal in a rare fit of buoyancy in June 1984. "They look great."[1] He is writing from Venice, California, on a break from performing during what would end up being his hardcore band's busiest year. The titles are but two of the *three* records Black Flag would release in the months that follow, having been both touring and recording incessantly for years but prohibited from releasing any of its material due to a legal injunction brought on by MCA Records as a result of the band's "anti-parent" album *Damaged*. Although this latest stint is technically supporting Black Flag's ambitious second long-player *My War*, before leaving for the present tour the group had been in the studio putting the finishing touches on *Slip It In*. As Rollins later explains, many of the unreleased album's songs—some of them improvisational tracks sounding less like hardcore than metal, even jazz—are already part of the band's set. So does a Black Flag show from summer 1984 include not only portions of *My War*, but its follow-up record's six-minute title track, which recalls the confusion of a young woman whose desire for chastity clashes with her inability to say no to anyone. "You decided to be all loose / It's what *you* choose," slobbers Rollins as a female voice behind him—L7 singer Suzi Gardner—moans, "Slip it in" suggestively. "You say you don't want it," Rollins adds with derision. "You don't want it?! / Say you don't want it—Then you slip it *in*."

5.1. Henry Rollins reads Henry Miller on stage in 1984. Still from *Black Flag Live* (1984).

Like most everything Black Flag produced, the new albums had been illustrated by the band's resident aesthetician Raymond Pettibon, Flag guitarist Greg Ginn's brother, who had developed a reputation in southern California since the middle 1970s for his crudely drawn punk album covers and handbills depicting unsettling and violent images of exploited women, bloodied children, and scads of naked, beastly men. Lots of penises. Keeping with tradition, the *Slip It In* cover imagines a lazy-eyed nun before a candy-apple red background. She is rubbing her face, the only exposed part of her body, against the hairy thigh of some pale-skinned, faceless brute. Her left arm wrapped around the man's bare leg, the nun is kneeling—perhaps genuflecting—and grimacing at the viewer, almost delighting in forcing the voyeur to witness the disintegration of her vows. She is disgusted with herself, too, for her incontinence, furrowing her brow and wondering how it is she had been made so low. "Nobody knows more than I," reads a caption floating inches from the sister's brassy crucifix, "that the less girls know the better they are likely to be."

It is as remarkable an image today is it was in 1984—irreverent and malicious, refusing to look away and demanding that the audience too acknowledge the violence of not only sex but the Church as an institution. Using the caption on Pettibon's cover as a point of entry, many critics bristled though, going so far as to connect the image to the title track's content and dwelling more on the rape culture allegedly enabled by the record than its overall merit or the cover's symbolic content. The album art and title track, wrote Stevie Chick in his Black Flag biography, echoes uncomfortably the chauvinism and phallogocentrism prevalent in rock: "['Slip It In'] remains a dark and somewhat troubling song, an only-slightly-ambiguous bolt of misogyny that rankles now, not least because of the language of its hookline."[2] Or as Robert Christgau put it in a pat sixty-five-word critique, *Slip It In* sounds like it was written by "somebody who learned about sex from movies."[3]

Missing in the reviews, however, was an exploration of the title's and image's literary origin. "Pettibon never stops working," Rollins had written earlier in his journal. "He rarely talks. He just draws and reads and he never stops." A voracious reader himself, Rollins, in his more lucid moments, had cited several authors and texts in *Get in the Van* that he claims shaped his punk self during those months and miles traveled, including some of Richard Hell's favorites—Edgar Allan Poe, Dostoevsky, and Lautréamont. Moving beyond the nineteenth century, Rollins confesses to obsessing over more recent writers as well—one in particular. In so doing he reveals Pettibon's inspiration. "I read *Black Spring* by Henry Miller for a few hours today," Rollins scribbled of the author who in many ways set the stage for Black Flag's often lewd critique of America. "This is the coolest book I have ever read." Later beaming with praise when a journalist links the two Henrys, Rollins adds that finishing one of Miller's books "is a grand occasion for me. It feels like the last day of school or something": "At the end of *The Tropic of Cancer, Black Spring* and *Tropic of Capricorn* it's like he packs you a lunch and sends you on your way. I sat outside the show in Vancouver, Canada and finished *Capricorn*. I read the last page over and over again. I hated finishing the book. I felt as if I was saying goodbye to a friend. I felt lonely when I had finished it. The man is totally endearing to me. I carry one of his books with me always." So infatuated with his namesake was Rollins at one point, so certain that the writer, who died mere weeks before Rollins joined Black Flag, was a kindred spirit, that the singer by that time in the band's arc had taken to reading Miller on stage, an act one documentarian captured for the *Black Flag Live* film from 1984, and aping Miller's style in his own spoken word tracks.[4]

Spreading to Rollins's colleagues, this fascination with Miller would make its way into the India ink sketches of Pettibon, whose father was a writer and English teacher. There is a scene early in *Tropic of Capricorn*, rather, where Miller describes getting a frantic call from his first wife while working at the "Cosmodemonic Telegraph Company." His wife's friend from convent school, Arline, had just been institutionalized, she tells Henry. Arline was but the latest of several girls from his wife's class to suffer a psychotic break since their time at the nunnery, and Mrs. Miller is afraid she might be next in line to be committed. Calming his wife down before relating the story to his loudmouth hound-dog friend MacGregor, who knows Arline, even Henry is shocked at his friend's laughing I-told-you-so conclusion that he always knew there was something askew with Arline. "Why?" Miller asks. "Because when [I] tried to force her one night she began to weep hysterically." As Miller quotes his chum:

> I said to her—well you don't need to do it if you don't want . . . just hold it in your hand. Jesus, when I said that I thought she'd go clean off her nut. She said I was trying to soil her innocence—that's the way she put it. And at the same time she took it in her hand and she squeezed it so hard I damn near fainted. Weeping all the while, too. And still harping on the holy ghost and her "innocence," I remembered what you told me once and so I gave her a sound slap in the jaw. It worked like magic. She quieted down after a bit, enough to let me slip it in, and then the real fun commenced.[5]

Astonishing for its violence, misogyny, obscenity, and irreverence, this scene is representative of many originally imagined by Miller that in one way or another would be translated into the several Pettibon-penned flyers, adverts, and album covers collected in Rollins's squalid memoir, which likewise imagines, ad nauseam, one sexually violent, humiliating, heretical, and abrasive punk scene after another.

If perhaps Miller's most *explicit* punk advocates, however, Black Flag and Pettibon are far from the only punks to celebrate the writer who called his prurient, audacious fiction "singing"—punk and post-punk groups have been reading Henry Miller for decades, referencing him routinely in their lyrics, band names, zines, and album art. Four years after *Slip It In*, for example, Bad Religion included a ninety-second reinterpretation of *Tropic of Cancer* on their "reunion" album *Suffer*, quoting the novel directly ("Life is the sieve through which my anarchy strains . . . chaos is the score upon which reality is written") before going on to paraphrase Miller's alternately millenarian-nihilist conclusion about the "Delirium of Disorder" that marks twentieth-century Being.

On the opposite side of the country, Sonic Youth's Thurston Moore was reading *Capricorn* as former Rodan singer Jeff Mueller (the German "Miller" who would eventually front a band named for E. Annie Proulx's novel *The Shipping News*) joined members of other slowcore pioneers Lungfish and Codeine to form the angular June of 44, whose name allegedly indicates the time Miller and American-born critic-diarist Anaïs Nin exchanged a series of particularly personal letters.[6] The group's first record, *Engine Takes to the Water,* in fact, unfolds not unlike Miller's career: after seeming to reference Miller's departure from first wife Beatrice in "Have a Safe Trip, Dear," the record offers listeners the paean "June Miller," whose nearly unintelligible lyrics eventually ask "Mona" to "restore ex-lover admiration"; the violent "Mindel," whose potential namesake Saul Mindel played a prominent role in defending Miller's publisher, Grove Press, against obscenity charges following its publication of D. H. Lawrence's *Lady Chatterley's Lover* and Miller's *Cancer;* and the reticent "Mooch," whose obsessive subject "is only in it for the work / And all he ever does is work." Finally, several punk and postpunk groups from disparate scenes have referenced Miller in their lyrics or liner notes, including Texas group At The Drive In, Sweden's Refused, and Baltimore's Candy Machine, who on its last record, *Tune International,* sing of a romance gone wrong being "translated by Henry Miller."[7]

Punk's affinity for Miller extends beyond recitation, however, emerging in the genre's jagged aesthetics and provocative politics. Like Miller, punks and postpunks have, from the start, sought a *lower* level of abstraction in their art, relying on obscenity and an often stylistic (if not literal) violence in articulating what feels to them like unspeakable social conditions. Rejecting the American approach to repression that he sensed as uniquely horrifying—"*always merry and bright!*"—Miller seems to have anticipated punk in calling his place of birth an "air-conditioned nightmare," and admitting in advance of the Sex Pistols that he wanted to see passersby—indeed his entire birthright—"destroyed, razed from top to bottom. I wanted to see this happen purely out of vengeance, as atonement for the crimes that were committed against me and against others like me who have never been able to lift their voices and express their hatred, their rebellion."[8] Furthermore, Miller's novels are less well-wrought masterpieces than impetuous, punky sketches of intellectually astute outsiders and threadbare rebels, himself included, who have discarded the status quo, particularly the market economy and the formal approach to art and knowledge. Or, as George Orwell put it, Miller is a "completely negative, unconstructive, amoral writer" (which was, of course, the point).[9] His scatological, sometimes dictated, and pastiche prose (Miller often intermingled biography, fiction, and dream content with news clippings and advertisements) is, as such, bombastic and crass, opposed to convention and cliché, seemingly "pointless," and reveling in its lack of revision—"I have made a silent compact with myself not to change a line of what I write" he once boasted.[10] Finally, Henry Miller, who, like punk, documents impatiently the boredom and banality of living, both describes repeatedly his own self-hate and adores music above all the arts, calling it "planetary fire, an irreducible which is all sufficient; it is the slate-writing of the gods."[11] But not just any music; Miller valorizes sound that screams and writhes, attacking the listener's very sense of self, rendering silent her spirit. Rejecting elegies, dirges, and anything approaching "pop," Miller endorsed, in perhaps the most ample definition of punk music ever articulated, sound as eschatology—music that made him feel as if "There's a madman inside me and he's hacking away, hacking and hacking until he strikes the final discord. *Pure annihilation*. . . . Nothing to be mopped up afterwards."[12]

Teasing out the thread that connects punk to Henry Miller, this chapter posits that punks have for decades looked to Miller as a model for not only their own anti-establishment aesthetics and politics but the self-injurious metaphysics of their romantic affairs. Seeing in Miller not just a literary and artistic template worth citing in song or to an interviewer, many punks have looked to Miller's relentlessly—if sometimes carelessly—fired ontological flares, particularly as they emerge in his relationship with June, as a guide for creating art and *love* in a culture wherein the refusal to tolerate the intolerable brands one as indecent, mad, or menacing. Specifically, it is in the violence and obscenity of Miller's prose and his agonizing and lost love for June that produced his obscenity and viciousness that the critic can see Henry and June as a prototype for many of the famously mutually abusive affairs that have both stereotyped and shaped punk culture for decades, from Sid and Nancy to Kurt and Courtney. In each case, one can see the attempt by marginalized ranters, fed-up and humiliated raw youth, and the walking wounded to explore the poverty of desire in the twentieth century not only by desiring poverty as such but by emphasizing what Alain Badiou once called the "agenda of contradictions and violence" embedded within "love" as an ontological posture.[13] So it is that "punk love" transforms its agents' depravity, shame, despair, and self-hate—all generated by the society in which punk is steeped—into art itself, making of masochism a genuine and aesthetically *productive* approach to being in a fragmented world in the throes of its own disintegration.

Henry and June

If Henry Miller serves as a touchstone for punks and postpunks around the globe, it is important to acknowledge first that it was Henry's second spouse who paved his coarse and crooked road to renown and remains an indispensable part of the calculus that birthed his prose and fame. Born Juliet Smerth in 1901 to a Roma family from the former Austro-Hungarian Empire, June Mansfield Smith would move to New York in 1906. A chance 1923 encounter in Manhattan brought Smith, now a dancer and self-styled courtesan who had a number of male "admirers" she insists never paid for her services, to Henry's door. Struck by June's beauty, her intellect, and the anarchism of her personality, Henry abandoned his first wife and daughter, inaugurating a decade-long affair that would convert a struggling writer, heretofore dismissed by the establishment, into the canonical author he is considered today—but only after June had abandoned him. "In the tomb which is my memory I see her buried now, the one I loved better than all else, better than the world, better than God, better than my own flesh and blood," Miller recalls longingly in *Tropic of Capricorn*, or, "the saga of June" as he later described the book to Nin and equating his love for June with the Hegelian wound that is its own balm.[14] "I see her festering there in that bloody wound of love, so close to me that I could not distinguish her from the wound itself."[15]

Serving as the signifier of several of Henry's desires simultaneously—sex and companionship, yes, but also freedom, a desire to annihilate the literary status quo and see America "razed from top to bottom"—the intrepid, mercurial, and self-governing June Miller, who was nobody's fool, unlocked the obscenity, violence, and blasphemy of both Henry's body and his writing, helping him clear away the suffocating debris of history, family, and culture to expose the truth for which not even Miller knew he was searching. She did so less through her presence than her sudden absence, however, cuckolding her husband by taking her lover Jean Kronski—who had been living in the Millers' flat—to France in 1927. "I thought, when I came upon her, that I was seizing hold of life," Miller continues in his novel, a decade after his desertion. "Instead I lost hold of life completely. I reached out for something to attach myself to—and I found nothing. But in reaching out . . . left high and dry as I was I nevertheless found something I had not looked for—*myself*."[16] Miller discovered himself only after the signifier of his desire had dissolved into the symbolic in what Lacan called the *aphanisis* (or fading) of the subject that coincides with the subject's reemergence in language as "meaning," in this case the *objet petit a* that is Miller's Obelisk trilogy. More precisely, June's disappearance forced Henry's febrile reconstruction of her on paper and thus her permanent eclipse as a subject by the object-novel that came to symbolize Henry's desire.

And not only Lacan, but Freud is at work in Miller's early fiction as well: although he loved her tremendously, June was also, in Henry's description, a controlling taskmaster who had made of him a despondent slave. Or, as a mousey Anaïs Nin put it in the middle of the affair she began with Henry in June's absence after Nin joined Henry in France, "More and more I realize that his life with June was a dangerous, shattering adventure"; "She humiliates him, she starves him, she breaks his health, she torments him."[17] Although Miller's fictionalization of the years Kronski lived with Henry and June in New York, *Crazy Cock*, best illustrates the torture Nin describes, she is here referencing *Cancer*, wherein "Mona" disapproves of Henry's friends, makes dates with him but fails to show, harasses him when she does keep a date—"Mona is losing her temper. Must have a bath. Must have this. Must have that. Must, must must"—and eventually abandons him altogether: "she left me here to perish . . . she put beneath my feet a great howling pit of emptiness."[18] Like a kick to the stomach, June's cold departure symbolized both the aphanisis that allowed Henry, alone, to sing out finally a vicious placeholder signifier in a voice that offended the reader with its obscenity and lust, *and* Freud's *The Ego and the Id*.

In this text from 1923 Freud not only argues that the size and severity of the subject's disciplinary superego directly relates to the ego's affection for its lost object of desire-authority—resulting ultimately in the subject's "need for punishment" and often its self-abuse—but contends that "for purposes of discharge the instinct of destruction [including of self] is habitually brought into the service of Eros."[19] That is to say, despite the humiliation and scorn he took from his spouse in her presence and his symbolization of her in his writing, Henry had come to *desire* punishment, signified in his lover, so far as it informed his ontological and aesthetic being, inflating his affection for this particular disciplinary master signifier in her absence, seeing its effect on his abject prose, which, flowing now, was also a sort of elegant self-punishment.

"This character Mona—she sposeduh be me? I struggled, suffered—fuh this?" Uma Thurman, as June, railed in Philip Kaufman's surreal picture *Henry & June*, waving the *Cancer* manuscript in her husband's face, her thick Long Island brogue nearly throwing Fred Ward's Henry from his chair. The question is a fair one: in creating the conditions for Henry's blossoming June had made *herself* into an object for another even in advance of the novels' publication, becoming an opium addict perhaps as a salve for having exchanged money for sex as she sought out wealthy suitors to support Henry as he dedicated himself to writing. "You make everything ugly! Beauty is a joke to you. You're so negative. You're a failure as a writer! You're not a man—you're a *child*!" Thurman hollers, all at once understanding how her subjectivity had been eclipsed—erased—in the symbolic order by a man who even in that moment seemed to find pleasure in her disapproval. "As Nietzsche said somewhere—'you have to first learn to love before you destroy,' or something to that effect," Miller wrote Nin in 1932 with a nervous smirk. And so did he continue to love his tormentor, all the while seething and itching at the opportunity to demolish, through his art, all the institutions he was taught to cherish that had rewarded his fealty with castration and humiliation: democracy, the free market, the publishing industry, family, love, the Judeo-Christian tradition, and most crucially, himself.[20]

Such a scenario would play itself out in a variety of ways with the irruption of punk in Miller's wake. Consider Miller's wardrobe. As Nin writes, Henry's proto-punk couture was shabby at best and mirrored the "brutality of his writing." For Nin, Henry's "stained hat and the hole in his coat," his "frayed suit," as drafty as Baudelaire's pants, are bound up with his prose. Rather, the paucity of Miller's attire cannot be separated from either his irreverent and septic novels or "his desire for punishment" in Freud's words. For even this style, Nin documents, originated with Henry's love for his wife. "June had a hole in her sleeve," writes Nin admiringly of the woman who initially shocked her for donning, in public, torn and stained dresses and hosiery, "June, who is not afraid of poverty and drabness." Obsessing over the crude American couple, whom Nin literally sees cannibalizing each other, the highborn diarist soon adopted apparel that too anticipated punk's safety-pinned and tattered style, acknowledging, "I am happiest in my black velvet dress because it is old and is torn at the elbows." Nin is here simulating Henry's and June's self-hate *as* art, a politically radical aesthetic form—embodied in the artist—which retains the ability to speak truth to and about not only power but Nature and self, Freud notwithstanding.[21]

Shabbiness, for the Millers, was itself a proto-punk refusal of capitalism and the bourgeois, effete intellectual class, a self-assailing, sexualized rejection of Romanticism *and* modernism and the post–Great War decadence that swarmed all around them in the 1920s despite the limbs that had been left in the mud only a few years before. It was a show of solidarity, even, with the Dust Bowl refugees and smudge-faced urchins of Miller's youth that were emerging even before the Roaring

Twenties came to a crashing end in 1929. His personal life mirroring the Great Depression, embodying the collateral damage of a market crash and symbolizing the emasculation he suffered under June, democracy, and capitalism, Miller thus *became* the Depression, inscribing the Fall in advance of Steinbeck's *The Grapes of Wrath,* whose author Miller considered pretentious. As such, Miller's body of work too serves as the proceedings of his existence with June, a life that fed on humiliation, insolence, emotional abuse, and violence, translating these experiences into signifiers that would shake up the literary world and inspire generations of future poets, outcasts, and cranks.

More specifically, Miller's saber-toothed prose and self-deprecating schizoanalysis served as a road map for a new generation of young musicians who began where Miller effectively ended. Having grown tired of the anomie and alienation that emerged alongside postwar capitalism in the West, particularly with regard to the inauthentic and contemptible youth-rock "counterculture" that was being sold to kids in the middle 1970s on both sides of the Atlantic, punks saw in Miller an escape from the paralyzing effects of glass-eyed decorum and consumer spectacle amid record unemployment, the perpetual threats of economic recession, environmental collapse, and nuclear apocalypse—and a willfully cynical entertainment industry that was ignoring each of these realities by peddling to pop fans little more than the Osmonds, disco, "prog" rock, and obsolete '60s icons (David Bowie notwithstanding). This escape route would be lit by both explosive and implosive violence, gratuitous vulgarity, and severe noise by teenagers fed up also with a hippy subculture too self-righteous or dazed and confused to recognize that it had merely replicated the social order it was ostensibly admonishing. As the Sex Pistols had frequently put it, "Never trust a hippy," to which Washington, DC's Teen Idles responded, in "Deadhead" from the first Dischord Records single in 1981, "Early to rise, early to bed / the only good deadhead is one that's dead!" Across time and place, punks have detested hippies, both references suggest, because they saw the call to tune in and drop out, to engage in "free love," as selfishly and licentiously apolitical—as an astoundingly naive ideological move. Rather than picking up the Youngbloods' egalitarian psalm "Get Together," *which seemed to have missed Miller's critique entirely,* groups like the sardonically named Flowers of Romance expressed if not a calculated loathing of self and Other, then a passionless anti-emotion: "I'm totally numb" Flowers drummer Sid Vicious would put it to the punk fanzine *SKUM* (not to be confused with Valerie Solanas's Society for Cutting Up Men) a year before he joined the Sex Pistols to perform songs like "No Feelings." "I'm more of robot than a person . . . I don't work on an emotional level."[22]

Following Miller's lead, whose response to the Romantic hedonism that had preceded his own version of modernism was to demystify sex, love, and the sublime with a "primitive honesty" as Nin puts it in her preface to *Cancer,* the anti-hippy punk reply was not only to see these phenomena for what they were—awkward, bestial, and embarrassing—but to seek out abuse as much as "love," and to *superimpose* the two. As the producers of New York's original *Punk* magazine declared in their January 1976 issue, "We don't believe in love or any of that shit."[23] Or, describing intercourse as "two minutes of squelchy noises . . . clumsy and deeply confusing," Rotten would go on to parrot Miller's take on June, writing that the woman who would become his wife, Ari Up's mother Nora Forster, "was so cruel, and I love cruel women."[24] Adding that he too seems to find himself only in the company of callous and dishonest females, Rollins would adopt Miller's mode of seeing in the feminine Other a signifier of his own desire for abuse, describing in his journal (a handful of pages after denying a rape accusation leveled at him from a woman in San Francisco) a dream wherein a young woman feigns interest in the singer before publicly emasculating him: "I remember a few girls who were like that. I remember this one girl. She said all kinds of nasty stuff about me to people. Luckily for me, I'm sub-human so this kind of thing just rolls off."[25] To these examples Los Angeles's Offspring add "Self-Esteem," their 1990s version of the self-hating punk masochist who continues to engage in abusive and manipulative couplings literally in spite of himself:

> When she's saying O! that she wants only me
> Then I wonder why she sleeps with my friends.
> When she's saying O! that I'm like a disease
> Then I wonder how much more I can spend.

"Well I guess I should stick up for myself / But I really think it's better this way / The more you suffer the more it shows you really care, right?" Offspring singer Dexter Holland concludes, directing the question more at himself than any sympathetic ear and too finding a certain libidinal satisfaction in his own mistreatment. In expressing such views, asking such degrading questions, and drawing attention to self-abuse, publicly and repeatedly, punks—both literally and politically the hippies' offspring—echoed Miller in shattering the image of the especial or hallowed nature of sex, romance, and a drug-induced sense of peace and love that not only the flower children, but, indeed, the culture industry generally had worked so hard to craft in the 1960s and 1970s—burying Miller in so doing.

Sid and Nancy

Seeing their hippy predecessors as having missed Miller's point, as verifying Walter Benjamin's dictum that behind every expression of fascism (for the punks, Reagan, Thatcher, and an emerging fundamentalist

Christianity) is a failed revolution, punks grabbed hold of Miller, finding particularly useful his recognition of the productive, enlightening, libidinally satisfying consequences of riveting oneself to another being whose ostensible love is simultaneously *destructive*, and how the debris of such a relationship might be reassembled into a new symbolic object. Although there is much in Iggy Pop's history worth exploring in this regard, or even in the short-lived, mutually abusive union of Dee Dee and Connie Ramone (who at one point knifed Dee Dee), there is no better case study of the punk desire for abuse than Sid Vicious and Nancy Spungen. The chronicle of the two—and all of its banalities—is well known. What is too often ignored in analyses of the couple, however, is how Sid's commitment to the woman who by all accounts harassed and abused him constantly, harping on and embarrassing the former bassist publicly and privately, was for the Sex Pistol an indispensable, constructive part of both his art and his punk ontology. Moreover, viewing Sid and Nancy *through* Henry and June gives lie to the hackneyed, misogynist reading of Spungen as some punk Yoko Ono who "deserved" her violent end or brought it upon herself, an attitude that remains current among many punks and postpunks, including, it seems, John Lydon.

A handsome, shy youth, John Simon Ritchie had lost, and thus internalized, two fathers before age ten. Left to navigate adolescence with his itinerant, ex-hippy mum Anne Beverley, who introduced her son to amphetamines, Sid began squatting and hanging out at Malcolm McLaren and Vivienne Westwood's boutique by age seventeen. To hear his friend Johnny Rotten tell it, Sid's interest in *SEX* and punk was, at least initially, sartorial. Sid was "an absolute fashion victim," wrote Lydon years after his friend's death—a lonely kid from a broken home who transformed his (dead) parents' neglect into a rather stylish self-hate. Seeing in punk an opportunity to further mask the control a terribly harsh superego had over him, Sid joined the Flowers of Romance with Viv Albertine before replacing Glen Matlock as Pistols bassist in 1977. In Lydon's view, the change in Sid's demeanor—cutting himself, constantly initiating brawls with footballers much larger than him, experimenting with heroin—while evident once he joined the band, grew particularly extreme after he began dating Spungen: "He disliked himself so much that he did the worst possible thing he could have ever done—hook up with that beast Nancy Spungen."[26]

One year Vicious's younger, the Pennsylvania-born Spungen was raised by middle-class Jewish parents in suburban Philadelphia. Highly intelligent—and possibly schizophrenic—Spungen was remembered by her mother as an extremely difficult child. Stretched to the breaking point by her erratic and violent daughter, Deborah Spungen effectively disinherited Nancy in her 1983 memoir, *And I Don't Want to Live This Life*, confessing, "We were desperately unhappy. . . . One night in bed, Frank and I actually discussed changing all the locks on the house after [Nancy] went out. . . . We realized she'd simply break a ground-floor window and get back in."[27] The Spungens got their wish, however. At age seventeen Nancy left home for New York City, where, before recasting herself as a professional groupie, she was a stripper and prostitute. "Nancy was in the S&M room," remembers photographer Bob Gruen (who accompanied the Pistols on their American tour) of the brothel where Spungen worked. "She would wear black leather garters and beat German bankers for money."[28] Nicknamed "Nauseating Nancy" by a sniping New York punk scene, Spungen to this day is remembered ignobly as the whining, tantrum-throwing harpy, the yang to David Berkowitz's yin during New York's Summer of Sam who, wearing out her welcome in the city, followed Richard Hell's Heartbreakers to London. Failing to seduce the Heartbreakers and Lydon, Spungen found the authentic, unconditional love she felt was denied her since childhood in

Vicious, who also represented the embodiment of Spungen's own desire for punishment.

"Sid and Nancy were great. They had a genuine affection for each other. I mean, there was that 'punk love' where they would put each other down . . . but it was real," former Television manager Terry Ork adds almost sentimentally. "You could tell there was a deep run of affection there. And you could also tell that Sid was like a fish out of water. He didn't have a clue about the big bad world really. He was like a child that depended on Nancy."[29] Or as Nora Forster put it, "Sid totally believed in her." Although he "beat her up so badly," Forster suggests too that Vicious acted as such in response to the abuse he suffered from Spungen, as part of some reciprocal, *necessary* arrangement.[30] Note especially Ork's categorization of a specific type of Eros—*punk love*—founded on a mutual desire for abuse: a collaborative, coequal "taking the piss." But punk love, modeled on the Millers, goes well beyond mere piss-taking, beyond sadomasochism, sliding comfortably into a handful of Freudian notions—most obviously his theory on the economic problem of masochism. Tapping into the (self-) violence-as-creativity meme punks find in Miller, both Forster and Ork too comment on not only the apparent seriousness of Sid and Nancy's relationship, but how its authenticity coincided with its *rational* and intentional indignity and ideological clarity.

For all its faults, then, this is what Alex Cox's dramatization of the relationship gets right: *Sid and Nancy* as a new *Henry and June*—the pair's love and death as the aesthetic, political, and ontological progression that the Woodstock Generation squandered, in its proto-fascist hedonism, and even Miller failed to sustain (becoming mostly a parody of himself after his initial burst of post-June prose). Early in the film, for example, there is a scene reproducing the Pistols' Brechtian performance on the Thames in mock celebration of the queen's Jubilee.

After the barge hauling the punk band and their mates is forced to dock, police board the vessel and attempt to detain—truncheons in hand—the frantically disembarking punks. Amid the chaos, Gary Oldman's pitch-perfect Sid Vicious and his American lover (played wonderfully by Chloe Webb, who had beat out Courtney Love for the title role) saunter casually off the boat and away from the melee, arms around each other, as one-by-one their colleagues—McLaren, Rotten—are handcuffed and escorted off-camera. The pair seems immune to the madness overtaking the nation in 1977, walking targets shielded at least for the moment by their brutal affection for each other, double negatives multiplying into something positive, even *protective*, through their self-loathing and codependence.

Jetting across the sea, the ramshackle pair later kiss passionately in some filthy New York alley, Sid pushing Nancy up against a dumpster as trash falls slowly from the sky around the lovers, missing them but leaving a decaying mess all around. It is here—America—that Sid tries hard to console an increasingly despondent Nancy, who has already told him that she no longer finds life worth living, particularly in a nation filled with little more than garbage. "Things'll be much better when we get to America," Sid quips hopefully in a paroxysm of volubility, smoking and nodding off in a grimy Hotel Chelsea suite. "*Siiiiiiiid*! We're *in* America!" Nancy shrieks back, realizing precipitously the depth of not only her own despair but her lover's stupefaction. Out of this traumatic realization would bloom, quite logically, the pair's conviction that their only solution, if they take not only their own rhetoric but their punk love, their *desire*, seriously, is death. So does a suicide pact come into being, and Cox imagines Nancy's stabbing by Sid as not intentional, yet not entirely accidental. Waking from a drug-induced phantasmagoria to find Nancy slumped under the bathroom sink in a pool of blood, a distraught Simon Ritchie would, less than a year after his lover's death, be cold, stiff, and bare himself, the former fashion victim becoming instead the pale incorporation of English historian Thomas Fuller's proverb, "Craft must have clothes, but Truth loves to go naked."

"I've been with Sid ever since the first day I ever got to England," Spungen explains in Lech Kowalski's 1980 documentary *D.O.A.* "And we're partners in crime. And we have good fun. We help each other out, you know." Recorded a few short weeks before her death, Spungen is in these scenes remembering Arthur Penn's *Bonnie and Clyde*—"They're young. They're in love. They kill people" read the poster for the film that romanticized the simultaneous death of love-struck vagrants—and understanding too how punk's attack on capitalism and the cultural status quo would probably kill them. Partners in crime, indeed: the clip is at first hilarious—Spungen cursing out a lethargic Vicious for burning her clumsily with his fag—then horrifying as the viewer realizes what would become of the woman who begins singing "Sid and Nancy at home" with a sad informality, recognizing the absurdly domestic, resigned quality of the scene in which the rubber-shirted addict eventually disrobes, without a thought for the roving camera as Vicious stares at her breasts. It is at this point that two abject subjects—abandoned by the external superegos that are their families and dismissed as pop burnouts in way over their heads by the crumbling culture that birthed them only to castrate them—took the self-hate, anger, and spectacle they had been fed their whole lives by the same firms that had appropriated the flower children and turned it, through a communal, inspired desire for abuse, into punk itself. Having already embodied punk as a cultural scheme, the couple soon took Miller's Freudian system—gratuitous violence, threadbare garments, mutual abuse as satisfying a libidinal need, and obscenity *founded on love and loss* as the source of new creation—to its logical conclusion: the annihilation of self. In this way the pair turned themselves into the signifiers of their own desire for punishment, the faded subjects eclipsed by the tabloid ink spilled over their "grotesque" coupling. Dead On Arrival. And although many postmortem accounts of the affair cast Sid and Nancy as a "punk *Romeo and Juliet*," a more fitting dramatic reference would be *Antigone*, wherein Spungen, the anti-matriarch and rebel sympathizer, rails against all symbolic law and politesse, suffering ultimately a public humiliation that leads to her private death. Finding his lover's body, Vicious plays the father-flouting Heamon, who falls on his sword rather than live without his fellow hysteric Antigone, an act duplicated by Anne Beverley's Eurydice, who mimed her son in overdosing on heroin in 1996, the same year the Sex Pistols re-formed without Sid for their "Filthy Lucre" world tour.

There had been deaths, even suicides, in punk before, of course; what made the passing of Sid and Nancy different was not only its integrity but the casualness with which the couple's conspirators reacted to the news. "It didn't seem to mean anything to me," Lydon admits with a trace of Catholic guilt in a statement that would have horrified Sophocles. "It's funny, that. I kept thinking, Should I feel something here? I didn't."[31] Or as Jon Savage put it, "If cynicism had greeted the death of Nancy Spungeon, then the reaction to the death of Sid Vicious was all the more terrible because it seemed so *expected*."[32] Expectations notwithstanding, the deaths of Sid and Nancy differed from earlier punk deaths in their channeling of the Millers. Vicious's attraction to that which could only hurt him, his astounding internalization of the superego and thus his commitment to his punk desire for annihilation, converted a heretofore mild-mannered boy into a sulphur-breathing embodiment of mutiny and refusal to tolerate the intolerable—not simply a *signifier* of the chaos, self-hate, and implosion cultivated by so-called civilization, but that implosion itself. In so doing, Vicious performed the most definite, absolute, even obvious punk act, the one Lydon (like

Miller) only condescendingly recommended his audience do at Winterland when he screamed "Be a man! Kill yourself!" to the American assembly. And the subculture has yet to come to grips with the ontological and political consequences of such expectations among its adherents. "We always knew that we would go to the same place when we died. We so much wanted to die together in each other's arms. I cry every time I think about that," Vicious, working on an emotional level after all, wrote to Deborah Spungen after her daughter's death. He is at this point out-Millering Henry Miller. "I promised my baby that I would kill myself if anything ever happened to her, and she promised me the same. This is my final commitment to my [punk] love."[33]

Love Will Tear Us Apart

Such words demonstrate the naked truth of punk: not only is punk's obscenity, self-hate, and destruction the result of its internalization of its abandonment and abuse by its parent culture and hippy predecessors, but that taking the piss (and having one's piss taken) serves as a satisfaction of punks' desire at the micropolitical level. Vicious's confession thus signals punk's reification of Freud, who not only associates the body's consciousness of pain with erotogenicity in *The Ego and the Id* and "On Narcissism: An Introduction," but in "The Economic Problem of Masochism," seems to envisage both Miller and punk in describing the varieties of masochism observable by the analyst: erotogenic, feminine, and moral. Combining the first two categories—since in studying the cases "one quickly discovers that [all types] place the subject in a characteristically female situation; they signify, that is, being castrated, or copulated with"—Freud postulates that the most significant of the three masochisms is moral, given both its frequent conclusion in suicide and its association with the subject's internalization of the disciplinary Name of the Father. In this last, as we have seen with Dostoevsky, the subject's monstrous superego has gone off the rails in response to its loss of an external object of desire, resulting in a subject that is "under the domination" of the superego and that expresses a certain *need* for punishment. In any case, Freud argues that all forms of masochism suffer from a particular economic conundrum: the subject's libidinal satisfaction in the service of Eros is directly joined to its death drive, its self-abuse. As Freud puts it, the irony of masochism lies in the fact that "even the subject's destruction of himself cannot take place without libidinal satisfaction." To be exact, for such subjects suicide not only serves to satisfy a certain longing, but may even be understood as "pleasurable."[34]

Few punk affiliates understand this notion better than Deborah Curtis. If Sid and Nancy represented punk's Bonnie and Clyde, its *Antigone,* the story of Ian and Deborah Curtis is closer to punk's version of *Samson and Delilah*. In 1975, at age nineteen, a would-be poet, self-hating Jim Morrison fan, and son of a policeman from Manchester married a woman named Deborah—whose namesake also plays a prominent role in the Hebrew Bible's bloody Book of Judges—after a brief courtship. Bored by the factory and civil service work that residents of heavily depressed northern England were lucky to find in the middle 1970s, Ian Curtis, who had always carried himself with an annoying air of destiny, saw punk as a way out. Ignoring Deborah's skepticism, the baritone-voiced teenager formed the punky Warsaw with three fellow Greater Mancunians in 1976. Realizing that fans and promoters were confusing the group with London's Warsaw Pakt, the troupe recast its glum melodies, morose lyrics, and fascination with Nazi culture into Joy Division, a reference to the Third Reich's concentration camp–stationed detachment of sex slaves. Jawbone in hand, Curtis and his band came to recognize—and thus exercise—the power of their music, taking Manchester, and soon London, by storm, playing on Tony Wilson's "Grenada Reports" program, releasing records on Wilson's Factory label, and soon outshining both Manchester's original punk product, the Buzzcocks, and Lydon's second act Public Image Ltd. Saddled with a newborn daughter and diagnosed with a worsening epilepsy just as his fame was growing, Curtis fell in with a skeletal Belgian attaché named Annik Honoré before bringing down the Temple he had built in May 1980, hanging himself on the eve of his group's departure for its first American tour as Iggy Pop's *The Idiot* played on the turntable nearby.

In her memoir *Touching from a Distance*, Deborah Curtis, both bitter and keeping an astonishing equanimity in the wake of Ian's suicide, nevertheless seems to go out of her way to recast her husband's infidelity, his self-abuse and violence, interpersonally or on vinyl, as an expression of his love for her and their daughter. In a letter Ian wrote her shortly before his suicide, Deborah says, the singer "talked of our life together, romance and passion; his love for me, his love for [our daughter] Natalie." At memoir's end she likewise describes how she can see, in her daughter's eyes, "how warm and loved I felt when [Ian] and I were sixteen." Such love was not only coupled with but likely a product of, the widow feels, a crippling obsession with anguish and desire for abuse that the bobby's son had for years cultivated: "He seemed to have a great deal of hate inside that was always directed at those closest to him," Deborah writes, remembering Ian's impropriety, the bruises on his body after Joy Division shows, his almost paranoid secrecy, and his irrational jealousy. "Hanging himself was only the final act in his plot of self-destruction." So it is, in Deborah's retelling, that Ian's marriage, his love, was both prelude to and reagent for his tortuous self-abuse; and it was out of this flagellating love, out of the notion anticipated by

Nietzsche, Freud, and Miller that a contrite-if-spiteful self-abuse was an act of love, of wish-fulfillment, that the idea of not only Joy Division but punk itself emerged.[35]

Such an idea, writes Deborah, was firmly embedded in her husband's constitution. Books on Nazism notwithstanding, the writing that consumed much of the singer's youth was primarily that of Dostoevsky, Nietzsche, Sartre, Hermann Hesse, and J. G. Ballard. "It struck me that all Ian's spare time was spent reading and thinking about human suffering," Deborah recalls. "I knew he was looking for inspiration for his songs, yet the whole thing was culminating in an unhealthy obsession with mental and physical pain."[36] And although there is little evidence Henry Miller was on Ian's reading list, Curtis's life and work bear a remarkable resemblance to the American writer: a doubting spouse in the process of leaving her husband, an adoring-if-badgering mistress, a refusal to paper over all that is ugly and brutal in the world, and a commitment to annihilation "as a fertilizing rather than a destructive event" as Ballard once put it, taking the words from Miller's foul mouth.[37] It is here, then, at the intersection of death and love, art and desire that Ian and Deborah too met Henry and June.

There is no better exhibit of such a statement than Joy Division's "Love Will Tear Us Apart," the pop version of Nietzsche's "you have to first learn to love before you destroy"—of Lacan's division of the subject into fading and meaning—and the phrase Ian's widow, in a final irony, chiseled into his gravestone after her husband had dissolved.[38] The song is not entirely timeless, though. From Bernard Sumner's keynote to the song's awkward fade, the melody becomes cemented to something periodized, even dismissed, today as "the Eighties"—MTV, synthesizers, coiffed manes atop androgynous, impassive pop faces. But the song is also a powerful, jarring burst of metaphysics, a paring down of Miller's Nietzsche reference and direct assault on love unmatched by any of

Joy Division's antecedents or contemporaries. "Why is the bedroom so cold? You've turned away on your side," Curtis wonders drearily, his voice ending the line nearly an octave below where it began. "Is my timing that flawed? Our *respect* runs so dry." Listening to the words today, hearing Curtis equate love with contempt, it is easy to envision an intense twenty-year-old paging through his dog-eared copies of not only *The Antichrist* or Ballard's *The Atrocity Exhibition*—the latter including the entry "Love and Napalm: Export U.S.A." and becoming the title of a Joy Division song—but Henry Miller's affront to love and American exceptionalism, *The Air-Conditioned Nightmare*. Anticipating the English song, Miller had left punk a breadcrumb trail years earlier, arguing as the original Joy Division was being dehumanized across Europe that "in the prison of life love takes on every form of mockery. *Are you suffering, little man?*"[39] Miller's logic would not have been not lost on Curtis, who, answering Miller's question in the affirmative, began dashing off fragmented and frantic words that remain some of the best in '80s pop from any genre: "And there's a taste in my mouth / As desperation takes hold / Just that something so good / Just can't function no more."

So does love tear Curtis apart. Surfacing as an afterthought to Sid and Nancy, however, the story of Ian and Deborah Curtis is but an interlude, a set-up for a third frayed punk couple who aped Henry and June in creating out of their mutual self-hating punk love a series of fragmented signifiers of their desire for punishment. If Terry Ork was right in identifying Sid and Nancy as the source of the type of love that thrived on self-hate and ontological cannibalism in the late twentieth century, it is Kurt Cobain and the uncannily named Courtney Love who extended the life of that philosophy nearly into the twenty-first century. By all accounts, Kurt and Courtney's torrid courtship, which began with a wrestling match on a barroom floor, was equal parts affectionate and punitive, less Samson and Delilah than *Salome*. "You better love me, you fucker," the woman born Courtney Michelle Harrison to Grateful Dead historian Hank Harrison once demanded of her blonde John the Baptist in a bit of graffiti scrawled in lipstick, bound with a heart, on her bedroom wall, to which Kurt would later respond, only moments after emerging from a failed suicide induced by a champagne-Rohypnol cocktail, "Fuck you. Get these fucking tubes out of my nose."[40] Such volleys were consistently paired with both seemingly sincere expressions of love by the couple, as in Kurt's admission to *Sassy* magazine in 1992 that "at times I even forget that I'm in a band, I'm so blinded by love," and their mutual admissions of *self*-hate.[41] "Well, here you are as ugly as me / Drill it in my good holes so that I can see," Love had sung in "Babydoll" from her band's debut album *Pretty On the Inside* as Cobain was working hard on convincing his band to christen what would be Nirvana's final album *I Hate Myself and Want to Die*.[42]

In these candid admissions one can almost smell, if not Ian and Deborah, certainly the punk twosome who more than a decade earlier had also loved each other to death. For almost any observer—those in the commercial mass media in particular—the temptation to connect Sid and Nancy to Kurt and Courtney was irresistible: Love looked and acted like Spungen and Cobain's heroin use and self-injurious demeanor were common knowledge. As *Vanity Fair* had gushed in 1992, in an article that accused Love of shooting heroin when pregnant with the pair's daughter, "Are Courtney Love, lead diva of the postpunk band Hole, and her husband, Nirvana heartthrob Kurt Cobain, the grunge John and Yoko? Or the next Sid and Nancy?"[43] Feigning fatigue with such associations, Kurt, sounding both indignant and resigned, complained, "It's just amazing that at this point in rock-and-roll history, people are still expecting their rock icons to live out these classic rock archetypes, like Sid and Nancy. To assume that we're just the same because we did heroin for a while—it's pretty offensive to be expected to be like that."[44]

As Cobain knew by this point, however, his and Love's association with Sid and Nancy was no mere media creation; Cobain is here mystifying the fact that both rockers had cultivated the connection intentionally, if perhaps ironically. Their mutual heroin use and punk personae notwithstanding, by 1992 Cobain, who like Vicious felt a profound shame in his parents' divorce, was reserving hotel rooms under the name "Simon Ritchie" (and had admitted that when he first met Love he "thought that she looked like Nancy Spungen").[45] Like the original punk couple, Kurt and Courtney too seemed as explosive and self-destructive as their forebears, antagonizing both fans and the record industry in a very public way. According to Cobain, he had fully intended, like the Sex Pistols, to "pose as the enemy to infiltrate the mechanics of the system to start its rot from the inside."[46] Furthermore, Cobain mirrored Vicious in being a fragile and painfully shy—if strikingly handsome—child of a broken home who had a terrible relationship with his father. Having discovered drugs and finding himself homeless as a teenager, Cobain too fell in with all manner of punks, misfits, and other members of the Aderdeen, Washington, underclass. Persistently and self-destructively rebellious, Kurt took his friends' admonitions to avoid Love both as evidence that she was the signifier for which he had been searching and as another opportunity to assert his autonomy, his symbolic opposition to and internalization of what Lacan called the big Other.

For Love's part, in a confrontational audition tape for *Sid and Nancy,* which failed to win her the female lead (earning her instead the role of Spungen's "best friend," Gretchen), Love virtually threatened Alex Cox: "You *should* pick me for Nancy, I mean, there is nobody else. I'm not going to leave you alone [until you cast me]," Love portends in a widely available video, ultimately asserting, "I *am* Nancy Spungen!" Even before auditioning for the role, Love had refined Spungen's style and been not only a stripper, rock groupie, and actor, but a very difficult child. Reading Deborah Spungen's *And I Don't Want to Live This Life* alongside the memoir penned by Love's mother, Linda Carroll, in fact, makes Love's claim to *be* a resurrected Nancy harder to laugh away. Witness the parallelism of both mothers' recollection of their daughters' toddler years:

> I began to carry [Nancy] to her stroller. In response she screamed at me angrily, her face turning bright red. I cuddled her. She reacted by suddenly stiffening her body like a board, arms and legs thrust out straight, head thrown back. She screamed even louder. I tried to relax her limbs but she fought me. . . . I tried to get her into her stroller—*bend* her in, really. She continued to fight me. I finally got her in, so stiff she was almost standing.[47]

> She woke up screaming, "No, daddy, no!" It was virtually impossible to soothe her afterward. The more I tried, the more she would stiffen, arching her back and resisting as though my touch were painful.[48]

The girls' shared stiffening aside, the grunge couple's adult relationship mimed both Sid and Nancy and Henry and June in being punctuated by what seemed to those closest to them and to journalists covering pop to be a reciprocal predilection for expressing love through self-hate and violence.

"[I've] read so many pathetic, second rate, Freudian evaluations from interviews, regarding our personalities and especially how im a notoriously fucked up heroine addict, alcoholic, self destructive, yet overly sensitive,frail,meek, fragile,compassionate, soft spoken, narcoleptic,

NEUROTIC,little,piss ant," Cobain, fed up finally, wrote with rage in his journal as his fame grew, "because I CANT HANDLE THE SUCCESS! OH THE SUCCESS! THE GUILT! THE GUILT!"[49] While it is unlikely Cobain had read much Freud, his admission of the "Freudian" nature of his character suggests a tacit recognition that for the masochist self-harm *is* love, is pleasurable in a problematic way. Such an idea saturates not only his marriage but both performers' art, documented in not only Love's lyrics—"I love him so much it just turns to hate" Love sings on "Doll Parts" from Hole's *Live through This*—but Cobain's emaciated journaling and songwriting. "She eyes me like a Pisces when I am weak," Cobain had written in "Heart-Shaped Box" from *In Utero*. Set in a hospital, Anton Corbijn's unsettling, poppy-strewn video for the song captures exquisitely the entire record's framing of love as a sort of disease that ultimately kills the subject: "I wish I could eat your cancer when you turn black." The song—much of the album in fact—is a coded enunciation of Cobain's craving for the cruelty of his spouse, who likewise had claimed in a journal that due to his having been born a Pisces, Cobain was "the object of my intense desires and repulsions at once."[50] This is all to say that with "Heart-Shaped Box," specifically, Cobain articulates, literally, his sense of having been degraded by Love from a subject into the object-cause of another's desire: he is the impossible Real trapped inside an objet petit a, shaped like a heart, whose protestations ooze out of the uterus in an effort to document his own fading as a subject. So did he, in response, follow Miller's lead and compose a place-holding signifier-song about his own Mona, ultimately demanding that she "throw down your umbilical noose so I can climb right back." Suicide would soon follow, leaving only the songs behind as signifiers for a person and relationship that had faded into meaning.

"Heart-Shaped Box" notwithstanding, the sonics, violence, and politics of *In Utero* caught many fans and journalists off guard. Clearing the pop landscape in 1993, the record bolted past the group's breakthrough *feminist* record *Nevermind* with songs like the sardonic "Rape Me," "Pennyroyal Tea" (which Cobain had cowritten with Love), and "Milk It," wherein Cobain mumbles "I am my own parasite / I don't need a host to live" over his noodling guitar, eventually reminding Love that "we feed off of each other." Giving these songs texture was the album's cover art—Cobain's own—which includes a series of pastiche works featuring piles of frozen bones, yawning pink fetuses, and perforated wombs nestled among all manner of flora, orchids in particular. So it is that the Kurt Cobain of *In Utero* is "riven by contradictions," wrote John Mulvey in a review of the record for England's *New Musical Express*, "so embarrassed by his touchingly blatant love for Courtney that he has to dress it up in doubt and infected imagery."[51] Mulvey is half right. On display in the record was less Cobain's embarrassed love for Love than his construction of her through music as a signifier for his own desire for abuse. As we have seen, by reading Ian and Deborah and Sid and Nancy through Freud, through Henry Miller, there is no contradiction in any of this. Or, as Cobain concludes quite judiciously at the record's end, "I'm married / Buried."

Indeed, as Cobain had already groaned in "Aneurysm," from his group's third album, *Incesticide*, "[I] Love you so much, it makes me sick," sounding very much like a contemporary Henry Miller, whose own health, according to Nin, was put to the test during his time with June. Even if the line was not directed at Love, having allegedly been penned for Bikini Kill drummer Tobi Vail, it anticipates *In Utero*, which shares much with Freud and Miller in terms of its corporal themes, contempt for consumerism, association of love with death, and self-deprecating narcissism, setting the stage for Cobain's ambiguously feminist-masochist parting words (in both "All Apologies" and the posthumously released "You Know You're Right") and his self-inflicted parting shot. It was Miller, after all, who had claimed in 1939 that "[I] suffered primarily because I was too honest, too sincere, too truthful, too generous."[52] As Cobain confessed to his journal in reply, "Have you ever felt like you cared so much that you wanted to kill everything?"—later striking out "everything" and replacing it with "your germs"—not long before theorizing in his final suicide note, "I think I simply love people too much. So much that it makes me feel too fucking sad."[53] It is no exaggeration, then, to claim that like Sid Vicious and Ian Curtis, *love killed Kurt Cobain.* Not Courtney Love—as was and remains the accusation of many distraught fans, paranoid Cobain colleagues, filmmakers, and lazy music journalists—but the lowercase signifier, which Cobain had identified as the source of many of his physical ailments and addictions.[54]

"I think I simply love people too much": such words would be the last penned by a bitter celebrity who had documented the interplay between his desire for destruction and his surplus love in dozens of journals over the course of his short life. Overflowing with short fiction, surrealist sketches and comics, news clippings, and pages of cultural commentary, the notebooks that remain seethe with a disgusted bitterness that Miller would have appreciated: the hatred for capitalism and "gluttony," a violent desire to smite what he called the American political establishment's "terrorist" mien, a repeated rejection of God, and an equally fascinated-ashamed celebration of biology and the blunt truth of human sexual relations—afterbirth, semen, blood, bile. For the reader taking in years' worth of Cobain's thought in a single sitting, it becomes easy to confuse the singer with if not a young Charles Bukowski, the lower-shelf punk animus who had detailed in *Women* his own masochism and self-hate in exploring what he called "slug love" (and whom Cobain cites in a piece of fiction from his journals), then an aging Henry Miller.[55] "It's hard to decipher the difference between a sincere entertainer and an honest swindler," Cobain sighs: "I've violently vomited to the point of my stomach literally turning itself inside out to show you the fine hairlike nerves I've kept and raised as my children, garnishing and marinating Each one as if God had fucked me and planted these precious little eggs and I parade them around in peacock victory and maternal pride like a whore relieved from the duties of repeated rape and torture, promoted to a more dignified Job of just plain old every day, good old, wholesome prostitution. My feathers are my pussy."[56]

So it is that, in the end, Sid and Nancy are a less useful referent for Kurt and Courtney than Henry and June. "She's wearing black stockings with runs in them, a vintage dress that's a size too small," wrote Lynn Hirschberg, sounding like a fawning Anaïs Nin in her smarmy *Vanity Fair* piece that inadvertently linked Love to a tattered and torn June Miller: "[The English press] adored her grunge-rock sound and her torn thirties tea dresses." Or, as Love's lawyer Rosemary Carroll put it to Hirschberg, speaking of the woman who was married in a decomposing white dress that had once belonged to 1930s American film star Frances Farmer, "The first time I saw her onstage, she was dressed like a soiled debutante. Her dress was ripped and she was a mess except for a perfectly pressed huge pink bow on the back of her dress. She was riveting to watch." Love's style notwithstanding, Carroll's comments show just how Love's persona draws heavily, if unconsciously, upon June's nondescript "feminism": a strong female in a ripped dress unafraid to exploit her sexuality and earn her own wage, stand ferociously up for herself, and retain an unapologetically imposing voice in her relationships. "It's sexy," Love explained to Hirschberg of her "kinder whore" style, "but you can sit down and say, 'I read Camille Paglia.'"[57]

Given form in these last four words is the core of Love's influence on Cobain's escalating desire for abuse, and the couple's metaphysical tie to the Millers. Within Love's ragged, *anti*-feminist Riot Grrrl acting as some Bizarro postmodern June Miller, rather, the distance between Nirvana's hysteric *Nevermind* and its little sister *In Utero* can be quantified. There is a moment just over halfway through *Nevermind,* for example, where a not yet strung out Kurt Cobain hands the microphone to his gangly bassist, the results of which are terrifically awkward. "Come on peeeepul now smile on yur *bruh*-ther," Krist Novoselic squeals in a biting parody of the Youngbloods' free-love anthem, "every-buddy get-tuh-GETHER—try to love one uh-*nutherrr* right *nahowww.*" Slouching back to his corner, Novoselic gives way to Cobain's distorted guitar and Dave Grohl's punitive snare before adding his own low end to "Territorial Pissings," the record's seventh cut. Stepping up, Cobain, moaning over his own feedback, issues a list of feminist demands and pulls the rug out from under patriarchy—from under himself—by admitting that he had never met a wise man, but "if so, it's a woman." It is the record's finest moment: a direct assault on hippy counterculture and the symbolic paternal in an unambiguously identifiable series of seconds that made it clear to any hearer—above and beyond "Smells Like Teen Spirit"—that pop music in 1991 was, as in 1977, suddenly in the hands of an extraterrestrial whose values, perspective, and ideas, and the violence they imply, would forever alter the cultural landscape.

In other words, if Cobain had not made his point clear in the previous six tracks, "Pissings" verifies that *Nevermind* is less a grungy call to arms for slackers around the globe than an homage—here flattering, there pained—not merely to Vail, whose Bikini Kill had established the Riot Grrrl scene an hour south of Seattle in Olympia in the early 1990s, but an emerging third-wave feminism generally. Despite its interpretation as an anthem for disaffected youth, the record owes its existence and vitality to Vail's sharing of feminist theory and praxis—bell hooks, Judith Butler—with her then-lover, offering many lyrics and scenes that simultaneously advocate contemporary feminist positions (as in "Breed" or "Drain You") and express a less anxious than relieved resignation at the loss of power—the castration—that such a position entails. On tour in support of the record, Cobain even took to playing such songs in a dress and kissed Novoselic on the lips following their performance of "Pissings" on *Saturday Night Live* in 1992.

Compare these expressions of feminist solidarity and anti-patriarchy with *In Utero*. In a torrent of unsettlingly indelicate positions dripping with Courtney's Camille Paglia–inspired "postfeminism," Cobain makes clear the shift in his own resolve, documented in his *Journals* as "I've learned to hate Riot Girrl" and referencing "Camille's vaginal/flower theory" in his notes for "Heart-Shaped Box."[58] From the bitter, infanticidal "Scentless Apprentice" to the terminal "All Apologies"—with "Rape Me," "Heart-Shaped Box," and "Milk It" in between—*In Utero* replaces Vail's emphases on identity politics and the broadening of the feminist scope to include race, gender, and social class with Love's only half-ironic thumb-in-the-eye to third-wave feminism generally, epitomized in her claim from stage shortly after Cobain had spent the night in jail for domestic assault that "we're donating all the money you paid to get in tonight to Domestic Violence Wife Beaters Fund. *Not*!"[59] That is to say, whereas *Nevermind* advocates for women, critiques phallogocentrism, and mocks homophobia (at the end of "Stay Away" Cobain shouts, "God is gay!"), its sour follow-up is much less certain of its big sister's politics, and, as such, more complex as a signifier of desire-as-self-hate. So does the aesthetic and ideological distance between the two records mirror the gap separating third wave from the postfeminism that was in many ways anticipated by June Miller.

Spinning these records sequentially, then, the analyst can see with astounding clarity what, to Cobain's chagrin, Freud adds to a reading of Kurt and Courtney: Cobain, the notoriously androgynous, skirted junkie-punk who combined feminism and LGBTQ advocacy with self-abuse, an excess of love, and eventual suicide, embodied much of what Freud theorized in the texts cited above. Knowing the end of Cobain's story, the analyst is not surprised to read in Freud's late essay on masochism that other psychoanalytical accounts of the phenomenon connect the masochist's association of love with its death drive to a concept called the "Nirvana Principle," or, the subject's attempt to reduce its ego-superego tension, and thus its "quantity" of excitation—its desire for pain—to zero.[60] "Punk rock is musical freedom," Cobain would go on to explain after Freud in a draft biography for his band. "Nirvana means freedom from pain and suffering in the external world and that's close to my definition of punk rock."[61]

We have seen this all before. Only the faces have changed. Like Sid and Nancy and Ian and Deborah, Love and Cobain took an affair founded on self-loathing, cooperative abuse, and a degrading public agency and converted it into a powerful, devastating, and literal pop corpse. In so doing, and in reveling in obscenity, blasphemy, and an opposition to the State as they paraded about the world in rags, they reminded the world of the lessons of not only *Salome* but Henry and June: "In the prison of life love takes on every form of mockery. *Are you suffering, little man*?" Beyond his addiction and shame, it is this pleasurable suffering and need for punishment—this garrulous recognition that love is the fertilizer of ruin—that killed Kurt Cobain. "Courtney, when I say I love you I am not ashamed, nor will anyone ever ever come close to intimidating, persuading, etc. me into thinking otherwise," Cobain had written his wife shortly before his suicide. "I spread you out wide open with the wingspan of a peacock, yet all too often with the attention span of a bullet to the head."[62] In his final suicide letter Cobain expands on this self-critique, defending his choice detailed in an earlier note to choose death, "like Hamlet," by arguing, "I have it good, very good, and I'm grateful, but since the age of seven I've become hateful toward all humans in general. Only because it seems so easy for people to get along, and have empathy. Empathy! Only because I love and feel for people too much I guess."[63] Echoing the "too honest, too sincere, too truthful, too generous" Miller, Cobain internalized the suffering he saw and experienced externally in the service of a bitter, desperate art that, as Nin described *Cancer*, fluctuates "between extremes, with bare stretches that taste like brass and leave the full flavor of emptiness. It is beyond optimism or pessimism. The author has given us the last *frisson*. Pain has no more secret recesses."[64] So it was with not only Kurt and Courtney but Sid and Nancy. And Ian and Deborah. And in time an equally punishing "punk" pair will again emerge in pop to convert their desire for abuse, signified in the Other, into a new, high-volume document to be broadcast to horrified hearers the world over, problematizing "love" and the phallogocentrism of pop in so doing.

In the end, then, punk and Henry Miller were always-already linked. And this union, it seems, was foreseen by the Brooklyn-born poet. There is a scene late in *Tropic of Cancer* where Henry Valentine Miller, thrashing and blaspheming, praising the words of his fellow Brooklynite Walt Whitman, recalls one formative Fourth of July when as a youth he purchased his first cache of firecrackers. Red, black, and gold paper littered the New York streets of his birth, Miller writes almost sentimentally of the nationalists' holiday, describing the swirling and smoking strings of explosives filling the American air with the sweetly acrid smell of gunpowder as he sought to explode his own purchase. More stunning than the fireworks though, Miller realizes as he sets flame to fuse, is the punk that sets them alight—the slowly burning object whereupon Chinese industry and American violence meet: "the long pieces of punk which break so easily, the punk that you blow on to get a good red glow, the punk whose smell sticks to your fingers for days and makes you dream of strange things." It sticks to you, the punk, writes Miller, burning slowly; it attaches itself to your skin, offends your nose and intellect, generating in your consciousness thoughts and dreams heretofore inaccessible. And try as you might, it refuses to wash away. Forsaking all astringents, the handler must let the punk *be*, advises Miller, who finds himself obsessed with the offensive and fragile object, "let it stick to your fingers, let it slowly infiltrate your veins."[65]

Despite its fleeting nature, its lack of a physical object, punk music, Miller prophesies without intending to, is thus tangible—it can be absorbed through the skin, into one's bloodstream. It *burns*. And like Cobain, Spungen, Curtis, and Vicious, it breaks easily. As such, it requires time and a careful, thoughtful patience to reveal its secrets. Only then can it convert slowly to words and symbols that emerge from the writer's pen, her mouth, and contribute to a (self-) destructive world critique, based on love and the desire for abuse, decades in the making. For embedded within punk's violence and obscenity, its nauseated and sacrilegious refusal of form and propriety, is the same ground-clearing Truth sought by not only Miller in his wicked attacks on his progenitors but Miller's own influences—Dostoevsky, Nietzsche, Baudelaire, Rimbaud, surrealism—and inheritors. On this list of heirs are not only William S. Burroughs, who like Miller has been highly influential to punks and postpunks (Cobain in particular), but other writers often categorized as science fiction: Philip K. Dick, Ballard, William Gibson. And so it is to Burroughs and punks' consistent captivation with all types of sci-fi that this study turns.

Notes

1. Henry Rollins, *Get in the Van* (Los Angeles: 2.13.61, 1994), 136.

2. Stevie Chick, *Spray Paint the Walls: The Story of Black Flag* (Oakland, CA: PM Press, 2009), 316.

3. Robert Christgau, *Christgau's Record Guide: The '80s* (New York: Pantheon, 1990), 58.

4. Rollins, *Get in the Van*, 121, 135, 238–39.

5. Henry Miller, *Tropic of Capricorn* (1939; New York: Grove, 1961), 93–94.

6. See David Browne, *Goodbye 20th Century: A Biography of Sonic Youth* (Philadelphia: Perseus/DaCappo, 2008), 95. One should also note that on June 5, 1944, Paul Verlaine's 1866 poem "Chanson d'automne" was broadcast over BBC radio, signaling the French Resistance that Operation Overlord had begun.

7. Candy Machine, "6 Months of Light," *Tune International*, Desoto/Dischord, DIS116.5CD, 1996.

8. Miller, *Tropic of Capricorn*, 12–13.

9. George Orwell, "Inside the Whale," *A Collection of Essays* (1940; Orlando, FL: Harvest, 1981), 251.

10. Henry Miller, *Tropic of Cancer* (1934; New York: Grove, 1961), 11.

11. Miller, *Capricorn*, 251.

12. Henry Miller, *Black Spring* (1936; New York: Grove 1963), 32.

13. Alain Badiou, *In Praise of Love* (2009; New York: New Press, 2012), 61.

14. Anaïs Nin, *Henry Miller Letters to Anaïs Nin* (1931–1946; New York: G. P. Putnam's Sons, 1965), 87.

15. Miller, *Capricorn*, 231.

16. Ibid., 13.

17. Anaïs Nin, *Henry and June* (1931–1932; San Diego: Harcourt Brace Jovanovich, 1986), 37, 242.

18. Miller, *Cancer*, 21, 250.

19. Sigmund Freud, "The Ego and the Id," in *The Standard Edition of the Complete Psychological Works of Sigmund Freud*, vol. 19, ed. James Strachey (London: Hoggarth Press, 1961), 41.

20. Nin, *Henry Miller Letters*, 24.

21. Nin, *Henry and June*, 23–25, 52, 101, 168, 187, 269.

22. Paul Brooks, "The Flowers of Romance," *SKUM #1*, January 1977, 4.

23. John Holmstrom and Bridget Hurd, *Punk: The Best of Punk Magazine* (New York: HarperCollins, 2012), 21.

24. John Lydon, *Rotten: No Irish, No Blacks, No Dogs* (New York: Picador, 1994), 162, 222.

25. Rollins, *Get in the Van*, 147, 195.

26. Lydon, *Rotten*, 56, 146.

27. Deborah Spungen, *And I Don't Want to Live This Life* (1983; New York: Villard, 1994), 209.

28. Legs McNeil and Gillian McCain, *Please Kill Me: The Uncensored Oral History of Punk* (New York: Penguin, 1996), 351.

29. Ibid., 348.

30. Lydon, *Rotten*, 147.

31. Ibid., 257.

32. Jon Savage, *England's Dreaming* (1991; New York: St. Martin's Griffin, 2001), 529.

33. Dorling Kindersley, *Punk: The Whole Story* (London: DK Publishing, 2006), 199.

34. Sigmund Freud, "The Economic Problem of Masochism," in *The Standard Edition of the Complete Psychological Works of Sigmund Freud*, vol. 19, ed. James Strachey (1923; London: Hoggarth, 1961), 162–70.

35. Deborah Curtis, *Touching from a Distance* (London: Faber & Faber, 2007), 22, 132–38.

36. Ibid., 90.

37. J. G. Ballard, *The Atrocity Exhibition* (1970; New York: Flamingo, 2002), 26.

38. Nin, *Henry Miller Letters*, 24.

39. Henry Miller, The *Air-Conditioned Nightmare* (New York: New Directions, 1945), 91.

40. Charles Cross, *Heavier Than Heaven* (New York: Hyperion, 2001), 192, 313.

41. Christina Kelly, "Kurt and Courtney Sitting in a Tree," *Sassy*, April 1992, 51.

42. Kurt Cobain, *Journals* (New York: Penguin/Riverhead, 2002), 218, 220.

43. Lynn Hirschberg, "Strange Love," *Vanity Fair*, September 1992, 230. See also Poppy Z. Brite, *Courtney Love: The Real Story* (New York: Simon & Schuster, 1997), 83–87, 110–11.

44. Kevin Allman, "The Dark Side of Kurt Cobain: Nirvana's Front Man Shoots from the Hip," *Advocate*, February 9, 1993, 37.

45. Allman, "The Dark Side," 36; Cross, *Heavier*, 192, 268; Cobain, *Journals*, 213.

46. Cobain, *Journals*, 168.

47. Spungen, *And I Don't Want to Live This Life*, 30.

48. Linda Carroll, *Her Mother's Daughter* (New York: Doubleday, 2006), 151.

49. Cobain, *Journals*, 185.

50. Cross, *Heavier*, 209.

51. John Mulvey, "Band of Fallopian Glory-*In Utero* Review," *New Musical Express*, September 4, 1993.

52. Henry Miller, *The Cosmological Eye* (New York: New Directions, 1939), 367.

53. Cobain, *Journals*, 104. See also Cobain's suicide note in Cross, *Heavier*, 338–39.

54. See Max Wallace and Ian Halperin, *Love and Death: The Murder of Kurt Cobain* (New York: Atria, 2005), and *Kurt & Courtney*, directed by Nick Broomfield (1998; New York: Fisher Klingenstein, 2012), DVD.

55. Cobain, *Journals*, 74, 82–84. See also Charles Bukowski, *Women* (1978; New York: Ecco, 2002), 37.

56. Cobain, *Journals*, 179.

57. Hirschberg, "Strange Love," 232, 297–98.

58. Cobain, *Journals*, 267, 222.

59. Cross, *Heavier*, 280.

60. Freud, "The Economic Problem," 159–60.

61. Cobain, *Journals*, 156.

62. Ibid., 237–38.

63. Cross, *Heavier*, 313, 339.

64. Miller, *Cancer* (see Nin's "Preface"), xxxi.

65. Ibid., 198–99.

THE DISMEMBERMENT PLAN 6

Burroughs, Dick, and the Portmanteaux

I am a recording instrument. . . . I do not presume to impose 'story' 'plot' 'continuity'. . . . I am not an entertainer.

William S. Burroughs, *Naked Lunch*

The image is as charming as it is mortifying: performing outside the United Kingdom for the first time—at the Plan K club in Brussels in October 1979—on a bill that included Cabaret Voltaire and headliner William S. Burroughs, Joy Division's Ian Curtis approaches the American junkie-writer, seated and signing hardcovers, for a word at the end of the show. Not quite star-struck, but certainly enamored, Curtis, who had just unveiled the song that would become his band's posthumous calling card, "Love Will Tear Us Apart," asks Burroughs for not an autograph but a desk copy of the expatriate's latest *The Third Mind*, written mostly in the 1960s but not published (in English) until 1978. "Yeah, kid, yeah. Whatever," Burroughs grumbles, ignoring Curtis in Joy Division bass player Peter Hook's retelling. Having already downed a pint or two, the singer persists. "Well, I'm in the band Joy Division who played tonight . . . I was wondering if I could have a book?" "*Have* a book?" Burroughs asks in his nasal delivery, finally looking up from his table: "Fuck off, kid."[1]

Like a clap on the ear, the unexpected rejoinder leaves Curtis pained —humiliated—and regretting immediately his approach. Slouching back to his mates, who roar with laughter as they repeat the line over and again the remainder of the night, Curtis, who would commit suicide fewer than eight months later, proceeds to get exceedingly drunk.

Although confirming that such a meeting certainly occurred, most recallers of the encounter, Hook included, in all likelihood exaggerate Burroughs's viciousness; the writer was among the last in a dying breed of genteel American aristocrats raised by his Southern progenitors to be polite in any company, even jittery junk addicts and raucous punks. "I very much doubt whether William told Ian Curtis to fuck off," Cabaret Voltaire's Richard Kirk later quipped, skeptical of Hook's version of the meeting. "I approached Mr. Burroughs at the Plan K event, and mentioned I was a friend of Genesis P-Orridge from Throbbing Gristle, who of course was known to William—he didn't know me or had heard of my band Cabaret Voltaire, but was very friendly and a very polite old gentleman."[2] Or as Chris Ott put it in his Joy Division book, Curtis was not so much sent away with a curse as merely "rebuffed" by the author, whom both Joy Division and Cabaret Voltaire allegedly idolized.[3]

Belligerent or not, Burroughs, as Kirk and Ott suggest, was nothing less than an icon within punk and postpunk circles, having been christened "the Godfather of Punk" not long after punk erupted, which for its part talked him up routinely, quoted him flagrantly, and took much from his often horrifying vision of society in constructing its own pastiche style, buying his notion that if one cuts into the present the future bleeds out. Burroughs-referencing punk groups the Soft Boys, Clem Snide, Throbbing Gristle, and Nova Mob notwithstanding, Iggy's *The Idiot* and *Lust for Life*, Cabaret Voltaire's "Control Addict," and Sonic Youth's "Dr. Benway's House" too reference Burroughsian characters and subjects, as does Joy Division's "Interzone," the song the band closed its Plan K set with as Burroughs smoked and mused in the corner. And as Jon Savage documents, Curtis had read Burroughs's *Naked Lunch* and *The Wild Boys,* as had Kurt Cobain, who would go on to provide a squelching soundtrack to Burroughs's *The "Priest" They Called Him.*[4] Such a collaboration was the best Cobain could do, having failed to entice the author to appear in Nirvana's "Heart Shaped Box" video. "William and I sitting across from one another at a table (Black and White) lots of Blinding sun from the windows behind us holding hands staring into each others eyes," Cobain had written in his journal, describing his vision for what would become Anton Corbijn's short film. The William in question is none other than Burroughs, whose cut-up method had infiltrated Cobain's own writing. "He gropes me from behind and falls dead on top of me. Medical footage of sperm flowing through penis. A ghost vapor comes out of his chest and groin area and enters me Body."[5]

Punks' interest in Burroughs was but a specific instance, however, of what several interviews, song titles, and lyrical allusions demonstrate is a broad punk penchant for literature typically categorized as science fiction by authors from Isaac Asimov, Anthony Burgess, and Philip K. Dick to J. G. Ballard, Ursula K. Le Guin, and William Gibson—never mind the graphic novel. "I say science fiction rules the world," Mary Monday's Vermillion put it in the first issue of *Search & Destroy* (which interviewed Ballard and Burroughs for issue #10) as on the opposite coast John Holmstrom and the other contributors to *Punk* magazine dedicated an entire issue (#15) to aping B-movies and sci-fi comics with a cut-up "Mutant Monster Beach Party" edition. This specific issue reified not only Suicide's celebration of *Ghost Rider* comics but Tommy Ramone's admission to *Search & Destroy* that "Dee Dee reads a lot: *Weird War* is his favorite [graphic novel]—and I've seen him read

Sergeant Fury and His Howling Commandos and *Battling Marines*. John's into monster magazines. I was into *Superman* and *Batman* and all that stuff when I was a kid. And I like underground comics—an *Arcade* series is real good."[6] Or, as Damon Locks of Chicago postpunk group Trenchmouth—whose drummer Fred Armisen went on to write and act for "Saturday Night Live" and "Portlandia"—told me, "I read comics in high school, *X-Men* in the Chris Claremont/John Bryne era. *Do Androids Dream of Electric Sheep*? was super important because of my love for *Blade Runner*. Also, *A Clockwork Orange* was big."[7] For their part, Sonic Youth offered nods to both Dick and cyberpunk author William Gibson over the course of several records, particularly *Sister* and *Daydream Nation*, while North Dakota group Imipolex G pored over Thomas Pynchon's *Gravity's Rainbow* and U.K. Subs brought Asimov's *I, Robot* to life decades before the Will Smith film of the same name. "He's the brave new world / For the boys and girls," Subs' singer Charlie Harper puffs as his mates chant, "I ro-bot" mechanically behind him, thinking too of Dick's androids. "He's gonna make you rich / Gonna make you jump and make you twitch." Finally, Daft Punk's spaceman aesthetic notwithstanding, self-evident are the cybernetic and techno-dystopian predilections of groups like the Human League, Devo, and Man or Astro-man?, who claim to be extraterrestrials sent to Earth to research humankind, the most inconspicuous method of so doing obviously being to impersonate a human surf punk band and tour the United States in a Ford Econoline van.

Nietzsche and Rimbaud, Genet and Dostoevsky notwithstanding, then, such repeated references suggest that much of punk's intellectual and phenomenological base is derived not (only) from philosophy and poetry, from the literary canon, so much as often pulpy, abstruse, cut-up, and fantastic future texts: dime store tales of space adventure, postapocalyptic cult comics, and dystopian technical writing. Surveying the diversity of punks' taste in science fiction, this chapter begins with punks' interest in Burroughs and the cut-up and moves into punks' guiltier literary pleasures, which nonetheless have both informed punk aesthetics and influenced the development of literature proper, which since at least 1984 has sprouted a series of loaded subgenres with the term "punk" in their title: cyberpunk, steampunk, splatterpunk. Whereas earlier punks looked to Burroughs and Dick—and to a lesser extent Ballard—to inform the beginning of what they saw as their effort to invade and dismantle the paternal consciousness, to slough off the superego by cutting it up and reassembling it, later punks turned their reading of comix, fanzines, and occasionally campy paperback novels into punk itself and, in so doing, came to complete the circle, influencing literature as much as pop music.

"The Godfather of Punk"

"I'm not a punk and I don't know why anyone would consider me the godfather of punk. How do you define punk?" So asked William Burroughs only half-rhetorically to the suggestion that his writing had become associated with punk music subculture in the late 1970s, answering his own question by surmising that if a punk is a young petty criminal, his fiction might be considered a bridge from the beats to punk rock so far as it focuses on such actors. But as a relentless critic of mass media and "official" discourse he remained skeptical of what he heard and read about the new wave—"I think the so-called punk movement is indeed a media creation. I have however, sent a letter of support to the Sex Pistols in England because I've always said that the country doesn't stand a chance until you have 20,000 people saying bugger to the

Queen"—and went so far as to add, tongue-through-cheek, "I always thought a punk was someone who took it up the ass."[8]

Although petty criminality, youth, and buggery can and have been applied to punk rock by advocates and critics alike, Burroughs is here being disingenuous; he knew from his association with Throbbing Gristle and Patti Smith—"She's really got it," Burroughs once told James Grauerholz of the poet—that the form and content of much of his work in many ways established the basis of what would become the early punk and postpunk aesthetic on both sides of the Atlantic.[9] Having internalized Burroughs's staccato and fissured word-images and steeped itself in his often "deviant" characters and extension of Tristan Tzara's "To Make a Dadaist Poem"—"Take a newspaper. Take some scissors. . ."—punk and postpunk seemed to be trying to give Burroughs's vision a soundtrack: not only Cobain's collaboration with Burroughs, but Iggy Pop admitting, "There's a lot of *Soft Machine* in *The Idiot*" and Genesis P-Orridge producing a recording of a Burroughs reading—"Nothing Here Now but the Recordings" in 1981—not long after yawning that Burroughs's "concepts of control through the word and media have got *so far* . . . cut-ups and collages and all the type-setting that's now punk cliché."[10] Porridge was quite right: so seriously did punk take the procedure developed by Burroughs, Brion Gysin, and "Subliminal Kid" Ian Sommerville—splicing together or "folding-in" disparate pages or lines of text in an effort to "rub out the word forever," as twelfth-century assassin Hassan-i Sabbah allegedly put it—that the punk cut-up, epitomized in Jamie Reid's graphics and handbills for the Sex Pistols, had become stale as early as 1978.

Attracted by the frighteningly prophetic character and *hostility* of such a method, punk internalized Burroughs's explanation that "the basic techniques of nova are very simple consist in creating and aggravating conflicts"[11] and began looking for ways of cutting up not only the written but the tape-recorded word in a manner similar to that described by Burroughs as:

> several hundred people recording and playing back in the street is quite a happening right there conservative m.p. spoke about the growing menace posed by bands or irresponsible youths with tape recorders playing back traffic sounds that confuse motorists carrying the insults recorded in some low underground club into mayfair and Piccadilly this growing menace to public order put a thousand young recorders with riot recordings into the street that mutter gets louder and louder remember this is a technical operation one step at a time here is an experiment that can be performed by anyone equipped with two machines connected by extension lead so he can record directly from one machine to the other.[12]

Taking Burroughs much more literally than the handful of counterculture or "progressive" rock bands (Steely Dan, the Insect Trust, Soft Machine) who allude to Burroughs but nonetheless produced rather conventional rock music, punk and postpunk saw themselves as the Nova Police of Burroughs's early "word hoard" Trilogy whose mission it is to identify and obliterate the patriarchal Nova Mob that had colonized human consciousness through the word-image virus, "a parasitic organism that invades and damages the central nervous system" via homogenizing political discourse, overt and subliminal messaging in advertising, current affairs broadcasting, and the spectacle of entertainment culture. So did they thrust two fingers upward at the recording industry and began experimenting with "instruments" and structures less listenable than irritating, less soothing than subversive.[13] Taking Burroughs to heart, as Kirk told Simon Reynolds, members of Cabaret

Voltaire would at one time "drive around in a van with tape loops playing out the back, or go into pubs with a tape machine and play weird stuff—just trying to wind people up, really."[14]

Consider not only Cabaret Voltaire or Throbbing Gristle—who put Burroughs into practice by generating a collection of singles and records comprising a *sound* hoard of reversed and reverbed lyric tracks over synthesized hums, buzzing found sounds, clipped television and radio bits, and monotonous beats—but Negativland. Coming out of San Francisco in 1979, the instrument-less and (initially) song-title-less group was both a hoax machine and live act whose cut-up soundscapes the recording industry rightly regarded as a direct assault on its cartel. After releasing their landmark album *Escape from Noise* in 1987, Negativland first hoaxed the press by issuing a news release that claimed the band had been forced to cancel its national tour in support of the record because the album's track "Christianity Is Stupid" had caused Minnesota teen David Brom to murder his family with an axe. And after a follow-up LP *Helter Stupid*, the band produced the *U2* EP, an amalgamation of obscenity-filled outtakes from Casey Kasem's "American Top 40" radio program, advertisement and B-movie bits, a kazoo version of Irish megaband U2's "I Still Haven't Found What I'm Looking For," and commentary from U2's Bono. Emerging at the same time as major record labels were just launching their legal assault on hip-hop for sampling, the record provoked an Island Records lawsuit for trademark infringement. "We're borrowing from everything and everywhere. We also have tools that allow us to grab stuff and manipulate it digitally, either sound or images—kids are now growing up with these tools," Negativland's Mark Hosler told *Punk Planet* in 1998, all but arguing that the jig is up for the recording industry by noting how the collage of Burroughs, of Cabaret Voltaire and Negativland, has gone mainstream. "You could say that all the stuff on a Negativland CD is stolen. But listen to our records. What do they sound like? Do they sound like other people's records? No. They sound like Negativland."[15]

The cut-up notwithstanding, punk, like Burroughs's early writing, is comprised of and valorizes junkies and madmen, strippers and provocateurs, anarchists, artists, and activists doing the necessarily violent and obscene work to preserve human freedom in the face of the swarming Insect People (both within Island Records and without) and their bureaucracies who are stifling consciousness and agency. That is to say, punk and postpunk too made explicit their resistance to the agents of control, offering, as Barry Miles describes the godfather's fiction, "a full-scale offensive against the deep-seated hypocrisy, arrogance, naivety and mindless futility" that characterized much of Anglophone society following the twentieth century's Great Wars.[16] Punk and postpunk were and are the insurrectionist Wild Boys, waging war on a soporific mass culture while sporting "expensive tailor-made rags" donned by "queens . . . camping about in wild-boy drag": "The wild-boy thing is a cult based on drugs, depravity and violence more dangerous than the hydrogen bomb," notes a Narc report on the Wild Boy movement in the novel that bears its name. "Some of the wild boys do not talk at all. Others have developed cries, songs, words as weapons. Words that cut like buzz saws. Words that vibrate the entrails to jelly. Cold strange words that fall like icy nets on the mind. Virus words that eat the brain to muttering shreds." Not only words, however, as we saw in the chapters above, but "*Idiot tunes* that stick in the throat round and round night and day" characterize the Wild Boys' multifarious assault on culture, Burroughs writes. So it is in punk, which like Burroughs revels still in its fractured *under*development as music, its "fucking with language" to quote Kathleen Hanna, and gnostic refusal of the agents of control whose stultifying word and image bank continue to blanket the modern subject with impunity.[17]

In each case—whether his resistance to State, Church, or what Jodi Dean would go on to call "communicative capitalism," or his attempt to make visible and reorder a fragmented unconscious—Burroughs exploits the signifier ("because essentially he's into linguistics" Devo's Gerald Casale once noted) in ways both violent and what the straight world would call offensive.[18] This vulgarism was appropriated not only by punk but by another Burroughs fan and science fictioner who also caught on with punks: J. G. Ballard. If Burroughs is the Freud of twentieth-century fiction, Ballard is its Wilhelm Reich, not so much articulating, deconstructing, and then reassembling the unconscious in an effort to drain the present of its lifeblood as exploring the latent desire of the unconscious made manifest by technology simply because it is an interesting thing to do. "Numerous studies have been conducted upon patients in terminal paresis (G.P.I.), placing [Ronald] Reagan in a series of simulated auto-crashes, e.g. multiple pile-ups, head-on collisions, motorcade attacks," Ballard writes in "Why I want to Fuck Ronald Reagan" from one of Ian Curtis's favorite novels. "Powerful erotic fantasies of an anal-sadistic character surrounded the image of the Presidential contender."[19] In a case of what Jean Baudrillard would go on to call "hyperreality," wherein the simulation both precedes and replaces a Real that never existed in the first place, Ballard is here anticipating his own aggressively prurient art installation of automobile wrecks that gave the writer all the information he needed to develop *Crash*. "I just put 3 crashed cars on display. Just there in [the New Arts Lab] gallery. I did it as a sort of test, actually, because I'd written my book *The Atrocity Exhibition* in which I'd had a character who'd put on a display of crashed cars, and I was thinking at the time of getting ready to write *Crash*,"

Ballard told Jon Savage not long after Joe Strummer had been caught reading *Crash* in hospital and Cabaret Voltaire too had begun exploiting the repressed, implicitly libidinal character of Western civilization's collective unconscious by performing in front of projected pornographic images and film sequences intercut with television news broadcasts, atrocity stills, advertisements, and other bits of cultural effluvia. As Ballard continues:

> I sent out invitations to art critics, invited a lot of people along. I've been to a lot of parties, but I've never been to one where everybody got drunk so quickly. . . . As we were setting up the show, where people'd walk into the gallery without realizing what was going on they'd see these crashed cars, and you'd get a kind of hysterical laugh. At the actual opening party I've never seen people getting drunk socially with so much more aggression and belligerence—I got nearly attacked Physically by a reporter from the *New Society*. I had a topless girl interviewing people, and . . . a closed-circuit TV going so people could see themselves being interviewed around these crashed cars by this topless girl—it was all too much. Everybody got overexcited, the girl nearly got raped in the back of the crashed Pontiac—it confirmed All my hunches, that show. During the month that the cars were on display, they were continually attacked—they were rolled over, splashed with white paint by communique men, windows that weren't broken were broken, wing mirrors ripped off these wrecks—it's absolutely amazing the amount of hostility. . . . Something about putting these crashed vehicles on display focused, pointed obviously a finger, at certain [psychological/pathological] areas that most people kept quietly concealed.[20]

Punk too is such a finger, if not the sugar in the petrol tank. As a result of this tapping into the latent eroticism of modernity (its failures and accidents in particular), Ballard, whose method too relied on what might be categorized as obscenity, was a natural referent for punk groups like Throbbing Gristle, Cabaret Voltaire, Negativland, and Devo, each of which tied to reverse Freud's *Civilization and Its Discontents* by utilizing the cut-up in an effort to *unleash* desires typically repressed by a highly ordered and mediated society, to uncork the modern subject's psychogeography and document the results.

Bracketing for the moment Devo's decidedly ungroovy and ambiguously erectile-cadaverous *Be Stiff* EP and debut long-player *Q: Are We Not Men? A: We Are Devo*!, which features not only "Uncontrollable Urge" as its lead track but the detumescent "Shrivel Up" and a wonderfully asexual version of the Rolling Stones' "(I Can't Get No) Satisfaction," Cabaret Voltaire represents perhaps the most illustrative case study of what the Burroughs-Ballard canon gave punk. Take the group's inaugural LP, *Mix-Up*. Combining rudimentary bass licks, synthesized beats, and distorted blows on a clarinet with both original "lyrics" and appropriated sounds from radio and film, *Mix-Up* is the droning radiator in David Lynch's *Eraserhead*: a terrifying soundscape that built on its predecessor *Extended Play* by noting on its record sleeve that the album contained "no rock and roll" and taking the EP's insectivorous closing track "The Set Up" to its logical Burroughsian conclusion: "I felt as though I owned Helsinki—We've got this other singer who can sing like a paranoid schizo, singing 1000 voices, sing like 100 men—It's pure genius—If the Rolling Stones could not play their Queen's music, they would be removed from the country—Why is it that the Institute of the Blind can tear a man to pieces and make him walk in the dark?—All your family is mad—I'm an artist—I could build you a three-tier wedding cake in forty seconds." So went a handful of the mumbled words to "Photophobia," the first track on *Mix-Up*'s dark second side, as behind the speaker woodwinds and synthesizers are essentially *weaponized*, lacerating the listener's unconscious with a string of signifiers and sounds that when assembled out of order tend to take on a threatening and visionary tenor, with or without music behind them. "He must've had the energy of 10,000 ballet dancers, [to] make the drive 3000 [unintelligible] across the Ardennes without a good fuck—Bodies of dead soldiers piled up like slabs of chocolate—Paranoid schizophrenics suffering from photophobia—[unintelligible] scientists or brain surgeons . . ." and so on. The song is disturbing and indecipherable simultaneously, as chilling as *The Soft Machine* or *Crash* in its effort to uncork a century's worth of bottled lust. And like Burroughs's or Ballard's contributions to literature, to political economy, "Photophobia" is almost untouchable as a result, terrifically successful in its prescient unlistenability, its unmarketable and uncanny ability to pull from the hearer heretofore crushed feelings of desire and aggression. In so doing the song bests even the band's very early "Bed Time Stories," whose speaker promises that "I'll hold a séance with Moroccan rapists masturbating end over end" and wakes up from a hallucinogen-induced sleep to discover in horror "the bodies of my comrades their legs and their intestines were strewn around the room."

Note in the above, however, the phallocentrism of Cabaret Voltaire's seedy discourse ("All the queers and all the greasers and those who'll never see the light—They stick their cocks in each other's assholes and tell you to steal to scream to die"), which saves little space, if any, for the feminine, the symptom. This, too, punk and postpunk take from Ballard's repetition of Freud's and Lacan's privileging of the phallus as such, from Burroughs's restriction of Wild Boy insurgency to a single sex. Burroughs especially, even if one ignores the fact that he shot his wife Joan Vollmer in the head in 1951 as part of a drunken "William Tell act," includes few female characters in any of his novels and wrote even after killing Vollmer that women "were a basic mistake, and the whole dualistic universe evolved from this *error*."[21] This reinvestment in the phallogocentric economy, even when it is problematized, carried over into what is elsewhere punk's more obviously hysteric character to its own ideological disadvantage (one that would not be addressed with any consistency until Riot Grrrl in the early 1990s).

That said, whether or not the prohibition on the feminine in his work and personal life amounts to a formal misogyny, Burroughs's (and thus punk's) cut-up remains a type of castration of the Logos also. Its absolute lack of women notwithstanding, the Nova Trilogy nonetheless emasculates the phallogocentric economy that had infected the Occident by shattering the signifying chain, enlarging and dismantling the violence and horror of the master signifier (here the Southern gentleman and flatfooted beat cop, there science, fascism, and the culture industry—advertising in particular), and emphasizing the depravity and humiliation that are symptoms of the word-virus. As Miles puts it, Burroughs reveals "the actual structure of writing itself, and, in his opposition to either/or dichotomies and his examination of texts (and not only texts) for hidden and repressed meanings, act[ed] as a precursor of the Deconstructionist philosophers."[22] This is not untrue. More useful in the present context, though, is to reframe Miles's reading to see in Burroughs, who had undergone years of psychoanalysis from a variety of Freudians, an appreciation for analysis and a revision of the notion that the subject comes into Being only through language: the cut-up text is literally the objectification of the unconscious at the same time that it is an attempt to dismantle and reconfigure—"disintoxicate" as Inspector Lee puts it in *Nova Express*—an unconscious mind that has been repressed and deformed by the superegotistical agents of control whose word-virus has become epidemic. In this way Burroughs quite openly sought to render the unconscious naked in its visibility and reconfigure it on paper in a way that not even the Dadaists and surrealists with their "automatic writing" and *détournement* accomplished.

"Dear Mom and Dad: I am going to join the wild boys. When you read this I will be far away," writes Johnny (Yen, Rotten, Ramone?) to the symbolic paternal, captivated by what seems a once-in-a-lifetime opportunity to snub not merely his biological but cultural progenitors, the genes and memes that are his birthright.[23] He sees the Wild Boys as a chance to move forward and backward in time and space, Johnny, to reclaim simultaneously both his own unconscious and the outside world that has filled his body and mind with parasites by inoculating himself against the virus of phallogocentrism—"Stopping [the] abdominal breathing holes of The Insect People."[24]

Jumping at such an opportunity were not merely those punks and postpunks holding instruments or tape machines, but the inheritors of Burroughs's typographical legacy who often emerged out of and helped cultivate punk as an idea: Kathy Acker, Mark Amerika, and the scores of editors who developed dozens of cut-up punk zines across the globe. Coming of age as punk came into being, Acker in particular picked up where Burroughs effectively left off in the middle 1970s, producing a series of experimental texts that reached their pinnacle in *Blood and Guts in High School*, an anti-linear pastiche of dramatic dialogues, genitalia sketches, appropriated poetry, and technical schematics, and her reimagined versions of *Don Quixote* and *Great Expectations* (whose inaugural section is entitled "Plagiarism"). Acker's colleague Amerika, whose *The Kafka Chronicles* is a Burroughsian collection of short stories, pornography, prose poems, advertisements, and word lists, later made the leap from the book-object to cyberspace, developing one of the earliest pieces of hyperfiction, *Grammatron*, which claims neither a beginning nor an end and allows each unique user to cut the text up at her discretion, jumping from "page" to "page," truly "writing" the novel anew with each reading in the way Roland Barthes theorized decades earlier.[25] Both writers have acknowledged that they cut their teeth, in one way or another, through an affiliation with punk in the 1970s.

Finally, as has been documented exhaustively elsewhere, punk was the impetus behind a series of cut-up, détourned, and intentionally *un*-edited fanzines that looked to not only Dada, Lettrism, and situationism for inspiration, but Burroughs and Gysin, including *Punk, Flipside, Profane Existence, Defiant Pose, Sniffin' Glue, Search & Destroy, Touch & Go,* and countless others.[26] "Fanzine culture was alive and well long before PUNK was published," *Punk*'s editor John Holmstrom wrote in a retrospective, noting the connection his magazine—which at one point was asked to publish a selection of Burroughs's *Junky*—held with the "comix" and sci-fi-oriented "zines" that predated his own magazine. "Dozens of fanzines devoted to comic books, sci-fi 'zines, and music were published during the mid-twentieth century. But punk rock became the first culture that both was inspired by other fanzines and DIY culture, and became a phenomenon and a movement of its own."[27] Each of these titles consisted, to varying degrees, of pastiche associations of often appropriated words and images, cut-up band interviews or record reviews, and comix, and were designed, like the Burroughsian cut-up, to make an author-editor of anyone with a scissors. Such a philosophy was embedded in the minds of punk documentarians and promoters from the start, as Reid's trademark "ransom note" iconography indicates.

Sleeping Androids Do Dream

But as Malcolm McLaren knew from his days schlepping around with anarchists and situationists like Reid, while the Burroughsian cut-up and "No future" made for powerful rhetoric, wonderfully simple bits of agitprop most effectively wielded by those who stood to inherit the future, such sloganeering was at times disingenuous. As Holmstrom understood, and groups like Jonathan Richman's Modern Lovers ("Astral Plane," "Here Come the Martian Martians"), Misfits ("I turned into a Martian," "Astro Zombies," "Science Fiction/Double Feature"), Six Finger Satellite, and Trenchmouth ("The Future vs. Centrifugal Force" from *Inside the Future*) imply, punk and science fiction have been concomitant from the subculture's birth. In the face of their politically motivated denunciation of the present by publicizing (even reveling in) their lack of a hereafter, in other words, dozens of punk—and especially postpunk—groups and their fans actually took great interest not only in campy sci-fi films but in the speculative fiction that made an earnest effort to imagine the future, Burroughs notwithstanding, which was described alternately as both worse and *better* than the present. After all, although quite understandably categorized as fantasy or science fiction, Burroughs's cut-ups of Rimbaud and Graham Greene, newsprint, advertising, medical journals, and his own prose were often little more than technical descriptions of a contemporary society that, when disassembled and reconfigured, took on a premonitory, "futuristic" ambiance even though the author had invested little energy in meditating on the shape of things to come. Burroughs and Gysin were, in fact, trying to bring prose up to date, to help it catch up to advances made in the plastic arts in the twentieth century.[28] In contrast, the several authors that punks have cited that are more easily categorized as science fiction proper—Robert Heinlein, Frank Herbert, Asimov, Anthony Burgess, Ursula Le Guin, and Dick—penned literally hundreds of often pulpy short stories and novels, typically aimed at young males, that openly grappled with the technical and philosophical aspects of travel through space-time, artificial intelligence and robotics, the colonization of other planets, and astrobiology.

Permeating the plurality of such stories are themes that in many ways shaped the punk worldview: a fear of and resistance to conformism and the cultural status quo; resistance to what Louis Althusser called the Repressive and Ideological State Apparatuses wielded at times haphazardly by the State, Church, and even Nature, including what much of science fiction sees as the planet's dystopian horizon; humans' displacement by machines; the simulated nature of Being writ large; and a vision of a future off-planet. All science fiction's earliest proponents explore these themes regularly over the course of their careers. Take Dick, who was and remains perhaps punk's most sought after sci-fi exponent, having even generated a small fan club–band known as the Dickies. "Have you ever read any Philip K. Dick? One of my favorites! . . . *Do Androids Dream of Electric Sheep*? is my favorite Dick book," Dickies singer Leonard Graves Phillips blathered breathlessly to *Search & Destroy* editor Vale in 1978, who for his part admits to admiring Dick's surveillance-oriented rumination on polarity *A Scanner Darkly,* barely getting in a word edgewise. "Ooh, have you ever read *The Man in the High Castle*? . . . A classic!"[29] Or, building on the Human League's "Being Boiled" b/w "Circus of Death" single, effectively a summary of Dick's *Ubik,* as Man or Astro-man? put it in "Philip K. Dick in the Pet Section of a Wal-Mart":

> I still thought I saw Philip K. Dick in that pet section
> He was yelling at all the mutant kids
> Imploring against the vile treatment of breeding
> He says "take a look at the algae eaters
> It's unethical."

"This is *twice* as weird as *A Scanner Darkly,*" adds Astro-man singer Birdstuff, whose group cast itself as the Nexus-6 replicants from if not *Androids* then Dick's short story "Explorers We," whose humanoid astronauts—near perfect facsimilia of a space team thought dead following a failed mission to Mars—are confused by the abuse they suffer upon their "return" to earth by the humans who refuse to accept the clones as authentic. Thus would Man or Astro-man? execute a "Genome Project" that ostensibly sent not original band members but a series of male Alpha clones out on tour in 1998 and all-female Gamma clones in 1999.

In Dick, punks have for years found a writer less demanding than either Burroughs or Ballard who nevertheless gives them all the anti-establishmentarianism, fast-paced dystopian pulp, and post-human Gnosticism (not to mention phallogocentrism) particularly attractive to smart, young, typically heterosexual males in the West, but without the camp of an Arthur C. Clarke, Heinlein, or Asimov. Where his early piece of short fiction "The Last of the Masters" imagines a near future where anarchism is taken seriously as a political philosophy, "The Minority Report" and *A Scanner Darkly* survey the limits of consciousness, determinism, and extrasensory perception, and *The Man in the High Castle* and *Do Androids Dream of Electric Sheep*? describe a bleak totalitarian present and future, respectively, a fascism always at the door or narrowly avoided due to mere accidents of history or technology.

A Scanner Darkly especially, published at the height of punk's first wave, tapped into the early punk and postpunk milieu that dripped with drug-fueled paranoia and punks' often puerile critique of the symbolic paternal, examining in one fell swoop notions of perception versus reality, subjectivity, neural disintegration, the physical and ideological control of the populace by a militarized class of neofascists, and the illusion of love and free will. "He felt, in his head, loud voices singing: terrible music, as if the reality around him had gone sour. Everything now—the fast-moving cars, the two men, his own car with its hood up, the smell of smog, the bright, hot light of midday—it all had a rancid quality," thinks undercover cop and "scramble suit" wearer Fred/Bob early in the novel, remembering with disgust the callousness of not the underclass he is tasked with surveilling but the elites, whose carelessness and brutality was summed up in one rich kid's ironic rejoinder to Fred, regarding an insect, "If I had known it was harmless I would have killed it myself."

As the novel reaches its depressing end Fred realizes that he had been used by his colleagues in the narcotics unit at the expense of his mental faculties, which have deteriorated following his necessary ingestion of the highly addictive "Substance D[eath]" to the degree that the two hemispheres of his brain can no longer filter fantasy from reality, even competing with each other to convince Fred of the "truth" of various images and experiences. "I've got two kids," Fred tells his superior after a team of psychologists have informed him that his brain is shot and he is being relieved of his duties. "I don't believe you do; you're not supposed to," Fred's boss, Hank, replies as Fred comes to understand that his fissured and fried brain has been seeing itself distorted, "through a mirror":

> A darkened mirror, he thought; a darkened scanner. And St Paul meant [in 1 Corinthians], by a mirror, not a glass mirror . . . but a reflection of himself when he looked at the polished bottom of a metal pan. . . . Not through a telescope or lens system, which does not reverse, not through anything but seeing his own face reflected back up at him, reversed—pulled through infinity. Like they're telling me. It is not *through* glass, but as reflected *back* by a glass. And that reflection that returns to you: it is you, it is your face, but it isn't.[30]

Recognizing the "punkiness" of *Scanner*'s tone, its austerity and contempt for bourgeois living, then, Richard Linklater's "animated" version of the novel makes a point of displaying a poster advertising angular postrockers June of 44 on a wall behind babbling Substance D addicts played by Robert Downey Jr. and Woody Harrelson.

And here, too, in not only Burroughs but Dick, is psychoanalysis. The alienation and objectification of the ego that accompanies this recognition that the self the mirror-gazing subject has been seeing is not the true ego but a distorted *reflection* of the self was theorized by Lacan as early as the 1930s. This "mirror stage" of human development is the foundational moment when the subject first recognizes itself as an image—as an Other external to itself or signifier to another signifier, most obviously the parent—thus generating the subject's sense of its own subjectivity and forever alienating the subject from herself. Or, as Darby Crash put it in "What We Do Is Secret," punks are the "aberrations / Defects in a defect's mirror." In this way does the child learn to assign libidinal value to the image-object at the same time as it becomes an object for another in a dialectic of self and other, master and slave, privileged signifier and abject signifier.

The curveball pitch and often paranoid politics of such stories fit in neatly with much early punk and postpunk, whose advocates likewise cover the above themes in song after song. Groups like Kraftwerk, the Human League, and the Fall aside, take, as the best and obvious example, Devo. Emerging out of Akron, Ohio, in the middle 1970s, brothers Jim, Bob, and Mark Mothersbaugh joined another pair of siblings, Bob and Gerald Casale, in what began as an art project by Kent State University undergrads but morphed into an angular pop chimera that would demythologize and castrate not only rock but American culture, turning a typically rhythmic, sexual, and danceable commercial product into a deliberately robotic, perhaps unsolvable, math equation. Devo accomplished this asexual reproduction of Americana both by consuming (to the point of surfeit) the desiring machine of industrial capitalism before defecating its products as recombinant "mutated" outputs and by grafting bits and pieces of capitalism's trash onto the band's distorted songs (see "Wiggly World") and band members' bodies—the "flower pot" hardhats, hazmat suits, too-tight polyester gym shorts, safety glasses, vinyl shoes, and so on. Calling itself "the fluid in the [punk, American, pop] enema bag," as Casale put it repeatedly to interviewers, Devo not only was pop as seen through a scanner darkly, but brought to life Dick's *Androids,* which paved the way for Devo by imagining a postwar planet where only the degenerates—"Emigrate or degenerate! The choice is yours!"—stay on a ruined Earth that is swarming with the trash of capitalism known as "kipple": the "useless objects, like junk mail or match folders after you use the last match or gum wrappers or yesterday's homeopape. When nobody's around, kipple reproduces itself. For instance, if you go to bed leaving any kipple around your apartment, when you wake up the next morning there's twice as much of it."[31] Such rubbish, both terrestrial and galactic—"She never saw it / When she was hit by—space junk! / She was smashed by—space junk!"—is resurrected in Devo, who, like Trash Heap from Jim Henson's *Fraggle Rock,* reanimates the detritus of Western civilization and serves as a festering oracle to chickenheads and replicants alike. Having too read Czech anthropologist Oscar Kiss Maerth's *In the Beginning Was the End,* which theorized that humankind evolved from a caste of brain-eating apes and was thus destined to consume itself in an increasing pandemic of sex and violence as the species foundered, Devo from its first rehearsals imagined itself as the degraded, pastiche product of a postindustrial capitalist economy designed to yield not high culture or durable goods but kipple: kitsch, disposable artifacts, and always-already obsolete rubbish, including gratuitous monster movies, plastics, pulp science fiction, professional sports, advertising, pop art, and pornography.

At the heart of Devo's degenerate mythology, then, was the claim that the band members were themselves the natural result of not merely refracted culture or cannibalism but "retrograde evolution: evolution which, instead of producing higher or more specialized organisms, has produced degraded or more generalized ones."[32] In becoming the cultural vivisection that Cabaret Voltaire and Negativland merely play with on tape—although Casale agrees that "for a lot of our songs if it wasn't for tape recorders we wouldn't have been able to create them"[33]—Devo came to embody and thus critique the effects of a really existing capitalism that too unsettled Burroughs, Le Guin, Dick, and other sci-fi authors so far as capitalism quite rationally devolves most anything it touches into a homogenized—thus retrograde—commercial product with broad appeal, no aura, and only simulated elegance. In satirizing the culture of the lowest common denominator, Devo made of itself the composite pop-punk version of several Dick novels—not only *Androids* but *The Simulacra,* with its interest in mutants and banning psychoanalysis, and *Flow My Tears, the Policeman Said,* whose genetically engineered subjects exist for the express purpose of spectacle in a future police state that has outlawed intellectuals.

Maerth and Dick in hand, so to speak, Devo set out to produce their own "anti-capitalist science fiction" texts—both records and films.[34] Notwithstanding its *Mechanical Man* EP and debut album, which featured, among other tracks punctuated by synthesizers grunting out blips and trills, the ironic take on modern medicine "Gut Feeling," the trashy "Space Junk," and the ode to kipple and the pleasure principle "Too Much Paranoias," the 1977 short film *In the Beginning Was the End: The Truth about De-evolution* remains Devo's first and best articulation of its argument. "In the past this information has been suppressed, but now it can be told. Every man, woman, and mutant on this planet shall know the truth about de-evolution," announces a wan éminence grise called General Boy from behind a chestful of military pins in what appears a classic sci-fi television broadcast-interrupt as his hysteric confederate and son, Booji Boy—masked and orange-suited—yelps with arms flailing, "Oh, dad, we're all devo!" The child had just conferred to his father "the papers the Chinaman gave [him]" verifying their theory on what a cynical class of powerful men familiar to readers of Dick had worked for decades to repress: behind viewers' constructed consumer culture, their distorted reality, resides a nefarious actuality of totalitarian ideological control operating amidst both genetic and ecological decay.

Dramatizing the return of the repressed, the film cuts precipitously to Mark Mothersbaugh, in his mad scientist getup, who jumps about awkwardly as his band's "Jocko Homo" begins and he professes, "We're pinheads now / We are not whole / We're pinheads all / [species] Jocko Homo." Borrowing the Sayer of the Law's query to his fellow Beast Folk—"Are we not men?"—from H. G. Wells's *The Island of Doctor Moreau* (which explores the cutting up and recombination of not graphical but organic signifiers) Mothersbaugh, the evil genius, lectures a standing-room-only class of "devotees"—some taking precise notes, others pounding on their desks—who quickly fall in line, answering Mothersbaugh's question with the mechanical rejoinder, "We are Devo!" Whipping his class into a frenzy, Mothersbaugh closes the lecture abruptly, sending his students out into a crumbling, synthetic world as the film cuts again to a bound Booji Boy, who has been captured now, and one assumes tortured, by the muscular functionaries of capitalism, the Gorgs of State, as on-screen tags read, "the littlest shall survive & the unfit may live . . . be like your ancestors or be different . . . we must repeat," and Booji Boy is unmasked and revealed as the professor himself as the reel runs out.

In crafting such films and records, Devo helped illustrate Dick's vision long before the visualization on film of any of his stories, which tend to follow a thematic pattern: nothing is as it seems; an ideology-generating (totalitarian) elite is behind the ruse; even the most fantastic products of capitalism are but distractions from the horrific reality lazing just out of the average pinhead's perception; and lifting the veil on the ruse and/or refusing to partake in the distraction can get one killed.

Taking Devo's appropriation of such content even further was Sonic Youth, the New York No Wavers less interested in kipple than in Dick's ideas of time and space. Included in the list of acknowledgements on its 1987 record *Sister* is "p.k. dick (the owl in daylight)." Ostensibly a meditation on Dick's life, the album, referencing both the author's incomplete last novel (*The Owl in Daylight*) and his twin sister who died less than two months after their premature birth, is the either/or soundtrack to Dick's late canon—*VALIS, Ubik, Radio Free Albemuth, Scanner*—at the same time as it is a meditation on what William James would have called Dick's "divided soul." That is to say, in their band's fifth album, Kim Gordon and Thurston Moore—with Lee Ranaldo getting in the way—explore Dick's broad, compulsive Manichaeism on a number of levels, not only the loss of his feminine Other self but schizophrenia and gnosticism ("[I Got A] Catholic Block," "White Cross"), mind-body astigmatism ("Cotton Crown"), and the ontology of time ("Stereo Sanctity," "Pipeline/Kill Time"). Accordingly, the record's music likewise heaves and swings precipitously between extremes of noise and silence, form and disorder, as in Gordon's "Pacific Coast Highway," in which an almost soothing instrumental bridge is sandwiched between the absolute chaos of Moore's and Ranaldo's guitars and the dissonance of Gordon's mocking words delivered without affect—"Come on baby . . . let's go for a ride somewhere . . . I won't hurt you." "Stereo Sanctity" in particular translates Dick's missing double, if not Lacan's mirror stage, into a sort of aural imbalance between the corresponding speakers on some home stereo, arguing in favor of an uncertain hylozoism—"your spirit is time-reversed to your body . . . it started growing up the day your body dies . . . real to irreal"—wondering as does Dick in multiple works if spirit can exist without matter, if the reel of time can be run backward. The song's line "I can't get laid 'cause everyone is dead" is allegedly a paraphrase from Dick's *Valis*.[35]

"[Dick is] like a modern day philosopher," Gordon once told an interviewer. "His books can be depressing, but I feel very centered whenever I read him."[36] Or, as Moore added later, keeping with his then-spouse's sophist analogy and discussing his approach to lyric writing in the late 1980s, "You didn't really have to read Kant or Hegel or the Bible or other things—you could read Philip K. Dick and get a lot of ideas through one writer. . . . I always liked the idea that writing lyrics was more of a subconscious attitude, in a way. It really came to fruition while reading Philip K. Dick for a couple of years, and also while writing *Sister*."[37] So does it come as no surprise that the Sonic Youth records produced when the band was taking regular hits of Substance Dick tend to sound not robotic or electronic like Kraftwerk or Devo, but nevertheless paranoid, schizophrenic, and *cold*—simultaneously binary and esoteric. Algorithmic. Like the sort of music a replicant might try to produce in imitation of what humans call "pop."

Punk Portmanteaux

Dick was hardly the only science fiction writer who influenced the words and music of Sonic Youth, however. "I'm a cool hunter making you my way / Like a brand name you'll replay," Gordon, her voice almost pretty now, whispers on the unnerving "Pattern Recognition" from her band's 2004 record *Sonic Nurse*, a song crystalizing the story of cool merchant Cayce Pollard in the novel of the same title by William Gibson. "Close your eyes and feel the fun / Pattern recognition's on the run." The song was not the first time that Sonic Youth referenced the author whose work defined a new genre; the group's landmark 1988 record *Daydream Nation* includes a track called "The Sprawl," borrowed from Gibson's *Neuromancer,* which also provided the names for bands good and bad laboring in the wake of punk, from the Panther Moderns to Straylight Run.

"My initial experience of punk was I went to Toronto, and I happened to go to a couple of nights of what historically turned out to be their first punk concert series. They had some bands from as far away as Los Angeles playing this kind of music I'd never heard before," Gibson, a Canadian by birth, told an interviewer in 2012. "Then a friend of mine who had been in art school in London returned with a knapsack full of British punk zines and everything that the Sex Pistols had released up to that point. And he pulled these records out of his knapsack. I had never heard of the Sex Pistols, and neither had anyone else in Vancouver. By the end of the evening we were all talking about them."[38] So did Gibson, now a full-fledged fan, go on to drop punk references in book after book, from the character named directly after Voidoid Bob Quine in *Neuromancer* to appropriating Arizona's Meat Puppets to describe a biological being under the sway of a cyber "cowboy" who had wired in to another's consciousness to his later novel *All Tomorrow's Parties,* taken from the Velvet Underground song of the same title. Accordingly, (post) punks like Moore and Gordon often ate up Gibson's books, reveling in stories obliquely about them.

Such reading on punks' behalf—closer to the twenty-first century than any other books or authors covered in this investigation—is interesting so far as it, a decade after the original cyberpunks Devo and Cabaret Voltaire and emerging too after Dick's death and Burroughs's waning, signals the emergence of a certain self-consciousness, even pretension, on punks' behalf: although influencing the shape of punk culture to come in marginal ways, Gibson's earliest and best work completes the circle by serving as the inscription of "postpunk" as an idea and would not have come to be *without* punk's first wave and would too shape subsequent punk aesthetics. So far as postpunks like Sonic Youth began consuming such fictional texts that further stylized their own subculture only to turn around and recreate "punk" music referencing sci-fi novels about themselves, then, they demonstrated the degree to which punk after Gibson if it was not truly dead, then at the very least had come to embody what Baudrillard called the "desert of the real." Put another way, if punk as an image and idea was the reflection of a profound reality, cyberpunk especially masked and denatured punks themselves and the reality to which punks were responding. The result was not only Sonic Youth but punk's splintering into dozens of variants that seem to render the very term "postpunk" meaningless, masking the *absence* of punk, of the fact that both the Real and punk are dead. To paraphrase Baudrillard's comment on anthropology, in order for punk to live, its object must die. And by dying punk takes its revenge for being "discovered" and appropriated by advocates and opponents by mutating into a hyperreal version of itself that renders both the original and the copy artificial.[39] Fretting at such a development are punks after Sonic Youth such as the (International) Noise Conspiracy, which in "Simulacra Overload" sings, "Save me won't you please / Save me from this hyper-reality."

The Noise Conspiracy's appropriation of Baudrillard's theorizing notwithstanding, this formal association of punk and science fiction resulted in the work of not only Gibson but Bruce Sterling, John Shirley (former member of punk group Sado-Nation), Rudy Rucker, and others being quickly categorized as "cyberpunk" for its application of the punk attitude and couture to dissident hackers and hipsters living on the margins of an often virtual networked economy. In Gibson's original "Sprawl Trilogy," for instance, alienated and disenfranchised, if incredibly street-smart and tech-savvy, young men and women navigate a sleazy postindustrial dystopian megalopolis where not representative governments but multinational corporations control all production and consumption, human geography, and digital information, which *is* the new currency. Such subjects, who pass their time jacking in and out of "cyberspace"—Gibson's neologism—are regularly described as characteristically punk in their manner and style. "The Panther Modern leader, who introduced himself as Lupus Yonderboy, wore a polycarbon suit with a recording feature that allowed him to replay backgrounds at will [on his outfit]." So Gibson describes his spike-haired "surreal terrorist" in a variegated post-Dick scramble suit whose cat-eyed associates, a collection of postmodern Duchamps and Bretons, simulate acts of mayhem for no other reason than to create situations in a way not unlike the Sex Pistols or Negativland. "He executed a strange little dance, his thin black arms whirling, and then he was gone. No. There. Hood up to hide the pink [hair], the suit exactly the right shade of gray, mottled and stained as the sidewalk he stood on. The [modified] eyes winked back the red of a stoplight."[40]

Taking both Gibson and Dick one step further by inserting Burroughs's idea that language is a virus into cyberspace is Neal Stephenson, whose *Snow Crash*, almost a parody of cyberpunk, imagines a computer virus that crashes hard drives at the same time as it infects the central nervous systems of human participants in the "metaverse." "In binary form, a [word-image] virus can bounce around the universe at the speed of light. It infects a civilized planet, gets into its computers, reproduces, and inevitably gets broadcast on television or radio or whatever," Stephenson's punky samurai-hacker Hiro Protagonist puts it, after realizing anarcho-capitalist and Pentecostal antagonist L. Bob Rife's intent to disseminate a computer virus—implied to be the lost Sumerian ur-language—to hackers *through* fiber optics. "When it is placed into a computer it snow-crashes the computer by causing it to infect itself with new viruses. But it is much more devastating when it goes into the mind of a hacker, a person who has an understanding of binary code built into the deep structures of his brain."[41]

This biolinguistic virus, created by the Levantine goddess of motherhood and fertility Asherah, was virtually eradicated in antiquity through the explosion of myriad tongues—what in Genesis the sons of Adam explain through the story of Babel—that prevented humankind from understanding and speaking the ur-language, Stephenson suggests. Rife had been hoping to resurrect and distribute what is hard to read as anything but *the* original Logos in binary form to hackers especially, who would be able to then spread the virus virtually, ostensibly converting anyone swimming through the ether to Rife's eschatological version of Christianity (which is also a simulation of a Real that no longer exists, if it ever did).

Like so much of punk and postpunk and the authors punks admire—Burroughs, Ballard, Dick—cyberpunk characters and the authors who produce them are too wrestling with, if not trying to undermine, the symbolic law, if not escape the horrors its administration of the planet has generated in a world of capitalism run amok: environmental collapse, political fragmentation, poverty for the majority, the privatization of natural resources, and techno-decadence for elites. Buying punk's critique of the symbolic paternal, many cyberpunkers, Gibson especially, have gone on to warn of the dangers of not only the surveillance state and technological determinism, but the turning over of traditionally public enterprises to the private sector. "Cyberspace, not so long ago, was a specific elsewhere, one we visited periodically, peering into it from the familiar physical world. Now cyberspace has everted. Turned itself inside out. Colonized the physical," Gibson wrote in a *New York Times* editorial in 2010, thinking perhaps of Baudrillard. "This is the sort of thing that empires and nationstates did, before. But empires and nationstates weren't organs of global human perception. They had their many eyes, certainly, but they didn't constitute a single multiplex eye for the entire human species." Behind Gibson's lament is a fear that much of what he and others prophesied is coming true (though he acknowledges science fiction failed to anticipate the Internet as it exists today), that the world is entering a new stage of declining in human rights, social justice, and privacy, never mind ecological collapse. "We are part of a postgeographical, postnational superstate, one that handily says no to China. Or yes, depending on profit considerations and strategy. But we do not participate. . . . We're citizens, but without rights."[42]

This fear that technology is outstripping the institutions that produced it, that political economy is resurrecting a past in which few citizens had privileges, cartels and organized mafias managed local economies, and democracy was but a pipedream (all of which is only obliquely criticized by Stephenson whose novels at times seem to endorse a certain libertarian capitalism), is at the heart of the second genre Gibson helped conceive. Rather than saying "yes" to the future by melding punk politics and style with cyberspace, computers hackers, and virtual reality, Gibson followed up his Sprawl Trilogy by teaming up with Bruce Sterling to pen *The Difference Engine*, less a mediation on the future than an alternate history in the vein of Dick's *High Castle*. Set in the nineteenth century, *Difference Engine* represents the authors' attempt to imagine not a virtual future but a pre-electronic—steam-powered—past, the gaslight realm of Baudelaire, Poe, and Dostoevsky, whose subjects ponce about in punky Victorian style (e.g., corsets with fishnet tights and spiked hair, top hats above not only coattails but gas masks or face piercings) as they simultaneously find themselves confronting many of cyberpunk's themes: alienation, technofetishism, and oligarchy as the dominant governing strategy. So did *Difference*, which catalyzed the production of a parade of similar novels, combine punk aesthetics with nineteenth-century technology and politics in a style that came to be regarded as "steampunk" by readers and critics. "The Byron men, the Baggage men, the Industrial Radicals, they own Great Britain! They own us, girl—the very globe is at their feet, Europe, America, everywhere," ex-Luddite and Dandy sellout Mick Radley lectures his protégé Sybil in Gibson's and Sterling's novel, reminding readers of the grip the symbolic paternal had on the levers of political economy more than a century ago as well. "The House of Lords is packed top to bottom with [Industrial Radicals]. Queen Victoria won't stir a finger without a nod from the savants and capitalists."[43]

Finding antecedents in H. G. Wells and Jules Verne, steampunk's relatively late development—*Difference* was published in 1991, the same year that Nirvana's *Nevermind* was released—means that punk and postpunk advocates have had much less time to read steampunk books and incorporate them into their music and performance aesthetics. But this is no terrible thing. As the aesthetics of twenty-first century groups like Vernian Process or Abney Park demonstrate, steampunk doubles down on punk's death, on Baudrillard, by literally creating the copy of an original ideogram that never actually existed and has no referent. In so doing, steampunk masks the fact that behind the highly stylized image of the new (post) "punk" is a vacuous nothingness.

The same is true of what came to be known as "splatterpunk," a pulpy genre that too emerged in the late 1980s through the melding of punk aesthetics and ideology with the gothic sensibilities of Mary Shelley, Bram Stoker, and Edgar Allan Poe, if not later "horror" writers like H. P. Lovecraft. And like cyberpunk, neither of these latter punk portmanteaux would have come to be without punk's first wave. Whereas steampunk carries punk aesthetics backward in time toward an alternate Victorian iteration of human development, though, splatterpunk brings Shelley, Poe, and Lovecraft forward in space-time, locating them in marginalized contemporary environs: a punk club in Hell's Kitchen, some back alley in the New Orleans French Quarter, and so on. Upping the ante on gothic and horror fiction's subtle gore, splatterpunk novels tend to describe a different sort of "cut-up," reveling in what is hard to describe as anything but a gratuitous enthusiasm for the spectacle of the dismembered body—its colors, fluids, and smells—only with "punks" wandering about in tattered cloaks and blue hair.

Take, if not Nick Blinko's aforementioned *The Primal Screamer*, Poppy Z. Brite's short story collection *Wormwood* as a case in point. Nearly each of the book's twelve tales, from the rock band-cum-carnies in "A Georgia Story" to the drunken punk necrophiles in "Xenophobia" to the musician-dad in the infanticidal "The Elder," is populated by leading characters who moonlight as members of underground bands and find their lives overturned by a series of supernatural and horrific occurrences. "Younger than Louis and myself, most of them were, and queerly beautiful in their thrift shop rags, their leather and fishnet cheap costume jewelry, their pale faces and painted hair," Brite describes the club-goers in *Wormwood*'s titular story, written in 1989. As for the club itself: "Feedback blasted us as we came in, and above it, a screaming battle of guitars. The inside of the club was a patchwork of flickering light and darkness. Graffiti covered the walls and the ceiling like a tangle of barbed wire come alive." As the story's narrator explains, after a night of absinthe, grave-robbing, and seeking out music that "was never loud enough," he awoke to find his compatriot Louis a brittle shell of a man, drained of his vitality by a punk vampire who had followed the pair home from the club and slinked away before dawn.[44]

Is this not an allegory for what steampunk and splatterpunk have done to punk and its original threat to the status quo, to the Father? In spite of Brite's skill as a stylist, such scenes—many of which revel in a certain apolitical and, again, morally conservative escapism that first-wave punks accused the hippies of exulting—were tired by the time the Misfits, Rudimentary Peni, Dead Moon, and even GWAR splattered onto the punk scene nearly a decade earlier in the early 1980s in the long wake of "shock rock" groups like Black Sabbath and Alice Cooper.

Breaking free of the camp of such acts, even the "punk" ones, which were often derivative too of groups like Devo and Throbbing Gristle, was a short-lived quartet from certifiably weird city Louisville. Although not "splatterpunk" in the generic sense, Slint nonetheless demonstrated the emptiness of splatterpunk before it had even caught on by crafting the most horrifying American record of the twentieth century without drawing a drop of blood. In so doing, Slint undermined the cultural dominant in ways splatterpunk merely fantasized about in its supernaturalism and mythologizing.

From the remnants of punk groups Squirrel Bait and Maurice, Brian McMahan, David Pajo, Britt Walford, and Ethan Buckler formed Slint in 1986. Named for one of the member's pet fish, and taking a page from the Big Black playbook, the quartet brought nineteenth-century gothic motifs, postpunk aesthetics, and despair together to create a music that was horrifying for both its originality and its refusal to condescend. After releasing the mostly instrumental record *Tweez* in 1989, which bristles with a tinselly bookishness and anxious timbre alluded to in tracks like "Ron" (the first of nine tracks named simply for the bandmates' parents), Slint went back into the studio to record its second and final album, *Spiderland*. Steeped in mystery and carrying with it a series of whispered anecdotes—that McMahan recorded his vocals in near darkness and would vomit after screaming certain verses, that the entire band checked itself into a psychiatric hospital following the recording sessions—*Spiderland* is an unnerving collection of intricate rhythms, screeching guitars, and disturbing narratives that are typically spoken rather than sung in what often seems an automatic effusion of unconscious thought that would have pleased Breton—or Poe.

"I stepped out onto the midway; I was looking for the pirate ship and saw this small, old tent at one end," McMahan begins on "Breadcrumb Trail," imagining himself a Hansel stuck in a nineteenth-century American near-South carnival, surrounded by dwarves, hucksters, and other grotesque dregs of America's opportunist doctrine. He is at home, though, this seeker, almost nonchalant and remembering all at once Poe's "The Cask of Amontillado"—"It was about dusk, one evening during the supreme madness of the carnival season, that I encountered my friend," Poe begins—and the Bob Dylan of "Desolation Row" as he takes pleasure in his wandering. Finding his estranged Gretel in the form of a fortune-telling girl, the speaker declines to have his future told, asking instead if the oracle would join him for a roller-coaster ride. With this abrupt question, this irrational and unexpected query that even the patron seems surprised to have had the courage to ask, *Spiderland* jolts into the thirty most terrifying minutes of pop music America has produced. "Creeping up into the *skyyyyyyyy*," McMahan shrieks as the song's initially jangly guitars become a broken ambulance siren, reproducing the dreamlike extremes—volume, pitch, attitude—of an amusement park ride. The song too is dizzying, moving up, then down, then up again, reproducing in the listener the singer's nauseating disorientation. "I shouted and searched the sky for a friend," the narrator remembers, "I heard the fortune-teller screaming *back* at me / We stuck out our hands and met the wind."

That the entire scene—words, music, and signifiers left unspoken—takes on a charged sexuality as it closes becomes clear the moment

McMahan, almost embarrassed at having lost his cool, admits in a whimper how the fortune-teller clutched her stomach and began to heave at the end of a surreal event that left both parties exhausted. Wobbling off the platform at ride's end, the pair grin sheepishly at each other as the grubby ticket-taker picks his teeth and offers the couple a second ride. "The sun was setting by the time we left," Hansel concludes, satisfied, if still trembling, as the fortune-teller walks her beau to the empty lot and leaves him alone in the dusk. "The carnival sign threw colored shadows on her face, but I could tell she was blushing."

Following that wholly unanticipated opening moment of tenderness and shame, *Spiderland* gets both more literary and progressively creepier, offering the Stokerian "Nosferatu Man," the equal parts suicidal-paranoid "Don, Aman," and the brooding "For Dinner . . . ," which like Whitman's *Leaves of Grass* nearly collapses under the pregnant weight of its crawling ellipsis. In each of these tracks, the band's literary background—and McMahan's and Walford's time at Louisville's K–12 progressive school J. Graham Brown—groans just below the layered (minor) chords. Although the group is cryptic in interviews, refusing to discuss lyrics in any detail, each of the songs on *Spiderland* suggests its writers' erudition, their half-remembered, jumbled consumption of not science fiction, not cyber- or splatterpunk, but American folklore, Romantic poetry, German Expressionist cinema, and gothic fiction—Poe in particular. That is to say, Slint's carnival psychic is Poe's murdered Madame L'Espanaye who "told fortunes for a living"; "Nosferatu Man" is not Stoker's *Dracula* necessarily but reminiscent of it, not to mention Poe's "Lenore"; "Don, Aman" fuses Poe's "The Sleeper" with Hawthorne's "Young Goodman Brown"; and "Washer" renovates "The House of Usher," whose namesake Poe describes as anticipating the disciplined and sparse "postrock" Slint is credited with inventing: "It was, perhaps, the narrow limits to which he thus confined himself upon the guitar which gave birth, in great measure, to the fantastic character of the performances. But the fervid *facility* of his *impromptus* could not be so accounted for. They must have been, and were, in the notes, as well as in the words of his wild fantasias (for he not unfrequently accompanied himself with rhymed verbal improvisations), the result of that intense mental collectedness and concentration." Poe is, with these words, calling Slint into being centuries before their birth, writing too in some dank unfinished cellar, vomiting after each line, and anticipating the bleak pop that sounds the way his stories read even to this day.[45]

Nowhere is Slint making direct reference to Poe, Hawthorne, Washington Irving, or Whitman; and nowhere in Slint's legacy is it apparent the band had read Brite or listened to shock rock (although elsewhere the Dickies' Stan Lee did tell Vale that "Edgar Allan Poe is great").[46] Furthermore, the group is not merely putting Hawthorne or Poe to music, as did Siouxsie and the Banshees, Lou Reed, and many other punk and postpunk groups. Instead, the band reconstructs, in a musty basement in western Kentucky, suggestively oblique stories born out of a miasma of gothic archetypes, tattered bits of twice-told tales, murder ballads, and indelible ghost stories from their (nation's) adolescence. The result is a clawfoot tub of anxious, self-conscious tales, dripping with despondency and bobbing along aimlessly in a sea of black blood, that achieve the psychological depth and intellectual terror of Poe's or Hawthorne's most memorable products.

Closing the creaking gate on the haunted house that is *Spiderland* is "Good, Morning Captain," Slint's answer to Samuel Taylor Coleridge's ghastly "The Rime of the Ancient Mariner." Gesturing also to Melville, Slint's ghost yarn of shattered vessels and spectral sailors describes the frail phantom of a ship captain haunting a child who recognizes in the captain's piteous "Help me" something unspeakable, perhaps unconscious, from his past. The song's rhythm is a stalker's walk; the beat: the sound of the repressed on its way to the surface. Terrified at the sight and sound of history—of the unconscious—on its way to confront him, the child tremblingly pulls down the "shade against the shadow" who, for his part, begins pleading, "I'm trying to find my way home" and crying, "I miss you!" as the song reaches its incoherent end. In this American take on the English canon, the dynamic music of which attacks the listener in rotating segments of gaunt pulses and violent crescendos of noise, the Ancient Mariner's curse is not so much having to relive his doomed voyage in verse as having to suffer the repeated rebellion of his former subjects, his children, who seem to be if not indifferent to his cries, then openly hostile to his suffering. Slint, in retelling this tale, accepts, on behalf of punk, Ralph Waldo Emerson's insistence in "The American Scholar" that American artists and poets slough off the yolk of European style, that they kill their fathers even as they confront their own ghosts. "Our days of dependence, our long apprenticeship to the learning of other lands, draws to a close," Emerson had decreed as much as he had yearned in 1837, to which Slint, as the song's alternately frightened-invigorated child, replies with a shrug a century and a half later, looking back at Coleridge through the eyes of American punk. As the captain and his issue mumble disjointedly and alternately, both desiring and hating the Other simultaneously,

> I miss you.
> I'm sorry.
> I've grown taller now [?]
> I want the police to be notified [?]
> I swear by this very song [?]
> I'll make it up to you,
> I miss you!

I swear by this song. In this mumbled penultimate line McMahan becomes the child back from having committed a pulverizing and necessary act of violence against the father—closing the shade on the searching superego—and feeling suddenly desperate at the thought of leaving his overlord behind even as he looks ahead to an untrammeled wilderness both boundless and perhaps more vicious than his former master.

But free. Having likely read their Poe and Coleridge, Walford and McMahan reproduce the former even as they reference the latter in *Spiderland,* reacting to capitalism's fabricated amusements and dehumanization of the subject—at a twinkling carnival, in a rural middle-American ghost town, on a busted English frigate spattered with blood—by refusing to have their future told, breaking the reflection of their image-object like Rollins on the *Damaged* cover and shrinking back only momentarily in terror at the memory of their own violent history. In so doing Slint finds itself in the position of the "Angelus Novus" in the Klee painting of the same title, about which Benjamin wrote, "Where we perceive a chain of events, he sees one single catastrophe which keeps piling wreckage upon wreckage and hurls it in front of his feet. The angel would like to stay, awaken the dead, and make whole what has been smashed. But a storm is blowing from paradise. . . . This storm irresistibly propels him into the future to which his back is turned, while the pile of debris before him grows skyward."[47]

In crafting such a narrative, in moving punk forward with its back turned as it sees the violence of its past, Slint created a record that not unlike Cormac McCarthy's *Blood Meridian* doubles as an allegory of American violence in the face of its own commitment to freedom, whether in 1776, 1863, 1944, 1968, or 1991; as such, it is a *nightmare,* conceived in a pit, not only for the bobbing heads on the record's cover but for its listeners and the businessmen and journalists charged with promoting an unmarketable, undanceable, and unsettling artifact: with no single to promote and composed by a group that disbanded before the record was even released, *Spiderland* is the ectoplasm left behind by a collection of ghosts from a New World that perhaps never even existed in the first place. In so doing Slint vaults past not only the horror punkers cited above, but steampunk and splatterpunk as literary genres, whose own anti-capitalism or refusal of the symbolic paternal collapse in on their own hedonism and conspicuous consumption, their surrender to the master's own commodification of violence and prurience.

All of this Slint embeds in its music and in so doing, obliquely references the European writer Franz Kafka, whose surreal and terrifying tales of transformation, isolation, and surveillance unfold like nightmares from which Josef K never seems to wake, and who cleared the ground for what would become the contemporary sci-fi launch pad. Amerika's *Kafka Chronicles*, Blinko's comparison of his punk protag to Kafka, and Dick's designation as "a kind of pulp-fiction Kafka" notwithstanding, even William Burroughs would not have come to be without Kafka.[48] Flinching at the horrors of bureaucracy at the same time as he birthed tales of human centipedes and other Insect People, Burroughs took a page from Kafka's playbook in never really "completing" a novel, but openly reworking tortuous narratives from one edition to the next, as in *The Soft Machine*, which exists in three different versions, and includes bits from earlier novels in later ones. Driving the connection home, Burroughs's *Nova Express* lifts entire paragraphs from Kafka's *The Trial*. Slint aside, then, if postpunk bands like Josef K and Kafka are any indication, Kafka too keeps his own shelf on the punk bookcase, influencing not only punk and postpunk bands but those punk *authors* like Acker and Amerika who would turn to crafting "punk fiction"—the subject of the next chapter—as a means of circumventing and dismantling the assemblages erected by the Name of the Father to isolate and inhibit the hysteric punk subject.

Notes

1. Peter Hook, *Unknown Pleasures: Inside Joy Division* (New York: HarperCollins/It, 2013), 231–33.

2. Alex Baker, "35 Years Ago Today Joy Division Played Live at Plan K, Brussels, Belgium," Post-Punk.com, October 16, 2014, http://www.post-punk.com/35-years-ago-today-joy-division-played-live-at-plan-k-brussels-belgium-live-debut-of-love-will-tear-us-apart/.

3. Chris Ott, *Unknown Pleasures* (New York: Continuum, 2004), 98.

4. Ian Curtis, *So This Is Permanence: Joy Division Lyrics and Notebooks*, ed. Deborah Curtis and Jon Savage (San Francisco: Chronicle, 2014), xviii.

5. Kurt Cobain, *Journals* (New York: Penguin/Riverhead, 2002), 244.

6. No author, "Vermillion Bitches," *Search & Destroy* #1, 1977, in *Search and Destroy 1–6: The Complete Reprint*, by V. Vale (San Francisco: V/Search, 1996),: 6; No author, "Ramones Go West," *Search & Destroy* #2, 1977, in *Search and Destroy 1–6: The Complete Reprint*, by V. Vale (San Francisco: V/Search, 1996), 22. Note also Steve Albini's post–Big Black group Rapeman, named for the Japanese manga series published 1985–92.

7. Damon Locks, personal communication with the author, June 29, 2015.

8. Victor Bockris, *Beat Punks* (New York: DaCapo, 1998), 182. See also Legs McNeil and Gillian McCain, *Please Kill Me: The Uncensored Oral History of Punk* (New York: Penguin, 1996), 208.

9. McNeil and McCain, *Please Kill Me*, 161.

10. Lynn X, "Iggy Pop," *Search & Destroy* #4, 1977, in *Search and Destroy 1–6: The Complete Reprint*, by V. Vale (San Francisco: V/Search, 1996), 66; Jon Savage, "Industrial Music for Industrial People," *Search & Destroy* #6, 1978, in *Search and Destroy 1–6: The Complete Reprint*, by V. Vale (San Francisco: V/Search, 1996), 122; William S. Burroughs, *Nothing Here Now but the Recordings*, vinyl LP, Industrial Records, IR0016, 1981.

11. William S. Burroughs, *Nova Express*, in *Three Novels by William S. Burroughs* (New York: Grove, 1980), 153.

12. William S. Burroughs, *The Ticket That Exploded* (New York: Grove, 1967), 210.

13. Ibid., 49.

14. Simon Reynolds, *Rip It Up and Start Again* (New York: Penguin, 2005), 90.

15. Joel Schalit, "Negativland," in *We Owe You Nothing*, ed. Dan Sinker (New York: Akashic, 2001), 203.

16. Barry Miles, *William Burroughs: El Hombre Invisible* (1992; London: Virgin, 2010), 103.

17. William S. Burroughs, *The Wild Boys*, in *Three Novels by William S. Burroughs* (New York: Grove, 1980), 51, 151, 165–66 (emphasis added).

18. No author, "Devo: 2nd Part of the De-Evolution Band Interview," *Search & Destroy* #3, 1977, in *Search and Destroy 1–6: The Complete Reprint*, by V. Vale (San Francisco: V/Search, 1996), 53.

19. J. G. Ballard, "Why I Want to Fuck Ronald Reagan," in *The Complete Stories of J. G. Ballard* (1968; New York: Norton, 2009), 757.

20. Jon Savage, "J. G. Ballard," *Search & Destroy* #10, 1978, in *Search and Destroy 1–6: The Complete Reprint*, by V. Vale (San Francisco: V/Search, 1996), 106–7.

21. Daniel Odier, *The Job: Interviews with William S. Burroughs* (New York: Grove, 1969), 116.

22. Miles, *William Burroughs*, 129.

23. Burroughs, *The Wild Boys*, 123.

24. Burroughs, *Nova Express*, 57–58.

25. Mark Amerika, *The Kafka Chronicles* (Normal: FC2/Illinois State, 1993), 169.

26. See, for example, Miriam Rivett's "Misfit Lit," in *So What?*, ed. Roger Sabin (London: Routledge, 1999), 31–48; Stephen Duncome, *Notes from Underground: Zines and the Politics of Alternative Culture* (London: Verso, 1997); and Vincent Bernière and Mariel Primois, *Punk Press: Rebel Rock in the Underground Press 1968–1980: Rebel Rock in the Underground Press 1968–1980* (New York: Abrams, 2013).

27. John Holmstrom and Bridget Hurd, eds., *Punk: The Best of Punk Magazine* (New York: HarperCollins, 2012), 159, 219.

28. Odier, *The Job*, 27.

29. V. Vale, "Dickies: LA Band Leaps to Punk Preeminence," *Search & Destroy* #5, 1978, in *Search and Destroy 1–6: The Complete Reprint*, by V. Vale (San Francisco: V/Search, 1996), 108.

30. Philip K. Dick, *A Scanner Darkly* (1977; Boston: Mariner, 2011), 84, 96–97, 220.

31. Philip K. Dick, *Do Androids Dream of Electric Sheep?* (1968; New York: Del Rey, 1996), 8, 65.

32. "Devo: 2nd Part of the De-Evolution Band Interview," 52.

33. No Author, "Devo's De-Evolution Decade," *Search & Destroy* #2, 1977, in *Search and Destroy 1–6: The Complete Reprint*, by V. Vale (San Francisco: V/Search, 1996), 31.

34. Vale, "Devo: Out West to Ride the Human Highway," *Search & Destroy* #8, 1978, in *Search and Destroy 1–6: The Complete Reprint*, by V. Vale (San Francisco: V/Search, 1996), 37.

35. Alec Foege, *Confusion Is Next: The Sonic Youth Story* (New York: St. Martin's, 1994), 163–64.

36. Erik Davis, "Bring the White Noise," *Spin*, January 1989, 48–50.

37. Foege, *Confusion Is Next*, 162–63.

38. Geeta Dayal, "William Gibson on Punk Rock, Internet Memes, and 'Gangnam Style,'" *Wired*, Wired.com, September 15, 2012, http://www.wired.com/2012/09/william-gibson-part-3-punk-memes/.

39. See Jean Baudrillard, *Simulacra and Simulation*, trans. Sheila Glaser (1981; Ann Arbor: University of Michigan Press, 1994), 7–9.

40. William Gibson, *Neuromancer* (1984; New York: Ace, 1986), 67–69.

41. Neal Stephenson, *Snow Crash* (New Uork: Bantam, 1992), 405.

42. William Gibson, "Google's Earth," *New York Times*, September 1, 2010, A23.

43. William Gibson and Bruce Sterling, *The Difference Engine* (New York: Bantam, 1991), 22.

44. Poppy Z. Brite, "His Mouth Will Taste of Wormwood," in *Wormwood* (New York: Dell, 1996), 34, 45, 44.

45. Edgar Allan Poe, "The Fall of the House of Usher," in *The Complete Tales and Poems of Edgar Allan Poe* (1839; New York: Modern Library, 1938), 237.

46. Vale, "Dickies: LA Band Leaps to Punk Preeminence," 108.

47. Walter Benjamin, "Theses on the Philosophy of History," in *Illuminations*, ed. Hannah Arendt (1940; New York: Schocken, 1976), 257–58.

48. Nick Blinko, *The Primal Screamer* (1995, Oakland: PM Press, 2012), 102. See also Eric Nash, "Existential Questions Plus Androids. Cool." *New York Times*, January 28, 1996, H9.

7 "A REPORT TO AN ACADEMY"

Punk Fiction

Don't feel guilty master-writing.

Nirvana, "Downer," *Incesticide*

"Mere bugle-blowing and drum-beating does not produce courage, and it would take a lot of trumpets before a fortress would tumble at their sound as the walls of Jericho did. It is enthusiastic ideas . . . the genius of generals which achieve this . . . and not music, for music can only count as a *support* for those powers which in other ways have already . . . captured the mind." So argued Hegel late in a sprawling series of lectures on aesthetics collated posthumously by his students. Believing that music, for all its beauty and power to evoke emotion from the listener, is but a supplement to both rigorous intellectual activity and physical strength, Hegel is, near the end of his life, none too shy in disparaging the value of music in particular as a force for social and political change, for the winning of wars. Harbor not illusions about the effectiveness of *sound*—which vanishes into memory instantly—to reform the world, advises the philosopher from Jena, building upon his groundbreaking *Phenomenology of Spirit*. It is music's very formlessness and annihilation of space, its pure subjectivity and temporal quality as movement in time—all of which separate music from architecture, sculpture, painting, dance, and poetry, and align music with History itself as a reflection of the perpetually evolving inner life of Spirit—that are negated the moment sound is embodied in the listener, who objectifies music, rendering it spatial and dissolving its infinity in so doing. Music remains a *political* failure so far as its principal task is affecting "not the objective world itself, but . . . the manner in which the inmost self is moved to the depths of its personality and conscious soul." Therefore, Hegel concludes, "we may not cherish a tasteless opinion about the all-powerfulness of music as such, a topic on which ancient writers, profane and sacred alike, have told so many fabulous stories."[1]

Such a conceit today appears not only misguided but pretentious and curmudgeonly, given music's—and in particular pop's—ostensible power to influence masses of youth, to inspire the listener to challenge the dominant discourse in acts of violence or resistance, solidarity or suicide: Stravinsky's *The Rite of Spring* caused a riot at its debut, as did Bill Haley as he and his Comets rocked around Europe in 1958. And then there were Elvis and the Beatles. Black Flag. Is it not the unique character of music as formless and subjective, as an expression of one's inner life and a reflection of one's soul, that contributes to its ability to express and shape human thought and behavior and thus the external world when the listener *acts* on her embodiment of music, the critic of Hegel is right to ask. "Music can change the world because it can change people," U2 singer Bono once quipped optimistically behind periwinkle glasses in a line premade for an Internet meme or college dorm poster, updating Jimi Hendrix's confident claim that "if there is something to be changed in this world, then it can only happen through music." Both rockers would be chagrined to learn that nearly two centuries before they had discovered rock and roll, Hegel had been especially hard on the popular music, which adds poetry to melody, that they would go on to champion. "In general, within this link between music and poetry the preponderance of one art damages the other," squints Hegel over his dais, his hairline receding, such that any music—folk songs, cantatas, choral incantations, pop—that emphasizes written lyrics over ephemeral music is always-already "meagre and of a certain mediocrity," and thus scarcely capable of contributing to the development of the world-historical Spirit.[2]

But while the proponents of pop, and even the most well-heeled composers of orchestral music, continue to insist on the power of their sounds to induce change in the material realm at least indirectly, punk, that most Hegelian of pop movements, typically knows better. Although a handful of punk groups and personalities have bought in to Bono's maxim, punk's very negationism, its character as the pessimistic and contradictory underside of pop and capitalism (which are one and the same), forced it to reject such rhetoric explicitly. "Anyone who would buy this is a fucking jerk," Darby Crash admitted on his band's first single as Bad Religion went on to acknowledge that "no Bad Religion song can make your life complete" and the Adolescents moaned "Can't Change the World with a Song." Punk had good reason to be skeptical of its own efficacy, after all, having overseen one failure after another early in its history. From punk's absorption by industry into "New Wave" and the dismantling of punks' early solidarity with women and the LGBTQ community by the misogyny and homophobia that peppered hardcore, to its appropriation by fascists and racists and, as a result of the above, punk's own descent into the conspicuous consumption typical of "streampunk" and internecine squabbling about who was and was not "punk," the subculture's members knew and continue to know how ineffective music in itself is at changing much of anything.

Despite his initial hope that punk might actually pierce the status quo's hard outer shell through its public negativity, John Lydon envisioned all of the above as he squatted on the stage at Winterland in 1978, looking blankly out into the audience of Americans who were already regarding the band as if not a novelty act then a freak show hardly worth taking seriously. "Ever get the feeling you've been cheated?" he would ask San Francisco fewer than two years before accusing his former colleagues of suckering him. "You make me feel ashamed," Lydon went on to yodel ahead of Public Image Ltd in "Memories," recalling his embarrassment at ever thinking punk could be more than an exhibitionist stunt. "Remember ridicule / It should be clear by now your words are useless / Full of excuses / False confidence / Someone has used you well." Whether the "you" in Lydon's charge is San Francisco, Malcom McLaren, Sid Vicious, the record industry, or the entire punk scene, his point is clear: his association with any of these entities—each of them—left him with a bitter shame in himself, his actions, his own naivety and gullibility. Not only is Lydon, in the wake of punk, *still* subject to the humiliating command and control of the institutions he had refused in song—Church, State, political economy—but he is (both at that single moment on stage in San Francisco and with a new group) coming to grips with the fact that even his best effort at resistance seems to have fallen short, even if each successive act failed better, to paraphrase Samuel Beckett, or Chairman Mao.

But while Lydon's response to the failures of punk—to his own failure—was to found not a band but a "company," as he told Tom Snyder, other punks have responded to the tenuous efficacy of their music by forsaking their subculture in a different way. As we have seen, while painting, poetry, and political activism have been a popular avenue for punks to take after dismantling their guitars, many punks have turned to *fiction*, and the novel in particular, as a way of better escaping the cultural dominant, recasting themselves not as "serious" musicians, poets, or activists but as writers of long-form narrative literature. Take Gideon Sams, who as early as 1977 gave the world *The Punk*, a pessimistic coming-of-age novella that follows spike-haired only child Adolph

Sphitz as he attends punk shows, evades roving gangs of frothing Teds, bickers with his parents, and searches fruitlessly for gainful employment. Subtitled "the first punk novel" by its publisher, *The Punk*, written when Sams was only fourteen, paved the way for what has become an identifiable subgenre of fiction in the Anglophone world: novels by punks—often about punk as an idea, lifeline, or failure.[3]

Following Sams are scores of current and former punks who have taken up fiction writing in an effort to succeed where their music subculture ostensibly failed: Richard Hell, Nick Cave, Billy Childish, Stewart Home, Nick Blinko, Frank Portman, Henry Rollins, and many other musician-authors both male and female. This transition to fiction, which emerged most vigorously in the 1990s, functions in two concomitant ways for punk subculture. Novelization first allows punks to formalize, document, and even classify both their opposition to and their attempted escape from the parent culture and their liturgy of failure, creating along the way a more cogent typology of punk desires: the punk bildungsroman, the anti-capitalist travelogue, and the coming-out novel, which constitute the bulk of tales whose narrator/subject affiliates with or expounds upon punk subculture. These novels form a more robust punk "assemblage of enunciation[s]," to quote Gilles Deleuze and Félix Guattari, who in their work on Franz Kafka also addressed the subject's desire to identify "lines of escape" from a variety of Names of the Father whose presence looms large in punks' lives.[4] Second, and more important as far as Hegel and Lacan are concerned, inscribing what a phonologically indistinct punk music merely makes implicit and fleeting, the punk novel turns the master's machine against itself—assuming his Logos—and thus better translates and subsequently dismantles the alienating assemblages to which punks are penitently joined. In so doing punk fiction moves through the shrill spectacle of punk music, too easily recuperated by industry, transcending punk subculture and more successfully reasserting its hysteric subjectivity and challenging the disciplinary institutions and Fathers identified as the source of punks' shame and desire for flight. Moreover, as we saw in the chapter on punk and Henry Miller, this creation of the object-novel invents a heretofore unanticipated signifier that stands for and gives meaning to the punk subject as she suffers from the "fading" of her being—whether her band dissolves in shame or her music simply resounds into nothingness once her song ends. The result of this shift is a punk corpus of always-already political, and much more effective and sustainable, "minor literature" that not only recalls what Deleuze and Guattari called Kafka's deterritorialization of language and mirrors his transition from short fiction to long-form novel, but confronts rather than avoids what has become for punks a twofold shame: both in their objectivity under the Name of the Father and the surplus shame they harbor in their inability to overcome him.

Lines of Escape

As punks' interest in fictionalizing their experiences suggests, music alone does not allow the punk to outrun the embarrassing selves or society to which they are bound. "Basically I have one feeling . . . the desire to get out of here," Richard Hell explained to Legs McNeil in 1976, expressing his core discomfort with Being even while performing with the Voidoids. "Any other feelings I have come from trying to analyze, you know, why I want to go away. See, I always feel uncomfortable and I just want to . . . walk out of the room. It's not going to any other place or any other sensation, or anything like that, it's just to get out of 'here.'"[5] His reading of Nietzsche notwithstanding, Hell was at the time of this statement not merely expressing a certain agoraphobia but anticipating Emmanuel Levinas's essay *On Escape*, which articulates the distress of being forever "riveted to oneself . . . the unalterably binding presence of the I to itself."[6] As psychoanalyst Joan Copjec later observed awkwardly, in reference to Levinas but echoing Hell, "The sentiment of being riveted to being is one of being in the forced company of our own being, whose 'brutality' consists in the fact that it is impossible either to assume *or* to disown it."[7] This riveting, if Hell's experience is representative, initiates punks' desire for "mobilization"—Levinas's term—in all its forms from their affection for obscenity of all types to their anti-capitalism, self-hate, and fascination with provocative signifiers (pierced faces, torn and threadbare clothing, swastikas, "bondage" gear).

Such binding also shapes punk reading and *writing*, which early on looked to Franz Kafka for inspiration. Long before they picked up the pen, punk and postpunk had been attracted to Kafka, of course: bands with an obvious Kafka bent include Brazilian group Kafka, Scottish punks Josef K, and Virginia's Gregor Samsa. In his *Punk Diary* George Gimarc reports that Howard Devoto of Buzzcocks and Magazine was attempting to "set Kafka to music."[8] And in an interview following Black Flag's bitter dissolution in 1987, Rollins describes life in Black Flag as reminiscent of Kafka's *The Trial*, explaining how "[Greg Ginn] would come up to you and say, 'Stop it!' I would say, 'Stop what?' He would say, 'You know what you're doing, stop. I'm not going to tell you again.' I would say, 'Oh, okay.' Welcome to the world of Kafka."[9] Kafka's attraction for punk is perhaps obvious: his absurdist, anxious, mechanical, "unfinished" tone describes accurately the punk worldview and ethic. Furthermore, as Deleuze and Guattari demonstrate, while Kafka was not interested in music as such in his work, he was committed to exploring sound, particularly sound "connected to its own abolition"—perhaps the best description of punk ever enunciated. After all, is not punk music, like most of the Czech author's prose, argue Deleuze and Guattari, stereotypically concise (when not intentionally interminable as in Lou Reed's *Metal Machine Music*), anti-metaphorical, self-defeating, cacophonous, and "meaningless"? Punk culture, furthermore, too connotes its subjects' often reactionary, inchoate stab at escaping from its humiliating milieu, serving as the articulation of its authors' "immanent" desire and attempted circumvention of the parent culture's bent-headed capitulation to bureaucracy and objectification. Punk and postpunk not only work to challenge popular culture in materialist terms, but seek the unqualified dismantling of the governing cultural landscape as a way of escaping "here," wherever here may be.[10]

Evidence of this restless outlook emerges in punks' own penchant for the "becoming-animal" theme Kafka describes in, among other stories, "The Metamorphosis," "Investigations of a Dog," and "Josephine the Singer, or the Mouse Folk." Each of these stories, Deleuze and Guattari tell us, functions as "absolute deterritorializations" which seek the dissolution of signification in full. Such narratives simultaneously serve to "flee the director, the business, and the bureaucrats, to reach that region where the voice no longer does anything but hum." So it is that punks' musical texts (records, performances) function like Kafka's briefer tales in that they often turn on the concept of becoming-animal, not only destabilizing and confounding popular music and a phallogocentric Western culture broadly, but seeking an acute, if unrefined, severance from the Name of the Father by dissolving the signifier-signified relation on several levels.[11]

Over the course of four decades, an evocative swell of punk songs both internalizing Georges Bataille's notion that it is only shame that separates humans from the animals and channeling Kafka's becoming-animal theme has surfaced: the Stooges' "Search and Destroy," wherein Iggy claims to be a "street-walking cheetah with a heart full of napalm" (this from man who often performed wrapped in dog collars and tail-pieces); Germs' "Manimal"; Wire's "I am the Fly"; the Cramps' "Human

Fly," composed primarily of guitarist Bryan Gregory's droning riff and singer Lux Interior's vocal buzz throughout; Nirvana's "Very Ape"; Candy Machine's "Animal Suit"; and, more recently, Q and Not U's "So Many Animal Calls," which wonders of the "people and animals all waiting around," "How do they make those sounds?"[12]

One particularly illustrative example is the Dickies' "You Drive Me Ape (You Big Gorilla)." During performances of this song, suggestive of Kafka's "A Report to an Academy," the band would don monkey masks as singer Leonard Phillips jumped around his mates pretending to pick and eat nits from their heads, singing: "Swinging around from every town to town / I swing around and I never come down / City is a jungle now this is it / Every time I look at you I go ape-shit." Groping about the stage, cursing the increasingly automated "civilization" that produced his bestiality, Phillips draws clear allusions to the simian narrator of Kafka's "Report," who explains calmly, in anticipation of Richard Hell, "No, freedom was not what I wanted. Only a way out; right or left, or in any direction; I made no other demand; even should the way out prove to be an illusion."[13] Consider also the Stooges' seminal "Now I Wanna Be Your Dog," Lou Reed's bow-wow-meowed "Animal Language," and the Dickies' "Poodle Party" (where Phillips barks throughout much of the track), all of which recall the "conclusion" of *The Trial*, wherein K laments the circumstances of his death—"Like a dog!"—and how his killers' stone-faced gaze guarantees "the shame of it must outlive him."[14]

As a quick study, though, Kafka realized early in his career that his more concise attempts at deterritorialization could not succeed due to the fact that they have, according to Deleuze and Guattari, "no room to develop." Lacking space and breadth, short stories are too easily "re-Oedipalized" by any symbolic paternal as a result of their very nature, which is "still too formed, too significative, too territorialized."[15] This scenario repeats itself in punk music culture to this day, having been converted by the recording industry, mass media, Church, and other mechanical Names of the Father into another banal commodity, from fashion accessory to Halloween costume to pop-punk to Christian punk. According to artist Frank Kozik, punk has been "taken over by the system and everything's punk rock now."[16] Like Kafka's short fiction, then, punk music and performance, with its brief, often overwhelming, bursts of inarticulate sound, is too limiting and limited, likewise failing to produce a sustained, tangible lifeline and requiring punks either to abandon the subculture, which many did and still do, or to alter their medium to better realize and overcome their ignominy.

In response, many punks have discovered the allure of the Logos, turning to fiction as a more effective tool for both articulating their shame and escaping the Name of the Father and selves to which they are bound. And in so doing they mimic Kafka's pivot to the novel. Take Blinko's *The Primal Screamer,* the story of suicidal teenager Nat Snoxell, who, reclusive like K and reticent about sex, is revealed exclusively through the haphazard and staccato dictation notes provided by his psychoanalyst. "The friends he chose were invariably outsiders, who eventually came to reject him. . . . This bad luck with relationships also dogged his father whose idea of helping Nat back to normality has been to recount in great detail his own entire life history," the psychoanalyst writes before referencing both Freud and Kafka and noting that Nat, who would go on to form a punk band and whose only friend is a contentious youth named Simeon, has been reading S. E. Hinton's *The Outsiders.* "Nat says there is a kind of bond between them: the inability to get on with other people, I gather. Simeon has visited Nat several times since hearing of [Nat's] suicide attempt. It seems he was thinking of doing something similar: patricide, I think." Not unlike Kafka's novels, *The Primal Screamer* is offered to the reader only in segments and half-thoughts; it does not end so much as stop as the clinician's highly technical prose takes on an increasingly surreal quality. As Nat allegedly devolves into a sharp-toothed and feral predator—like a dog, perhaps—Blinko tells readers that the psychoanalyst himself adopted his patient's deterritorializing language, rendering him incapable of reiterating the Father's Logos and quite literally vanishing from the territory: "Rodney H. Dweller disappeared on the 30 April 1986. . . . [Diary] Entries after the 21 November 1985 were made in a script and language which have yet to be identified."[17]

Making perhaps too obvious what Blinko accomplishes with more subtlety is Jamie S. Rich, whose *Cut My Hair* acknowledges explicitly its debt to Kafka. Rich's protagonist Mason—who constantly devalues himself, noting his weakness, foolishness, and self-resentment—takes to following a punk group called Like A Dog and relating Kafka to his own experience throughout.[18] "I got through *The Metamorphosis* rather quickly and wasn't quite sure if I had gotten the right book. 'Like a Dog' didn't appear once." Mason muses with confusion after punk group Like A Dog's singer Tristan had advised the young punk to pick up Kafka as a clue to the meaning of his band's name. "I could see why Tristan had chosen Like A Dog as the band's name," Mason later realizes after reading *The Trial*, nearly hitting the floor as he reads the novel's last page. "It was so powerful, said so many things. Perhaps that was why his lyrics dealt so much with fear and cowardice."[19] What Mason fails to appreciate that authors Rich and Blinko recognize, however, is that Tristan's reading of Kafka would be more productive were it to direct him to make a Hegelian move away from punk music and in the direction of the symbolic law. Here in the beginning, as John's Gospel clarifies, to write is to assume a certain infinity, to assume the Father's Logos—that privileged signifier—as one's own by creating meaning and form out of what was before only the formlessness and subjectivity of punk music. Or, as Derrida put it in *Writing and Difference*, to write is to acknowledge that the subject is "incapable of making meaning absolutely *precede* writing."[20]

On the heels of its own failure, its shame in both its objectivity and its inability to undermine the status quo or make meaning out of its rage, punk finds in its own fictionalization an avenue for making sense of all that noise while simultaneously undermining phallogocentrism. Writing is thus foundational and positive, Derrida adds, in that "it is dangerous and anguishing. It does not know where it is going, no knowledge can keep it from the essential precipitation toward the meaning that it constitutes and that is, primarily, its future."[21] In articulating its accusations against the Father, its subjectivity and shame, on paper, in spurning sound for the written word in an unpredictable act of creation, punks better identify and animate any and all lines of escape by aligning themselves with the Logos. To put it another way, in seizing inscription as her own, the punk author gestures toward creation itself (if not the Christian's so-called resurrection) not only by becoming her own master signifier but by creating a tangible, "significant" work product out of her failure and shame that better than any performance or artifact captures and makes meaning of the punk subject's desire in the wake of her (music's) "fading."

A Minor Literature / A Literature of Minors

Calling Kafka's fiction a *new* collection of statements that signal an innovative development in writing and reading, Deleuze and Guattari posit that both the writer's short stories and purposefully unfinished novels "insert themselves into old assemblages and break with them." Penetrating the dominant discourse, the minority's distorted and distorting use of Logos makes writing part of a "minor literature" that retains three imperative features: it is highly deterritorializing, always-already political in nature, and collective. On this last, the "collectivity" of minor literature is a result of the very scarcity of formal talent within the group. Such a dearth, which mirrors punk musicians' repudiation of aptitude vis-à-vis their instruments and voices, is palpable in punk fiction, if the frequent grammatical and editorial errors, "bad language" celebrated in the punk fiction anthology *Gobbing Pogoing and Gratuitous Bad Language*, and general poor quality of many of the works is any indication. It is also beneficial in that the minor literature's broadly unceremonious character "allows the conception of something other than a literature of masters" so far as the enunciation of each individual author "constitutes a common action . . . even if others aren't in agreement," making inscription itself a unifying, revolutionary enunciation for a marginalized community.[22]

Take, as examples of its creation of a highly disruptive minor literature, punk fiction's chronic subversion of the master's very tongue, a subversion often conducted by young people in tales about themselves. "So okay, maybe shaving's still a novelty to yours coolly, here and now in the flutter and wow, mourning in America, year one, A.D. After Darby," admits fourteen-year-old narrator Rockets Redglare in Thorn Kief Hillsbery's *What We Do Is Secret*, a punk novel bursting with all varieties of cant, referential winks, and neologisms. "But am I over and I mean cradle to 45 Grave my thirst for the worst, oh most defiantly."[23] Or consider if not the Estuary vulgarisms of Chris P.'s "Portentous Speed Ahead" from *Gobbing*—"They sed I cud be the singer cos I cudnt do nuffing else and they fought I was punk cos of me mohecan"—then Billy Childish's dyslexic, phonetic writing, epitomized in his chapbook *The First Creacher Is Jellosey* but described in his novel *Notebooks of a Naked Youth* as so much nonsense: "Whole sentences jostle for position on the page, colliding mid-paragraph, tumbling over each other and then spreading out into an inky mass to merge into the margins and out across the bottom of the page. Unpronouncable words appear in thickets, which are then joined by sparse hedgerows of fiercely hatched letters that ramble on for page after page in no particular order whatsoever, until they finally die out or get incorporated into a whole new forest of meaningless sentences." "I hold the pages in my hands and kiss them," writes Childish ecstatically, calling his scrabbling, which early in his career went uncorrected, "a miracle of God! Every word a gift from some magical unknown place." In the Beginning was the Word, indeed.[24]

Unremarkable as such discourse initially seems as the basis for literature, it epitomizes punks' attempt to create a new assemblage dedicated to "fucking with language," and phallogocentrism more specifically, in ways unavailable to punk musicians and further allowing for the hysteric abject subject's reclamation of her agency.[25] In so doing, as Sams demonstrates, punk novelists often adopt the bildungsroman as a useful paradigm for their radical inscription and critique of both the status quo and punk subculture. An incomplete list of additional coming-of-age novels by or about current and former punks includes Bad Al's *Punk Novel*, Joe Meno's *Hairstyles of the Damned*, the aforementioned *Cut My Hair*, John King's *Human Punk*, John Sheppard's *Small Town Punk*, Childish's "creative confession" *My Fault*, Michael Muhammad Knight's *The Taqwacores*, and Joshua Furst's *The Sabotage Café*.

In developing narratives of teenage rebellion against the parent culture's social, political, and economic value systems, punk authors often mime and/or critically reinterpret J. D. Salinger's premier tale of adolescent angst and growing up. Punks have long been enamored of *The Catcher in the Rye*, referencing it not only in song—the Beastie Boys (whose first record is a blistering manifestation of New York hardcore) once boasted "I got more stories than J. D.'s got Salinger," to which Green Day replied, "Who Wrote Holden Caulfield?" which inspired Screeching Weasel's "I Wrote Holden Caulfield" and Piebald's "Holden

Caulfield"—but appropriating it for their band names, as New Jersey's Pency Prep suggests.[26] Where such references are typically complimentary of Salinger's wayward youth and critique of postwar America, however, punk authors regularly problematize Salinger's novel even as they legitimize it. "I hate the Bible and J.D. Salinger and Kurt Vonnegut," Rockets spits early in Hillsbery's novel, even as Meno names the girl upon whom his punk loner-narrator Brian Oswald has a crush after Salinger's "For Esmé."[27]

Such riffs reached their apex in Frank Portman's *King Dork*, which was described by one reviewer as a "deeply nuanced . . . teen novel in the way that Mark Twain wrote teen novels. Or J. D. Salinger."[28] Perhaps the premier punk bildungsroman, Portman's novel displaces what has become a tired genre at the same time as it adds to the deterritorialization of Salinger as a privileged signifier. In so doing it shatters the signifying chain of language that generates the subject position to which the hysteric is bound. In *Dork*, narrator Tom Henderson and his lone friend, Sam, who don't fit in with the rest of the "fake people" comprising the Hillmont High student body, spend their days listening to punk records, working on album covers for their imaginary bands, enduring the insults of both Hillmont jocks *and* their girlfriends, and dozing through insufferable literature courses that focus on improving students' vocabulary and lauding *The Catcher in the Rye*, upon which *Dork* hinges and which Tom has "been forced to read . . . like three hundred times." Putting aside Tom's sardonic, intentional mimicking of Holden Caulfield throughout—he repeatedly quips such Caulfieldian lines as "I swear to God" and "[goddam] phony"—what allows *Dork* to rise above its cohorts in subverting its primogenitor is Tom's discovery of a dog-eared *Catcher* in a box in his basement inscribed with the initials of his dead father. "It was very old, very beaten up, not a paperback but not exactly a hardcover book," Tom explains of the novel-signifier

7.1. Lacan's notion of *aphanisis* as illustrated by Daniel Chang for the *King Dork* cover, 2006. Used by permission.

that Portman makes clear is nearing the end of its usefulness—becoming as dead as Tom's father, as dead as Salinger. "The title on the spine had been rubbed off, but was legible on the front cover, which was only hanging on by a few threads. Some of the bunches of pages were loose. The whole thing was falling apart."[29]

This connection of the Father's death with his signification as Logos had been noted by Freud in essay after essay, recalls Lacan in *Écrits*, calling Freud's theory of primordial patricide, true or not, a productive metaphor that shows how "if this murder is the fertile moment of the debt by which the subject binds himself for life to the Law, the symbolic father, insofar as he signifies this Law, is truly the dead Father."[30] Furthermore, as we saw in previous chapters, the emergence of such a signifier—the novel—subordinates the subject and catalyzes its "split" into fading (as speaking subject) and meaning (as object). This division is ineluctable in the dialectic between subjects, continues Lacan in *The Four Fundamental Concepts of Psychoanalysis,* arguing that "there is no subject without, somewhere, *aphanisis* of the subject, and it is in this alienation, in this fundamental division, that the dialectic of the subject is established."[31] Here then, is the crux of punk's turn to fiction: in a world where the punk subject and her music have already been subordinated—faded—by the master signifier and even bound to him despite his death, it is only through the object-novel, the appropriation of Logos, that her meaning emerges.

Making brilliant, and surprisingly subversive, use of *Dork*'s content, the novel's hardcover jacket designer put Lacan into practice by appropriating the 1966 crimson-covered *Catcher* for *Dork,* duplicating the *Catcher* cover but "erasing" the original novel's title and author and replacing them with a blue pen–scribbled "King Dork" title with "Frank Portman" taking Salinger's byline. If *King Dork* itself is the *objet petit a* representing the subject's desire in what might be read as a

Salinger-Portman dialectic, then, or rather a juxtaposition of their novels as signifiers, it is clear that Portman's novel is helping erase, literally, the original *Catcher.* So does Portman take Salinger's place as the "master" of alienated teen fiction as much as Portman's inscription makes meaning of his band's fading. In so doing he "rubs out" not just *Catcher,* but Salinger himself, in spite of finding his own subjectivity contingent upon the clandestine author. Such is the scenario, at least, that Portman develops *inside* his novel. Upon not only finding his dead father's dog-eared *Catcher,* but using it to solve the mystery of his father's "murder," Tom remarks how his quest to generate meaning from his father's death, his signification as a beat-up coming-of-age novel, led not to his knowing better the Law or man who produced him, but to their further alienation. As Tom later acknowledges, after briefly entertaining the notion of "solving" the mystery of his hysteric (m)other: "My mom is sad, distant, goofy, mysterious, and beautiful, and part of me feels like I'd prefer to leave her that way. . . . I know I wouldn't like it if investigating her caused her to fade even more from view, which is what basically happened when I tried to investigate my dad [via Salinger's novel]."[32]

Not the investigation, but the Father's signification as Logos, as a book, is what "faded" the physical Charles Evan Henderson. Such, ostensibly, is the punk author's goal, Portman's publishers would have us believe, apropos *Dork*: as Portman's phallogocentric signifier emerges as the representation of his abject punk desire, *Catcher in the Rye*—Salinger himself—fades into nonbeing, giving up the ghost not long after *King Dork* was published in 2006 and named a "Best Book" for Young Adults by the American Library Association in 2007.

If such a "Hegelian murder," as Lacan puts it in his "Mirror Stage" essay, were not enough, Portman too demonstrates how his novel serves as the bellwether for a minor literature that subverts language, characterizing his subject as given to an at times brilliant *misuse* of Logos, which ultimately deterritorializes not simply Salinger's novel, but his entire tongue and the industry that exploits it to fasten hysterics like Tom to the Father's legacy, whether cultural, familial, political, or socioeconomic. When, for example, Tom's mother discusses with Tom her dead husband's relationship with Tom's pedophilic Associate Principal Teone (Holden's Mr. Antolini) near the novel's end, Tom explodes, ejaculating almost instinctually that Teone is, among other soubriquets, "mal-efficient." Having meant "maleficent," Tom shows the degree to which he has internalized psychoanalysis, noting sarcastically, "The trick is to make the mispronunciation have a totally different meaning from the correctly pronounced word. My education was starting to bear fruit."[33]

This disruption of the signifying chain has been part of the novel all along. Earlier, Tom and his classmates mime their octogenarian English teacher in turning "bête noire" into "bait-no-our-eh" and "wanton" into "wawntawn," dismantling not French clichés or Cantonese dumplings but the superegotistical public school system as a whole, whose job it is to discipline and objectify the hysteric and subordinate her to its Law. Later, Tom translates from French a note, tucked inside another of his father's books, containing the term *ramonée,* a conjugation of the infinitive *ramoner,* or "to sweep a chimney." In the context of the note, Tom discovers that his father was not, in fact, a chimney sweep, but used the term as a sexual euphemism. The significance of this pun in the context of punk—the Ramones—requires little elucidation.[34]

Not to be outdone, Michael Muhammad Knight's *The Taqwacores*—"a *Catcher In the Rye* for young Muslims"—describes the growing pains, and various embarrassments (of accent, religion, and skin color) of narrator Yusef Ali, a Pakistani American student living in a *Muslim* punk house in upstate New York. The novel opens, following an epigraph entitled "Muhammad Was A Punk Rocker," with Yusef stumbling into his living room late one night to find, among other passed-out punks, a spike-haired punker kneeling silently on a flattened pizza box and facing an easterly hole in the wall (baseball bat–induced) indicating qibla—the way to Mecca. Explaining the origin of term "taqwacore"—a portmanteau combining the Arabic word for "piety" or "divine consciousness" with hardcore—one of Yusef's friends suggests the pair head west to catch a few punk shows: "Get a van, make like an interstate jam'aat. . . . And along the way we'd round up all the queer alims, drunk imams, punk ayatollahs, masochistic muftis, junkie shaykhs, retarded mullahs, and gutter-mouthed maulanas we can find, just load up the van 'til we can't fit no more and then have guys hangin' off the side like in Rawal-fuckin'pindi! Shit man, down the I-90. And it all ends in Khalifornia." Challenging Portman's best effort, Knight, a Caucasian convert to the faith, takes pains, with much effrontery and on behalf of both punks and a marginalized Muslim American community, to twist, invert, and deconstruct his progenitors' symbolic law and culture both linguistically and thematically even as he remains bound to it, forcing his way into the master's discourse in order to disassemble and escape it.[35] Thus is the grammar and syntax of punk fiction necessarily extreme, difficult, and "bad": in taking not only the master's language but his narrative formula to its limit, in subverting it, punk fiction ceases to be the representation of punk (a book "about" punk) but is itself a punk signifier as much as bondage gear and spiked hair.[36] Through a flexible, offensive, creative use of diction, such enunciation, as we saw as well in the work of Kathy Acker and Mark Amerika, deterritorializes, resists, and offends the master-father.

The punk bildungsroman in particular is symbolic of what Lacan called a "cut" in the real offered only through language.[37] As such it updates Hegel, whose *Phenomenology* represents, in the words of Mark C. Taylor, "an all-inclusive Bildungsroman that simultaneously recapitulates the emergence of individual identity on both a personal and a cultural scale and inscribes the end of self-consciousness."[38] Portman's rubbing out of Salinger notwithstanding, *The Taqwacores* signals how such inscribed enunciation can better help its producers and consumers generate new, significant lines of escape at the Father's expense: writing in 2003 Knight imagined and then inscribed his novel in advance of any actual, identifiable Muslim-punk subculture in the United States. It was this object-novel itself and Knight's assumption of the Logos, contend members of the movement's best known bands the Kominas ("Bastards" in Urdu), Secret Trial Five, and Vote Hezbollah that inspired them to form Muslim punk bands and start an actual scene.[39] In so doing, punk writers like Portman and Knight transcend not only their musical but their literary forebears, and Salinger in particular, who merely identified the postwar subject's hysteric urge to escape her increasingly alienated self and her embarrassment in riveted being as early as the 1950s.

Adult Books

In fact, Salinger's eventual reclusion reflected, despite his protagonist's revolt and institutionalization, his *acceptance* of the master's segregating discourse, his capitulation. Rather than drawing inward, writers after Salinger moved out methodologically and ideologically, in America at least, the result of which was the Beat movement personified in writers like Ginsberg and Jack Kerouac, whose Sal Paradise displaced Holden Caulfield in the American consciousness long before Portman. Much in the way Kerouac followed Salinger's rejection of postwar American consumerism and McCarthyism by offering a more grown-up Holden—who takes to the road in search of not merely sex, drugs, and rock and roll but himself—punk fiction also opted not for the coming-of-ager but the prurient travelogue. Aping and deterritorializing *On the Road,* which too is referenced by punks in song from Bad Religion to Jawbreaker to (again) the Beastie Boys, are several punk novels on the market that feature caution-to-the-wind and philandering narrators who, disenchanted with their boring, repressive, bourgeois, white lives, abandon their girlfriends-wives, jobs, and relative comfort for the road, often with a band in tow.[40] Henry Rollins's embellished tour diary notwithstanding, consider Aaron Cometbus's *Double Duce;* Michael Turner's *Hard Core Logo,* an account of fictional punk band Hard Core Logo's debasing reunion tour; Stewart Home's *Cunt;* Nick Cave's *The Death of Bunny Munro;* and Steve Wishnia's serial novel *Exit 25 Utopia,* a collection of punk "road" stories one reviewer described as "a cross-pollination between Henry Rollins' *Get In The Van* and Jack Kerouac's *On The Road.*"[41]

Exemplary in this regard is Richard Hell's first novel, *Go Now,* wherein punk-junkie-writer Billy Mud is charged with driving a 1957 DeSoto Adventurer convertible from Los Angeles to New York in order to reunite the car with its owner, a publishing industry entrepreneur known only—perhaps not coincidentally—as Jack. Accompanying Billy on the journey is French photojournalist and Billy's former lover Chrissa. Jack has commissioned the trip with the intent of developing a piece of creative nonfiction out of the adventure: Billy's interpretation of "Big mongrel America" circa 1980 paired with Chrissa's photographs of Americans both urban and rural. Jack's goal, he brazenly admits, is that the pair recapture, in the interest of selling nostalgia to aging baby boomers, the "rockabilly" America of the 1950s, the America of Elvis and Kerouac, "especially in the pockets that are still practically like the nineteenth century electrified." As the narrative evolves, however, Billy finds himself participating in one degrading scene after another: much casual and dirty sex, the physical horrors of heroin withdrawal coupled with an inability to kick his drug habit, and the long-distance dissolution of his band. In the end, the punk comes to a certain realization of himself—particularly his humiliating meaninglessness—as the couple's journey ends in Billy's hometown when the Adventurer suffers an irreparable breakdown and Chrissa abandons her beau for a second time.[42]

He is a failure, this punk: no band, no companion, no transportation, and, in the end, no book deal. The shame of yet another botched plan only intensifies Billy's desire to escape "here," to locate the source of his binding and finally dismantle it. So it is that Billy's search leads him directly to Freud's "*Wo es war, soll Ich werden*"—Hell's hometown of Lexington, Kentucky—where the novel reaches its wretched climax at the home of Billy's aunt.[43] Wandering about the literal place of his birth, Billy searches for his childhood home. Finding the house, Billy describes the structure as "a perfect representation of a child's idea of a house," and it is at this moment Billy is confronted by his Lacanian Real: the line of escape he had been pursuing for thousands of miles was impossible all along, having only infantilized him and returned him to the Father's door.[44] Disoriented by this realization, Billy, with perhaps a nod to Kerouac's repeated reference to aunts, stumbles over to his aunt's home. Making one last effort at escape and taking the Name of the Father for himself, Billy reinterprets Oedipus by seducing his mother's sister in the town of his birth. Just as the scene is reaching its climax, Chrissa, who had been away taking photographs of the city, intrudes on the couple and obliterates—fades—Billy's subjectivity by snapping several images of his act, immortalizing Billy's blank two-dimensionality and objectifying his disgraceful Being in perpetuity, forever riveting it to the photograph.

In the end, then, Hell, who too lost his father at a young age, not only replicates Kerouac's abstruse conclusions on having sought one's self on the road, but, in a stark rebuke, reduces the Beat's mystical, and ultimately paternal, elitism to dust: Billy never "found himself" on the road, or anywhere. Or if he did, that self was nothing more than a disgrace and failure still subject to the (dead) Father. But in order to make sense of this failure, Billy nonetheless picks up the pen. In so doing, in miming Kerouac, he attempts to articulate that which resists symbolization through semiotics, through Logos, reinterpreting his own subjectivity and reconstructing for himself a viable, or at least conceivable, line of escape on paper as his subjectivity faded—not the journey but the physical (if embellished) signifier of his desire itself, which inscribes his refusal of capital and Kerouac, his failure and shame. As Hell, at this point looking back on punk from a distance of twenty years, puts it in the novel's phallogocentric conclusion: "I'm on my knees before you. The words are on their knees. . . . All the words. All the words since the beginning of time. The ending is words. The person in a cloud of them, like a cloud of bugs. Step back, the person is emerging, elsewhere, emerging like a creature from a dead carapace or cocoon or a penis from a foreskin to resume his life outside our observation. The deformations he suffered for being inaccurately described are shuffled off."[45] Emerging *elsewhere*, insists Hell. For a riveted being whose construction of self and binding have been subject to symbolic law all along, it is the Logos rather than music that Billy eventually exploits to escape the Name of the Father, to combat his fading by being born again somewhere else as Logos itself. Through writing, Billy-Hell not only recuperates his subjectivity and the "meaning" of his recent history, but illustrates the failure of punk music culture, which is simply too territorialized, too ineffable, and too bound to the parent culture to create the conditions for an escape. Putting Lacan, Deleuze, and Derrida into practice, he creates instead a concrete, deterritorializing metasubject, manufacturing a more stable and critical dialectic and giving himself a sense of unbound, endowed being that ironically appears only alongside *inscribed,* narrative enunciation on paper that, as Judith Butler puts it, "although dependent on the symbolic, can neither be reduced to it nor figured as its unthematizable Other."[46]

Nick Cave and Stewart Home accomplish as much, if with less overt philosophizing and more egregious sex, in their novels. A beauty product salesman and womanizer who eats and breathes exploitation (of his clients, spouse, employer, and various female service industry workers), Cave's Bunny Munro responds to his wife's suicide by taking a gauche nine-year-old Bunny Junior on a sales trip wherein he visits a dozen clients in their homes over the course of several days in southern England, unloading his wares, among other things, on nearly each of them as Junior waits in the car. Home's narrator is pulp novelist David Kelso, who has been tasked with amassing experiential material to help him rewrite the last installment of his *Countdown to Chaos* trilogy as a certain roman à clef, which requires that he "persuade the first thousand women I'd fucked to have sex with me *again*."[47] Putting the *Letters to Penthouse* series to shame, both novels are absolute fantasies so far as the phallocentric exploits of their protagonists are categorically impossible, taking on the form of what Deleuze and Guattari called the "exaggerated Oedipus." In enlarging to the point of absurdity Kerouac's (or capitalism's) libertinism, however, Cave, and especially Home, not only parody *On the Road* but update both Sade's *Justine-Juliette* compendium, referenced in Home's novel, and Bukowski's *Women* (published at the height of punk in 1978). A lower-shelf punk referent, having influenced San Pedro's Minutemen and Kurt Cobain, Bukowski and his work have been referenced by "punks" as varied as Modest Mouse, NOFX, Hot Water Music, and former *Heckler* magazine music editor Donald Bell, who noted in an article on the band Hot Water Music, "Like almost everything else that's worthwhile, Bukowski is too offensive for the establishment (parents, schools, mass media), but too beautiful to be ignored."[48] *Women,* in particular, a novel overflowing with intimate depictions of what Bukowski calls "slug-love," documents the author's sexual awakening in middle age—"It was entertaining and a bit funny, but also a bit sad—like laughing at someone who's pathetic," Childish noted of Bukowski[49]—offering a series of often self-deprecating chapters wherein Henry Chinaski drinks and fucks his way across Los Angeles.[50]

The equally overt, seedy sexuality represented by Hell, Cave, and Home was new in punk, as of the 1990s, so far as punk and postpunk music, for all their obscenity, traditionally confronted sex by treating it if not comically, as in Hell's "Love Comes in Spurts" or the Cramps' "Hypno Sex Ray," then as embarrassing (Violent Femmes' "Blister in the Sun" or Green Day's "Basket Case"), exploitive (Bad Brains' "Pay to Cum!" or Kathleen Hanna's "Riot Grrrl Manifesto"), disgusting (Lydon's "two minutes of squelchy noises" or Nirvana's "Mexican Seafood"), violent (X's "Johny Hit and Run Paulene," the Gun Club's "Sex Beat," and Germs' "Sex Boy"), and even with a certain Puritanism (Minor Threat's "Out of Step"). Recognizing that punk attempts at undermining the commodification and mystification of sex that is at the heart of capitalism—not to mention the so-called counterculture inspired by Kerouac and the Beats—has been fruitless, though, punk storytellers problematize sex in a different way.

Exaggerating the signifier of difference that Lacan asserts is not merely a male sex organ but an inaugural or privileged link in the signifying chain—the phallus—in punk fiction allows the heretofore dismembered punker, dominated by the Father through his Law and prohibition of *jouissance,* to experience a regeneration of sorts that functions in a multiple way. Taking descriptions of heterosex to their absolute extreme, the (male) punk writer of road fiction finally "grows a pair," so to speak, turning the master's claim to the phallus against him and engaging in an act of subversion inaccessible to punk bands used to only watching as the impenetrable master penetrates, controls, and even creates punk subculture itself. The punk author "uncastrates" herself, in other words, by miming and distorting the master's almost literal attempt to fuck everyone in his field of vision, seizing the signifier par excellence and throwing it around with abandon—taking her hands off the wheel in so doing as the road machine veers quickly off-course. Forcing the reader to hold the punk novel at arms' length, in either disgust or embarrassment as we also saw in the case of Iggy, Dostoevsky, and performers like David Thomas, Darby Crash, and GG Allin, the punk author exploits the Father's Logos through not performance or music but his own language so as to produce the hysteric's own inscribed, phallogocentric discourse of exploitation, which reifies the shameful nature of the master signifier's abusive immoderation.

In the cases described above, the sex-obsessed mercenary salesman and self-confident literary "bull," to quote Dostoevsky, those against whom punk has for much of its existence directed its vitriol, collapse under the weight of their own excesses and find themselves made low—and literally shamed to death in at least one case. Confessing his sudden "burning attendant shame" is Bunny, who in a Ballardian auto wreck–induced hallucination late in the novel sees the disappointed faces of each of the persons, predominantly women, he had manipulated, abandoned, and cheated over the course of his life. "I am truly sorry," the lotion seller sobs, rainbow tears streaming down his cheeks as he looks, "with a shamed stricture of the heart," one by one into the faces of those he had objectified over the course of two decades, his wife included. "Can you please find it in your hearts to forgive me?" They do forgive the contrite Bunny, this mass—at least in Bunny's mind. Finding no such forgiveness in waking life, Bunny, as Cave's title tells us, awakes in his son's arms only to give up his now self-conscious ghost moments later, a victim of what might be interpreted as a certain indirect patricide. So does Cave, coming off the release of his band's resurrectionist *Dig, Lazarus, Dig*!!! but anticipating its gorgeous and phallic follow-up *Push the Sky Away*, kill the heretofore shameless Father, transferring agency and moral authority to Bunny Junior.[51] This transference was anticipated, in fact, by Cave's first novel, the Book of Numbers–referencing *And the Ass Saw the Angel*, whose young male narrator, Euchrid, living a cloistered oddball life in the American South, too dispenses gruesomely with his animal-torturing father and abusive mother in a manner that would have pleased if not Flannery O'Connor then Poppy Brite.[52]

Fucking his way across England, Germany, Finland, and Estonia, Home's Kelso ends his journey at ground zero in Aldeburgh, where instead of murdering his first-ever sexual partner—the "chaos" in *Countdown to Chaos*—he assumes the role of returned prodigal son, unexpectedly remembering Jesus of Nazareth's Sermon on the Mount, converting to Christianity on the spot like Augustine of Hippo on the cusp of his two-thousandth coupling, and asking his first and only love to marry him. "Now that we're married I pray for her every night. I pray that she will let Jesus into her heart," Kelso admits with an abrupt, appalling sense of shame in having spent weeks and hundreds of pages articulating his impossible number of conquests in graphic detail for an audience he is suddenly revolted at having to satisfy: "I couldn't prevent Shadow Books from issuing these wretched tomes. I'd signed a three book contract with them. I didn't want the royalties, so I gave half the money to the church and the other half to my wife. I have a good marriage and I love my wife but I wish that she could find God. Now I'm submitting this diary as it was written to a Christian publisher. I want people to read the words of a sinner and see how even the lowliest of men came to be redeemed." Ending his confession with the admission that

"The Christian life is the only good life, it has enabled me to atone for all the wrongs I've done," Kelso not only undermines the political economy that generated the shame he had embodied—giving it to charity—but complicates the Church as the literal source and arbiter of symbolic law, framing this particular master as a cynical and manipulative guardian of good ethical conduct whose benevolence is too a shambles.[53]

What We Do Is Secret

The shambles that is phallogocentrism is what led other writers of punk fiction to go in a different direction than either the male-dominated bildungsroman or the oat-sowing road novel. Suggesting that Kafka's own fascination with "deviant" relations and tight clothing is a type of punk precursor—including the buckled-and-belted policemen of *The Trial,* who are in turn whipped by a flogger donning a "dark leather garment which left his throat and a good deal of his chest and the whole of his arms bare"—Deleuze and Guattari further explain that "today still, these are the clothes of American sado-masochists," which signal in both Kafka and punk a "Homosexual effusion" that leaks out of the cracks in the assemblage's undercarriage, as it were.[54] So it is in punk fiction, which, too remembering Foucault's point that the superficial flourishing of discourse on sex in the West is less the sign of liberal awakening than a regulatory reinforcement of the heterosexist economy and the master's patronizing discourse, responds to the phallogocentric scripts of Home, Cave, and Hell with a more radical narrative. Seeing a certain bolstering of the Father's hegemony over the hysteric in Billy Mud and Bunny Munro, in the sexually violent cover band Australian Whitehouse from Home's entry in *Gobbing Pogoing and Gratuitous Bad Language,* are the writers of the punk coming-out novel, whose gay and lesbian authors and subjects grapple with their displacement by not only the penetrating and castrating Father but the (heterosexist) punk male. The Father notwithstanding, the very materiality of Hell's or Home's version of punk fiction recreates within punk culture a class of "abject beings" whose subjectivity, in Butler's estimation, emerges only in "those 'unlivable' and 'uninhabitable' zones of social life which are nevertheless densely populated by those who do not enjoy the status of the subject." Such an abject being, although existing, is essentially transparent: she has no matter and does not matter, wrote Butler as Riot Grrrl was reaching the height of its rhetorical and political power. Thus do the gay and lesbian authors of punk coming-out fiction repudiate those punk writers whose attempt at assuming the phallus poses no threat to the cultural dominant and does nothing for women or the (punk) LGBTQ community either ontologically or politically. In an effort instead to help marginalized gay street kids and abject lesbian musicians emerge as subjects, as bodies that matter, through what Butler calls a "politicization of abjection," these "punk" authors too seize both the Logos and phallus, which are one and the same, in an effort to develop a more destabilizing and radical challenge to the Father and their own subculture.[55]

Although Kathy Acker is an obvious referent in this regard, as we have seen, punk subculture plays little role in her fiction's content. Acker nevertheless inspired several writers who likewise explore the queer side of their punk identities through the novel. Channeling both Acker and Butler, who notes that the very humanity of abject beings is too often called into question, is J. D. Glass, whose *Punk Like Me* offers a lesbian narrator wondering, after sharing an intimate moment with her best friend following their visit to CBGB, "Was I still Nina? Was I still even a girl? Still human?"; Kristyn Dunnion, whose lesbian subject, in *Mosh Pit,* abandons punk culture in the end; Lorrie Sprecher, whose narrator, Melany, describes, in *Sister Safety Pin,* her initial embarrassment in browsing lesbian books at a women's bookstore and her abuse at the hands of some overzealous cops—"My cheek grinding into concrete . . . I felt my arms almost crack"—who had shut down a Pride rally she attended; "A Georgia Story" from *Gobbing,* written by the same Poppy Brite who although assigned the female gender at birth now identifies as a male named Billy Martin and went on to write a sympathetic biography of Courtney Love; Hell's second novel *Godlike,* which to Hell's credit inverts *Go Now* by offering a sober update of the Rimbaud-Verlaine tryst; and Abram Himelstein and Jamie Schweser's *Tales of a Punk Rock Nothing,* which gives voice to queer poets and lesbian Riot Grrrls and otherwise explores punk homosexuality.[56] Or as Rockets describes the heretofore shameful "secret" he harbors from his foster home days in Hillsbery's *What We Do Is Secret,* in which over the course of a single night Rockets comes out, escapes an attempt on his life, serves as tour guide to two middle-aged closet cases from Minnesota, and abandons punk in one fell swoop:

> I reckon the secret's the part you can't tell. Like I can put in words how scared Jake was that day, the physical signs I mean. His lower lip trembled and a twitch started winking one of his eyes and how the blood just drained from his face. . . . I can't tell you what it felt like, being there, touched by his fear, and shame too it must have been, sharing it. Or what passed between us, besides words. How for the first and only time, after living in the same house for ten years, breaking bread and breaking wind and breaking promises, we somehow connected.[57]

More than any other novelist exploring punk subculture, Hillsbery achieves the tone, complexity, and radical alterity of the best of queer literature, whether the Genet of *Our Lady of the Flowers* or James Baldwin's *Giovanni's Room,* which details not only its characters' shame in their orientation, but their inability to escape both homosexuality and the society that marginalizes them and directs them to feelings of inadequacy, guilt, and indignity.

Upping the ante on such authors is Hillsbery, whose narrator, when not trying to make sense of Darby Crash's suicide or suffering the mischief of his trick-turning lesbian compatriots Squid and Siouxsie, fawns over "just your typical All-American lesbian folksinger" Phranc, who played guitar with early Los Angeles punk bands Nervous Gender and Catholic Discipline before single-handedly dismantling fascism in perhaps the punkest of punk moments in the history of the L.A. scene. Remembering the night Phranc took the stage at the Whisky A Go Go in 1980 with an *acoustic* guitar to belt out "Punks, Take Off Your Swastikas," Rockets recalls how the tiny, flat-topped lesbian stared down a roomful of surf Nazis: "And a few jerks finally yelled out 'Sieg Heil' but it was still mostly silent night unholy night, and then she started singing in this voice that wasn't growling like Darby or screeching like Alice Bag but more like real music, the kind that takes you places where you've never been. And it got quiet quiet quiet again and stayed quiet quiet quiet all the way through the song, so you could hear every word, and before she even finished I took off mine."[58]

Here is a heretofore abject lesbian punker, Hillsbery writes, who without a hint of fear talks back to the heterosexist bias embedded within (hardcore) punk. In so singing, Phranc undermines punk's own phallogocentric fascism and its signifiers in the heart of that uninhabitable zone of social life—the punk club—and creates for herself a formidable and impenetrable subjectivity well in advance of Butler. Such a bold speech-act, muses Rockets, "proved what Darby said about the power of words, that language could physically affect you." Both coming out and coming to the realization that punk in many ways contributes to the reinforcement of the phallogocentric cultural dominant, Rockets follows Phranc's lead, eventually melting his X record, *Los Angeles*, and ditching his nascent hustler-cum-lover Blitzer and punk in full. That is to say, over the course of a single song Phranc helps Rockets understand that even punk subculture is but another unlivable space for the abject punk subject, given its ideological posturing and heterosexist metaphysics that only temporarily deteriorated with the rise of Riot Grrrl and queercore (both of which ostensibly did to punk what another of Phranc's short-lived groups—Castration Squad—threatened).

Exploiting what she sees as a flaw in Lacanian psychoanalysis, however, Butler argues that if the phallus is the privileged signifier of the symbolic order, it gains its status as such, as generative, only by denying its own status as an "imaginary effect," fantasy, and object. As a pure signifier, without fixed meaning or form, the phallus can be manipulated by anyone and everyone, for any purpose, "deprivileging the phallus and removing it from the normative heterosexual exchange," notes Butler.[59] Such an appropriation not only "castrates" the Father, in a way, but fundamentally breaks the signifying chain that gave the phallus its power. When, therefore, it falls into the hands of not only gay men but lesbian Riot Grrrls or transgender persons like Brite—whose homosexual vampires-punks in "A Georgia Story" too deterritorialize both the symbolic paternal and punk discourse—the phallus itself is both radically distended and ultimately "trimmed." So emerges what Butler calls the "lesbian phallus": "When the phallus is lesbian, then it is and is not a masculinist figure of power," she writes, remembering Phranc's Castration Squad, Tessa Pollitt's the Castrators, and perhaps Meir Zarchi's *I Spit on Your Grave*, "for it both recalls and displaces the masculinism by which it is impelled. And insofar as it operates at the site of anatomy, the phallus (re)produces the spectre of the penis only to enact its vanishing, to reiterate and exploit its perpetual vanishing as the very occasion of the phallus. This opens up anatomy—and sexual difference itself—as a site of proliferative resignifications."[60]

Such reproduction and resignification is, of course, the point of Zarchi's *feminist* film, released in the immediate wake of punk. Having taken up residence in rural Connecticut to write her first novel, Camille Keaton's Jennifer Hills is raped by a quintet of cromags who not only humiliate her sexually but mock her effort *to inscribe Logos,* to appropriate and undermine the master's phallogocentrism, destroying the draft manuscript before her eyes. Later piecing her novel together, Jennifer murders the five men in terrifically brutal fashion, including through the literal castration of one of her assailants with a dull knife in what seems a play on Bukowski's "Praying Mantis," from *Hot Water Music,* whose femme fatale bites the penis off her lover. "Suck it, bitch!" commands Jennifer in a role reversal as her rapist bleeds out in a bathtub from the void where his penis had been (having been removed by another phallic signifier) before she moves into the living room to enjoy a high-fidelity opera, whose aria is punctuated by the castrato's screams in a bolted bathroom.[61]

Punk coming out fiction is equally neutering, at least as a metonymy, if Butler is right that the "lesbian phallus" functions as a shadow of the Lacanian Real that reinterprets that which remains "outside" the symbolic, as the impossible Real that cannot be signified and thus controlled by Logos. In this way punk coming-out fiction overcomes not only the cultural dominant but the heterosexist punk travelogue and its sheepish bildungsroman so far as it represents "a poetic mode of signifying that, although dependent on the symbolic, can neither be reduced to it nor figured as its unthematizable Other."[62] For this very reason punk's early association with gay bars, strip clubs, and brothels as performance venues must not be read by critics as evidence of punk's depraved and obscene character; such a working relationship between punkers and sex workers, between shoegazing teenagers and transsexuals from Candy Darling to Wayne/Jayne County to Phranc to Brite to Against Me!'s Laura Jane Grace, which still exists, simultaneously undermines the authority that generates and sustains the heterosexist economy at the same time as it validates punks' crucial evolution into Riot Grrrl and queercore.

This is not to claim the lesbian phallus always succeeds where the punk travelogue or punk music inevitably fail. Butler is quick to add that the lesbian phallus specifically, and the embodied abjection of the homosexual position generally, too often results in an oversimplified binary, a simple disavowal of what is its unavoidably constitutive relationship with heterosexuality as the status quo. "This very disavowal, however, culminates paradoxically in the weakening of the very constituency it is meant to unite," Butler writes, warning that "a full-scale denial of that interrelationship can constitute a rejection of heterosexuality that is to some degree an identification *with* a rejected heterosexuality." To clarify, any clear-cut denial of a position or framing of oneself as opposed to the master signifier in particular, as Hegel too documented in the master-slave dialectic, vests authority in the Father, only bolstering his status as such.[63]

Nonetheless, taken as a self-contained, complex, and evolving minor literature, punk fiction—whose widely inconsistent authors each speak for an abject community—in the end forms an appropriated assemblage of always-already political literature that expresses its alienation, anger, shame, and anxiety with the cultural dominant and more effectively displaces the symbolic law than punk's too easily re-Oedipalized, effluvial music culture. The result is a cacophonous and "rhizomatic" corpus of texts that actively dissemble and disassemble the master's discourse and, like Kafka, resist the urge to surrender to nationalist impulses or a trite symbolism. As *Cut My Hair, Go Now,* and *Bunny Munro, King Dork, My Fault, Punk Like Me,* and *What We Do Is Secret* all demonstrate, punks accomplish this occupation and dismemberment through an overbearing emphasis on shame—that of both the abject hysteric subject and the master signifier. More than any punk record or performance, in appropriating, inscribing, and inverting the Logos punk fiction both states its community's abjection more productively and improves upon its forebears' resistance and failure by expressing, even cultivating, punks' deep sense of shame not only in Being itself, but in their inability to disengage themselves effectively from the master's discourse—which the typically white, middle-class punk community reluctantly recognizes as its birthright. And it does so by overcoming punk music's fading through the manufacture of a symbolic object. To understand finally the dynamics of this move, then, one must mine specifically Lacan's seventeenth seminar in more detail, which is what this book's conclusion does in order to provide a more detailed ontological and political rationale for what punks' literary expression of shame accomplishes.

Notes

1. G. W. F. Hegel, *Aesthetics: Lectures on Fine Art,* vol. 2, trans. T. M. Knox (1835; Oxford: Clarendon, 1975), 891, 908–9.

2. Ibid., 900.

3. Gideon Sams, *The Punk* (London: Corgi, 1977), back cover.

4. Gilles Deleuze and Felix Guattari, *Kafka: Toward a Minor Literature,* trans. Dana Polan (1975; Minneapolis: University of Minnesota Press, 1986), 18.

5. John Holmstrom and Bridget Hurd, eds., "Richard Hell," in *Punk: The Best of Punk Magazine* (New York: HarperCollins, 2012), 62.

6. Emmanuel Levinas, *On Escape,* trans. Bettina Bergo (1982; Stanford, CA: Stanford University Press, 2003), 64.

7. Joan Copjec, "May '68, The Emotional Month," in *Lacan: The Silent Partners,* ed. Slavoj Žižek (London: Verso, 2006), 90–114.

8. George Gimarc, *Punk Diary* (San Francisco: Backbeat, 2005), 85.

9. David Grad, "Black Flag," in *We Owe You Nothing,* ed. Dan Sinker (1997; New York: Akashic, 2001), 88.

10. Deleuze and Guattari, *Kafka*, 6.

11. Ibid., 13.

12. See Georges Bataille, *Erotism: Death and Sensuality*, trans. Mary Dalwood (1957; San Francisco: City Lights, 1986), 30–31.

13. Franz Kafka, *The Complete Stories*, trans. Willa and Edwin Muir (New York: Schocken, 1971), 253–54.

14. Franz Kafka, *The Trial*, trans. Willa and Edwin Muir (1925; New York: Schocken, 1968), 229.

15. Deleuze and Guattari, *Kafka*, 15.

16. John Brady, "Frank Kozik," in *We Owe You Nothing*, ed. Dan Sinker (1999; New York: Akashic, 2001), 177.

17. Nick Blinko, *The Primal Screamer* (1995; Oakland: PM Press, 2012), 18–19, 122.

18. Jamie S. Rich, *Cut My Hair* (Burbank, CA: Crazyfish, 2000), 64.

19. Ibid., 61, 64.

20. Jacques Derrida, *Writing and Difference*, trans. Alan Bass (1967; Chicago: University of Chicago, 1978), 8 (emphasis added).

21. Ibid., 11.

22. Deleuze and Guattari, *Kafka*, 17, 83.

23. Thorn Kief Hillsbery, *What We Do Is Secret* (New York: Villard, 2005), 9.

24. Billy Childish, *Notebooks of a Naked Youth* (Northville, MI: Sun Dog, 1998), 79, 98.

25. Dan Sinker, "Kathleen Hanna," in *We Owe You Nothing*, ed. Dan Sinker (1998; New York: Akashic, 2001), 64.

26. See "Shadrach" on the Beastie Boys record *Paul's Boutique*. This record also contains the track "Looking Down the Barrel of a Gun," which references Burgess's *A Clockwork Orange*.

27. Hillsbery, *What We Do*, 4; Joe Meno, *Hairstyles of the Damned* (New York: Akashic, 2004), 97.

28. Joel Stein, "The Revenge of the Dork," *Time*, December 4, 2006, 116–17.

29. Frank Portman, *King Dork* (New York: Delacorte, 2006), 12, 48.

30. Jacques Lacan, "On a Question Prior to Any Possible Treatment of Psychosis," in *Écrits: A Selection*, trans. Bruce Fink (1956; New York: Norton, 2002), 189.

31. Jacques Lacan, *The Four Fundamental Concepts of Psychoanalysis* (1964; New York: Norton, 1978), 221. See also Lacan, *Écrits*, 301.

32. Portman, *King Dork*, 320.

33. Ibid., 266.

34. Ibid., 16, 174, 342.

35. Michael Muhammad Knight, *The Taqwacores* (Berkeley, CA: Soft Skull, 2004), back cover, 28.

36. Deleuze and Guattari, *Kafka*, 22–23.

37. Lacan, *Écrits*, 260–61.

38. Mark C. Taylor, *Erring: A Postmodern A/theology* (Chicago: University of Chicago, 1984), 35.

39. Christopher Maag, "Young Muslims Build a Subculture on an Underground Book," *New York Times*, December 23, 2008, A16.

40. See "3 Minute Rule" on the Beastie Boys record *Paul's Boutique*.

41. See the back cover of Steve Wishnia's *Exit 25 Utopia* (East Setauket, NY: Imaginary Press, 1999).

42. Richard Hell, *Go Now* (New York: Scribner, 1996), 44, 91.

43. "Where the Id was, the Ego shall be." See Sigmund Freud, "New Introductory Lectures on Psycho-Analysis," in *The Standard Edition of the Complete Psychological Works of Sigmund Freud*, vol. 22, edited by James Strachey (1933; London: Hogarth Press, 1964), 80.

44. Hell, *Go Now*, 153.

45. Ibid., 174.

46. Judith Butler, *Bodies That Matter* (New York: Routledge, 1993), 70.

47. Stewart Home, *Cunt* (London: Do-Not Press, 1999), 8.

48. See Anna Goldfarb, "Hot Water Music Rocks Out," *Heckler* #40, Spring 2000, 96–97.

49. Vale, "Billy Childish," in *Real Conversations No. 1: Henry Rollins, Jello Biafra, Lawrence Ferlinghetti, Billy Childish* (San Francisco: RE/Search, 2011), 85.

50. Charles Bukowski, *Women*, 1978 (New York: Ecco, 2002), 37.

51. At the risk of taking the analysis too far, Cave lost a son in 2015, a traumatic event captured in oblique ways in the Bad Seeds' 2016 record *Skeleton Tree*.

52. Nick Cave, *The Death of Bunny Munro* (New York: Farrar, Straus and Giroux, 2009), 267–68, 272.

53. Home, *Cunt*, 181–82.

54. Kafka, *The Trial*, 84; Deleuze and Guattari, *Kafka*, 68–69.

55. Butler, *Bodies That Matter*, 3, 21.

56. J. D. Glass, *Punk Like Me*, 2nd ed. (Johnsonville, NY: Boldstroke, 2006), 89; Butler, *Bodies That Matter*, 8; Lorrie Sprecher, *Sister Safety Pin* (Ann Arbor: Firebrand Books, 1994), 33, 143, 203–12; Abram Himelstein and Jamie Schweser, *Tales of a Punk Rock Nothing* (New Orleans: New Mouth from the Dirty South, 1998), 42–43, 134–37.

57. Hillsbery, *What We Do*, 169.

58. Ibid., 36.

59. Butler, *Bodies That Matter,* 88.

60. Ibid., 89.

61. *I Spit on Your Grave,* directed by Meir Zarchi (1978; Burbank: Anchor Bay, 2011), DVD.

62. Butler, *Bodies That Matter,* 70.

63. Ibid., 113.

EPILOGUE

The Loveliest of Passions

Alexis Tsipras was tired. A mere forty years of age at the time his radical-left Syriza party was given the reins to Greece in January 2015, having won *half* of the seats in the Hellenic Parliament, the olive-skinned prime minister inherited a colossal debt that in June 2015 would reach €323 billion. Six months into Tsipras's tenure it is Independence Day one ocean and several seas to his West; Barack Obama is somewhere giving a confident speech about his nation's exceptionalism as Tsipras finds himself instead feeling older than his age on the eve of a July 5 referendum that will determine not only the future of his nation but possibly of Europe as a *union*. At the behest of the "Troika"—the German-led European Central Bank, European Commission, and International Monetary Fund, whose clients include American companies and the American government—Greece was all but forced into the referendum asking its people whether or not they should accept the latest Troika "bailout" offered to Syriza that included more of the same austerity measures that had already brought the country to the brink of ruin. Raise taxes and curb pensions, the masters of the universe again told Greece, privatize public assets, eviscerate health spending, and pare down social services and student aid.

Fed up with such demands, with his people's suffering for what he saw as the result of their good-faith effort to join the European Union and adopt a common currency, Tsipras assembled his parliament to deliver a critical message to his people in advance of the referendum, and ultimately encourage them to vote *Oxi*. "The institutions' persistence that we follow a program of austerity that has obviously failed, and their insistence on measures that they know we won't accept cannot simply be a mistake, or a result of overzealousness. Chances are, their insistence serves political motives, as well as a political plan to *humiliate* not only the Greek government but also, our country," said the man trained as not an economist but an engineer, in a powder blue shirt sans tie, his face showing the fatigue it has endured from too many late nights and punitive conferences since January. "The time has come for Europe to seriously discuss Greece's future—and the future of the Eurozone itself. Does it want, by insisting on its stance, to lead a country and its people to humiliation and impoverishment or does it want to reach an agreement and to further democracy and solidarity? This is Europe's dilemma. This is the critical question awaiting an answer."[1]

Despite an overwhelming "No" vote in July—no to continued austerity, no to the master's finger in the face of Greek pensioners, women, and children, the Greek people said definitively—Tsipras knew the answer to his own question: the architects of global capitalism had every intention of treating one of their own as they do the global South, of humiliating Greek leaders for daring to stand up to the Troika. As American economist Paul Krugman had put it before the vote, "creditors have come to expect the symbolism of debtor governments abjectly abandoning their campaign promises in the name of responsibility, and are waiting for the new Greek government to pay the usual tribute of humiliation."[2] But when Syriza stood up to the ECB and IMF, when it stood up to capitalism as an ideology, the Troika's response—its answer to Tsipras's question—made it clear that capitulation was not enough. The Troika was seeking a total humiliation of the nation and its leaders.

In this way was the Syriza government, whose perfectly rational Thessaloniki Programme intended to reject austerity at the same time as it reduced Greek debt through the promotion of "tax justice," increased employment, and a transformed political system that would "deepen democracy," made an example. Chastened, Tsipras yielded unexpectedly a week following the referendum, agreeing to an *even more severe* austerity package on July 12 despite his people's overwhelming refusal of austerity, a turn of events that is difficult to describe in any other way than an economic and ideological coup, if not a complete betrayal on Tsipras's part. Worse than the initial demands of austerity from the Troika that would impoverish a majority of Greek citizens, rather, was the fact that the voices of the citizens—the populist leadership of a democratically elected government—meant nothing, that the global elite was still going to get its way through overt economic coercion, in the birthplace of Western democracy no less.

Calling the Troika's demands "madness," Krugman went off the rails in the *New York Times,* mere blocks from Wall Street, in a column some of his colleagues likely considered unfit for print in the paper of record. "The trending hashtag #ThisIsACoup is exactly right," fumed Krugman. "This goes beyond harsh into pure vindictiveness, complete destruction of national sovereignty, and no hope of relief. It is, presumably, meant to be an offer Greece can't accept; but even so, it's a grotesque betrayal of everything the European project was supposed to stand for."[3] Or, as a more conservative writer put it without irony from London after Tsipras's turnaround, "What a relief that the Greeks have finally seen sense, and agreed to Angela Merkel's demand that their Prime Minister Alexis Tsipras must scrub Berlin with a dishcloth, and crawl along the banks of the Rhine in a thong barking like a dog."[4]

There is that phrase again, the one Kafka used to close his tale of the humiliating nature of the market-oriented modern bureaucratic state:

like a dog. Only one symptom of the twenty-first-century malaise the master signifier has helped intensify through his infectious boorishness and ruthless displacement of the subordinated and abject subjects it has created, Tsipras's fall reflects at the same time as it heralds the humiliation that has been and will continue to be the fate of any contemporary subject who would dare challenge the patronym's right to behave as he pleases. It is at such an historical moment, when the shamelessness of the symbolic paternal—here multinational capital and corrupt political institutions, there a murderous state police, rabid nationalism, and the incontinence of so many priests—meets head-on the shame of the hysteric, that punk and postpunk are at their most relevant as *revolutionary* movements. "Shame is already revolution of a kind," Marx had written Arnold Ruge in 1843, anticipating not only Fugazi's Guy Picciotto, who asked in "Nightshop," "Is capital's incontinence causing you embarrassment?," but Greece's refusal to accept a condescending "bailout" that reinforced its own powerlessness. "Shame is a kind of anger which is turned inward. And if a whole nation really experienced a sense of shame, it would be like a lion, crouching ready to spring."[5]

As it was for Kafka, so it is in Greece. And so it is that, as we have seen, those same politicians, priests, police, professors, and punks themselves all agree: punk too is a disgrace, an openly mortifying, explicit valorization of the sort of humiliation common to twenty-first-century Greeks, Iraqi and Syrian refugees, American Indians, and Palestinians. Seething for decades at the shame with which they are confronted daily by the Name of the Father, punk and postpunk are not merely such a lion, but blackened canaries in a carcinogenic coal mine embodying not only the upheaval to come, but that which is already here. And so have they taken to heart Brian Eno's advice that they "Be dirty. . . . Look closely at [your] most embarrassing details and amplify them," almost from the moment global capital began its amplification in the 1970s, serving as the avant-garde in an army of dispossessed whose casualties have been and will continue to be high for their willingness to face such dehumanization head-on, to publicize it.[6] Or as one fretting mother admitted to the police in an episode from the final season of a certain Reagan-era crime drama, *Quincy, M.E.*, she had of late been mortified to come home from work only to find her daughter "burning cigarette holes in her arms, shredding her clothes to bits, taking pills, and locking herself in her room listening to that violence-oriented punk rock music that does nothing but reinforce all those bad feelings."[7]

Grasping the revolutionary mechanics of humiliation, punks across time and place have gone to great lengths to out the indignity of the status quo by making the shame generated by the Father their legacy, too taking to heart Marx's suggestion that the shame of German economics masquerading as national religion, of capitalism as such, must be "made still more shameful by making it public."[8] "[We learned] from our recent American tour that it was embarrassing to go on stage and do gigs," Keith Levene told Tom Snyder on *The Tomorrow Show* following Public Image Ltd's release of its second album, *Metal Box*, wherein Lydon yodels on "Memories," "You make me feel ashamed / At acting attitudes / Remember ridicule." That same year, 1980, also saw Madness's "Embarrassment" b/w "Crying Shame" single and Ian Curtis's admission that "I'm ashamed of the things I've been put through / I'm ashamed of the person I am." Or, as Henry Rollins notes in *Get in the Van*, wondering why he continues to endure the suffering that is part and parcel of being Black Flag's singer, "Maybe it's because it's the most alienating, humiliating, emptying thing I have found."[9] Feeling the same shame in success made possible by the debasing star system that fed his addictions and depression, Kurt Cobain would admit on his band's final studio album, *In Utero*, "I'll take all the blame / Aqua sea-foam shame." These lines followed the moaning "I was shamed" of Nirvana's "Floyd the Barber" from the band's first album and set the stage for Brett Morgen's biopic *Montage of Heck,* which makes Cobain's lifetime of disgrace the hub around which the story of Nirvana revolves. "[Don Cobain] belittled and ridiculed Kurt, and Kurt would be shamed. And it hurt him; he would be embarrassed," Cobain's mother, Wendy O'Connor, explains early in the film, to which Krist Novoselic adds, "Kurt hated being humiliated. He *hated* it."[10] As we have seen, even punk fiction has joined in the lamentation: beside Jamie Rich wondering if punk represents "a banding together of the shamed"[11] and Frank Portman reminding his young adult readers by way of a Lord Alfred Douglas epigraph that "Of all sweet passions Shame is loveliest,"[12] as Mark Perry notes in his entry in the *Gobbing Pogoing and Gratuitous Bad Language* anthology:

> a punk life—a sad life
> the lure of the flesh
> something to take us out of the shit
> coming home from work drunk
> getting felt up by some sad old bar queen
> crying of shame . . . what am I?
> what are we here for?[13]

Or, admitting to feeling "queasy and shameful" for no reason quite regularly, Cheryl, the runaway punk protagonist of Joshua Furst's debut novel, *The Sabotage Café,* scoffs at the idea of inking herself with a Logos-based tattoo, preferring instead "something harder on the eyes, something that would make people look away in shame . . . a splotch."[14]

Finally, around the same time Yeah Yeah Yeahs reminded the master signifier that "Shame is soft they say / Lose when I play your game" on "Shame and Fortune" (on a record that also contains the track "Hysteric") and Norway's Turbonegro described the view from "Humiliation Street," Thomas Gabel/Laura Grace of Against Me! admitted that

"Because of the shame . . . I am numbing myself completely," Seattle's Tacocat recalled the "Shame Spiral" of a drunken reverie, and Q and Not U jack-of-all-instruments Harris Klahr argued in "Recreation Myth" from his band's album *Different Damage*, "Dip your head in the water / Hands up and over / Head down in shame / Give in, give in." Never sure himself whether he is talking theology or economics, the Book of Genesis or Max Weber, Klahr, seeing in market economics a certain catechism and reminded perhaps of Walter Benjamin's suggestion that capitalism has become not merely its own religion but the most extreme *cult* in history, laments the complicity with which the contemporary citizen has been born again involuntarily into the pure object of capitalism: "Is this the cup that's worth more than me?" he asks, and chanting now, "Hands up—give in to modernism." That is to say, give in to capital, a cynical bureaucracy, and a repressive superegotistical "Civilization" broadly—the master signifier.[15]

As this browsing of the punk bookshelf has argued, then, punk and postpunk music culture from their beginning have made an effort both to invert rock and roll's anti-intellectual tradition, often to their own detriment as "products," and have been virtually obsessed with the shame of their hysteric and castrated "abject" subjectivity from at least the moment Iggy and the Stooges took to performing publicly in the United States in the late 1960s and well into the new century. Punk's predilection with not only anger, melancholy, and anxiety, but shame specifically is unique in popular culture so far as punk has from its inception articulated, contemplated, and internalized not only the disgrace that is an effect of its marginalized and subordinated subjectivity that emerged simultaneous to its creation by the master signifier—who *creates*, *names*, and *commands* in words and acts forbidden to the hysteric—but the shame of its participation in the market and its inability to escape either the master or itself.

For even if Ruth Benedict was correct to call America specifically—and the market-oriented Occident more generally—"guilt" cultures as opposed to the "shame" cultures more typical in the East in the middle of the last century, the emergence of punk long after Benedict published *The Chrysanthemum and the Sword* signals how Western guilt, with its bourgeois individualizing character and internalizing of the subject's agency that forces the subject to blame herself for her failures, is giving way to the externalized locus of control typical of shamed subjects increasingly under the thumb of any number of effluvial forces over which individual subjects have little control: economic upheaval, environmental ruin, automation, bureaucracy, state and nonstate terrorism, the erosion of privacy and national sovereignty, and global immigration. Punk shame is thus instructive in that while many citizens of the Global North—those used to colonizing—are just waking up to the humiliation associated with these effects, punks have, not unlike the colonized, been wrestling with them for decades. Having grappled with such horrors for years, punks show their compatriots a number of ways out of the shame of contemporary Being under the Father, including, as we have seen, plunging into (embodying) their shame to reify the horror and consequences of their hysteric and abject lives, mimicking and exaggerating the Father's animal shamelessness by acting in shameless ways publicly and repeatedly, if ineffectively, and even sticking a shiv in the source of punk shame in each of his sites of repose.

(H)ontology

Articulating their disgrace not only through aliases, words, or performances, but their bookshelf—Dostoevsky, Nietzsche, Rimbaud, Freud, Kafka, Bukowski, Salinger—punk "plunge[s] into shame," as Genet put it, in order to attempt to escape and transcend their abject subjectivity.

For only by diving into shame head-first, by identifying, embracing, and exploiting awfulness and inadequacy, Genet wrote in one work after another, can one *escape* shame and make something useful of it. This notion nourishes Claire and Solange, the maids humiliated daily by their Madame, whose own shamelessness reflects that of her class and whose service economy guarantees that the maids can never actualize their fantasy of murdering Madame, but who can only kill *themselves* while portraying Madame in her stead in a suicidal transference: "*Her* joy feeds *our* shame. Her carnation is the red of our shame," Solange tells her sister of their clueless Madame.[16] It encourages Green Eyes and his fellow convicts in *Deathwatch*, who takes his creator's advice, finding pride in deciding, as Genet put it in his *Journal*, "to be what crime has made him." It gives impetus to the Johns in *The Balcony* who become the fetishist Magistrate, Bishop, and General they had, with some embarrassment, been merely impersonating in the brothel. "The veil of modesty torn, the shameful parts shown, I know—with my cheeks aflame—the need to hide myself or die," Genet later explained, knowing personally the indignity of the convict, thief, hustler, and derelict, of the love that dare not speak its name, "but I believe that by facing and enduring this painful anxiety I shall, as a result of my shamelessness, come to know a strange beauty."[17]

Having spent weeks sketching out his four psychoanalytical discourses (master, hysteric, university, and analyst), Lacan, writing in Genet's shadow, ultimately made this exact point at the end of his seventeenth seminar. While Derrida was off musing on Rousseau's shame in bucking tradition by valorizing writing over speech, Lacan was asking his students tough questions about their own discomfiture in the wake of May '68, which by 1970 seemed to him to have been a total failure. Remembering the activism that was unable to topple the de Gaulle administration, Lacan asks, in *The Other Side of Psychoanalysis*, why his audience of student radicals is not *more* ashamed of its seemingly inept emotionalism. Why has the master's discourse, which produces the embarrassing hysteria of the "castrated" and abject subject, maintained its power in spite of his audience's sustained, agitated opposition?[18] Answering his own question in the wake too of Fanon's *The Wretched of the Earth* (which in quoting from Aimé Césaire's *Les armes miraculeuses* gives voice to the humbled colonial subject: "My name—an offense; my Christian name—humiliation; my status—a rebel"[19]), Lacan slogs into a homily on Hegel's *Phenomenology*, noting that since it is evident nearly two centuries after Hegel and Marx that in no way is the world "approaching the ascendancy of the slave," a fresh approach to the master signifier is in order. That approach, Lacan contends, is not merely psychoanalysis as a practice but the emphasizing and publicizing of the hysteric's shame, which he calls the "hole from which the master signifier arises." You should be embarrassed of your failure and your heritage, Lacan tells his white middle-class audience, so far as shame is useful to the hysteric if she would only *enter the pit whence her shame emerged*. So must hysteric subjects meet shame on its own terms without reservation, and even be willing to die of shame, "if one wants to have anything to do with the subversion . . . of the master's discourse." Become shame and dismember yourself, says Lacan after Hegel and Genet (but before Brendan Mullen's Masque) to his clients of largely bourgeois upbringing, who after all may well function as the master signifier one day: in a shameless market culture where affect, autonomy, and perhaps meaningful Being are increasingly prohibited by the Name of the Father, to embody the shame of an emotional outburst, to follow Hegel, Marx, and Genet by publicizing your own shame while participating in a shameful institution, economy, or unjust and fracturing society, is to immerse oneself into Being itself and more effectively muffle the symbolic law, to *change* the Law. In making this argument, Lacan posits a neologism, pairing the French "shame" [*honte*] with ontology to produce *hontology*: shame *is* Being as much as Being is shame, and the hysteric does herself a favor in recognizing, broadcasting, and exploiting this fact.[20] After all, as Lacan had argued long before this latest seminar, is it not the Greek goddess of shame Aidos (Αίδως) who emerges uninvited in the frescoes at the Villa of the Mysteries at Pompeii to strike a female initiate as she reaches for a hidden phallus, that signifier of Logos and Law? "The function of the phallic signifier touches here on its most profound relation: that by which the Ancients embodied therein the Nous and the Logos," writes Lacan, a relation resurrected in punk, which too emerged in pop quite unexpectedly, almost mystically, to grasp the phallus in the 1970s in an effort not only to assume it with embarrassment, but to distend it.[21]

For as we have seen, many punks and postpunks, being the children of English teachers, university professors, and other professionals, were raised in a culture of literacy by a class that had valorized the Logos: Iggy's father was a schoolteacher, Joe Strummer's father was a diplomat in the British Foreign Service, Greg Ginn's and Raymond Pettibon's father was a teacher and novelist, Jello Biafra's father was a psychiatric social worker whose profession hinged on language, Ian Curtis's father was a lawman, Greg Graffin's parents were academics, Ian MacKaye's father was a journalist for the *Washington Post* and other publications, Pat Smear's mother was an opera singer and his father in film, Henry Rollins's father held a doctoral degree in economics, and so on. What these children of the postwar (often intellectual) middle class, the inheritors of the bourgeoisie and their symbolic law, seem to have done in filling their bookshelves is explore not only the canon that was fed to them but the more radical authors who wrote in opposition to that class whose values punks learned very quickly to question as the economy crumbled in the 1970s. So it is that punk provides a useful case study in how literature and knowledge circulated in the late twentieth century, at least within a certain class, how it was reproduced and *détourned* among baby boomers' children in the wake of Vietnam and Thatcherism. No surprise is it, then, that given this heritage, more than a few punk and postpunk luminaries (and countless lesser-known former punkers) have gone on to careers in academia, film, writing, and publishing: Graffin's (Bad Religion) doctorate in evolutionary biology, Milo Aukerman's (Descendents, All) biology PhD, Dexter Holland's (the Offspring) post-doc work in oncology, Zack Furness's *Punkademics* anthology, punk fiction as a self-contained genre, and the countless scholarly conferences, publishing houses, and symposia dedicated to punk around the globe. Each of these examples speaks to ease with which many punk exponents, given the formality of their educations, slide into and out of the world of writing and scholarship—Logos—as youth and adults.

And although a further exploration of punk education is beyond this book, the above examples show how punk had fallen into its particular literary regimen, at least initially, not necessarily through its reading of psychoanalysis or poststructuralism or even the traditional canon but the more radical texts that spoke to the *shame* these same punks felt in their birthright. Remembering Marx's comments on shame was Patti Smith's and Richard Hell's model Rimbaud, whose poem "*Honte*" insists that so long as the master's blade, stone, and flame have not killed the subject, (s)he "In brute stupidity / Must not an instant cease his wild / Deceit and treachery."[22] To this, Dostoevsky added his self-referential *Humiliated and Insulted* and Kafka imagined the awkward K, who is not only marginalized and humiliated unto death in *The Trial* but in *The Castle* is demoted from land surveyor to janitor, flogged by a schoolteacher, and humiliated by the marginalizing and faceless administration of the foreboding castle on the hill. And finally Nietzsche, who in

Beyond Good and Evil quipped that the allure of knowledge would be paltry "if one did not have to overcome so much shame on the way" (§65), made shame the sun around which Zarathustra orbits in the book bearing his name as he sought desperately to overcome himself, to transcend humankind and emerge as a higher man.[23] "To him who has knowledge, man himself is 'the animal with red cheeks.' How did this come about? Is it not because man has had to be ashamed too often? O my friends! Thus speaks he who has knowledge: shame, shame, shame—that is the history of man!" states Zarathustra in Darby Crash's favorite book, desiring self-transcendence in an entry that goes on to pronounce the death of God. "And that is why he who is noble bids himself not to shame [others]: shame he imposes on himself before all who suffer."[24]

The idea that at the core of punk's undignified elegy is a rather embarrassed and embarrassing agency permeates Viv Albertine's punk book as well. A filmmaker and guitarist for the Slits, Albertine, who was *tired* of blushing a century after Nietzsche, gave the world a tremendous gift in 2014 by publishing a memoir that took to heart Legs McNeil's suggestion that the point of punk is to turn "everything embarrassing, awful, and stupid in your life to your advantage."[25] Beginning with a first chapter entitled "Masturbation" and proceeding to document her almost unbelievable lifetime of disgrace—her abandonment by her father, her messy adolescent menses, her sexual indiscretions and infections, an abortion she later regrets, her failure as an artist, her public incontinence, two miscarriages, a near rape and multiple assaults both onstage and off, a failed marriage, a crippling anxiety/depression, cervical cancer, and her consistent mistreatment by men in the music, film, and publishing industries—Albertine (a surname reserved for servants in France), in her own reconstruction, becomes a certain punk peony, that fabulous flower of shame whose blooming consistently attracts only the crawling ants who bend its blossom to the dirt. As the woman who at one time patronized frequently McLaren and Westwood's shop puts it repeatedly: "My humiliation was overruled by terror"; "I feel so exposed, it's unbearable, I'm horrified, ashamed"; "I'm embarrassed by my lack of ability in every area, technically, intellectually and creatively"; "*I'm still cringing now*"; "I am so humiliated: I've never been treated like such a piece of dirt before"; "I feel pathetic and uptight"; "I have no confidence . . . I've lost my identity. I haven't a clue who I am. I feel like nothing"; "I feel stiff and awkward around them"; "I'm embarrassed"; "Ari and Tessa go mad. They're furious and I'm really embarrassed"; "How embarrassing"; "I'm back in the cold white room. So ashamed"; "Am I shallow? Immoral?"[26]

And that is only the book's *first half*. As her band dissolved, Albertine found herself unmoored and often despondent, leading to her making two decades worth of desperate choices—"I feel ashamed. I got carried away" she admits after drifting away from her husband and having an "emotional affair" with actor and director Vincent Gallo—and eventually returning to her music. But even in more familiar territory Albertine, no longer a young woman, finds self-consciousness and embarrassment in asserting herself, in speaking up in a roomful of strangers: "I can't sing . . . it's excruciatingly embarrassing for me," Albertine confesses as she begins rehearsing for a solo performance at some open mic night. "The voice I have absolutely no confidence in. The voice I've been embarrassed about since I was a child . . . I don't have to put myself through the humiliation"; "I am embarrassingly awful. I am shit." Taking on a book project, in between trying to forget "the humiliation that I've just suffered performing to a bunch of guys who can play the blues" and extirpating herself from an abusive partner for whom she still has feelings—"*I miss the psycho*. I'm deeply ashamed of myself"—Albertine too comes to admit, "I can't write. The book will be shit."[27]

But despite her self-doubt, the consistency of her self-hate, Albertine completes the text that is almost abusive to any reader with a modicum of empathy. And this is the point: its facetious title notwithstanding, Albertine all but admits that *Clothes Clothes Clothes Music Music Music Boys Boys Boys* is her last best hope for plunging into her chronically abject being and working through—redirecting—the pile of shame that had been heaped upon her in each case by the Name of the Father (whether her biological father, the pop industry, various husbands/boyfriends, or the Academy) for half a century. As we have seen, this is not something Albertine could accomplish through music; not merely the plunging into but coming out the other side requires, not unlike Dostoevsky, Acker, Genet, or punk fiction, 400 pages worth of self-effacing inscription, of appropriating the Logos, if Albertine hopes to threaten seriously the master signifier, if she hopes, as Lacan put it, "to have anything to do with the subversion . . . of the master's discourse" that has threatened her dignity her entire life. The book, in other words, serves as a reclamation of the Logos enunciated not through amplifiers but the printed page—a *mute* voice of interiors that communicates a deafening shame with not sound but silence.

Walk Away in Silence

Like the pause in Richard Hell's "Blank Generation," like Henry Miller's claim that "to *be* is music, which is a profanation of silence in the interest of silence, and therefore beyond good and evil," Albertine's catalogue of shame is significant so far as its self-conscious combination of *jouissance* and shame is representative of not simply a single punker but an entire phalanx of despondent and stoop-shouldered youth whose shrieking expression of the repulsion they feel in simply existing is a sort of speech designed to leave the listener speechless.[28] Such, then, is the effect punk and postpunk have been seeking all along: not only the screaming refusal of the cultural dominant, but the silencing of the Father—which often requires the eventual re-silencing of themselves—who shames the subject with a relentless violence day in and day out. Or, as Wallace Stevens had argued years before Exene Cervenka and John Doe formed a band, "Tell X that speech is not dirty silence / Clarified. It is silence made dirtier still. / It is more than an imitation for the ear."[29] Remembering that punk, aligning itself with the typically mad and marginalized subjects caught up in Foucault's Great Confinement, had initially reacted to their forced silence with an almost primal screaming, reimagined on the Slits' *Cut* album, punks' emphasis on the shame of Being and the shamelessness of the master, in the end, exhausts itself in a pile of dirty noises, signifiers and signifieds, that is simultaneously equivalent to and ends in absolute silence: "*Pure annihilation*. . . . Nothing to be mopped up afterwards," in Miller's words.[30]

Nick Blinko's theft of the analyst's voice in *The Primal Screamer* notwithstanding, this call to silence had been initiated if not by Lydon's despondent and closed-mouthed squatting at Winterland then by Joy Division, whose indecisive "Atmosphere" pleads that his fellow postpunks "Walk in silence / Don't walk away in silence." Anton Corbijn's grayscale advertisement for the song, wherein a coven of robed Druids—each branded with a plus or minus symbol—literally dismantle a phallic spire and bury it on the beachfront, is astounding for not only visualizing Curtis's words—"Always danger / Endless talking"—but aestheticizing Curtis's silencing of himself as the Druids hush the privileged signifier. In a precarious move for Corbijn, his actors first separate themselves—repelled by their opposite charges—only to force themselves awkwardly together to lug through the sand several icons of the singer who, dead mere weeks after the funereal song's release, seems to be waving goodbye to both an abject punk scene whose shame he helped identify and the moneyed architects of civilization whose authority the postpunk scene Curtis helped build calls into question.

Silencing songs by Rudimentary Peni, Rites of Spring, All, Refused, Trail of Dead, and countless other punk and postpunk bands notwithstanding, this quieting of the symbolic paternal too was Kurt Cobain's garbled object. Understanding not only that punk was dead but that "punk is dad," as Czech screamo band Donnie Darko noted much later, Nirvana recorded the sludgy, loud-quiet-loud "Endless, Nameless" in one take during its *Nevermind* sessions in 1991. "Silence / Here I am / Silent," Cobain screams in between chugging and screeching bursts from his guitar. "Bright and clear / It's what I am / I have / *Died*," the singer then groans before the song becomes airier, almost a warbling ditty, showcasing Cobain's sing-song cries of "mama" for a handful of measures before more noise. Surprised by the quality of the seven-minute jam, the band asked that "Endless, Nameless," the performance of which was captured in David Markey's documentary of Sonic Youth's 1991 European tour, *The Year Punk Broke*, be included on *Nevermind* as a hidden track. Almost on cue—as if predetermined by Cobain's cystic demand for silence—a "misunderstanding" kept the track *off* early pressings of the album, leaving the record's first listeners themselves ruminating in an uninterrupted, stunned silence following Cobain's mumbled end of the already barely audible "Something in the Way."

Such self-hating entreaties to silence have not only been made by punks and postpunks lyrically, but conjured by punk and postpunk *music* for decades, from Lou Reed's *Metal Machine Music* to the noise rock of New York's "No Wave" groups or bands like the Boredoms, Swans, and Lightning Bolt, among others, whose violent desecration of silence and overwhelming of the chatter of pop is designed to pull if not the listener then the master toward noiselessness. "I use destruction creatively . . . always aiming towards a real, inner harmony, an inner peace—and silence," Henry Miller had asserted forty years before *Metal Machine Music* or Einstürzende Neubauten. "I prefer music above all the arts, because it is so absolutely sufficient unto itself and because it tends toward silence."[31] Or, as Burroughs put it at the end of his most popular novel, "*Naked Lunch* demands silence from the reader."[32] In its extreme emphasis on volume, shrillness, and dismemberment as an attempt to drown out—thus silence—all the meaningless noise that had come before it, punk too was and remains a violent exercise in the death and rebirth typical of the punk bookshelf, the subject's violent and discordant recognition of her shame in the service of the purifying silence that follows her purging of shame at the same time as she calls out the master for his shamelessness. It is, as such and necessarily so, an eschatological rejoinder to pop broadly, and Simon and Garfunkel in particular: the actual sound of silence.

"In this century," Egyptian-American literary critic Ihab Hassan wrote in his book on Miller, "the immoderate reaction against reason, society, and history, which finally swept into a reaction against all forms, against language itself, carried with it, covertly, the hopes of a saner world."[33] So with Miller's, Kafka's, Acker's, or Burroughs's "anti-literature" can the contemporary critic see punk and postpunk as explicitly anti-music: in seeking "the absolute end of rock and roll," as Lydon told Tom Snyder was his goal with the Sex Pistols, punks hoped and continue to hope to use the culture industry's tools against itself in an effort to dissolve the discourse of pop and demand that civilization be held accountable for its relics and the distress and shame it has generated in its subjects.[34] Put another way, punk had picked up the notion that art is at its best when squeezing the throat of its own audience—and of itself—not from any musical influence, but from books. Biting the hand that feeds. And in clutching with one hand pop's gullet and with the other its own, both punk hands created the conditions for the mute refusals of the master exploited by new art movements and political programs around the globe as one century melted into the next.

"Words cannot express anything that matters—the alternative is silence," argued members of CrimethInc., the Ex-Workers' anarcho-punk collective that picked up where Cobain left off, carrying the shame of capitalism and bureaucracy into the new century by publishing scores of anti-capitalist books, websites, pamphlets, zines, and albums *anonymously*, speaking up and back to the master in piece after *détourned* piece without a sound. "Cain accepts the judgment that has been pronounced upon him, but reverses the values upon which it is predicated," the group goes on, seeming to reference both Genet and Sartre: "Against all counsel, he chooses to assume responsibility for what he is, for what others have made him—to become, in defiance of all, what all say he is: a thief, a cheat, a beast, a devil. Shame is the only distinction between above and below: he does away with this distinction and thus knows his triumph by his defeat, his worth by his worthlessness, his riches by his poverty. By this inversion, he survives." So must songs go written but unsung as "our throats remain mute," notes the collective, whose list—thief, cheat, beast, devil—is punk's Genet, Burroughs/Miller, Kafka, and Dostoevsky, respectively. After all, embedded within the dialectic of consumer capitalism is the hysteric's own gripe, which is expected by capital as a byproduct of its activity: her screaming refusal is anticipated. In this way the truly disorienting response is not shrieking speech or amplifiers turned to eleven but a sober, voiceless, embodied finger in the face of the Father. For in that silent accusation resounds the future of humankind, "if you have ears for it," as CrimethInc. puts it.[35]

This the participants in Occupy Wall Street understood as well in the new century. Modeling themselves perhaps after Melville's Bartleby, who simply "prefer[s] not to," and taking much from CrimethInc. and punk, Occupy demonstrated in 2011 how in refusing to assume any subject position and keeping one's mouth *shut* the subordinated signifier confounds and terrifies the symbolic paternal better than any screaming abject subject frothing at the mouth—which anyway only calls attention to the hysteric's powerlessness. As the Father's representatives, the same masters who would shame Greece into submission, asked repeatedly on television and in print, grinding their teeth in rage that year as bodies massed in lower Manhattan, "But what does the Occupy Wall Street movement *want*?" The question was even articulated by some Occupy supporters, who on occasion admitted, "I'd prefer to see a list of demands," asking also for "specific, tangible goals."[36] As the situation's nonorganizers knew up front, though, there would be no demands, no concrete goals from the movement, only a swelling, disturbing mass of subordinated bodies asking for nothing and everything in a stare and leaving unanswered its own question—"What is our one demand?"—from the *Adbusters* handbill that was the catalyst for the occupation that drilled into the American psyche the idea of the "1 Percent" and the unsustainable level of income inequality in America. No demands, only a simple reminder to the Name of the Father that his place *is* occupiable, that his position is never secure.

For as Hell and Miller, Curtis and Burroughs, Cobain and CrimethInc. knew years before, such a question requires no answer, being always-already a void when posed "before the Law," writes Judith Butler, so far as the query "concerns the tacit cruelties that sustain coherent identity, cruelties that include self-cruelty as well, the abasement through which coherence is fictively produced and sustained."[37] So does Butler both point to bisexuality and the transsexuals of Jennie Livingston's film *Paris Is Burning* as a less restricted, more destabilizing identification—after Jayne County but long in advance of Laura Grace, Poppy Brite, and Bradley Manning's transition to Chelsea as she languished in a military prison for stealing and disseminating the master's most secret

Logos—and jump head first into Occupy Wall Street, speaking not to but *with* the mass of bodies in New York's Liberty Plaza, of all places, on October 23, 2011, explaining its silence. "People have asked, so what are the demands? What are the demands all these people are making?" Butler asks, speaking to the news media in a brief enunciation available widely online. "Either they say there *are no demands* and that leaves your critics confused, or they say that the demands for social equality and economic justice are impossible demands. And impossible demands, they say, are just not practical. If hope is an impossible demand, then we demand the impossible—that [if] the right to shelter, food, and employment are impossible demands, then we demand the impossible."[38] In a full reversal, the several hysteric punk and anarchist participants in Occupy finally stopped screaming at the Father but simply stared at him in silent solidarity, not as abject, subordinate subjects, but as subjects coequal and unafraid of making impossible demands with their *bodies* alone, *without* the Logos, without speech, but as a powerful symbol—often literally a signifying chain—nonetheless.

Such grappling and contemplation, such shame in Being, is as present in the punk lyric, performance, and bookshelf as it is absent in any other commercial pop genre—excepting hip hop, with which punk has maintained an obvious affinity for decades and which also faces the chronic dehumanization of its advocates head-on, grasping too the revolutionary mechanics of humiliation explored not only by Fanon but Malcolm X, James Baldwin, Maya Angelou, Cornel West, and Ta-Nehisi Coates. Less ironic than obvious it is, then, that in having long appropriated blues and reggae rhythms and signifiers, punk—which *is* truly dead—has found itself being most infectious half a century after its birth not as an irritating standalone subculture in the twenty-first century, too often a parody of itself, but as a *specter*, as the recuperated residue to music produced by other abject subjects. To be more exact, not only hip hop but the purveyors of electronica have come to understand that punk's scream is most effective when it comes not from the mouths of typically white middle-class kids, but untouchables: Sri Lankan-born Londoner M.I.A. making Suicide's "Ghost Rider" the basis for her anti-colonialist song "Born Free"; Saul Williams lifting Bad Brains' "Supertouch/Shitfit" for his self-flagellating "Telegram" to hip hop; Death Grips sampling Black Flag; Danny Brown tipping his hat to both Joy Division and J. G. Ballard on *Atrocity Exhibition*; and countless other hip hop groups appropriating dozens of punk songs in a resuscitated effort to help them kill the Father, to "cut his nuts off" as Jesse Jackson hoped to do to Barack Obama in 2008.

Through such a reappropriation, accomplished as it interrogates and dismembers itself as a genre, hip hop and its variants help salvage meaning out of punk's intentional and necessary, if Lydon is to be believed, fading-silencing. That is to say, the meaning of the vanishing punk subject emerges not only in the punk manuscript—novels, memoirs, poetry chapbooks, and collections of polemic essays by scores of punks from Albertine, Lydon, and Patti Smith to Cervenka, Lunch, Penny Rimbaud, Rollins, Richard Hell, Cave, Frank Portman, and half of Sonic Youth—but on the self-critical hip hop artifact, which breathes new life into punk's embarrassing/embarrassed complaint against the master signifier. So should it come as no surprise that hip hop groups would eventually begin to lift the punk aesthetic for themselves, and come to be described by critics as "punk." If their stage diving, inconsistent lineup, and provoking of their own audience are any indication, Odd Future Wolf Gang Kill Them All is a case in point. Describing a 2010 Odd Future concert wherein Future founder Tyler, the Creator openly antagonized music journalists and record label functionaries—"Fuck every label and magazine here, suck my dick!" shouted a then-nineteen-year-old raw youth from behind a green ski mask—Chris Schultz noted with delight that the haphazard group's performance "felt more like a sweat-soaked punk rock teenage riot than a rap show." Such violence and energy is paired with its speakers' punky reveling in not their prowess—typical of early hip hop—but the shame of their sexual or material inadequacies. Building on Saul Williams's laying bare his embarrassments ("I used to hump my pillow at night," "My complexion had me stuck in an emotional rut," "I think I'm too black," and so on—in the same record that writes a critical "Telegram" to hip hop), Tyler, writes Schultz, awkwardly and without reservation "took an on-stage hit of his asthma inhaler."[39]

It is at this exact moment, when the hysteric subject's recognition of itself as a subordinated and self-conscious signifier stops being a private humiliation and instead goes very public, that punk and hip hop—*pop music*—is most potent. Likewise, the degree to which any artist participating in "pop" refuses to engage in Marx's "revolution of a kind," in Lacan's *hontology*, in at least a cursory way cannot ever be anything but a mouthpiece for phallogocentrism, for the master signifier, for despotism. "I think there are many Rimbauds in this world and that their number will increase with time," Henry Miller submitted in 1946 as the Second Great War's victors were restructuring the world economy to their exclusive benefit in Bretton Woods, New Hampshire, expecting not only punk but hip hop and predicting that the shame-soaked "Rimbaud type" will come to replace "the Hamlet type and the Faustian type": "His example has cast a spell on us. Let us not look for disciples among the literary figures of our time, let us seek them rather in the obscure, eclipsed ones, among the young who are forced to stifle their genius. Let us look first of all to our own country, America, where the toll is heaviest."[40] That such a prophecy has come to pass needs no further justification. In fulfilling what was written by not only Rimbaud but Nietzsche, Miller, Kafka, Burroughs, Marx, Dostoevsky, and

Genet, punk especially anticipated the humiliation that, if Greece and Haiti, Black Lives Matter and Brexit, the American Indian reservation and Donald Trump are any indication, is now touching humankind on an unprecedented level. This is punk's warning to the world. And as the soundtrack to the dehumanization and humiliation on the horizon, punk and postpunk, both within and without hip hop, have been and are likely to remain a necessary contributor to the odd future to come.

Notes

1. Joseph Cotterill, "Sovereign Default: How to Do It in Rhetorical Style," *London Financial Times*, FT.com, June 18, 2015, http://ftalphaville.ft.com/2015/06/18/2132096/sovereign-default-how-to-do-it-in-rhetorical-style/.

2. Paul Krugman, "Greece: The Tie That Doesn't Bind," *New York Times*, February 9, 2015, http://krugman.blogs.nytimes.com/2015/02/09/greece-the-tie-that-doesnt-bind/.

3. Paul Krugman, "Killing the European Project," *New York Times*, July 12, 2015, http://krugman.blogs.nytimes.com/2015/07/12/killing-the-european-project/.

4. Mark Steel, "Poor Tsipras, Forced to Crawl along the Banks of the Rhine in a Thong," *London Independent*, July 17, 2015, 32.

5. Karl Marx, "On the Barge to D. in March 1843," in *Writings of the Young Marx on Philosophy and Society*, ed. D. Easton and Kurt H. Guddat (Indianapolis: Hackett, 1997), 204.

6. Brian Eno and Peter Schmidt, "Oblique Strategies," *Search & Destroy* #3, 1977, in *Search and Destroy 1–6: The Complete Reprint*, by V. Vale (San Francisco: V/Search, 1996), 43.

7. *Quincy, M.E.*, "Next Stop, Nowhere," NBC. Several other popular programs from the 1980s dealt with the embarrassing "punk problem" for an episode, including *Mama's Family, Alice*, and *Silver Spoons*.

8. Karl Marx, *Critique of Hegel's "Philosophy of Right,"* ed. and trans. Joseph O'Malley (1843; Cambridge: Cambridge University Press, 1977), 134.

9. Henry Rollins, *Get in the Van* (Los Angeles: 2.13.61, 1994), 175.

10. *Kurt Cobain: Montage of Heck*, directed by Brett Morgen, HBO Documentary Film, 2015, television.

11. Jamie S. Rich, *Cut My Hair* (Burbank, CA: Crazyfish, 2000), 64.

12. Douglas quoted in Frank Portman, *King Dork* (New York: Delacorte, 2006), as an epigraph, no page. The line is from Douglas's poem "In Praise of Shame" (1894).

13. Mark Perry, "Punk Life," in *Gobbing Pogoing and Gratuitous Bad Language*, ed. Robert Dellar (London: Spare Change, 1996), 5–8.

14. Joshua Furst, *The Sabotage Café* (New York: Vintage, 2007), 117, 100.

15. Walter Benjamin, "Capitalism as Religion," in *Selected Writings*, vol. 1: *1913–1926*, ed. Marcus Bullock and Michael W. Jennings (Cambridge, MA: Belknap Press, 1996), 289.

16. Jean Genet, *The Maids, Deathwatch* (New York: Grove, 1954), 81.

17. Jean Genet, *The Thief's Journal*, trans. Bernard Frechtman (1949; New York: Grove, 1964), 97, 163.

18. Jacques Lacan, *The Other Side of Psychoanalysis*, trans. Russell Grigg (1970; New York: Norton: 2007), 181.

19. Frantz Fanon, *The Wretched of the Earth* (1961; New York: Grove, 1963), 86.

20. Lacan, *Other Side*, 171, 180, 189.

21. Jacques Lacan, "The Signification of the Phallus," in *Écrits: A Selection*, trans. Bruce Fink (1958; New York: Norton, 2002), 277, 280.

22. Arthur Rimbaud, "Shame," in *A Season in Hell / The Illuminations*, trans. Enid Rhodes Peschel (Oxford: Oxford University Press, 1973), 13.

23. Friedrich Nietzsche, *Beyond Good and Evil*, trans. Walter Kaufmann (1886; New York: Vintage, 1989), 79.

24. Friedrich Nietzsche, "Thus Spoke Zarathustra," in *The Portable Nietzsche*, ed. Walter Kaufmann (1891; New York: Penguin, 1976), 200.

25. Legs McNeil and Gillian McCain, *Please Kill Me: The Uncensored Oral History of Punk* (New York: Penguin, 1996), 334.

26. Viv Albertine, *Clothes Clothes Clothes Music Music Music Boys Boys Boys* (New York: Thomas Dunne, 2014), 59, 60, 62, 115, 123, 129, 194, 200, 204, 222, 279, 293–94.

27. Ibid., 322, 340, 347–49, 385, 397.

28. Henry Miller, *Tropic of Capricorn* (1939; New York: Grove, 1961), 332.

29. Wallace Stevens, "The Creations of Sound," in *The Collected Poems* (1947; New York: Vintage, 1990), 310.

30. Henry Miller, *Black Spring* (1936; New York: Grove 1963), 32.

31. Henry Miller, *The Cosmological Eye* (New York: New Directions, 1939), 371.

32. William S. Burroughs, *Naked Lunch* (1959; New York: Grove, 1966), 224.

33. Ihab Hassan, *The Literature of Silence* (New York: Knopf, 1967), 205.

34. "Public Image Ltd," *The Tomorrow Show with Tom Snyder*, NBC, June 1980.

35. CrimethInc., *Expect Resistance* (Salem, OR: CrimethInc. Workers' Collective, 2008), 143, 233, 242.

36. Tina Susman, "Settling in on Wall Street: Almost Two Weeks into an Anti-Greed Sit-In, a 'Leaderless Resistance Movement' Is at a Crossroads," *Los Angeles Times*, September 30, 2011, A1.

37. Judith Butler, *Bodies That Matter* (New York: Routledge, 1993), 115.

38. Butler's 2011 speech *with* her audience is available widely online, but see the video by "Luke Taylor" here: https://www.youtube.com/watch?v=rYfLZsb9by4. Accessed January 10, 2017.

39. Christopher Schultz, "The Live Insanity That Is Odd Future Wolf Gang . . . ," *Spin*, November 9, 2010, SpinMedia online, http://www.spin.com/2010/11/live-insanity-odd-future-wolf-gang/. Accessed January 10, 2017.

40. Henry Miller, *Time of the Assassins* (New York: New Directions, 1946), 6, 132.

BIBLIOGRAPHY

A Scanner Darkly. Directed by Richard Linklater. 2006. Burbank: Warner Home Video, 2006. DVD.

Acker, Kathy. *Blood and Guts in High School*. 1978. New York: Grove, 1994.

——. *Don Quixote*. 1986. New York: Grove, 1994.

——. *Great Expectations*. 1982. New York: Grove, 1994.

Adolescents. "Can't Change the World with a Song." *The Fastest Kid Alive*. Compact Disc. Concrete Jungle, 0206556CJR. 2011.

Adorno, Theodor. "Culture Industry Reconsidered." 1963. In *The Culture Industry: Selected Essays on Mass Culture*, edited by J. M. Bernstein, 85–92. London: Routledge, 1991.

Adverts, the. "Bored Teenagers." *Crossing the Red Sea with the Adverts*. Vinyl LP. Bright Records, BRL201. 1978.

AFI. "De Profundis Clamavi." *Black Sails in the Sunset*. Compact Disc. Nitro, 15824–2. 1999.

Aflalo, Agnès. *The Failed Assassination of Psychoanalysis: The Rise and Fall of Cognitivism*. 2009. Translated by A. R. Price. London: Karnac, 2015.

Against Me! "Because of the Shame." *White Crosses*. Compact Disc. Sire, 522739–2. 2010.

——. *Transgender Dysphoria Blues*. Compact Disc. Total Treble, TTM003. 2014.

——. "Violence." *Searching for a Former Clarity*. Compact Disc. Fat Wreck Chords, FAT684–2. 2005.

Albertine, Viv. *Clothes Clothes Clothes Music Music Music Boys Boys Boys*. New York: Thomas Dunne, 2014.

All. "Silence." *Mass Nerder*. Compact Disc. Epitaph, 86531–2. 1998.

Allan, Jon. "The Rocket from the Tombs Story (1973–1975)." *Late Night Magazine*. Ubu Projex. 2001. http://www.ubuprojex.com/rftt/rfttstory.html.

Allin, GG. [See also GG Allin & the Murder Junkies.] "Bored to Death." *Always Was, Is and Always Shall Be*. Vinyl LP. Orange Records, ORA-777. 1980.

Allman, Kevin. "The Dark Side of Kurt Cobain: Nirvana's Front Man Shoots from the Hip." *Advocate*, February 9, 1993, 35–43.
Amerika, Mark. *Grammatron*. 1997. AltX Network. http://grammatron.com/.
——. *The Kafka Chronicles*. Normal: FC2/Illinois State, 1993.
. . . And You Will Know Us by the Trail of Dead. "Baudelaire." *Source Tags & Codes*. Compact Disc. Interscope, 069493236–2. 2002.
——. *Worlds Apart*. Compact Disc. Interscope, B0003290–02. 2005.
Annex. "Chinas Comidas." *Search & Destroy* #8, 1978. In *Search and Destroy 1–6: The Complete Reprint*, by V. Vale, 39. San Francisco: V/Search, 1996.
Artaud, Antonin. *Antonin Artaud: Selected Works*. Edited by Susan Sontag. Berkeley: University of California Press, 1976.
——. *The Theatre and Its Double*. New York: Grove, 1958.
At the Drive In. "Lopsided." *In/Casino/Out*. Compact Disc. Fearless, F034. 1998.
Bachelder, Chris. *Bear v. Shark*. New York: Scribner, 2001.
Bad Al [Al Saperstein]. *Punk Novel*. New York: Macmillan, 1980.
Bad Brains. "Fearless Vampire Killers." *Bad Brains*. Vinyl LP. ROIR, A106. 1982.
Badiou, Alain. *In Praise of Love*. 2009. New York: New Press, 2012.
Bad Religion. "Delirium of Disorder." *Suffer*. Vinyl LP. Epitaph, E-86404. 1988.
——. "No Direction." *Generator*. Compact Disc. Epitaph, E-86416–2. 1992.
——. "The Positive Aspect of Negative Thinking." *Against the Grain*. Compact Disc. Epitaph Records, E-86409–2. 1990.
——. "Sanity." *No Control*. Compact Disc. Epitaph, E-86406–2. 1989.
——. *Stranger Than Fiction*. Compact Disc. Atlantic, 82658–2. 1994.
Bad Religion/Noam Chomsky. "New World Order: War #1." Vinyl Single. Maximumrocknroll, MRR006. 1991.
Baker, Alex. "35 Years Ago Today Joy Division Played Live at Plan K, Brussels, Belgium." *Post-Punk.com*. October 16, 2014. http://www.post-punk.com/35-years-ago-today-joy-division-played-live-at-plan-k-brussels-belgium-live-debut-of-love-will-tear-us-apart/.
Bakhtin, M. M. *Problems of Dostoevsky's Poetics*. 1963. Translated by Caryl Emerson. Minneapolis: University of Minnesota Press, 1984.
Baldwin, James. *Giovanni's Room*. New York: Dell/Laurel, 1956.
Ball, Hugo. *Flight Out of Time: A Dada Diary*. 1927. Translated by Ann Raimes. New York: Viking, 1974.
Ballard, J. G. *The Atrocity Exhibition*. 1970. New York: Flamingo, 2002.
——. *Crash*. 1973. New York: Picador, 2001.
——. "Why I Want to Fuck Ronald Reagan." 1968. In *The Complete Stories of J. G. Ballard*. New York: Norton, 2009.

Bangs, Lester. *Psychotic Reactions and Carburetor Dung*. Edited by Greil Marcus. New York: Vintage, 1988.

Bataille, Georges. *Erotism: Death and Sensuality*. 1957. Translated by Mary Dalwood. San Francisco: City Lights, 1986.

Baudelaire, Charles. *Les Fleurs Du Mal*. 1857. Translated by Richard Howard. Boston: David R. Godine, 1982.

Baudrillard, Jean. *Simulacra and Simulation*. 1981. Translated by Sheila Glaser. Ann Arbor: University of Michigan Press, 1994.

Beastie Boys. *Paul's Boutique*. Compact Disc. Capitol, CDP7917432. 1989.

Beeber, Steven Lee. *The Heebie-Jeebies at CBGB's*. Chicago: Chicago Review Press, 2006.

Benedict, Ruth. *The Chrysanthemum and the Sword: Patterns of Japanese Culture*. Boston: Houghton Mifflin, 1946.

Benjamin, Walter. "Capitalism as Religion." In *Selected Writings*, vol. 1: *1913–1926*, edited by Marcus Bullock and Michael W. Jennings, 288–91. Cambridge, MA: Belknap Press, 1996.

——. "The Paris of the Second Empire in Baudelaire." 1938. In *The Writer of Modern Life*, edited by Michael W. Jennings, 46–133. Cambridge: Belknap Press, 2006.

——. "Paris, the Capital of the Nineteenth Century." 1935. In *The Writer of Modern Life*, edited by Michael W. Jennings, 30–45. Cambridge, MA: Belknap, 2006.

——. "Surrealism." 1929. In *Selected Writings*, vol. 2: *1927–1934*, edited by Michael W. Jennings, 207–21. Cambridge, MA: Belknap Press, 1999.

——. "Theses on the Philosophy of History." 1940. In *Illuminations*, edited by Hannah Arendt; translated by Harry Zohn, 253–64. New York: Schocken, 1976.

——. "What Is Epic Theatre?" 1939. In *Illuminations*, edited by Hannah Arendt; translated by Harry Zohn, 147–54. New York: Schocken, 1976.

Berger, George. *The Story of Crass*. Oakland, CA: PM Press, 2009.

Bernière, Vincent, and Mariel Primois. *Punk Press: Rebel Rock in the Underground Press 1968–1980*. New York: Abrams, 2013.

Bey, Hakim. *T.A.Z. The Temporary Autonomous Zone, Ontological Anarchy, Poetic Terrorism*. Brooklyn: Autonomedia, 1991.

"Beyond Good and Evil." *Human, All Too Human*. Directed by Simon Chu, et al. BBC Television. EuroArts, 1999.

Bikini Kill. "Daddy's Lil Girl." *Revolution Girl Style Now*! Cassette. Self-published, no catalogue number. 1991.

Black Eyes. *Black Eyes*. Compact Disc. Dischord, DIS135CD. 2004.

Black Flag. *Damaged*. 1981. Vinyl LP. SST, SST007. 1984.

——. *Family Man*. Vinyl LP. SST, SST026. 1984.

——. *Nervous Breakdown*. Vinyl EP. SST, SST001. 1979.

——. *Slip It In*. Vinyl LP. SST, SST029. 1984.

Black Flag Live. No director given. 1984. Lytham St. Annes: Visionary Communications, 2000. DVD.

Black Randy. "Black Randy." *Search & Destroy #3*, 1977. In *Search and Destroy 1–6: The Complete Reprint*, by V. Vale, 39. San Francisco: V/Search, 1996.

Black Star. *Mos Def & Talib Kweli Are Black Star.* Compact Disc. Rawkus, RWK1158–2. 1998.

Blinko, Nick. *The Primal Screamer.* 1995. Oakland, CA: PM Press, 2012.

Blush, Steven. *American Hardcore.* Port Townsend, WA: Feral House, 2010.

Bockris, Victor. *Beat Punks*. New York: DaCapo, 1998.

Bowie, David. *Diamond Dogs*. Vinyl LP. RCA Victor, CPL1–0576. 1974.

BoySetsFire. *This Crying, This Screaming, My Voice Is Being Born*. 1997. Vinyl EP. Magic Bullet Records, MBL001–1. 2011.

Brady, John. "Frank Kozik." 1999. In *We Owe You Nothing*, edited by Dan Sinker, 173–82. New York: Akashic, 2001.

Breadcrumb Trail. Directed by Lance Bangs. Chicago: Touch & Go, 2014. DVD.

Brecht, Bertolt. "A Short Organum for the Theatre." 1948. In *Brecht on Theatre*, 179–205. New York: Hill & Wang, 1964.

——. "Baal." 1922. In *Collected Plays*, vol. 1, 1–58. New York: Pantheon, 1970.

Breton, André. *Manifestoes of Surrealism*. 1924. Ann Arbor: University of Michigan Press, 1969.

——. *Nadja*. 1928. Translated by Richard Howard. New York: Grove, 1960.

Brite, Poppy Z. *Courtney Love: The Real Story.* New York: Simon & Schuster, 1997.

——. *Wormwood*. New York: Dell, 1996.

Brooks, Paul. "The Flowers of Romance." *SKUM* #1, January 1977, 3–5.

Brown, Danny. *Atrocity Exhibition*. Compact Disc. Warp Records, WARPCD276D. 2016.

Browne, David. *Goodbye 20th Century: A Biography of Sonic Youth*. Philadelphia: Perseus/DaCappo, 2008.

Bukowski, Charles. *Hot Water Music*. Santa Barbara, CA: Black Sparrow Press, 1983.

——. *Women*. 1978. New York: Ecco, 2002.

Burgess, Anthony. *A Clockwork Orange*. 1962. New York: Norton, 1987.

Burroughs, William S. *Naked Lunch*. 1959. New York: Grove, 1966.

——. *Nothing Here Now but the Recordings*. Vinyl LP. Industrial Records, IR0016. 1981.

——. *Nova Express*. 1964. In *Three Novels by William S. Burroughs*. New York: Grove, 1980.

——. *The Soft Machine*. 1961. In *Three Novels by William S. Burroughs*. New York: Grove, 1980.
——. *The Ticket That Exploded*. New York: Grove, 1967.
——. *The Wild Boys*. 1969. In *Three Novels by William S. Burroughs*. New York: Grove, 1980.
Burroughs, William S., and Kurt Cobain. *The "Priest" They Called Him*. Compact Disc. Tim/Kerr, TK92CD044. 1993.
Butcher, Raegan. "A Half-Step." In *Rusty String Quartet*. Olympia: CrimethInc. Ex-Workers' Collective, 2005.
Butler, Judith. *Bodies That Matter*. New York: Routledge, 1993.
——. *Gender Trouble: Feminism and the Subversion of Identity*. 1990. New York: Routledge, 1999.
Buzzcocks. "Boredom." *Spiral Scratch*. Vinyl EP. New Hormones, ORG-1. 1977.
Cabaret Voltaire. "Bed Time Stories." 1976. *Methodology '74/'78 Attic Tapes*. Compact Disc. Mute, CABS17CD. 2002.
——. *Extended Play*. Vinyl EP. Rough Trade, RT003. 1978.
——. "Photophobia." *Mix-Up*. Vinyl LP. Rough Trade, Rough4. 1979.
Candy Machine. "*A Modest Proposal*." Compact Disc. Eastwest/Skene, 92489–2. 1994.
——. "6 Months of Light." *Tune International*. Compact Disc. DeSoto/Dischord, DIS116.5CD. 1996.
Carlson, Zack, and Bryan Connolly. *Destroy All Movies!!! The Complete Guide to Punks on Film*. Seattle: Fantagraphics, 2010.
Carroll, Jim. "Rimbaud Scenes." In *The Book of Nods*, 32–35. New York: Viking, 1986.
——. "Withdrawal Letter." 1973. In *Living at the Movies*, 71–72. New York: Penguin, 1981.
Carroll, Linda. *Her Mother's Daughter*. New York: Doubleday, 2006.
Cave, Nick. *And the Ass Saw the Angel*. 1989. New York: Penguin, 2013.
——. *The Death of Bunny Munro*. New York: Farrar, Straus and Giroux, 2009.
——. *King Ink*. Los Angeles: 2.13.61, 1996.
Cervenka, Exene. *Virtual Unreality*. Los Angeles: 2.13.61, 1996.
Cervenka, Exene, and Lydia Lunch. *Adulterers Anonymous*. San Francisco: Last Gasp, 1996.
Chalmers, Robert. "No Holds Bard." *Independent on Sunday*, November 8, 2009, 14.
Chick, Stevie. *Spray Paint the Walls: The Story of Black Flag*. Oakland, CA: PM Press, 2009.
Childish, Billy. "banging the clay from my knees." 1992. In "*i'd rather you lied*." Hove, UK: Codex, 1999.

———. *My Fault*. London: Virgin, 2005.
———. *Notebooks of a Naked Youth*. Northville, MI: Sun Dog, 1998.
———. "People Don't Need Poetry." *Poems of Laughter and Violence*. Vinyl LP. Hangman, HANG-16UP. 1988.
Chris P. "Portentous Speed Ahead." In *Gobbing Pogoing and Gratuitous Bad Language*, edited by Robert Dellar, 90–92. London: Spare Change, 1996.
Christgau, Robert. *Christgau's Record Guide: The '80s*. New York: Pantheon, 1990.
———. "Spins: Platter Du Jour." *Spin*. March 1996, 107.
Citizen Fish. "Alienation." *Short Music for Short People*. Compact Disc. Fat Wreck Chords, FAT591–2. 1999.
Clarke, John Cooper. "Evidently Chickentown." *Snap, Crackle & Bop*. Vinyl LP. Epic, ELPS4071. 1980.
Clash, the. *The Clash*. Vinyl LP. CBS, CBS82000. 1977.
Class of 1984. Directed by Mark Lester. 1982. Burbank: Starz/Anchor Bay, 2006. DVD.
Class of Nuke 'Em High. Directed by Richard W. Haines and Lloyd Kaufman. 1986. New York: Troma, 2010. DVD.
Cobain, Kurt. *Journals*. New York: Penguin/Riverhead, 2002.
Cometbus, Aaron. *Double Duce*. San Francisco: Last Gasp, 2003.
Constantines. "Arizona." *Constantines*. 2001. Compact Disc. SubPop, SPCD652. 2004.
Copjec, Joan. "May '68, The Emotional Month." In *Lacan: The Silent Partners*, edited by Slavoj Žižek, 90–114. London: Verso, 2006.
Corbeil, Carole. "Angelic Yearnings from Poet, Rocker." *Toronto Globe and Mail*, December 29, 1981, A15.
Cotterill, Joseph. "Sovereign Default: How to Do It in Rhetorical Style." *London Financial Times*. FT.com. June 18, 2015. http://ftalphaville.ft.com/2015/06/18/2132096/sovereign-default-how-to-do-it-in-rhetorical-style/.
Cramps, the. "Human Fly." Vinyl Single. Vengeance, 668. 1978.
———. "Hypno Sex Ray." *Big Beat from Badsville*. Compact Disc. Epitaph, 86516–2. 1997.
Crandall, Beverly. "Decline in Reading of the Classics Causing Concern about Students' Intellectual Grasp." *New York Times*, May 29, 1977, A1, A36.
Crass. *Christ—The Album*. Vinyl LP. Crass, BOLLOX2U2. 1982.
———. "Where Next Columbus?" *Penis Envy*. Vinyl LP. Crass, 321984/1. 1981.
CrimethInc. *Expect Resistance*. Salem, OR: CrimethInc. Workers' Collective, 2008.
Cross, Charles. *Heavier Than Heaven*. New York: Hyperion, 2001.
Curtis, Deborah. *Touching from a Distance*. London: Faber & Faber, 2007.
Curtis, Ian. *So This Is Permanence: Joy Division Lyrics and Notebooks*. Edited by Deborah Curtis and Jon Savage. San Francisco: Chronicle, 2014.
Davis, Erik. "Bring the White Noise." *Spin*, January 1989, 48–50.

Dayal, Geeta. "William Gibson on Punk Rock, Internet Memes, and 'Gangnam Style.'" *Wired*. Wired.com. September 15, 2012. http://www.wired.com/2012/09/william-gibson-part-3-punk-memes/.
Dead Kennedys. *Frankenchrist*. Vinyl LP. Alternative Tentacles, VIRUS45. 1985.
———. *In God We Trust, Inc.* Vinyl EP. Alternative Tentacles, VIRUS5. 1981.
Dean, Jodi. *Democracy and Other Neoliberal Fantasies: Communicative Capitalism and Left Politics*. Durham, NC: Duke University Press, 2009.
Deathfix. "Dalí's House." *Deathfix*. Compact Disc. Dischord, DIS178CD. 2013.
Death Grips. "Klink." *Exmilitary*. MP3/Digital file. No Label/Self-Released. 2011.
———. "Punk Weight." *The Money Store*. Compact Disc. Epic, 88691963512. 2012.
Decline of Western Civilization, The. Directed by Penelope Spheeris. 1981. Culver City: Media Home Entertainment, 1985. VHS.
Deleuze, Gilles. "Postscript on the Societies of Control." *October* 59, Winter 1992, 3–7.
Deleuze, Gilles, and Félix Guattari. *Anti-Oedipus: Capitalism and Schizophrenia*. New York: Viking, 1977.
———. *Kafka: Toward a Minor Literature*. 1975. Translated by Dana Polan. Minneapolis: University of Minnesota Press, 1986.
Derrida, Jacques. "Cogito and the History of Madness." In *Writing and Difference*. 1967. Translated by Alan Bass. Chicago: University of Chicago, 1978.
———. *Of Grammatology*. 1967. Translated by Gayatri Spivak. Baltimore: Johns Hopkins University Press, 1976.
Descendents. *Milo Goes to College*. Vinyl LP. New Alliance, NAR-012. 1982.
Devo. *Q: Are We Not Men? A: We Are Devo*! Vinyl LP. Warner Bros., BSK3239. 1978.
———. *Be Stiff*. Vinyl EP. Stiff, ODD1. 1978.
———. "Whip It" b/w "Turnaround." Vinyl Single. Warner Bros., WBS49550. 1980.
"Devo's De-Evolution Decade." *Search & Destroy #2*, 1977. In *Search and Destroy 1–6: The Complete Reprint*, by V. Vale, 30–31. San Francisco: V/Search, 1996.
[Devo's De-Evolution Decade, pt. 2] "Devo: 2nd Part of the De-Evolution Band Interview." *Search & Destroy #3*, 1977. In *Search and Destroy 1–6: The Complete Reprint*, by V. Vale, 52–53. San Francisco: V/Search, 1996.
Dick, Philip K. *A Scanner Darkly*. 1977. Boston: Mariner, 2011.
———. *Do Androids Dream of Electric Sheep*? 1968. New York: Del Rey, 1996.
———. *Flow My Tears, The Policeman Said*. 1974. New York: Vintage, 1993.
———. "Last of the Masters." In *The Early Work of Philip K. Dick*, vol. 2. Rockville, MD: Prime, 2010.
———. *The Man in the High Castle*. 1962. Boston: Mariner, 2011.
———. *The Simulacra*. 1964. Boston: Mariner, 2011.
Dickies, the. *The Incredible Shrinking Dickies*. Vinyl LP. A&M, SP-4742. 1979.

Dils, the. "Class War." *198 Seconds of the Dils*. Vinyl Single. Dangerhouse, SLA268. 1977.

D.O.A.: A Rite of Passage. Directed by Lech Kowalski. 1980. Tokyo: King Records, 2003. DVD.

Doll by Doll. *Remember*. Vinyl LP. Automatic, K56618. 1979.

Donnie Darko. "Punk Is Dad." *Supertramps*. MP3/Digital file. No Label/Self-Released, 2014.

Dostoevsky, Fyodor. *The Brothers Karamazov*. 1880. Translated by Richard Pevear and Larissa Volokhonsky. New York: Vintage, 1991.

———. *Crime and Punishment*. 1866. Translated by David McNuff. London: Penguin, 2003.

———. *Demons*. 1870. Translated by David Magarshack. London: Penguin, 1971.

———. *The Dream of a Ridiculous Man and Other Stories*. 1877. Translated by Constance Garnett. West Valley City, UT: Waking Lion, 2006.

———. *Humiliated and Insulted*. 1861. Translated by Ignat Avsey. Richmond, England: Alma, 2012.

———. *Notes from Underground*. 1864. Translated by Serge Shishkoff. New York: Thomas Crowell, 1969.

Drohojowska, Hunter. "Drawn to Words: Pairing Sketches with Texts, Raymond Pettibon Keeps His Art between the Lines—Where His Mother Could Find It." *Los Angeles Times*, June 16, 1991, 90.

Duncome, Stephen. *Notes from Underground: Zines and the Politics of Alternative Culture*. London: Verso, 1997.

Dunnion, Kristyn. *Mosh Pit*. Markham, Ontario: Red Deer Press, 2004.

Dwarves. "Oozle." *Horror Stories*. Vinyl LP. Voxx, VOXX200.037. 1986.

Dylan, Bob. "Desolation Row." *Highway 61 Revisited*. Vinyl LP. Columbia, XSM110641. 1965.

Einstürzende Neubauten. *Kollaps*. Vinyl LP. ZickZack, ZZ65. 1981.

Emerson, Ralph Waldo. "The American Scholar." 1837. In *The Essential Writings of Ralph Waldo Emerson*, edited by Brooks Atkinson, 43–62. New York: Random House, 2000.

Eno, Brian, and Peter Schmidt. "Oblique Strategies." *Search & Destroy* #3, 1977. In *Search and Destroy 1–6: The Complete Reprint*, by V. Vale, 43. San Francisco: V/Search, 1996.

Ex, the. *Dizzy Spells*. Compact Disc. Touch & Go, TG221CD. 2001.

Exploited, the. *Punks Not Dead*. Vinyl LP. Secret, SEC1. 1981.

Fall, the. *Bend Sinister*. 1986. Compact Disc. Beggar's Banquet, BBL75CD. 1997.

Fanon, Frantz. *The Wretched of the Earth*. 1961. New York: Grove, 1963.
Filth and the Fury, The. Directed by Julian Temple. 2000. Los Angeles: New Line Home Video, 2005. DVD.
Flying Lizards, the. *The Flying Lizards*. Vinyl LP. Virgin, VA13137. 1979.
F-Minus. "Party's Over." *F-Minus*. Compact Disc. Hellcat, 80423. 1999.
Foege, Alec. *Confusion Is Next: The Sonic Youth Story*. New York: St. Martin's, 1994.
Foster, Ben. *Like Hell*. Chicago: Hope and Nothings, 2001.
Foucault, Michel. *History of Madness*. 1961. Translated by Jonathan Murphy and Jean Khalfa. London: Routledge, 2006.
——. *The History of Sexuality*. Vol. 1: *An Introduction*. 1976. Translated by Robert Hurley. New York: Vintage, 1990.
——. *Madness and Civilization*. New York: Pantheon, 1965.
Frank, Joseph. *Dostoevsky: The Stir of Liberation 1860–1865*. Princeton, NJ: Princeton University Press, 1986.
Freud, Sigmund. "Civilization and Its Discontents." 1930. In *The Complete Psychological Works of Sigmund Freud*, vol. 21, edited by James Strachey, 59–145. London: Hoggarth Press, 1961.
——. "Dostoevsky and Parricide." 1928. In *The Complete Psychological Works of Sigmund Freud*, vol. 21, edited by James Strachey, 175–96. London: Hoggarth Press, 1961.
——. "The Economic Problem of Masochism." 1924. In *The Standard Edition of the Complete Psychological Works of Sigmund Freud*, vol. 19, edited by James Strachey, 157–70. London: Hoggarth, 1961.
——. "The Ego and the Id." 1923. In *The Standard Edition of the Complete Psychological Works of Sigmund Freud*, vol. 19, edited by James Strachey, 3–66. London: Hoggarth Press, 1961.
——. "New Introductory Lectures on Psycho-Analysis." 1933. In *The Standard Edition of the Complete Psychological Works of Sigmund Freud*, vol. 22, edited by James Strachey, 3–182. London: Hogarth Press, 1964.
Fricke, David. "Iggy Pop." *Rolling Stone*, April 19, 2007, 54–59.
Fugazi. "Lusty Scripps." *Instrument*. Compact Disc. Dischord, DIS120CD. 1999.
——. "Nightshop." *The Argument*. Compact Disc. Dischord, DIS130CD. 2001.
Furness, Zach. *Punkademics*. London: Minor Compositions, 2012.
Furst, Joshua. *The Sabotage Café*. New York: Vintage, 2007.
Gang of Four. *Entertainment*! 1979. Vinyl LP. Warner Bros., BSK 3446. 1980.
Gardner, Gilson. *Lusty Scripps: The Life of E. W. Scripps (1854–1926)*. New York: Vanguard, 1932.

Genet, Jean. *The Maids, Deathwatch*. New York: Grove, 1954.
——. *Our Lady of the Flowers*. 1943. Translated by Bernard Frechtman. New York: Grove, 1963.
——. *The Thief's Journal*. 1949. Translated by Bernard Frechtman. New York: Grove, 1964.
Germs. "Forming/Sex Boy." Vinyl EP. What? Records, What01. 1977.
——. *(GI)*. Vinyl LP. Slash, SR103. 1979.
——. "Lexicon Devil/No God." Vinyl EP. Slash, SCAM101. 1978.
GG Allin. [See Allin, GG.]
GG Allin & the Murder Junkies. "Kill Thy Father, Rape Thy Mother." *Brutality & Bloodshed for All*. Compact Disc. Alive, ALIVE001CD. 1993.
Gibson, Alexander. *The Religion of Dostoevsky*. Philadelphia: Westminster Press, 1973.
Gibson, William. "Google's Earth." *New York Times*, September 1, 2010, A23.
——. *Neuromancer*. 1984. New York: Ace, 1986.
Gibson, William, and Bruce Sterling. *The Difference Engine*. New York: Bantam, 1991.
Gimarc, George. *Punk Diary*. San Francisco: Backbeat, 2005.
Ginsberg, Allen. "Howl." 1959. In *Howl and Other Poems*. San Francisco: City Lights Books, 1996.
"Ginsberg SEZ." *Search & Destroy* #1, 1977. In *Search and Destroy 1–6: The Complete Reprint*, by V. Vale, 13. San Francisco: V/Search, 1996.
Glass, J. D. *Punk Like Me*. 2nd ed. Johnsonville, NY: Boldstroke, 2006.
Gogol Bordello. "Start Wearing Purple." *Voi-La Intruder*. Compact Disc. Rubric, RUB38. 1999.
Goldfarb, Anna. "Hot Water Music Rocks Out." *Heckler* #40, Spring 2000, 96–97.
Gordon, Kim. *Girl in a Band*. New York: Dey/HarperCollins, 2015.
Grad, David. "Black Flag." 1997. In *We Owe You Nothing*, edited by Dan Sinker, 77–93. New York: Akashic, 2001.
——. "Jello Biafra." 1997. In *We Owe You Nothing*, edited by Dan Sinker, 33–47. New York: Akashic, 2001.
Graffin, Greg. *Anarchy Evolution*. New York: HarperCollins, 2010.
Green Day. "Basket Case." *Dookie*. Compact Disc. Reprise, 945529-2. 1994.
——. *Bullet in a Bible*. Compact Disc. Reprise, 49466-2. 2005.
——. "Good Riddance (Time of Your Life)." *Nimrod*. Compact Disc. Reprise, 946794-2. 1997.
——. "Who Wrote Holden Caulfield?" *Kerplunk*! Compact Disc. Lookout!, Lookout46. 1992.
Grimes, William. "Jim Carroll, 60, Poet and Punk Rocker Who Wrote 'The Basketball Diaries.'" *New York Times*, September 14, 2009, A19.

Gun Club, the. "Sex Beat." *Fire of Love*. Vinyl LP. Ruby, JRR102. 1981.
Hanna, Kathleen. "Riot Grrrl Manifesto." *Bikini Kill* #2, 1991.
Harron, Mary. "Theresa Stern." *Punk* #4, 1976. In *Punk: The Best of Punk Magazine*, edited by John Holmstrom, 90–91. New York: HarperCollins, 2012.
Hassan, Ihab. *The Dismemberment of Orpheus*. New York: Oxford University Press, 1971.
——. *The Literature of Silence*. New York: Knopf, 1967.
Hebdige, Dick. *Subculture: The Meaning of Style*. 1979. London: Routledge, 1999.
Hegel, G. W. F. *Aesthetics: Lectures on Fine Art*. Vol. 2. 1835. Translated by T. M. Knox. Oxford: Clarendon, 1975.
——. *Phenomenology of Spirit*. 1807. Translated by A. V. Miller. Oxford: Oxford University Press, 1977.
Hell, Richard. *Godlike*. New York: Akashic, 2005.
——. *Go Now*. New York: Scribner, 1996.
——. *I Dreamed I Was a Very Clean Tramp*. New York: Ecco, 2013.
——. *The Voidoid*. 1973. Hove, UK: Codex, 1996.
Henry & June. Directed by Philip Kaufman. 1990. Los Angeles: Universal Studios Home Entertainment, 1999. DVD.
Heylin, Clinton. *From the Velvets to the Voidoids: A Pre-Punk History for a Post-Punk World*. New York: Penguin, 1993.
Higgs, Daniel. *The Book of Antennae*. 2000. Chicago: Now Testament, 2015.
Hillsbery, Thorn. *What We Do Is Secret*. New York: Villard, 2005.
Himelstein, Abram, and Jamie Schweser. *Tales of a Punk Rock Nothing*. New Orleans: New Mouth from the Dirty South, 1998.
Hirschberg, Lynn. "Strange Love." *Vanity Fair*, September 1992, 230.
Hole. "Babydoll." *Pretty on the Inside*. Compact Disc. Caroline, CAROL1710-2. 1991.
——. "Doll Parts." *Live through This*. Compact Disc. DGC, DGCD-24631. 1994.
Holmstrom, John, and Bridget Hurd, eds. *Punk: The Best of Punk Magazine*. New York: HarperCollins, 2012.
Home, Stewart. "Cheap Night Out." In *Gobbing Pogoing and Gratuitous Bad Language*, edited by Robert Dellar, 76–78. London: Spare Change, 1996.
——. *Cranked Up Really High*. Hove, UK: Codex, 1995.
——. *Cunt*. London: Do-Not Press, 1999.
Hook, Peter. *Unknown Pleasures: Inside Joy Division*. New York: HarperCollins/It, 2013.
Human League, the. "Being Boiled" b/w "Circus of Death." Vinyl Single. Fast Product, FAST4. 1978.
Hüsker Dü. *Zen Arcade*. Vinyl LP. SST, SST027. 1984.

"Iggy Pop." *The Tomorrow Show with Tom Snyder: Punk and New Wave*. NBC. February 1981. Louisville, KY: Shout Factory, 2006. DVD.
(International) Noise Conspiracy, the. "Capitalism stole My Virginity." Vinyl Single. G7 Welcoming Committee, HD5005–7. 2001.
——. "Simulacra Overload." *The Reproduction of Death*. Vinyl EP. SubPop, SP558. 2001.
In the Beginning Was the End: The Truth about De-Evolution. Directed by Chuck Statler. 1976. New York: Rhino Home Video, 2003. DVD.
I Spit on Your Grave. Directed by Meir Zarchi. 1978. Burbank: Anchor Bay, 2011. DVD.
Jam, the. "The Modern World." *This Is the Modern World*. Vinyl LP. Polydor, 2383–475. 1977.
Jarry, Alfred. "Theatre Questions." In *Selected Works of Alfred Jarry*, edited by Roger Shattuck and Simon W. Taylor, 82–85. London: Jonathan Cape, 1965.
——. *Ubu Roi*. 1896. Edited by Drew Silver. Mineola, NY: Dover, 2003.
Jawbreaker. "Boxcar." *24 Hour Revenge Therapy*. Compact Disc. Communion, COMM49–4. 1994.
Jetton, Jeff. "The Secret of Noam: A Chomsky Interview." *Brightest Young Things*. BYT Media, Inc. March 9, 2011. See Chomsky.Info, Anthony Arnove Admin. http://chomsky.info/20110309-2/.
Jim Carroll Band. "People Who Died." *Catholic Boy*. Vinyl LP. ATCO Records, SD 38–132. 1980.
Joan of Arc. *Joan of Arc Presents: Joan of Arc*. Vinyl LP. Joyful Noise, JNR88. 2012.
"John Lydon." *The Tomorrow Show with Tom Snyder: Punk and New Wave*. NBC. June 1980. Louisville, KY: Shout Factory, 2006. DVD.
Johst, Hanns. *Schlageter*. 1933. Translated by Ford B. Parkes-Perret. Stuttgart:Akademischer Verlag Hans-Dieter Heinz, 1984.
Jonathan Richman and the Modern Lovers. *Jonathan Richman and the Modern Lovers*. Vinyl LP. Beserkley, BZ-0048. 1976.
Jones, Malcolm. *Dostoevsky and the Dynamics of Religious Experience*. London: Anthem Press, 2005.
Jones, Peter. "Anarchy in the U. K.: '70s British Punk as Bakhtinian Carnival." *Studies in Popular Culture* 24, no. 3 (2002): 25–36.
Joy Division. "Isolation." *Closer*. Vinyl LP. Factory, FACT25. 1980.
——. "Love Will Tear Us Apart." Vinyl Single. Factory, FAC23. 1980.
——. "She's Lost Control" b/w "Atmosphere." Vinyl Single. Factory, FACUS2. 1980.
Jubilee. Directed by Derek Jarman. 1977. New York: Criterion/Janus: 2010. DVD.
Julie Ruin. "On Language." *Julie Ruin*. Compact Disc. Kill Rock Stars, KRS297. 1998.
June of 44. *Engine Takes to the Water*. Compact Disc. Quarterstick, QS32CD. 1995.
——. "Henry's Revenge." *In The Fishtank 6*. Compact Disc. Konkurrent, Fish6CD. 1999.

Justin(e). "Médisance après." *Du Pareil Au Même*. Compact Disc. Guerilla Asso, KYE009. 2006.
Kafka, Franz. *The Castle*. 1926. New York: Knopf, 1969.
——. *The Complete Stories*. Translated by Willa and Edwin Muir. New York: Schocken, 1971.
——. *The Trial*. 1925. Translated by Willa and Edwin Muir. New York: Schocken, 1968.
Kelly, Christina. "Kurt and Courtney Sitting in a Tree." *Sassy*, April 1992, 51.
Kerouac, Jack. *On The Road*. 1959. New York: Penguin, 1976.
Killdozer. *Uncompromising War on Art under the Dictatorship of the Proletariat*. Compact Disc. Touch & Go, TG082CD. 1994.
Kindersley, Dorling. *Punk: The Whole Story*. London: DK Publishing, 2006.
King, John. *Human Punk*. London: Vintage, 2001.
Klein, Howie. "Clash in the Hospital." *Search & Destroy #6*, 1978. In *Search and Destroy 1–6: The Complete Reprint*, by V. Vale, 123. San Francisco: V/Search, 1996.
Klosterman, Chuck. *Sex, Drugs, and Cocoa Puffs*. New York: Scribner, 2003.
Knight, Michael Muhammad. *The Taqwacores*. Berkeley, CA: Soft Skull, 2004.
Kristiansen, Lars J., Joseph R. Blaney, Philip J. Chidester, and Brent K. Simonds. *Screaming for Change: Articulating a Unifying Philosophy of Punk Rock*. Lanham, MD: Lexington, 2010.
Krugman, Paul. "Greece: The Tie That Doesn't Bind." *New York Times*, February 9, 2015. http://krugman.blogs.nytimes.com/2015/02/09/greece-the-tie-that-doesnt-bind/.
——. "Killing the European Project." *New York Times*, July 12, 2015. http://krugman.blogs.nytimes.com/2015/07/12/killing-the-european-project/.
Kurt & Courtney. Directed by Nick Broomfield. 1998. New York: Fisher Klingenstein, 2012. DVD.
Kurt Cobain: Montage of Heck. Directed by Brett Morgen. 2015. HBO Documentary Film. Television, 2015.
Lacan, Jacques. "Discourse To Catholics." 1960. In *The Triumph of Religion*, translated by Bruce Fink, 3–52. Cambridge: Polity, 2013.
——. *The Four Fundamental Concepts of Psychoanalysis*. 1964. New York: Norton, 1978.
——. "On a Question Prior to Any Possible Treatment of Psychosis." 1956. In *Écrits: A Selection*, translated by Bruce Fink, 169–214. New York: Norton, 2002.
——. *The Other Side of Psychoanalysis*. 1970. Translated by Russell Grigg. New York: Norton: 2007.
——. "The Signification of the Phallus." 1958. In *Écrits: A Selection*, translated by Bruce Fink, 271–80. New York: Norton, 2002.
Laing, Dave. "Interpreting Punk Rock." *Marxism Today*, April 1978, 123–28.

——. *One Chord Wonders: Power and Meaning in Punk Rock*. 1985. Oakland, CA: PM Press, 2015.
Lautréamont, Comte de. *Maldoror*. 1869. Translated by Alexis Lykiard. Cambridge, MA: Exact Change, 1994.
Lehmann, Chris. "The Dustbin of Theory: Greil Marcus's Hipster Historicism." *Baffler* 8, 1996, 90–98.
Levinas, Emmanuel. *On Escape*. 1982. Translated by Bettina Bergo. Stanford, CA: Stanford University Press, 2003.
Lydon, John. *Rotten: No Irish, No Blacks, No Dogs*. New York: Picador, 1994.
Lynn X. "Alejandro Is a Maverick." *Search & Destroy #6*, 1978. In *Search and Destroy 1–6: The Complete Reprint*, by V. Vale, 115–16. San Francisco: V/Search, 1996.
——. "Iggy Pop." *Search & Destroy #4*, 1977. In *Search and Destroy 1–6: The Complete Reprint*, by V. Vale, 64–66. San Francisco: V/Search, 1996.
——. "Talking Heads." *Search & Destroy #6*, 1978. In *Search and Destroy 1–6: The Complete Reprint*, by V. Vale, 132–33. San Francisco: V/Search, 1996.
——. "Tom Verlaine/Eno." *Search & Destroy # 3*, 1977. In *Search and Destroy 1–6: The Complete Reprint*, by V. Vale, 43. San Francisco: V/Search, 1996.
Maag, Christopher. "Young Muslims Build a Subculture on an Underground Book." *New York Times*, December 23, 2008, A16.
Madness. "Embarrassment" b/w "Crying Shame." Vinyl Single. Stiff, BUY102. 1980.
Magazine. *The Correct Use of Soap*. Vinyl LP. Virgin, VA13144. 1980.
Man or Astro-man? "Birdstuff Explains" b/w "Philip K. Dick in the Pet Section of a Wal-Mart." Cassette Single. No Label/Self-Released, 1994.
Marcus, Greil. *Lipstick Traces: A Secret History of the Twentieth Century*. Cambridge, MA: Harvard University Press, 1989.
Marquis de Sade. "Back to Cruelty." *Rue de Siam*. Vinyl LP. EMI/Pathé-Marconi, C070–72302. 1981.
Martinsen, Deborah. *Surprised by Shame*. Columbus: Ohio State University Press, 2003.
Marx, Karl. *Capital*. 1867. Translated by Samuel Moore and Edward Aveling. Chicago: C. H. Kerr, 1906.
——. *The Communist Manifesto*. 1848. Translated by Samuel Moore. New York: Chartwell, 2010.
——. *Critique of Hegel's "Philosophy of Right."* 1843. Edited and translated by Joseph O'Malley. Cambridge: Cambridge University Press, 1977.
——. "On the Barge to D. in March 1843." In *Writings of the Young Marx on Philosophy and Society*, edited by D. Easton and Kurt H. Guddat, 203–4. Indianapolis: Hackett, 1997.

———. "Private Property and Communism." In *The Economic and Philosophic Manuscripts of 1844*, edited by Dirk J. Struik. New York: International Publishers, 1964.
McCay, George. "'I'm So Bored with the USA': The Punk in Cyberpunk." In *Punk Rock: So What?*, edited by Roger Sabin, 49–67. London: Routledge, 1999.
McNeil, Legs. "Patti Smith." *Punk* #2. 1976. In *Punk: The Best of Punk Magazine*, edited by John Holmstrom, 32–36. New York: HarperCollins, 2012.
McNeil, Legs, and Gillian McCain. *Please Kill Me: The Uncensored Oral History of Punk*. New York: Penguin, 1996.
Meno, Joe. *Hairstyles of the Damned*. New York: Akashic, 2004.
Metallica. *. . . And Justice for All*. Vinyl LP. Elektra, 60812-1. 1988.
M.I.A. "Born Free." *Maya*. Compact Disc. XL/Interscope, B0014344-02. 2010.
Miles, Barry. *William Burroughs: El Hombre Invisible*. 1992. London: Virgin, 2010.
Miller, Henry. *The Air-Conditioned Nightmare*. New York: New Directions, 1945.
———. *Black Spring*. 1936. New York: Grove 1963.
———. *The Cosmological Eye*. New York: New Directions, 1939.
———. *Time of the Assassins*. New York: New Directions, 1946.
———. *Tropic of Cancer*. 1934. New York: Grove, 1961.
———. *Tropic of Capricorn*. 1939. New York: Grove, 1961.
Minor Threat. *Out of Step*. Vinyl EP. Dischord, DIS010LP. 1982.
Misfits. *Walk Among Us*. Vinyl LP. Ruby, JRR804. 1982.
Mission of Burma. "Max Ernst's Dream." *ONoffON*. Compact Disc. Matador, OLE 613-2. 2004.
———. *The Obliterati*. Compact Disc. Matador, OLE683-2. 2006.
———. *Signals, Calls, and Marches*. Vinyl EP. Ace of Hearts, AHS 1006. 1981.
Mochulsky, Konstantin. *Dostoevsky: His Life and Work*. 1947. Translated by Michael A. Minihan. Princeton, NJ: Princeton University Press, 1967.
Modest Mouse. "Bukowski." *Good News for People Who Love Bad News*. Compact Disc. Epic, EK87125. 2004.
———. *The Lonesome Crowded West*. Compact Disc. Up, Up44. 1997.
———. "Never Ending Math Equation." *Building Nothing Out of Something*. 1998. Compact Disc. Up, Up73. 2000.
Moon, Tom. *1,000 Recordings to Hear before You Die: A Listener's Life List*. New York: Workman, 2008.
Moore, Thurston. *Alabama Wildman*. Marlborough, MA: Water Row, 2000.
Mr. T Experience. "Boredom Zone." *The Thing That Ate Floyd*. Vinyl LP. Lookout!, Lookout11. 1988.
Mullen, Brendan, Don Bolles, and Adam Parfrey. *Lexicon Devil: The Fast Times and Short Life of Darby Crash and the Germs*. Los Angeles: Feral House, 2002.

Mulvey, John. "Band of Fallopian Glory—*In Utero* Review." *New Musical Express*, September 4, 1993.
Nabokov, Vladimir. "Letters: The Strange Case of Nabokov and Wilson." *New York Review of Books*, August 26, 1965, 25–26.
——. *Pale Fire*. 1962. New York: Vintage, 1989.
Nadeau, Maurice. *The History of Surrealism*. Translated by Richard Howard. New York: Collier, 1965.
Nash, Eric. "Existential Questions Plus Androids. Cool." *New York Times*, January 28, 1996, H9.
Negativland. *Negativland*. Vinyl LP. Seeland, SEELAND001. 1980.
——. *U2*. Compact Disc. SST, SSTCD272. 1991.
Nehring, Neil. *Flowers in the Dustbin: Culture, Anarchy, and Postwar England*. Ann Arbor: University of Michigan Press, 1993.
Nervous Gender. *Music from Hell*. Vinyl LP. Subterranean, SUB21. 1981.
"Next Stop, Nowhere." *Quincy, M.E.* Directed by Ray Danton. NBC. December 1, 1982. Television.
Nick Cave and the Bad Seeds. *Dig, Lazarus, Dig*!!! Compact Disc. Anti-, 86943-2. 2008.
——. *Push the Sky Away*. Compact Disc. Bad Seed Ltd., BS001CD. 2013.
——. *Skeleton Tree*. Compact Disc. Bad Seed Ltd., BS009CD. 2016.
Nietzsche, Friedrich. "The Antichrist." 1888. In *The Portable Nietzsche*, edited by Walter Kaufmann, 565–656. New York: Penguin, 1976.
——. *Beyond Good and Evil*. 1886. Translated by Walter Kaufmann. New York: Vintage, 1989.
——. *The Birth of Tragedy*. 1872. Translated by Douglas Smith. Oxford: Oxford University Press, 2000.
——. "Letter to Overbeck." 1887. In *The Portable Nietzsche*. Edited by Walter Kaufmann. 454–55. New York: Penguin, 1976.
——. "Thus Spoke Zarathustra." 1891. In *The Portable Nietzsche*. Edited by Walter Kaufmann, 103–439. New York: Penguin, 1976.
Nin, Anaïs. *Henry and June*. 1931–1932. San Diego: Harcourt Brace Jovanovich, 1986.
——. *Henry Miller Letters to Anaïs Nin*. 1931–1946. New York: G. P. Putnam's Sons, 1965.
1991: The Year Punk Broke. Directed by Dave Markey. 1993. Santa Monica: Geffen, 2011. DVD.
Nirvana. *Bleach*. Vinyl LP. SubPop, SP34. 1989.
——. *Incesticide*. Compact Disc. DGC, DGCD24504. 1992.
——. *In Utero*. Compact Disc. DGC, DGCD24607. 1993.

——. *Nevermind*. Compact Disc. DGC, DGCD24425. 1991.
NOFX. "The Marxist Brothers." *Wolves in Wolves' Clothing*. Compact Disc. Fat Wreck Chords, FAT711–2. 2006.
O'Brien, Lucy. "The Woman Punk Made Me." In *Punk Rock: So What?*, edited by Roger Sabin, 186–98. London: Routledge, 1999.
Odd Future Wolf Gang Kill Them All. *The Odd Future Tape*. MP3/Digital file. No Label/Self-Released. 2008.
Odier, Daniel. *The Job: Interviews with William S. Burroughs*. New York: Grove, 1969.
Offspring. "Self-Esteem." *Smash*. Compact Disc. Epitaph, 86432–2. 1994.
Ohana. "Birth of the Clinic." *Dead Beat*. Compact Disc. Imperative Residence, IR001. 2008.
O'Hara, Craig. *The Philosophy of Punk: More Than Noise*! 1999. Oakland, CA: AK Press, 2001.
Orange County Keith. "Good Times with Bad Religion." *The Orange County Keith Netzine*. The Bad Religion Page. 1996. http://www.thebrpage.net/media/item.asp?itemID=558.
Orchid. "Tigers." *Gatefold*. Compact Disc. Ebullition, Ebullition51. 2002.
Ordway, Nico. "Anarchy, Surrealism & New Wave." *Search & Destroy* #5, 1978. In *Search and Destroy 1–6: The Complete Reprint*, by V. Vale, 111. San Francisco: V/Search, 1996.
——. "De Sade." *Search & Destroy* #4, 1977. In *Search and Destroy 1–6: The Complete Reprint*, by V. Vale, 68. San Francisco: V/Search, 1996.
Orwell, George. "Inside the Whale." 1940. *A Collection of Essays*. Orlando, FL: Harvest, 1981.
Ott, Chris. *Unknown Pleasures*. New York: Continuum, 2004.
Panic, June. *Horror Vacui*. Compact Disc. Secretly Canadian, SC015. 2000.
——. "On H's 'They.'" *I Hope You Fail Better*. Compact Disc. Secretly Canadian, SC087. 2003.
Passion of Joan of Arc, The. Directed by Carl Theodor Dreyer. 1928. New York: Criterion/Janus, 1999. DVD.
Patti Smith Group. *Horses*. Vinyl LP. Arista, AL4066. 1975.
——. *Radio Ethiopia*. Vinyl LP. Arista, AL4097. 1976.
Pere Ubu. *Dub Housing*. Vinyl LP. Chrysalis, CHR1207. 1979.
——. *Elitism for the People 1975–1978*. Vinyl LP. Fire Records, FIRELP406. 2015.
——. "Final Solution" b/w "Cloud 149." Vinyl Single. Hearthan Records, HR102. 1976.
——. *The Modern Dance*. Vinyl LP. Blank Records, 001. 1978.
Perry, Mark. "Punk Life." In *Gobbing Pogoing and Gratuitous Bad Language*, edited by Robert Dellar, 5–8. London: Spare Change, 1996.

Piebald. "Holden Caulfield." *When Life Hands You Lemons. . . .* Compact Disc. Hydra Head, HH666–20. 1997.
Pierson, John R. *Weasels in a Box*. Chicago: Hope and Nothings, 2005.
Pigface. *Notes from Thee Underground*. Compact Disc. Invisible, CDINV028. 1994.
Pixies, the. "Where Is My Mind?" *Surfer Rosa*. Vinyl LP. 4AD, CAD803. 1988.
Poe, Edgar Allan. "The Fall of the House of Usher." 1839. In *The Complete Tales and Poems of Edgar Allan Poe*, 231–45. New York: Modern Library, 1938.
Police, the. *Synchronicity*. Vinyl LP. A&M, SP-3735. 1983.
——. *Zenyatta Mondatta*. Vinyl LP. A&M, SP-3720. 1980.
Pop, Iggy. *The Idiot*. Vinyl LP. RCA, PK12275. 1977.
——. "Louie, Louie." *American Caesar*. Compact Disc. Virgin, 724383900220. 1993.
——. *Lust For Life*. Vinyl LP. RCA Victor, AFL1–2488. 1977.
Pop Group, the. "We Are All Prostitutes." Vinyl Single. Rough Trade, RT023. 1979.
Portman, Frank. *King Dork*. New York: Delacorte, 2006.
Preoccupations. *Preoccupations*. Compact Disc. Jagjaguwar, JAG290. 2016.
Proletariat, the. "Religion Is the Opium of the Masses." *Voodoo Economics and Other American Tragedies*. Compact Disc. Taang!, 127. 1998.
Propagandhi. *Where Quantity Is Job #1*. Compact Disc. G7 Welcoming Committee, G7007. 1998.
Public Image Ltd. *Metal Box (Second Edition)*. Vinyl LP. Warner Bros./Island, 2WX3288. 1979.
"Punk and History." In *Discourses: Conversations in Postmodern Art and Culture*, edited by Russell Ferguson, Karen Fiss, William Olander, and Marcia Tucker, 224–45. Cambridge, MA: MIT Press, 1990.
Q and Not U. *Different Damage*. Compact Disc. Dischord, DIS133CD. 2003.
Raincoats, the. "No Looking." *The Raincoats*. Vinyl LP. Rough Trade, ROUGH 3. 1979.
Ramones, the. "Pinhead." *Leave Home*. Vinyl LP. Sire, SA-7528. 1977.
——. *Ramones*. Vinyl LP. Sire, SASD-7520. 1976.
"Ramones Go West." *Search & Destroy #2*, 1977. In *Search and Destroy 1–6: The Complete Reprint*, by V. Vale, 22–23. San Francisco: V/Search, 1996.
Rancid. . . . *And Out Come the Wolves*. Compact Disc. Epitaph, 86444–2. 1995.
——. "The Wolf." *Life Won't Wait*. Compact Disc. Epitaph, 86497–2. 1998.
Randy. "Karl Marx and History." *The Human Atom Bombs*. Compact Disc. Epitaph, 82019–2. 2001.
Reed, Lou. "Animal Language." *Sally Can't Dance*. Vinyl LP. RCA, CPL1–0611. 1974.
——. *Metal Machine Music*. Vinyl LP. RCA, CPL2–1101. 1975.

Refused. *The Shape of Punk to Come*. Compact Disc. Burning Heart/Epitaph, 82001–2. 1998.
Reynolds, Simon. *Rip It Up and Start Again*. New York: Penguin, 2005.
Rich, Jamie S. *Cut My Hair*. Burbank, CA: Crazyfish, 2000.
Richard Hell and the Voidoids. *Blank Generation*. Vinyl LP. Sire, SR6037. 1977.
Rimbaud, Arthur. *Complete Works*. Translated by Paul Schmidt. New York: Harper & Row, 1976.
——. *A Season in Hell / The Illuminations*. Translated by Enid Rhodes Peschel. Oxford: Oxford University Press, 1973.
Rimbaud, Penny. *The Diamond Signature*. Oakland, CA: AK Press, 2001.
——. *Shibboleth: My Revolting Life*. Oakland, CA: AK Press, 1999.
Rites of Spring. *Rites of Spring*. Vinyl LP. Dischord, DIS16LP. 1985.
Rivett, Miriam. "Misfit Lit.: 'Punk Writing,' and Representations of Punk through Writing and Publishing." In *Punk Rock: So What?*, edited by Roger Sabin, 31–48. London: Routledge, 1999.
Rock and Roll High School. Directed by Allan Arkush. 1979. Louisville, KY: Shout Factory, 2010. DVD.
Rocket from the Tombs. *The Day the Earth Met the Rocket from the Tombs*. Compact Disc. Smog Veil, SV37CD. 2002.
Rockwell, John. "Rock Poet: Jim Carroll." *New York Times*, December 31, 1980, A36.
Roderick, John. "Punk Rock Is Bullshit." *Seattle Weekly*, March 6, 2013. Sound Publishing, Inc. http://archive.seattleweekly.com/arts/830007-129/punk-rock-music-art-culture-self.
Rodi, Robert, and Dennis Polkow. "Music 45: Who Keeps Chicago in Tune 2015." *Newcity* 30, no. 1330 (July 16–23, 2015), 9.
Rollins, Henry. *Get in the Van*. Los Angeles: 2.13.61, 1994.
——. "Three Short Stories." *The Portable Henry Rollins*. Los Angeles: 2.13.61, 1997.
Rollins Band. *The End of Silence*. Compact Disc. Imago(3), 72787–21006–2. 1992.
Romalotti, Charles. *Salad Days*. Austin: Layman Books, 2000.
Rudimentary Peni. "Vampire State Building." *Death Church*. Vinyl LP. Corpus Christi, Christ It's 6, 1983.
——. "Voice." *Echoes of Anguish*. Compact Disc. Outer Himalayan Records, Boob006CD. 1998.
Sade, Marquis de. *Philosophy in the Boudoir*. 1795. Translated by Joachim Neugroschel. New York: Penguin, 2006.
Salewicz, Chris. *Redemption Song: The Ballad of Joe Strummer*. New York: Faber & Faber, 2006.

Salinger, J. D. *The Catcher in the Rye*. 1951. New York: Bantam, 1966.
Sams, Gideon. *The Punk*. London: Corgi, 1977.
Sands, Vermilion, and Annette Weatherman. "Clash Landing." *Search & Destroy #2*, 1977. In *Search and Destroy 1–6: The Complete Reprint*, by V. Vale, 28. San Francisco: V/Search, 1996.
Sartre, Jean-Paul. "An Interview with Sartre." *New York Review of Books*, March 26, 1970, 22–31.
——. *Saint Genet*. 1952. Translated by Bernard Frechtman. New York: Pantheon, 1963.
Savage, Jon. *England's Dreaming*. 1991. New York: St. Martin's Griffin, 2001.
——. "Industrial Music for Industrial People." *Search & Destroy #6*, 1978. In *Search and Destroy 1–6: The Complete Reprint*, by V. Vale, 122. San Francisco: V/Search, 1996.
——. "J. G. Ballard." *Search & Destroy #10*, 1978. In *Search and Destroy 1–6: The Complete Reprint*, by V. Vale, 106–7. San Francisco: V/Search, 1996.
Schalit, Joel. "Negativland." 1998. In *We Owe You Nothing*, edited by Dan Sinker, 195–205. New York: Akashic, 2001.
Schamus, James. "Dreyer's Textual Realism." In *Rites of Realism: Essays on Corporeal Cinema*, edited by Ivone Margulies, 315–25. Durham, NC: Duke University Press, 2002.
Schill, Brian James. "June Panic." *Punk Planet #57*, September–October 2003, 64.
Scholder, Amy, ed. *Pussy Riot: A Punk Prayer for Freedom*. New York: Feminist Press/ CUNY, 2013.
Schultz, Christopher. "The Live Insanity That Is Odd Future Wolf Gang." *Spin*, November 9, 2010. SpinMedia online. http://www.spin.com/2010/11/live-insanity-odd-future-wolf-gang/. Accessed January 10, 2017.
Screeching Weasel. "I Wrote Holden Caulfield." *How to Make Enemies and Irritate People*. Compact Disc. Lookout!, LK97CD. 1994.
Scritti Politti. "Wood Beez (Pray Like Aretha Franklin)." Vinyl Single. Warner/ Virgin, VS657–12. 1984."
——. The Word Girl." *Cupid & Psyche 85*. Vinyl LP. Warner/Virgin, I-25302. 1985.
Sex Pistols. *Never Mind the Bollocks*. Vinyl LP. Warner Bros., BSK3147. 1977.
Shepard, Sam. "Buried Child." 1979. *Seven Plays*. Toronto: Bantam, 1986.
——. "The Tooth of Crime." 1974. *Seven Plays*. Toronto: Bantam, 1986.
Shepherd, Julianne. "Black Eyes." *Punk Planet #57*, September–October 2003, 44.
Sheppard, John L. *Small Town Punk*. 2nd ed. Brooklyn: Ig Publishing, 2007.
Shipping News. "Books on Trains." *Save Everything*. Compact Disc. Quarterstick, QS50CD. 1997.

Sid & Nancy. Directed by Alex Cox. 1986. Beverly Hills: MGM, 2000. DVD.
Silkworm. "Lily White & Cherry Red." *Chokes*! Compact Disc. 12XU, 12XU028–2. 2006.
Sinker, Dan. "Ian MacKaye." 1999. In *We Owe You Nothing*, edited by Dan Sinker, 15–31. New York: Akashic, 2001.
———. "Kathleen Hanna." 1998. In *We Owe You Nothing*, edited by Dan Sinker, 59–75. New York: Akashic, 2001.
Six Finger Satellite. *The Pigeon Is the Most Popular Bird*. Compact Disc. SubPop, SP215b. 1993.
Sleepytime Gorilla Museum. "Sleepytime (Spirit Is a Bone)." *Grand Opening and Closing*. Compact Disc. Seeland, Seeland523. 2001.
Slint. *Spiderland*. Compact Disc. Touch & Go, TGLP64CD. 1991.
———. *Tweez*. Compact Disc. Touch & Go, TG138CD. 1989.
Slits. "Spend, Spend, Spend." *Cut*. Vinyl LP. Island, ILPS9573. 1975.
Smith, Patti. *Auguries of Innocence*. New York: HarperCollins, 2005.
———. *Early Work: 1970–1979*. New York: Norton, 1994.
———. *Just Kids*. New York: HarperCollins, 2010.
Sofianos, Lisa, Robin Ryde, and Charlie Waterhouse. *The Truth of Revolution, Brother*. London: Situation Press, 2014.
Sok, G. W. *A Mix of Bricks & Valentines: Lyrics 1979–2009*. London: PM Press, 2011.
Sonic Youth. *Daydream Nation*. Compact Disc. Enigma, D2–575403. 1988.
———. *Goo*. 1990. Compact Disc. DGC, B0000845–02. 2005.
———. "Pattern Recognition." *Sonic Nurse*. Compact Disc. DGC, B0002549–12. 2004.
———. *Sister*. Compact Disc. SST, SSTCD134. 1987.
Sontag, Susan, ed. *Antonin Artaud: Selected Works*. Berkeley: University of California Press, 1976.
Spaceballs. Directed by Mel Brooks. 1987. Beverly Hills: MGM, 2012. DVD.
Spitz, Marc, and Brendan Mullen. *We Got the Neutron Bomb*. New York: Three Rivers, 2001.
Spoon. "Quincy Punk Episode." *A Series of Sneaks*. Compact Disc. Elektra, 62199–2. 1998.
Sprecher, Lorrie. *Sister Safety Pin*. Ann Arbor: Firebrand Books, 1994.
Spungen, Deborah. *And I Don't Want to Live This Life*. 1983. New York: Villard, 1994.
Steel, Mark. "Poor Tsipras, Forced to Crawl along the Banks of the Rhine in a Thong." *London Independent*, July 17, 2015, 32.
Stein, Joel. "The Revenge of the Dork." *Time*, December 4, 2006, 116–17.
Stephens, Simon. *Punk Rock*. London: Bloomsbury, 2009.

Stephenson, Neal. *Snow Crash*. New York: Bantam, 1992.
Stevens, Wallace. "The Creations of Sound." 1947. In *The Collected Poems*, 310–11. New York: Vintage, 1990.
——. "Extracts from Addresses to the Academy of Fine Ideas." 1942. In *The Collected Poems*, 252–59. New York: Vintage, 1990.
Stinnett, Caskie. "I Know It's Only Rock 'N' Roll, But I Hate It." *Atlantic Monthly*, August 1977, 26–27.
Stooges, the. "Search and Destroy." *Raw Power*. Vinyl LP. Columbia, KC32111. 1973.
——. *The Stooges*. "Now I Wanna Be Your Dog." Vinyl LP. Elektra, EKS-74051. 1969.
Strauss, Julius. "We Will Face the Tanks If We Have to." *London Daily Telegraph*, November 24, 2004, 14.
Subb. "A Little More of Chomsky (A Little Less of You and Me)." *The Motions*. Compact Disc. Stomp, Stmp049. 2006.
Suicide. *Suicide*. Vinyl LP. Red Star, RS1. 1977.
Sum 41. "Billy Spleen." *Does This Look Infected*? Compact Disc. Island, 440063492–2. 2002.
Susman, Tina. "Settling in on Wall Street: Almost Two Weeks into an Anti-Greed Sit-In, a 'Leaderless Resistance Movement' Is at a Crossroads." *Los Angeles Times*, September 30, 2011, A1.
Svenonius, Ian. *The Psychic Soviet*. Chicago: Drag City, 2006.
Tacocat. "Shame Spiral." *Shame Spiral*. Compact Disc. Don't Stop Believin' Records, DSBR–013. 2010.
Talking Heads. "I Zimbra." *Fear of Music*. Vinyl LP. Sire, SRK6076. 1979.
Taylor, Mark C. *Erring: A Postmodern A/theology*. Chicago: University of Chicago, 1984.
Taylor, Steven. *False Prophet: Field Notes from the Punk Underground*. Middletown, CT: Wesleyan, 2003.
Teen Idles. *Minor Disturbance*. Vinyl EP. Dischord, DIS001EP. 1981.
Television. *Marquee Moon*. Vinyl LP. Elektra, 7E-1098. 1977.
They Live. Directed by John Carpenter. 1988. Los Angeles: Universal Studios Home Entertainment, 2003. DVD.
Thomas, Dave. *Bring Me the Head of Ubu Roi*. Utica, PA: Hearpen, 2011.
Thompson, Stacy. *Punk Productions*. Albany: SUNY Press, 2004.
Threepenny Opera, The. Directed by G. W. Pabst. Written by Bertolt Brecht. 1931. New York: Criterion/Janus: 2007. DVD.
Total Eclipse. Directed by Agnieszka Holland. 1995. Burbank: New Line Home Video, 1999. DVD.

Trenchmouth. *Inside the Future*. Compact Disc. Skene!, Skene!30. 1993.
Trynka, Paul. *Iggy: Open Up and Bleed*. New York: Broadway Books, 2007.
Turbonegro. "Humiliation Street." *Apocalypse Dudes*. Compact Disc, Man's Ruin, MR149CD. 1999.
Turner, Isaac. "SKWM." *Agricouture #2*, July 2002, 8–9.
Turner, Michael. *Hard Core Logo*. 1993. Vancouver, BC: Arsenal Pulp, 1996.
TV On The Radio. *Desperate Youth, Blood Thirsty Babes*. Compact Disc. Touch and Go, TG254CD. 2004
———. "Wolf Like Me." *Return to Cookie Mountain*. Compact Disc. Interscope, B0007466-02. 2006.
20,000 Days on Earth. Directed by Iain Forsyth and Jane Pollard. 2014. Los Angeles: Cinedigm, 2015. DVD.
U.K. Subs. "I Robot." *Endangered Species*. Vinyl LP. Nems, NEL6021. 1982.
United Nations. "Serious Business." *The Next Four Years*. Compact Disc. Temporary Residence, TRRCD234. 2014.
Vale, V. "Devo: Out West to Ride the Human Highway." *Search & Destroy #8*, 1978. In *Search and Destroy 1–6: The Complete Reprint*, by V. Vale, 37. San Francisco: V/Search, 1996.
———. "Dickies: LA Band Leaps to Punk Preeminence." *Search & Destroy #5*, 1978. In *Search and Destroy 1–6: The Complete Reprint*, by V. Vale, 108. San Francisco: V/Search, 1996.
———. "Nuns' Switchblade." *Search & Destroy #1*, 1977. In *Search and Destroy 1–6: The Complete Reprint*, by V. Vale, 10. San Francisco: V/Search, 1996.
———. *Real Conversations No. 1: Henry Rollins, Jello Biafra, Lawrence Ferlinghetti, Billy Childish*. San Francisco: RE/Search, 2011.
———. "Screamers from LA: A Better World Begins with You." *Search & Destroy #5*, 1978. In *Search and Destroy 1–6: The Complete Reprint*, by V. Vale, 88–90. San Francisco: V/Search, 1996.
Various Artists. *(Coles) Notes from Underground*. Compact Disc. Underground Operations, UOPJ2001-2. 2002.
Vaselines, the. "Jesus Wants Me for a Sunbeam." *Dying for It*. Vinyl Single. 53rd & 3rd, AGAAF 17. 1988.
Velvet Underground, the. *The Velvet Underground and Nico*. 1966. Compact Disc. Polydor, 3145312502. 1996.
"Vermillion Bitches." *Search & Destroy #1*, 1977. In *Search and Destroy 1–6: The Complete Reprint*, by V. Vale, 6. San Francisco: V/Search, 1996.
Vernian Process. *Behold the Machine*. MP3/Digital file. No Label/Self-Released. 2010.

Viet Cong. *Viet Cong*. Compact Disc. Jagjaguwar, JAG260. 2015.
Violent Femmes. "Blister in the Sun." *Violent Femmes*. Vinyl LP. Slash, 1–23845. 1983.
Wallace, Max, and Ian Halperin. *Love and Death: The Murder of Kurt Cobain*. New York: Atria, 2005.
Walters, Chris. *Punk Rules OK*. Vancouver, BC: Burn Books, 2002.
Weakerthans, the. "Our Retired Explorer (Dines with Michel Foucault in Paris, 1961)." *Reconstruction Site*. Compact Disc. Epitaph, 86682–2. 2003.
Wild Billy Childish and the Chatham Singers. "I Am the Strange Hero of Hunger." *Heavens Journey*. Compact Disc. Damaged Goods, DAMGOOD255CD. 2005
Wilde, Jon. "Every Night I Thought I'd Be Killed." *London Guardian*, August 1, 2008, 5.
Williams, Saul. "Black Stacey." *Saul Williams*. Compact Disc. Fader, 09042. 2004.
Willis, Ellen. "The Velvet Underground." 1978. In *Out of the Vinyl Deeps*, 53–65. Minneapolis: University of Minnesota Press, 2011.
Wilson, Edmund. "The Strange Case of Pushkin and Nabokov." *New York Review of Books*, July 15, 1965, 3–6.
——. *To the Finland Station*. 1940. New York: Farrar, Straus and Giroux, 1972.
Wire. "I Am the Fly" *Chairs Missing*. Vinyl LP. Harvest, SHSP4093. 1978.
Wishnia, Steve. *Exit 25 Utopia*. East Setauket, NY: Imaginary Press, 1999.
X. "Adult Books" b/w "We're Desperate." Vinyl Single. Dangerhouse, D88. 1978.
——. *Los Angeles*. Vinyl LP. Slash, SR104. 1980
X-Ray Spex. "Oh Bondage Up Yours!" Vinyl Single. Virgin, VS189. 1977.
Yankovic, Alfred. "Happy Birthday." *"Weird Al" Yankovic*. Cassette. Rock 'n' Roll Records, PZT38679. 1983.
Yeah Yeah Yeahs. "Shame and Fortune." *It's Blitz*. Compact Disc. Interscope, B001273502. 2009.
"Young Actress Ends Life in Hollywood." *Lewiston Daily Sun*, September 20, 1932, 11.
Youth Brigade. "Alienated." *Sound & Fury*. Vinyl LP. Better Youth Organization, BYO 002. 1982.
Žižek, Slavoj. *For They Know Not What They Do*. 1991. London: Verso, 2002.

INDEX

Page numbers in italics refer to illustrations

BRIAN JAMES SCHILL is a researcher and writer working at the University of North Dakota. He is Founder and Editor of Agricouture.org.